My Paper     Due Wednesday

Values - people
        be
  why
  beliefs ar

• Welfare
, Education

6 sentences
3 bibliography
2 or 3   author
              title year publication

# POWER
# AND
# CHOICE

## AN INTRODUCTION TO
## POLITICAL SCIENCE

D0777755

# POWER AND CHOICE

## AN INTRODUCTION TO POLITICAL SCIENCE

FIFTH EDITION

## W. Phillips Shively
University of Minnesota

THE McGRAW-HILL COMPANIES, INC.

New York   St. Louis   San Francisco   Auckland   Bogotá   Caracas
Lisbon   London   Madrid   Mexico City   Milan   Montreal   New Delhi
Paris   San Juan   Singapore   Sydney   Tokyo   Toronto

# McGraw-Hill

*A Division of The **McGraw·Hill** Companies*

**POWER AND CHOICE**
An Introduction to Political Science

2 3 4 5 6 7 8 9 0   FGR   FGR   9 0 9 8 7

ISBN 0-07-057187-2

This book was set in Times Roman by Ruttle, Shaw & Wetherill, Inc.
The editors were Lyn Uhl and Monica Freedman;
the production supervisor was Annette Mayeski.
The cover was designed by Rafael Hernandez.
The photo researcher was Anne Manning.
Project supervision was done by Ruttle, Shaw & Wetherill, Inc.
Quebecor Printing/Fairfield was printer and binder.

**Library of Congress Cataloging-in-Publication Data**

Shively, W. Phillips, (date)
    Power and choice : an introduction to political science / E.
  Phillips Shively. — 5th ed.
      p.    cm.
  Includes bibliographical references.
  ISBN 0-07-057187-2
    1. Political science.    I. Title.
JA66.S47   1997
320—dc20                      96-13836

# ABOUT THE AUTHOR

W. PHILLIPS SHIVELY is Provost for Arts, Sciences, and Engineering at the University of Minnesota, where he moved in 1971 after teaching at the University of Oregon and Yale University. He has also served as Visiting Professor at the University of Oslo in Norway. His research, which has appeared in numerous articles, deals with the comparative study of elections, and he has written *The Craft of Political Research,* an introduction to research techniques. He has also had practical political experience as a lobbyist in Minnesota. His true love is bird-watching.

To Ruth Phillips Shively
and
Arthur W. Shively

# CONTENTS

# PREFACE

This book provides a general, comparative introduction to the major concepts and themes of political science. For a number of years I had taught a course that attempted to accomplish this aim, and that experience had shown me how badly we need a text that is conceptually alive and that engages students with concrete examples of analysis without losing them in a clutter of definitional minutiae. That is what I aimed for when I first wrote this book, and I've been most pleased at the response it has elicited.

The title of the book, *Power and Choice,* indicates a subsidiary theme that recurs at intervals. Politics may be seen as (1) the use of power or (2) the production of a public choice. Often one or the other is heavily emphasized in approaching the subject. Marxism emphasizes politics as the use of power, while pluralism and much formal modeling work emphasize the emergence of public choices. For our present purpose I have defined politics as the use of power to make common decisions for a group of people, a definition that obviously demands that one hold both perspectives simultaneously. At various stages of my presentation I note instances in which an emphasis on just one of the two halves of the definition may yield a distorted interpretation.

Behind this subsidiary theme lies a broader theme that remains largely implicit—that political analysis is best conducted eclectically, rather than being straitjacketed into a single approach. My own research is squarely in the "behavioral" realm, for instance, but I found as I was working on this book that necessities of exposition and understanding pulled me toward a greater emphasis on policy and institutions than I had originally intended. Similarly, the state as an organizer of politics thrust itself more to the fore than I had anticipated. Distinctions that provide useful boundaries for research proved unhelpful in my efforts to build an understanding of politics among students; I think this is a healthy sign.

Material in the book is presented topically rather than on a country-by-country basis; but in order to add the sort of detailed contextual grounding that students gain from a country presentation I have included within each substantive chapter a couple of extended examples from countries that particularly display the conceptual material of that chapter. For instance, Chapter 2, which deals with the state, concludes with detailed sections on the European Union and on the establishment and maintenance of the

Nigerian state. Similarly, Chapter 15 (Bureaucracy and the Public Sector) gives detailed treatment to France, Saudi Arabia, and Brazil.

## NEW TO THE FIFTH EDITION

The world has been in such flux for the last several years that this book has needed to be revisited fairly often. Beyond general updating, I have also taken advantage of the chance offered by this new edition to carry forward the evolution of *Power and Choice* into a new world and have made a number of minor corrections and revisions. "Third World," which became a particularly meaningless term with the end of the Cold War, has been dropped in favor of the more useful "South"; I Have noted that modern political parties originated in the United States; I have somewhat expanded my treatment of state and society and so forth. Finally, I wrote the third edition in the midst of the wave of post-1989 optimism; this view darkened in the fourth edition, and darkens still more in this edition.

I have also added three new country examples: "*A Failure of the New World Order: Ethnic Conflict in Rwanda,*" "Interest Groups in Japan: Attenuated Neocorporatism," and "Fragile Democratization in Peru." And, I have taken advantage of the establishment of Transparency International to present their rankings of the level of political corruption in forty countries.

I have been very pleased by the response to this book. It is a wonderful experience to run into people who have used it and felt that it had helped them. I am grateful to the many people who have given me suggestions or corrections. And in particular, I am grateful to the following reviewers, who will notice many of their suggestions incorporated: Alwyn Rouyer, University of Idaho; Elizabeth Burrow, University of Northern Iowa; Manwoo Lee, Millersville University; Neil Harvey, New Mexico State University; Charles H. Winslow, Indiana University Purdue University Indianapolis. I am also deeply indebted to David Frisch for his help in gathering materials and for his creative ideas.

*W. Phillips Shively*

# ACKNOWLEDGMENTS

Kendall Baker, et al., tables from pp. 40, 183 of *Germany Transformed*. Copyright © 1981 by the President and Fellows of Harvard College. Reprinted by permission of Harvard University Press.

Pauline H. Baker, map from p. 78 of "Nigeria: Lurching Toward Unity," *The Wilson Quarterly* (Winter 1980). Copyright © 1980 by the Woodrow Wilson International Center for Scholars.

Morris P. Fiorina, table from p. 93 of *Congress: Keystone of the Washington Establishment.* Copyright © 1977 by Yale University Press.

Robert Kvavik, table from p. 42 of *Interest Groups in Norwegian Politics.* Copyright © 1976 by Universitetsforlaget.

Albert Speer, excerpts from pp. 300–302 and pp. 389–393 of *Inside the Third Reich.* Copyright © 1969 by Verlag Ullstein GmbH; translation copyright © 1970 by Macmillan Publishing Company. Reprinted by permission of Macmillan Publishing Company.

Sidney Verba, et al., table from p. 58 of *Participation and Political Equality.* Copyright © 1978 by Cambridge University Press.

Frank L. Wilson, table from p. 898 of "French Interest Groups: Pluralist or Neocorporatist?" *American Political Science Review* (December 1983). Reprinted by permission.

Allen L. Otten, "Back Bencher Blues" from *The Wall Street Journal,* August 5, 1980. Reprinted by permission of Dow Jones & Company, Inc.

Article on bureaucracy in Brazil from *The World Development Report 1987.* Copyright © 1987 by the International Bank for Reconstruction/The World Bank. Reprinted by permission of Oxford University Press, Inc.

# POWER AND CHOICE

## AN INTRODUCTION TO POLITICAL SCIENCE

# PART ONE

# INTRODUCTION

# 1

# POLITICS:
# SETTING THE STAGE

Everyone knows something about politics, and many people know a great deal about it. It is an interesting, amusing, and moving spectacle that ranks not too far behind professional sports in the eyes of many. Political scientists, however, *study* politics and *analyze* it. This involves doing pretty much the same sorts of things that other people do who follow politics: we read the newspapers and listen to press conferences, take part in political campaigns, and so on. But we also do some things differently. We usually try to see both sides of any question and to keep our emotions in low key, because emotions can cloud judgment. We borrow deliberately from other disciplines—such as economics, history, sociology, psychology, and philosophy—to help us understand what is going on politically. And above all, as you will see later in this chapter, we try to be precise about the meanings of the words we use. Many words having to do with politics—such as "liberal," "represent," and even "politics" itself—are quite complex, but most people use them unthinkingly. Political scientists are careful to analyze the varied meanings of such words and to use them precisely, partly because it is important to know exactly what we mean by the words we use and partly because careful examination of a richly complex word may teach us a lot about the things it describes.

What do political scientists study? Over recent years we have seen work in which political scientists:

- Measured just how much it actually costs a country to lose a war
- Devised a new system of voting in primaries that might have led to a different set of candidates for most presidential elections
- Analyzed and explained the various styles that members of the U.S. Congress adopt in dealing with their constituents
- Studied the spread of welfare reforms across the states

• Showed that the roots of successful government may go back to social institutions several centuries ago

• Showed why most nations will ignore warnings about surprise military action by hostile nations

• Studied why democracies almost never wage war on other democracies

These are the sorts of things political scientists do. In this book you will be introduced to the broad principles of what we have learned about politics, especially about the politics of democracies like the United States. We hope the study will sharpen and enrich the more general understanding of politics that you already have.

This first chapter, in particular, involves the precise definition of several words with which you are already somewhat familiar. We must examine these definitions because you should start your study with some basic terms in place. You may also find it intriguing to see complexity in words, such as "politics," that have probably not struck you before as being particularly complicated.


## POLITICS

What is politics? What is it that makes an act political? Consider the following questions, all of which involve political circumstances. What do these have in common?

• How was Hitler able to take power through a series of supposedly democratic elections?

• Why does the U.S. Congress so often disagree with the president in framing energy policies?

• Why should workers sort letters the way their boss directs if they know a more efficient way?

• Why were southern blacks denied the vote and placed in segregated schools throughout the 1950s while at the same time their housing was not as segregated as that in the North?

• Should communists be barred from teaching in the schools?

• Should fascists be barred from teaching in the schools?

• Why does the United States have only two major political parties when most democracies have more?

• Should state and local governments have the right to force landholders to sell them land that is needed for public purposes?

• Was Harry Truman right to bomb Hiroshima and Nagasaki?

• Why do people so often feel guilty about not doing what their parents want them to do?

These questions all deal with politics. The questions about bosses and parents may not have looked to you as if they belonged in this group, but their connection with politics should become clearer by the end of this chapter.

What is it that all these questions have in common? There are two main things, and both have often been used as the defining characteristics of politics. First, all the questions involve the *making of a common decision for a group of people*, that is, a uniform decision applying in the same way to all members of the group. Second, all involve *the use of power* by one person or a group of people to affect the behavior of another person or group of people. Let us look at both of these in more detail.

## POLITICS AS THE MAKING OF COMMON DECISIONS

Any group of people must often make decisions that will apply to all of them in common, as a group. A family must decide where to live, what sorts of rules to set for children, how to balance a budget, and so on. A class in a college or university must decide what reading material to require, how students are to be graded by the instructor, how bright the light should be in the classrooms. A country must decide where to locate parks, what allies to seek out in case of war, how to raise revenue by taxing its citizens, how to care for the helpless, and many other things. Each of these requires the setting of some sort of common policy for the group, a single decision that affects all members of the group.

Not all human actions, of course, involve the making of a common policy for a group. When one brother teases another, he is not carrying out a family policy, nor is a family member who decides to write the great American novel. A student who decides to read extra material on one section of the course (or, perhaps, to skip a bit of the reading) is not executing a policy of the class. A person's decision to build a new house is not part of any common national policy, although the country may have policies—on interest rates, the regulation of building, land use, zoning, and so on—that affect this person's decision. Ford Motor Company's decisions on new-car styling are not part of a common national policy.

Those actions that contribute to the making of a common policy for a group of people constitute politics, and questions about those policies and the making of those policies are political questions. The political/nonpolitical distinction is not always easy to draw. The example of the Ford Motor Company, above, is tricky because Ford is so large that its decisions verge on being common policy for the whole United States, even though the company has no formal role in the nation's government. In other words, one might argue that because the U.S. government tolerates the concentration of our automobile industry among three giant corporations and because (as a result of this) the decisions of any one of the three bulk so large in American life, those decisions have a quasipublic character and are "sort of" political. In 1980 the quasipublic nature of large corporations was underlined when the government found that it had to become intimately involved in Chrysler Corporation's financing in order to prevent Chrysler from going out of business. Chrysler was so large that the economic health of the country was unavoidably bound to its economic decisions; therefore the government decided it had no choice but to support Chrysler's loans. In this sense, decisions made by the management of Chrysler were to a degree binding on the country as a whole and became, to some extent, U.S. political decisions.

Another tricky aspect of the "political/nonpolitical" distinction is that it is partly a matter of perspective. Ford's design decisions are not (except via Ford's quasipublic nature) political decisions for the *United States*; but they *are* political decisions for Ford's stockholders, managers, and workers, inasmuch as they set a common policy for the company. A family's decision to build a house is not a political decision for the *country*, but it is a political decision for the *family* as a group inasmuch as it involves a common policy for the family. "Company politics" is involved in Ford's decision, and "family politics" is involved in the family's decision. Neither, however, is a national political decision. Society consists of groups within groups within groups. Ford Motor Company is a group within the United States, and a family may be a group within the larger group of those dependent on Ford. Politics exists within any of these groups whenever a decision that will apply to all the members of the group is made. So depending on which group you are thinking of, a given decision—the decision of the Clauski family to build a house—may be treated as either political or nonpolitical. The Clauski decision is political for the family as a group but not political for the nation.

## POLITICS AS THE EXERCISE OF POWER

A second characteristic of politics, one that runs through all the questions at the start of this chapter, is that politics always involves the exercise of *power* by one person or persons over another person or persons. "Power" is the ability of one person to cause another to do what the first wishes, *by whatever means*. Politics always involves this: one person causing others to do what that person wants either by forcing or convincing them to do so. Looking back to our list of questions, we note that Hitler rose to high office by convincing many Germans to vote for him; the U.S. Congress disagrees with the president so often about energy policy because the president does not have much power either to force or to convince Congress to go along with his wishes in that area; and so on. In such ways, each of these questions involves the power of one person or persons over another or others.

The two defining characteristics of politics, then, are that (1) politics always involves the making of common decisions for groups of people *and* (2) those decisions are made by some members of the group exercising power over other members of the group. Power can consist of a wide variety of tools that help one person affect the actions of another. Power may be stark, as when a police officer stops a demonstrator from marching up the street; or it may be subtle, as when a group of poor people, by their very misery, elicit positive governmental action on their behalf.

Power may be exercised as *coercion* when we force a person to do something he or she did not want to do, as *persuasion* when we convince someone that that is what she or he really wishes to do, or as the *construction of incentives* when we make the alternative so unattractive that only one reasonable option remains. The ability to exercise any of these forms of power may be based on all sorts of things—money, affection, physical strength, legal status (the power of a police officer to direct traffic, for instance), the possession of important information, a winning smile, strong allies, determination, desperation (which helped North Vietnam to defeat the United States in the 1960s), and many more. Any of these can help some people get other people to act as they wish.

It is not necessary to learn the specific bases of power listed above. They are meant to provide a sense of the variety and complexity of power, not as an exhaustive list of all its important sources. The point is that all politics involves the use of power, and such power may take varied forms.

A business planning session. These people are conducting politics—using power to reach collective decisions. (Beringer/Dratch/The Image Works)

## IMPLICIT AND MANIFEST POWER

In fact, power need not consist of any observable link between the people or groups involved. Scholars distinguish between *manifest* power and *implicit* power. Manifest power is based on an observable action by A that leads B to do what A wants. A police officer's signal that causes a driver to stop and wait is an example of manifest power. In the case of implicit power, B does what A desires not because of anything A says or does but because (1) B senses that A wants something done and (2) for any of a variety of reasons B wishes to do what A wants done. Many examples of implicit power are found in families, whose members are so attuned to one another that there is often no observable communication between members of the family who yet manage to "read" and comply with one another's wishes. A father may toss the car keys to his daughter on Saturday morning completely unprompted except by his knowledge of her habits and his desire to comply with her wishes. As she drives, the daughter may obey the 55-miles-per-hour speed limit because she knows that her parents feel strongly about it. In neither case is there any overt signal from one family member to the other.

A famous example of implicit power in a broader sphere of politics comes from the reign of King Henry II of England. The king had been involved in a series of disputes with Thomas à Becket, the Archbishop of Canterbury. Henry exclaimed one day. "Will no one rid me of this man?" Four of his knights overheard what the king said and proceeded to murder Becket. Historians still dispute whether the king really wished to have Becket killed. Frequent examples of implicit power occur in modern politics. Many issues never get raised in Congress, for example, simply because their proponents know they would have no chance. We never *see* the power that has led to the quashing of such proposals, but it is nonetheless real.

What is most important and interesting about implicit power is that an observer would have a hard time deciding whether or not such power has been exercised in any particular instance. The source of implicit power may lie far away from its exercise. To understand why the daughter drives 55 miles per hour, for instance, we might have to look back to her early childhood, to observe the hugs and admonitions she received years before. Power can be analyzed easily in the case of one country telling another "Cede the province Anemone to us or we'll invade you." It cannot be so easily analyzed if the resources on which it is based are varied and complex, as in the power of a defeated Germany to draw economic aid from the United States after World War II; or if it is in whole or in part implicit, as in the king's muttered remark in the presence of his soldiers.

### An Example of the Difficulty of Analyzing Power

Because power is so important to politics and because it is so difficult to measure precisely how and when power is exercised, there are recurrent disputes within political science about how much power various groups have. A famous dispute of the 1950s and 1960s centered on American cities, about which the following question was asked: "Is there a small group of people [the "downtown people," the political bosses, or what have you] who run things in American cities?" This might seem to be a simple question, but it was difficult for political scientists to answer, and we still have not gotten a clear answer to it.

In a study of Atlanta, Georgia, Floyd Hunter attempted to answer the question by asking journalists, officials, business leaders, and others who the most important people in the city were.[1] When all his varied sources named roughly the same set of leaders, he concluded that Atlanta was run by a small group of "insiders."

In response, however, Robert Dahl observed that all Hunter's respondents might be mistaken in the same way; they might all *think* that the downtown corporate elite ran Atlanta because that idea was part of the conventional wisdom about the city, but they might all be wrong. That the downtown people had a *reputation* for power did not prove to Dahl's satisfaction that they really *had* power; rather, he said, we must actually see power being used. As a response to the earlier Atlanta study, he performed a new study of his own based on New Haven, Connecticut.[2] He chose a set of major issues that faced the community—education, urban renewal, and so on—and recorded who actually participated in making decisions on each type of issue. Since he was restricting himself to observable power, he had to ignore the possibility of implicit power; other than that, his procedure was straightforward. He found that quite different groups of people were active on the different issues. Parents and "society people" were especially involved in ed-

---

[1]Floyd Hunter, *Community Power Structure* (Chapel Hill: University of North Carolina Press, 1953). Note that the politics of Atlanta today is very different from that which Hunter described in 1953. The most obvious difference is that Atlanta has now had a black mayor for a number of years; the power structure Hunter described was all white.

[2]Robert Dahl, *Who Governs?* (New Haven: Yale University Press, 1961).

ucation, for example, while downtown people were especially involved in urban renewal. He concluded that New Haven was not run by a single group of insiders but that
all sorts of groups were involved.

Still a third position was then staked out in the dispute. Two scholars criticizing
Dahl's study of New Haven noted that it is not enough just to see who was active in various kinds of decisions but that we must also investigate why particular issues get raised
in the first place.[3] Perhaps the really important decision is the one that governs which
issues will be brought before the public. For instance, during the period Dahl studied,
New Haven did not consider any policies for taking over utilities and running them publicly, for breaking up the residential racial segregation of the city, or for cutting property
taxes sharply. At this level, decisions may or may not be controlled by a small "power
elite"; we simply cannot tell from a study such as Dahl's.

Peter Digeser has added what he calls a "third face of power," drawing on the work
of Steven Lukes and (implicitly) Antonio Gramsci. Taking Bachrach and Baratz beyond
the notion of an elite controlling the agenda of discussion about different groups' needs
and wants, he points out that the process they describe might consist of an elite controlling ideas and public opinion such that it does not even occur to some groups to want
the things they should want:

> Lukes contended that power *could* be exerted even if B consciously wants to do what A de-
> sires. Lukes claimed that if B acts contrary to her objective, real interests then power is being
> exercised.[4]

In other words, the elite might exercise power not just by preventing discussion of proposals they do not want to see on the table, but by determining what people want so that
inconvenient proposals never occur to them in the first place. The test for Digeser
(based on Lukes) is not whether people have proposals that never reach the table, but
whether the things people want are contrary to their real interests. Such a disjunction
between people's wants and their real interests, for Digeser, is the footprint of elite
power. In other words, the way the elite maintains its power is to maintain control over
communications and ideas (Gramsci calls this control "hegemony"), such that people
do not want (do not realize they need) things that threaten the elite. Of course, this becomes remarkably difficult to analyze, since it requires us to identify what people really
need as distinct from what they merely think they need. And academics, who have very
distinctive values themselves, are not always in a good position to judge other people's
"true" needs.

Notice how complex the question of power in American cities has become. Hunter
gave us a very straightforward assessment of Atlanta. Dahl complicated the issue by

---

[3]Peter Bachrach and Morton S. Baratz, "The Two Faces of Power," *American Political Science Review* 56
(1962): 947–953.

[4]Peter Digeser, "The Fourth Face of Power," *Journal of Politics* 54 (November 1992): 977–1007, p. 980.
Digeser goes on to describe still another approach to power (this is his "fourth face")—that of Michel Fou-
cault, who develops a rich but elusive concept in which our definition of ourselves and of our very interests results from others' exercise of power over us. That is, the elite can maintain hegemony not only over what people want, but over what they identify themselves as. At this point, analysis becomes difficult—some would
say it collapses—because nothing is anchored. References to Lukes and Gramsci are: Steven Lukes, *Power: A
Radical View* (London: Macmillan, 1974); Antonio Gramsci, *Letters from Prison* (New York: Columbia University Press, 1994).

pointing out that in New Haven different types of people had dominant power with respect to different kinds of issues. Bachrach and Baratz reminded us that we must also consider who controls which issues will even come before the public. And Lukes added the consideration that this control might operate at an unconscious level, in elite control of how people form their very desires. In the end, it is difficult to say anything general and conclusive about the concentration of power in our cities because it is difficult to study what might have been—what issues might have entered public discussion but did not. This series of studies clearly illustrates the inherent complexity of power.

Although these studies certainly show that there are few blanket truths about power, one should not therefore conclude that power is impossible to study. Rather, an understanding of the complexity of power and the difficulty of measuring it can lead us to detailed examinations of very specific instances of power. In response to the Bachrach and Baratz article, for instance, several interesting studies have appeared on the setting of agendas in American politics. These are a direct result of the argument that the most important power is that which decides what issues will be up for debate.

## POLITICS AND POWER

Despite the complexity and elusiveness of power, we *can* say that all politics is based on some form of power and that its sources may be highly varied. For most questions about politics, however, it is not necessary to specify in detail exactly what sort of power is involved. For all political analysis, it is helpful to bear in mind that you are dealing with power of one sort or another; but that realization may often serve as a background or setting for your analysis. For instance, most of the questions posed at the opening of this chapter can be addressed without conducting precise analyses of the power relationships that form contexts for the questions.

Before we leave our consideration of power in politics, we might draw attention to the surprising universality of the use of power to determine common decisions for groups of people. People around the world vary remarkably little in physical strength and intelligence; they are also more or less equal in their basic talents. Yet millions of them will fear and obey another person whose intrinsic capacities are little superior to theirs.

Because of the weakness and inexperience of children, it is understandable that this should be so within families. The adult members of a family are stronger than the children, and it is perhaps natural that they should be able to control them. But it is astounding that large numbers of adults will grant this sort of control over their own actions to a military officer, a member of Congress, a dictator, or a religious leader. How is it that political power is so universal and often so concentrated in small numbers of people?[5]

Simply posing the question in this way demonstrates once again that the bases of power must be varied and complex. Physical compulsion alone would not be sufficient to ensure the obedience that people all over the world give to their political leaders.

---

[5]R. M. MacIver, *The Web of Government* (New York: Macmillan, 1947), Chapter 1.

"Congratulations, keep moving, please. Congratulations, keep moving please. Congratulations. . ." **(Drawing by B. Tobey: © 1974 The New Yorker Magazine Inc.)**

## POWER AND CHOICE

Politics, then, consists of the making of common decisions for a group through the use of power. Though the concept involves some complexity, it will usually be clear to everyone concerned whether a given action is or is not political in this sense. There are two very basic ways of looking at the making of such common policies, and people often use one or the other of these in evaluating any particular political action. In so doing, they may fail to consider how their viewpoint colors their conclusions. The two alternative viewpoints are as follows:

**1** Political action may be interpreted as a way to work out rationally the best common solution to a common problem—or at least a way to work out a reasonable common solution. That is, politics consists of *public choice*. (Note that even though this perspective emphasizes the cooperative aspect of decisions, power will still be involved in the making of choices; if nothing else, the power to persuade will be involved.)

**2** Political action may be interpreted as a way to accomplish the domination of some people by other people. That is, politics consists simply of the use of *power*. Here power is primarily thought of as power through coercion.

In other words, two people who observe the same political action from these opposing viewpoints will each have a different idea of what is going on. For instance, a person operating from the "public choice" viewpoint might look at the large number of people who fail to vote in American presidential elections and conclude that this is a reasonably healthy situation, because if such a large number of people have chosen not to bother voting, they must be tolerably satisfied with things as they are. Someone else, operating from the "power" viewpoint, might look at that same large number of nonvoters and conclude that American elections are a sham, that they are meant to give the appearance of popular choice without providing the voter with significantly different options (i.e., many voters do not bother to vote because their choices have been restricted).

Most often, *both* viewpoints are partly accurate. Politics generally involves considering at least the broad needs of the group for whom policy is being made: Pure tyranny is rare and is difficult to maintain. At the same time, the making of common policy generally means that one part of a group will be dominating another part to at least some extent. In the presidential voting example above, both characterizations probably have some truth to them.

It is good to bear these two perspectives in mind, because we may then be able to avoid misjudging a particular political situation as being all one or the other. For example, a college or university class is a group for which common policies must be made and in which a single person (the instructor) is formally charged with responsibility. Thus the group's politics will largely consist of domination of the students by the instructor. However, it is not solely or simply a system of domination because there are a number of informal mechanisms by which students participate in decision making, and these should not be overlooked. In short, the politics of a classroom also includes aspects of a rational working out of solutions to common problems. Such questions as the timing of tests, whether or not doors should be closed or the lights on, or the nature of special projects and examinations are often decided by the instructor in consultation with the students. In less direct ways, students—by their expressions of interest—often influence the very content of a class. Thus, although the politics of a classroom consists primarily of domination, there is also some element of a common search for solutions to common problems. This might be overlooked if one were not alert to the two sides of politics.

It is especially important to bear these two points of view in mind when we consider political actions about which we have strong feelings and about which we may expect to be prejudiced. Until the opening up of democratic elections in the Soviet Union, for instance, Americans tended to dismiss elections in communist countries as fraudulent. Yet, as you will see in Chapter 10, there was evident in the elections of most such countries a surprising element of broad participation in a search for common solutions. For instance, even during the period of noncompetitive elections, when only a single candidate appeared on the ballot, 28 percent of Soviet citizens reported that they had at one time or another attempted to persuade others to vote as they did; 19 percent had even contacted a state or national government official about some problem.[6] "The weeks preceding the election see the formation of countless study circles, discussion groups, campaign meetings, door-to-door canvassing, rallies, demonstrations and speeches."[7] Thus

---

[6]Richard D. Little, "Mass Political Participation in the U.S. and the U.S.S.R.," *Comparative Political Studies* 8 (January, 1976), p. 439.

[7]Ibid., p. 439.

there appears to have been more to the Soviet Union's uncontested elections in some ways than we had commonly been able to see. Bearing in mind that it is rare, if not impossible, for a political choice to consist solely of the use of power can help us to remain alert to such possibilities even when we know we are strongly prejudiced about a subject.

To sum up this section of the chapter: Politics consists of the making of a common decision for a group of people through the use of power. Any act of politics may be viewed from either of two perspectives, either as a cooperative search for an answer to common problems or as an act by which some members of a group impose their will on other members of the group. It is important to remember that generally both viewpoints are valid, especially when we might be prejudiced about the subject at hand, because keeping both viewpoints in mind can help us to avoid thinking about the subject in narrow, prejudiced ways. Power and choice, the two major themes by which we organize our views of politics, have provided the title of this book. And they will recur in succeeding chapters as we examine various aspects of politics.

## POLITICS OF THE STATE

One thing that has probably seemed odd to you in this chapter, right from the set of questions on page 4, is that things we do not always think of as "politics" have been described under this heading. There is some variation in common usage of the word. Family, workplace, church, and so on are not often thought of as political places, though they are *sometimes* thought of in that way. When we refer to "office politics," "campus politics," and "church politics," we mean activities that fit under the definition of politics presented in this chapter: the use of power to make common decisions for groups or people. When Kate Millett wrote a book about the relations between men and women, she titled it *Sexual Politics* explicitly to underscore her claim that men use various sorts of power to dominate the making of common decisions involving women:

> . . . a disinterested examination of our system of sexual relationship must point out that the situation between the sexes now, and throughout history, is a case of that phenomenon Max Weber defined as *herrschaft*, a relationship of dominance and subordinance. What goes largely unexamined, often even unacknowledged (yet is institutionalized nonetheless) in our social order, is the birthright priority whereby males rule females. . . . The fact is evident at once if one recalls that the military, industry, technology, universities, science, political office, and finance—in short, every avenue of power within the society, including the coercive force of the police, is entirely in male hands. As the essence of politics is power, such realization cannot fail to carry impact.[8]

This broad usage of the word "politics" fits the general definition presented in this chapter, but a much more common usage of the word is slightly narrower. If we say, "Frank went into politics," or "I'm fascinated by politics," we are not thinking of the

---

[8]Kate Millett, *Sexual Politics* (Garden City, N.Y.: Doubleday, 1970), pp. 24, 25. Note that Millett approaches politics almost exclusively from the standpoint of power, not choice.

family or corporation or church. In this sense of the word we are referring only to the kind of politics that has to do with government of the state.

"State" has a special meaning in political science. It is not the same thing as the states of the United States; instead, it is what we commonly call a country. The United States is a state in this sense, as are France, Russia, Algeria, Mexico, and so on.

In the next chapter we will look at the state in more detail, but for now it is enough to note that the state is a particular kind of social group. Over the last few centuries, people have focused more and more on the state of which they are citizens, and the state has determined more and more of what goes on in their lives. Several centuries ago, most people were almost unaware of the state in which they lived; they noticed it only if the king's soldiers marched through their fields. In fact, at that time, many large geographic areas could hardly be said to have been organized as states at all. Gradually states have become more thoroughly organized and have demanded more and more from us. First, states became the prime focus of peace and war, maintaining peace within their borders and waging war with other states. Then, states became the organizers of commerce and industry within their borders, regulating prices and the quality of products, constructing roads and canals, and so on. Only for the last several decades has the state generally been expected by its citizens to maintain stability in the economy, guarantee employment, and keep the value of currency stable. A century or so ago events in the economy were treated as "acts of God," and the state was not involved in them, but today the state is generally held responsible for economic conditions. The responsibilities of the state continue to grow. In the future might the weather, which is now treated as an "act of God," become part of the responsibility of the state?

For better or worse, the state has become critically important to us, and its politics has taken on great importance. In fact, when we say "politics" today, we usually mean by it simply "politics of the state." Political science shares this general preoccupation with politics of the state. Though we will occasionally look at other sorts of politics in this book, most of our attention will be directed to the politics of the state. It is good to remember the more general meaning of "politics," however, and to remember that in dealing with the state we will be looking at politics only in one of its forms, albeit its most important and most complex form.

## POLITICAL SCIENCE

Political science is the academic field that takes as its sole and general task the analysis of politics, especially the politics of the state. There has been continuing debate over how "scientific" political science should be. Some political scientists think that politics is so complex and involves such basic personal values that we should not try to pin it down to exact regularities. Rather, we should interpret each political event and idea more or less in and of itself, in a personal, subjective way. Such political scientists would model themselves upon historians, who interpret a particular sequence of events more or less in and of itself, seeking to retain the richness of its detail while making a general patterned interpretation of what process unfolded through the events.

Other political scientists think that their discipline should be more scientific than this, seeking out the basic essence of regularities across a whole set of events, even though this means sacrificing some of the rich detail with which each single event is laden. They think that the only way we will be able to explain and predict what happens in politics is to emphasize the underlying processes that a number of disparate events may have in common. These political scientists would model themselves on other social scientists such as economists, who analyze events simply as instances of general processes, which they treat in the abstract. Economists, for instance, prefer to deal abstractly with supply-and-demand theories rather than analyze specifically what happens in a given used-car lot.

The first kind of political scientists are sometimes called "interpretivists," the latter "behavioralists." Interpretive political scientists are most likely to deal in historical and philosophical aspects of politics and to seek detailed, nonnumerical information on a few cases. Behavioralists lean more to abstract, mechanical theories of politics and to statistical analyses of numerical information. They find numerical information especially attractive because it distills a set of complex details down into something very simple and basic—a number. Thus, since behavioralists are looking for simple descriptions of basic processes, they see it as more useful to summarize party competition in many congressional districts with a single index number for each district than to try to digest masses of biography, newspaper accounts, and so on from a few congressional races.

This picture should not be seen as starkly black and white. Political science does not consist of two warring camps, and most political scientists combine some element of "interpretivism" with some element of "behavioralism." However, there are nevertheless different *degrees* of these among political scientists, which adds greatly to the variety of materials available in the field.

Whatever their preferred way of gathering information about the political world, political scientists tend, in their *thinking* about politics, to emphasize broad generalization and abstraction. Political scientists pursue generalization through *theory*.

A theory is a statement linking specific instances to broader principles. *Empirical theories* are theories describing how things work in the world we observe. They are usually explanatory; that is, they have to do with why things happen as they do. This means they consist of causal statements of the form "X causes Y." (For more on causation, see the discussion in the appendix, pp. 344–346.) An example of an empirical theory addressing one of the questions from page 4—why does the United States have only two major political parties—would be: "Single-member-district-plurality electoral systems, by disadvantaging small parties, tend to reduce the number of political parties to two." You will meet the single-member-district-plurality electoral system in Chapter 10. For now, the point is that this is a *causal* statement (SMDP causes two-party systems) and it links the specific case (United States parties) to a general principle.

*Normative* theories involve making a judgment about the world, not describing how it works. They address the question: "What should X be or do?" Again, these theories link specific cases to general principles. An example would be, "What sort of public health care plan should the United States have?" Normative theories would answer this question by applying general principles, such as "governments should intervene as little as possible in people's lives" or "societies are good to the extent that everyone has equal chances in life," to the specific policy question.

The important thing to note here is that both of our major kinds of theory—normative and empirical—are statements that deal with specific instances by linking them to general principles. Our relatively strong reliance on theory is what sets political scientists apart from others, especially historians, who also deal with politics as a subject. Theories are the building-blocks of political science, and you will find them throughout this book. A good example of normative and empirical theories is found in the box on page 97.

For practical purposes of curriculum and organization, the field of political science is divided into subfields according to the subjects in which political scientists specialize.[9] The major subfields are:

• *American political behavior:* The study of individuals and nongovernmental organizations involved in politics and of why they do what they do. Studies of public opinion, elections, interest groups, and political parties would fall under this heading.

• *American political institutions:* The study of national governmental bodies, the Congress, the presidency, the bureaucracy, and—in part—the courts.

• *American public law:* The study of legal reasoning and of why courts hand down the decisions they do.

• *American public policy:* The analysis of the product of politics, the kinds of policies that are laid down.

• *American state and local politics:* The study of all of the above, but at the level of "states" (such as California or Minnesota) and localities rather than the nation as a whole.

• *Comparative politics:* The study of all of the above in any place but the United States. To lump all aspects of politics outside of the United States together is obviously parochial, but that is what is usually done. In other countries, political scientists may differentiate their own politics and lump that of the United States together with the rest as "comparative."

• *International politics:* The studies of politics between states—the making of common decisions for a group of states through wars, diplomacy, and so on. All of the subfields listed above deal with politics *within* states, not between them.

• *Political theory:* The history of ideas about politics and critical discussion of political values.

This book reviews the general findings of political science but blends U.S. politics and "comparative politics," treating the politics of all parts of the world (including the United States) comparatively.

## THE PLEASURES OF POLITICS

I have led you through some rather dry material in this chapter because it was necessary to start you off with clarity on a number of concepts. And frequently throughout this

---

[9]This listing shows American political science to be fairly parochial, setting up most subfields as parts of American politics and lumping all the rest of the world simply as "comparative politics." Political scientists in other countries are just as bad; Swedish political scientists have many subdivisions of the study of Sweden, as do the French for France, the Japanese for Japan, etc.

book you will find that we are working toward greater precision than is found in every-day language; this usually requires abstraction and may also seem a bit dry. I hope, however, that as we do this, you will remember—and I can communicate—what a fascinating and dramatic thing we are studying.

"The use of power to reach collective choices"—think what this phrase means. We are talking here about struggles for the souls of nations. The "use of power" has meant Thoreau going to prison to protest the United States' invasion of Mexico; underground resistance by the Catholic church and the Communist party against Nazi occupation troops in the Second World War; students braving police dogs and murderous assaults to integrate American businesses and public facilities in the 1960s; Mikhail Gorbachev and Boris Yeltsin juggling political coalitions to create democracy in the Soviet Union, where it had never been seen before. "Collective choices" have included the invention of democracy as a way to accomplish government by the people; the development of public education, park systems, public health; and also such horrors as the Nazis' murder of millions of Jews and other "undesirables."

I try in this book to write dispassionately about politics, because it is easier to keep a clear head that way, but a love of politics lies behind all of it. I switched from another undergraduate major to political science in the early 1960s because I was excited by John Kennedy. And I have remained a news "junkie" and sometime participant in politics ever since. The things we will be analyzing in the pages that follow involve real people devoting their energies to things they want and things they believe in. While you learn how to analyze what is happening in these events, and learn to deal with the events dispassionately, I hope you will not lose your feeling for the humanity that is moving through them.

## FURTHER READING

### Politics and Power

Dahl, Robert. *Modern Political Analysis.* 4th ed. New York: Prentice-Hall, 1984, Chapters 3 & 4.

Digeser, Peter. "The Fourth Face of Power." *Journal of Politics* 54 (November 1992): 977–1007.

Lasswell, Harold D., and Kaplan, Abraham. *Power and Society.* Yale Law School Studies. Vol. 2. New Haven, Conn.: Yale University Press, 1950.

Maier, Charles S., ed. *Changing Boundaries of the Political.* New York: Cambridge University Press, 1987.

MacIver, R. M. *The Web of Government.* rev. ed. New York: Free Press, 1965.

Nagel, Jack H. *The Descriptive Analysis of Power.* New Haven, Conn.: Yale University Press, 1975.

"Power." In *The International Encyclopedia of the Social Sciences.*

Wrong, Dennis. *Power.* New York: Harper & Row, 1979.

### Political Science

Almond, Gabriel A. *A Discipline Divided: Schools and Sects in Political Science.* Newbury Park, Calif.: Sage, 1990.

Easton, David, and Gunnell, John G., and Graziano, Luigi, eds. *The Development of Political Science: A Comparative Survey.* New York: Routledge, 1991.

Fenno, Richard. *Home Style: House Members in Their Districts*. Boston: Little, Brown, 1978. (The appendix to this book provides a good argument for qualitative social science.)

Lave, Charles A., and March, James G. *An Introduction to Models in the Social Sciences*. New York: Harper & Row, 1975. (Chapters 1–3 provide a good nontechnical argument for quantitative social science.)

"Political Science." In *The International Encyclopedia of the Social Sciences*.

Wahlke, John C. "Liberal Learning and the Political Science Major." *PS* 24 (March 1991): 48–60.

Wiarda, Howard, ed. *New Directions in Comparative Politics*, rev. ed. Boulder, Colo.: Westview Press, 1991.

PART **TWO**

## THE STATE AND
## PUBLIC POLICY

# 2

# THE MODERN STATE

Nation - large group of people who are bound together because of a common culture, usually with a common language.

In this book, we have chosen to focus on the politics of the *state*—rather than on "office politics," politics in the family, and so on—simply because the state has come to play such a central role in modern politics.[1]

The extent to which the state has come to dominate our attention is evident even in the way we treat individuals. When we think about a person who comes from a different country, we are likely to think of him or her primarily in terms of this—to the exclusion of other characteristics that may actually have more to do with what the person is like. If you knew a Danish engineer named Ole, for instance, and were asked to say quickly, in one word, what Ole is, you would be very likely to say "a Dane." The other likely answer would be "a man"; gender has not given way even to the state in the amount of attention we give it. Ole is an engineer, and that should say a lot about him; but not many people would choose that over his nationality as a label for him. He may be a Lutheran or a Jew, pious or apathetic, tall or short, a charmer or a clod; still, most people who know him would characterize him first as a Dane. This does not really make much sense, since almost all the other things mentioned would have told you more about Ole's personality or person than does the fact that he is a Dane. It is a result not of logic but of our modern fixation on nationality and the state.

If you have ever lived abroad, you will have noticed this phenomenon in a particularly striking way. Most of us do not ordinarily think of ourselves in terms of the state to which we belong. But let us reside in a different state, and suddenly our native state becomes a most important aspect of our identity. Canadians living in the United States or

[1]As noted in Chapter 1, the word "state" as used here does not refer to a place like California or Pennsylvania. Rather, it means approximately what is often called a "country," such as Canada, Nigeria, or the United States of America.

21

(Drawing by S. Harris; © 1981 The New Yorker Magazine Inc.)

Europe begin to think of themselves much more as Canadians than they ever have before, Nigerians studying or working in the United States suddenly begin to think of
themselves as Nigerians, Americans living in Europe or Asia suddenly feel themselves
to be vividly American, and so on.

Our fixation on the state goes beyond what reason would dictate. We have seen that
we could really say more about Ole if we characterized him as tall or university educated than merely as a Dane, as most people would nevertheless begin by doing. Another paradoxical result of our fixation on the state is that most people pay a good deal
more attention to the national government, which is remote and inaccessible to them,
than they do to their relatively more accessible local governments. In America, politics
and attention to politics reach a peak every four years at the election of a new president.
This national event so seizes our attention that enrollment in political science courses at
American universities generally follows a four-year cycle, rising 10 to 20 percent in a
presidential election year! Americans turn out to vote in considerably larger numbers at
presidential than at local elections.

The paradox in such attention to national politics is that in a country as large as the
United States, an individual voter has virtually no chance of affecting the outcome of a
national election. As a character in Skinner's *Walden Two* remarks to his friend,

"How is the people's will ascertained? In an election. But what a travesty! In a small committee meeting, or even a town hall, I can see some point in voting, especially on a yes-or-no question. But fifty million voters choosing a president—that's quite another thing."

"I can't see that the number of voters changes the principle," said Castle.

"The chance that one man's vote will decide the issue in a national election," said Frazier, speaking very deliberately, "is less than the chance that he will be killed on his way to the polls."[2]

By contrast, an individual voter in a modest-sized city has a small but significant chance of casting the deciding vote in a local election, where perhaps ten or twenty thousand other people will vote in the same election. One can also reasonably argue that the policies of local government are just as important as the policies of the national government. It is true that foreign policy and issues of war or peace, the state of the national economy, and the broad issues of social policy—all the purview of the national government—are extremely important to people's lives. But the policies of local government are also important. The public schools, the condition of the street in front of your house, the purity and taste of your drinking water, how you are treated by police officers—all these and more are decided by your local government.

How odd, then, that most people pay so much more attention to their national than to their local government! This is just another proof that our focus on the state and its operations goes beyond the demands of reason.

The people of the world have not always been so thoroughly organized into states. In the remainder of this chapter, we shall look at the history of how the modern system of states arose; we shall then consider the relationship between the modern state and "nationalism"; finally, we shall look at emerging political forms that might serve as alternatives to the state.

## THE DEVELOPMENT OF THE MODERN STATE

The invention of this thing to which we pay so much attention, the state, is fairly recent. Just six or seven hundred years ago people simply did not think of themselves as belonging to a state or nation as we know it today. Most people lived on subsistence farms, intimately concerned with the village in which they lived but not caring much about the world beyond. Armies sometimes raided the village, but it did not make much difference to the villagers whether the army was hired by the king of France, by the pope, or by the Inca king. Barbara Tuchman's picture of what we now call "France" in the fourteenth century depicts a geographic region carved into various political divisions that might be controlled now by the English king, now by the French, and whose populations did not seem to care much which of these was their ruler.[3]

In the fourteenth and fifteenth centuries, as European kings began to claim greater powers and to tighten their control over large territories, these shifting political divisions began to coalesce into states. Even in Europe, however, it was not until the early nineteenth century that states were well established in the form we now know.

[2]B. F. Skinner, *Walden Two* (New York: Macmillan, 1948), pp. 220–221.
[3]Barbara W. Tuchman, *A Distant Mirror: The Calamitous Fourteenth Century* (New York: Knopf, 1978).

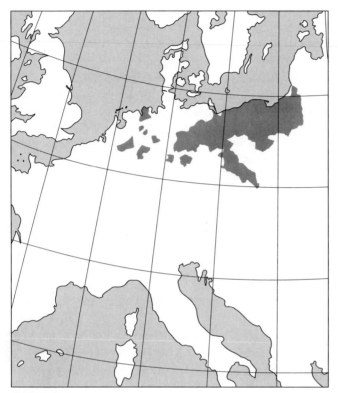

**FIGURE 2–1**
Prussia in 1789.

Throughout the early period of state building in Europe, populations continued to be largely indifferent about the state to which they belonged. During the early stages of its formation, for example, the state of Prussia was spread in little smears and droplets all over the map of northern Europe (see Figure 2–1), and this did not especially concern the Prussians. Some of these regions had been acquired for the crown by royal marriages, others by settlements of war or debt, and the people living in them were simply transferred like property from one ruler to another.

If ordinary people did not care much about the state, the leaders and the educated elite also saw it more as a convenience than as something special. This was particularly true early in its formation, but to some extent it remained true even as late as the eighteenth century. At the beginning of the period of state building, most members of the elite, if they could write at all, wrote in Latin rather than in their local tongue. Although daring writers such as Dante were breaking out in their local languages by the fourteenth century, most writers still tended to think of themselves well into the seventeenth century as belonging primarily to a cosmopolitan, European literary world rather than to a local English, French, or Spanish community.

The kings who were creating these new states often had family ties or other interests that took priority over their state. As late as 1714, a German line of kings whose members could not even speak English for the first generation came to power in England. Later, during World War I (after Britain and Germany had evolved into modern states), it would prove an embarrassment to the British royal house that the kaiser of Germany was their cousin—so much so that they changed their name from Hanover to Windsor.

Even military affairs were not as clearly divided by state through much of this period as they were at the end. Foreign mercenaries were an important part of most wars: Bands of English soldiers could be hired by the French king to fight the English, and vice versa. In the American Revolution, the king of England hired German troops (the Hessian soldiers) to do some of the fighting in America.

It was not until the early nineteenth century that the state as we know it today could be seen—a relatively large territory with stable boundaries, whose people were bound together by intricate political ties and who thought of themselves distinctively in terms of the state to which they belonged.

The invention of modern states in Europe may be said to have been completed by Napoleon from 1800 to 1815. In France, he created one of the first recognizably modern states by joining the excitement and the passions of the French Revolution to an active and efficient bureaucracy and army. The resulting state was nearly invincible and succeeded in conquering most of Europe. Its power rested partly on the first European army whose members fought not only for what they themselves might gain but for their nation—*France*. The modern state had finally emerged. Even after Napoleon eventually overreached himself and was defeated, things could never be the same. He had demonstrated what could be accomplished by a full-fledged state, and the new or remaining states that emerged after 1815 tried, some eagerly and some with more hesitation, to emulate his method of organization.

Although the modern state had finally been invented in Europe and North America by the early nineteenth century, most other peoples of the world still lived under a variety of other arrangements. But a great surge of European colonial expansion during the eighteenth and nineteenth centuries had divided the rest of the world into colonies organized somewhat as subsidiary states. When, in the twentieth century, European power waned as a result of two disastrous world wars, these colonies were able to break away and establish themselves as independent. Then their new leaders, almost all of whom had been educated in Europe, adopted the state as their own form of political organization. Thus the modern state became the universal form of political organization.

## THE ORIGIN OF STATES

What was it that led to the invention of the state over the last several centuries? Perhaps an exploration of this question will help us to better understand the nature of the state. There is a vigorous debate among scholars as to why states developed in Europe.[4] However, one thing is clear: The modern state developed there along with the coming of in-

---

[4]A good introduction to this debate may be found in Charles Tilly, ed., *The Formation of National States in Western Europe* (Princeton, N.J.: Princeton University Press, 1975). See especially Tilly's introductory chapter.

dustry and of complicated commercial arrangements. Large-scale industry and commerce could be carried on most easily among large populations whose members could be held together with minimal difficulty and who were willing to have their economic activities coordinated. As long as most economic activity consisted of subsistence farming, cottage weaving, coastal fishing from small boats, and so on, almost any form of political organization would do. But as larger-scale, more complicated economic operations developed, something like the state offered important advantages.

With the development of the state, merchants and industrialists could draw on a large, uniformly treated population as their pool of laborers, and they could sell their products across a large market subject to a single set of laws. Goods could be transported readily, without being subject to special taxes or duties as they passed from one part of the state to another. On the greater scale made possible by the modern state, large factories and ships could be built, and these could be involved in complex nets of transactions. Industry and commerce thus benefited from the development of the state.

In this sense, then, modern industry and commerce *needed* something like the state, and this partly explains why it developed when it did. But modern industry and commerce also made the state *possible* by providing the hardware, the technology, and above all the ease of communication by which a large, widespread population could be readily controlled by an army. Before the coming of modern communications, it was difficult for the government of a state of even moderate size to control the population with any exactness. As late as the early nineteenth century, it took a stagecoach three days to cross southern England. Under those circumstances, the government's control was necessarily loose. But with the coming of the railroad and the telegraph in the nineteenth century, governments could keep an instantaneous check on what was happening throughout their realm and could move troops rapidly to any trouble spot.

We can see that the relationship between the modern state and modern commerce and industry can be interpreted in two ways. On the one hand, commerce and industry needed something like the state, and so the state was invented. It emerged because it was an appropriate choice. On the other hand, modern commerce and industry made it easier to control people and seize taxes from them, and so the state was able to develop. Governments were able to spread their power more widely. Probably both explanations carry part of the truth. These interpretations embody "power" and "choice," the two sides of politics introduced in Chapter 1. To the extent one believes that the state emerged because it was made necessary by the modern economy, its invention represents politics as choice. To the extent one believes that it developed because people could now be controlled more easily, it represents politics as power.[5] Different scholars will lean more to one or another of these points of view. In extreme cases, like that noted in the box headed "The Marxist Theory of the State," some may hold that one of the viewpoints is totally false; but to go wholly one way or another is probably a distortion.

---

[5]Tilly takes somewhat more the viewpoint of politics as choice. For a view that emphasizes politics as power, see John H. Herz, *The Nation-State and the Crisis of World Politics* (New York: McKay, 1976), especially the third and eighth essays.

THE MARXIST THEORY OF THE STATE

In this chapter the state has been interpreted partly as being made possible by modern military technology and communications and partly as required by modern commerce and industry. Another way of interpreting the rise of the state is offered by Marxist socialism. (A fuller treatment of Marx and of socialism is offered in Chapter 3.)

Marx thought that modern society consisted of one class (the capitalists) dominating another (the workers). Because of the tensions caused by this domination, the workers had to be controlled, and for this the state was needed. The state keeps the workers under control partly by repression (the police) and partly by integrating them into the prevailing system by convincing them, in school and by other means, that their current situation is good.

Marx thought that eventually the workers would revolt and set up a socialist system in which one class would no longer dominate another. Then the state would have become unnecessary and would wither away through disuse.

Note that this theory sees the state solely as an instrument of power and that it does not analyze public choice at all. As you will see in Chapter 3, this is generally true of Marxist theory, which interprets politics solely as a matter of power.

Further readings in the Marxist theory of the state are Ernest Mandel, *Late Capitalism* (London: NLB, 1975), Chapter 15; and V. I. Lenin, "State and Revolution," in *Sources in Twentieth-Century Political Thought*, ed. Henry Kariel (New York: Free Press, 1964).

## NATIONALISM

One striking and disturbing thing about the modern state is the way it has been able to enlist its people in its cause. Citizens of a state generally identify themselves strongly with it and will defend it with passion. This passionate identification with the state is called "nationalism," and like any passion, it can make people either noble or base. Some have performed great acts of courage and self-sacrifice under the influence of this sentiment, and others have carried out cowardly assassinations and brutal massacres under the same influence. Whether it makes people noble or ignoble, nationalism is undeniably convenient for governments. It predisposes a large and varied population to obey the single government of the state; and if the state is attacked from outside, nationalist passion makes the defending soldiers a much more formidable force than they would otherwise be. Therefore all governments try to encourage nationalism—not necessarily a hate of others, but at least a national pride—by holding parades, using national symbols like the flag, presenting the state's history to schoolchildren, and so on.[6]

We have always been ambivalent about nationalism. Consider the two sides of it presented in the following quotations. The first is Sir Walter Scott's celebration of patriotism in his *Lay of the Last Minstrel:*

---

[6]There is considerable room for disagreement as to what causes nationalism and how nationalist sentiments are maintained. See Chong-do Hah and Jeffrey Martin, "Towards a Synthesis of Conflict and Integration Theories of Nationalism," *World Politics* 27 (April 1975): 361–386; E. J. Hobsbawm, *Nations and Nationalism Since 1780* (Cambridge: Cambridge University Press, 1990).

Breathes there the man, with soul so dead,
Who never to himself hath said,
    This is my own, my native land!
Whose heart hath ne'er within him burned,
As home his footsteps he hath turned,
    From wandering on a foreign strand!
[Such a man] concentered all in self,
Living, shall forfeit fair renown,
And, doubly dying, shall go down
To the vile dust, from whence he sprung,
Unwept, unhonoured, and unsung.[7]

The second gives the view of a cynical spy, portrayed in a novel by Eric Ambler:

Love of country! There's a curious phrase. Love of a particular patch of earth? Scarcely. Put a German down in a field in Northern France, tell him that it is Hannover, and he cannot contradict you. Love of fellow-countrymen? Surely not. A man will like some of them and dislike others. Love of the country's culture? The men who know most of their countries' cultures are usually the most intelligent and the least patriotic. Love of the country's government? But governments are usually disliked by the people they govern. Love of the country, we see, is merely a sloppy mysticism based on ignorance and fear. It has its uses, of course. When a ruling class wishes a people to do something which that people does not want to do, it appeals to patriotism. And, of course, one of the things that people dislike most is allowing themselves to be killed.[8]

## GOVERNMENT AND THE STATE

Who is the state? We have talked here of "the state" acting in various ways. (Look back to the opening sentence of the preceding section, "Nationalism," for example.) But who in fact does the acting?

A *government* is a group of people within the state who have the ultimate authority to act on behalf of the state (see Chapter 6). They are a unique group in the state; they, and only they, have the right to make decisions that everyone in the state has a duty to accept and obey. An influential current of thought in political science has sought to sensitize us over the last decade to the fact that governments and their bureaucracies are often self-starters in questions of policy—that they actively develop problems and seek solutions to them, rather than waiting for the population to come to them with problems. To understand politics properly, according to this current of thought, we must think of the government and bureaucracy itself as a participant and claimant in politics, rather than as a kind of adjudicator over a political process which comes from outside it; this is often referred to as the theory of the "autonomous state."[9] The idea is that the

---

[7]Walter Scott, *The Lay of the Last Minstrel,* canto 6, 1807.
[8]Eric Ambler, *Journey into Fear* (New York: Knopf, 1943; rpt. Bantam), p. 166.
[9]P. B. Evans, D. Rueschmayer, and Theda Skocpol, eds., *Bringing the State Back In* (Cambridge, England: Cambridge University Press, 1985).

state apparatus may itself participate autonomously in political conflict and decision making.

There is a creative ambiguity here, because this theory treats the government and bureaucracy as if they *are* the "state." Actually, the government/bureaucracy acts on behalf of the state, but the state obviously consists of more than just the government and bureaucracy. However, recognizing the ambiguity at least helps us to address the inherent vagueness in our notion that the "state" acts, does things. The first sentence in the section on nationalism is inevitably fuzzy because it refers to the state "enlisting its people in its cause." But this sounds as if the state is doing something to itself, since in the most usual sense, the people *are* the state. In this case the actions of the state in fostering nationalism come largely from government and bureaucracy (in outlawing burning of the flag, for instance), but also to some extent from a broader group including television announcers, religious leaders, teachers, and writers (as in the quotation from Sir Walter Scott). The theory of the autonomous state helps sensitize us to this problem, but it cannot answer it finally, because there is an inherent ambiguity in whom we mean when we refer to the state as acting.

Another good thing about the theory of the autonomous state is that it does emphasize for us the fact that the government and bureaucracy may often participate in politics directly, as claimants on their own behalf.[10] Especially in new states where diverse populations have been thrown together into a state, and where there is little consensus about proper directions to take, the state apparatus may be forced to (or, find itself free to) govern in an authoritarian way.[11] Under these circumstances, free from the constraint of shared traditions and norms, governments sometimes pursue policies benefiting their own personal or class interests in a fairly direct way, which simply adds further to the problems of the new state. This is part of what is going on in the example of Nigeria at the end of this chapter. Another example is the Philippine government's charge that Ferdinand Marcos stole several billion dollars from the government during the period of his rule. Some governments have even savaged the people of their state to further their own ends. Between 1975 and 1979, the government of Cambodia killed about 3 million people (out of a population of 9 million) in its effort to establish a new socialist society. From 1991 to 1994, Haiti's military government encouraged a systematic terror of the democratic opposition by troops and thugs.

Thinking of the government (and associated bureaucracy, media, public institutions, etc.) as "the state" is also useful because it allows us to draw a distinction between "state" and "society." As we have seen, the state is a set of legal arrangements involving sovereignty and embodied in a government. But the people of the state have a *society* of personal, social, and economic interactions that is partially independent of the people's organization into a state. For instance, from 1989 to 1993 Czechoslovakia was orga-

---

[10]This is especially relevant to the discussion of "pluralism" in Chapter 12.

[11]Here is another nice contrasting example of alternative "choice" and "power" interpretations of a political situation. Note in this sentence that I was uncertain whether to characterize the government as "forced" to govern in an authoritarian way (which would suggest that they were simply seeking the best public outcome and that circumstances forced them into authoritarian rule: a choice perspective) or to characterize them as "free" to govern in an authoritarian way (which would suggest that they were self-seeking and took advantage of the chance that was available to them to initiate authoritarian rule: a power perspective).

Opening Olympics ceremonies, Los Angeles, California. (Douglas Kirkland/Sygma)

nized as a single state. In 1993 it split into two states: the Slovak Republic and the Czech Republic. But before and after the split the people of Czechoslovakia were involved in families, friendships, clubs, and economic arrangements (jobs, investments, etc.) that were only indirectly affected by the nature of state organization. A family that was spread across the new border did not cease to function as a family, for instance, merely because of the new state arrangements.

There is usually some tension between society and state. It is often thought that if "society" is too strong—that is, if pressure groups and special interests can easily force their views on the government—the state will be ineffective and will not be able to make clear policies. This is often cited as the reason why the United States has difficulty setting clear economic policies and energy policies, for example. A reverse problem is that totalitarian states sometimes seek total control of society (this is why they are called "totalitarian"). Hitler's Germany abolished many private clubs and all labor unions, setting up instead its own organizations; it tried to undermine the family by drawing children away from their parents and into the Hitler Youth organizations.

This subtle distinction between state and society is hard to express other than through the theory of the autonomous state.

## "STATE" AND "NATION"

Up to this point the word "state" has not been defined precisely, although we have considered the modern state, its development, and its characteristics at some length.

We must distinguish between "nation" and "state." We often use these terms loosely as synonyms, along with the more common word "country," and they are clearly related. As one example of the relationship between the two, we have earlier in this chapter labeled as "nationalism" a passionate identification with the state. In fact, in ordinary conversation, most people use the words "state," "nation," and "country" interchangeably.

But "nation" and "state" have more precise meanings for political scientists. A nation is *a large group of people who are bound together, and recognize a similarity among themselves, because of a common culture; in particular, a common language seems important in creating nationhood.* A state, on the other hand, is *a political unit that has ultimate sovereignty—that is, a political unit that has ultimate responsibility for the conduct of its own affairs.* France is a state, Brazil is a state, the United States of America is a state. The Jewish people do not make up a state, since they are not a political unit, but Israel is a state. General Motors and Exxon are not states, though they are very large organizations. Chicago is not a state; although it is a political unit, it lacks sovereignty (the ultimate responsibility for the conduct of its own affairs) because another government, represented by the Supreme Court and the U.S. Army, has the right to intervene and force decisions on Chicago should that be necessary. A nation is a *cultural* and especially a linguistic grouping of people who feel that they belong together; a state is a *political* unit with sovereignty.

Nations do not necessarily coincide with the political boundaries of states, although the two do go together sufficiently well that we often simply refer to the *nation-state* when talking about states. Figure 2–2 shows a linguistic map of Europe. Notice that some apparent nations spread across the boundaries of states. For instance, the German language and culture spread well beyond the boundaries of Germany. Austria, a large part of Switzerland, and a small part of Italy are German, and there are pockets of German population across eastern Europe. The Basques are spread across northwest Spain and southwest France. Switzerland encompasses a variety of linguistic groups that might qualify as nations.

Correspondence between nation and state is particularly loose in Africa and Asia. The boundaries of many African and Asian states are left over from the older colonial era, when they were drawn by the colonizing powers to suit their own convenience.[12] Thus a crazy quilt of boundaries was superimposed on the land, with little regard for the culturally coherent groups of people living there. Once they regained their independence, of course, those people inherited these peculiar boundaries. The map of Nigeria in Figure 2–3 illustrates the loose correspondence between nation and state that exists in much of Africa today. In the Mideast, Turkey, Iraq, and Iran are all home to some of the Kurdish people, who are a minority in each of these countries and have made attempts to break away and form their own unified state. India includes fifteen official linguistic groups. And many other former colonies exhibit similar mixtures of state and nation.

With the modern importance of nationalism, we have come to think it a right of people, if they feel that they have a common nationality, to have a state to match that na-

---

[12]The correspondence between state and nation is reasonably close in South and Central America, for an unhappy reason: Here the native population was exterminated or enslaved, to be replaced by a reasonably coherent population of settlers from Europe; or, over a period of centuries they have been absorbed culturally in a *mestizo* blend of natives and Europeans.

**FIGURE 2–2**
Linguistic map of Europe.
  *Source:* Norman J. G. Pounds and Robert C. Kingsbury, *An Atlas of European Affairs* (New York: Praeger, 1964), p. 23.

tionality. This "right" has become a constant source of political tension and conflict for two reasons. As just pointed out, many state boundaries do not coincide with the geographic distribution of nations. But beyond this, the sense of nationhood is a subjective thing. A "feeling" on the part of a group of people may be stimulated or laid to rest by persuasive leaders and is therefore liable to change. Even if state boundaries could ever at any one time be brought into a perfect fit with the distribution of nations, this benign situation could not last, because new nations would gradually be invented and some old ones would fade and be forgotten. The once influential although small black nationalist

**FIGURE 2–3**
Tribal map of Nigeria.
   SOURCE: Pauline H. Baker, "Nigeria: Lurching Toward Unity," *Wilson Quarterly* 4 (Winter 1980): 78.

movement in the United States is just one example of an attempt to arouse a "nation" (the nation of blacks) among a people who had not generally thought of themselves as belonging to a separate nation.

   At any given time, then, the system of states will not coincide with the system of nations. Points at which state and nation fail to coincide are likely to be hot spots politically; indeed, many intense political struggles of recent years have resulted from such situations. The movement to separate Quebec from the rest of Canada; the war between East and West Pakistan, which resulted in the formation of a new state, Bangladesh; the Basque nationalist movement in Spain; the conflict between French- and Dutch-speaking Belgians; the civil war in Nigeria in 1967; the activities of the Palestine Liberation Organization, which embodies the desire of Palestinians for a state of their own; the chronic unrest among Kurds in Iraq, Iran, and Turkey; the attempt by the region of Chechnya to secede from Russia in 1994; above all, the bloody ethnic wars of the 1990s in Bosnia and Croatia—these are only a few examples of hot political conflicts occasioned by a disparity between state boundaries and people's sense of nationhood.

## CHALLENGES TO THE STATE

The state may have evolved over the last few centuries to be the dominant form of political organization, but today it is under strong challenge from both above and below.

Above the state, world leaders are groping for structures which would replace many functions of states and operate over a wider geographic range than the state. This has developed especially in economic matters. In Europe, a European union established by fifteen states (with another dozen or more trying to get into it) is in the process of taking over much of its member states' control of their own economies (see the discussion below). In North America, the United States, Canada, and Mexico have established a free trade zone within which trade will not be regulated by the governments. Worldwide, the International Monetary Fund (IMF) puts restrictions on its members' policies (Russia and other parts of the former Soviet Union joined in 1993, which will expand the influence of the IMF). In the area of environmental regulation, many cross-state bodies have been formed through which states give up their individual control of migratory species of wildlife, the production of pollutants, and so on.

The state is also under attack from below. Far from fading away with the development of modern economies, as most scholars of all stripes thought they would do, ethnic and regional separatist movements have exploded in the past couple of decades. From the Walloons in Belgium to Tamil separatists in Sri Lanka, to French Canadians in Quebec, to the Croatians and Slovenians in former Yugoslavia, to the Eritreans in Ethiopia, to the Baltic republics in the former Soviet Union—the list could include dozens of further examples—regional or ethnic aspirations, which twenty-five years ago were quiet, built up over the 1980s and 1990s into serious political movements capable at the least of paralyzing their states. At the same time—across North Africa, the Middle East, and southern Asia—militant Islam, the most dynamic religion of today's world, seeks to replace the secular states of the postwar period with religious political structures in which the state plays a relatively minor role, state boundaries would (ideally) fade, and the Islamic community would be ruled throughout by its religious leaders.

What has been happening? Why the challenges to the state? One way to look at it is to note ways in which the state may have become less valuable in meeting societies' needs. This could help explain both the challenge from "above" and the challenge from "below." From above, a series of environmental problems have appeared in recent years that are clearly going to become even more pressing in future years and are not readily dealt with by individual states. Swedish trees are dying because of pollution from industry in Britain, Germany, and other states; the chimney swift which breeds in Canada and the United States may cross the boundaries of eleven states in its annual migration; "greenhouse" gases warm every state in the world, regardless of whether they helped to produce them. These are problems that need broader, more overarching political structures.

Economically, the appropriate scale of industry has increased in the twentieth century. Few small states were ever able to develop an automobile industry. There is no Norwegian auto company or Dutch auto company, for instance; auto companies developed mostly in such large states as the United States, Britain, France, Italy, and Japan. Nuclear technology, the aircraft industry, and space technology require an even larger scale to work economically. Is it any wonder that states are banding together?

From the other end, the experience of the latter half of the twentieth century is that centralized states have been rather clumsy structures for fine-tuning responses to varying local needs in housing, education, health care, and so on. This has helped to fuel pressures for local and regional autonomy. Perhaps, too, with a waning of the symbols of nationalism in a world in which most states cannot control their own destinies militarily, ancient local symbolic attachments or religious symbolic attachments have risen more to the fore and have come to satisfy people's yearning for symbolic identity. Thus both from "above"—problems too big for states to deal with—and from "below" at the local level, states find themselves challenged.

The above paragraphs give rather a "choice"-oriented explanation of challenges to the state: Other structures can meet some of the people's needs better than the state, and so they have begun to rival the state. One might also develop a "power"-based explanation: The state really evolved as a military structure; the one thing that defined a state— that still defines "sovereignty," in fact—was that the state wielded a military force that could protect its people against invasion from outside its boundaries and could put down any internal challenge to the government's authority as well. Two developments in the latter half of the twentieth century, both born in the Second World War, have weakened this claim by the state to a monopoly of military power. First, nuclear weapons were invented. In the nuclear age, no government can protect its people against destruction from abroad; it may be able to reply in kind, but it cannot prevent its own destruction. Nuclear weapons are just too devastating for that. From the other end, guerrilla warfare came into its own in the Second World War; techniques for local, sustained military effort against superior central forces were developed that are being used today by insurgent local forces in dozens of places around the world. Militarily, the ability of states to control their destinies both against other states and against internal insurgency has diminished.

Economically, also, states are no longer able to control things as they once could. Just in the last decade, financial markets have ceased to be local to a given state, and thus controllable by the state's government. This has largely been a result of the invention of the computer—which makes it possible to conduct large-scale, complex transactions instantaneously across large distances—plus the invention of new financial and organizational strategies for business. The result is that governments, now placed in competition among themselves, must shape their economic, environmental, and other policies to attract capital rather than to regulate it.[13]

Whether we can better understand this from a "choice" or a "power" perspective, it is clear that the state is now seriously challenged.

## SOME POSSIBLE ALTERNATIVES

The world is still groping for alternatives to the state. And the state still has a lot of life left in it; by no means is it clear that it will go away! However, three possible alternatives of varying sorts are presented below:

[13]"The Stateless Corporation," *Business Week*, 14 May 1990, pp. 98–105.

## 1. Regional Integration

Many regions in the world have attempted to establish regional organizations that would have at least limited power to overrule and coordinate the actions of their member states. The Organization of American States in North and South America, the African unity movement, occasional attempts at economic union in Central America, and several abortive attempts to form a united Arab republic all attest to this wish, though none of these have succeeded very well. The European Union, which includes most of western Europe, has had considerable success at integrating the politics of its member states, so much so that one can at least conceive of a time at which one might ask whether its members were still sovereign states. (The European Union is discussed in greater detail later in this chapter.)

At its best, regional integration would only represent a consolidation of the system of states into a smaller number of larger states. But this might represent progress in its own right, and the process by which states were brought to yield up portions of their sovereignty voluntarily to a higher organization might teach us much about how the world system as a whole could begin to coordinate its members' activities.

## 2. The United Nations

There does exist an organization of almost all states of the world which is supposed to stand above them and lead them into peaceful coordination of their activities. The United Nations has little power to force states to cooperate, but it does have considerable persuasive power and has helped at least modestly to defuse several crises that could have led to war. And with the decline of Soviet-American rivalry in the 1900s it has seemed at least conceivable that the United Nations could emerge as a major structuring force in international relations. The United Nations is discussed in more detail in Chapter 17.

## 3. Communications and a "World Culture"

As electronic communication makes it possible to send messages easily from one end of the world to another, as people travel more widely and observe cultures that are new to them, the world is beginning to develop a more common set of attitudes. Different nations are becoming slightly less distinctive in their points of view. Blue jeans have become almost an international uniform of young people, and English has become an almost universal second language in which business is conducted among strangers. Much cultural richness may be lost in this homogenization, but it may become easier for populations of different states to understand each other's point of view. Too much faith should not be placed in this, since conflicts may as easily arise from understanding as from misunderstanding; remember, most murders occur within families. Still, it may be a hopeful sign.

## THE WEST, THE EAST, AND THE SOUTH

The states of the world have generally been grouped into three broad regions: the West, the East, and the South, the three regions indicated on the map in Figure 2–4. This is a set of categories that originally was based on the now-vanished "Cold War" between the Soviet Union and the United States. While the categories still make general sense, they are certainly not ideal. In particular, as you will see below, the term "South" covers a very diverse set of states.

The "West" comprises the industrialized states of North America and western Europe, plus Australia, New Zealand, and (probably) Japan. These are economically prosperous states, with a moderate degree of governmental direction in their economies, linked in fairly similar foreign and military policies, often with leadership from the United States.

The "East" comprises the erstwhile Soviet Union and its former eastern European satellites. These states are also modestly prosperous, though not so well off as the West. They are all involved in a massive effort to democratize their governments and reorient their economies from heavy governmental direction to more open systems like those of the West. Eventually the "East" may look a lot like the "West," but for now its states bear the mark of seventy years of a very different history.

These two regions make a good deal of sense, in that the states in each have a good deal in common with each other and are different in important ways from the world's other states. The remaining region, the "South," is something of a catchall region. During the Cold War the region was often called the "Third World," as the thing that distinguished its members was that they were neither of the West nor of the East. At that time, when both the United States and the Soviet Union were trying to enlist other states to join their "side," this distinction may have been important enough in itself; but beyond that, the states had little uniquely in common. In effect, the term "Third World" just meant "none of the above."

"South" is not a perfect term, either. As you see in Figure 2–4, the states of the South are generally south of those in the West and East, but Australia and New Zealand are great exceptions. "South" also refers to what is often called North–South conflict: a set of economic conflicts over trade and natural resources that generally divide less industrialized states of the South and the industrialized states of the West.

Whatever term one picks, however—"Third World," "South," or something else—this is a region of quite varied states. Over two-thirds of the world's population lives in the South. Politically, the region ranges from still-communist states like Cuba to conservative monarchies like Saudi Arabia. Western culture is relatively new to most of the region, except that many Latin American states have made active cultural contributions for centuries. Most states of the South are poor, but a number of them have great mineral wealth (like Saudi Arabia and other oil-producing countries), and some have become rather heavily industrialized (like Argentina, Brazil, Singapore, Malaysia, Thailand, and South Korea). With several exceptions, states of the South depend heavily on exports of raw materials or agricultural products—often on a single product, like Honduras's bananas or Bolivia's tin—which makes them subject to jolts when commodity prices swing. Most states of the South have rather new political structures, and their populations are generally not broadly involved in politics.

**FIGURE 2–4**
The West, the East, the South

### Example: State Building in Nigeria

No state's experience has been "typical," but it is useful to look at some examples in order to flesh out the concepts and analyses you have read so far in this chapter. In this section we will take a brief look at how the Nigerian state was established; in the next section, we will consider the European Community and how it is drawing a number of west European states into something new, which is a bit like a much broader "state."

Nigeria is a populous state on the west coast of Africa, with a population of 92 million. One out of five Africans lives in Nigeria, and its gross national product is second on the continent only to that of South Africa. The country is rich in oil, but it has so many people to feed that the average Nigerian is not especially well-off; in 1993, the average annual income was $310 per person.

Until 1960, Nigeria was a British colony; like most colonies, it was not constructed for internal coherence, but rather for the administrative convenience of the British. Over 250 different languages and dialects are spoken within its borders, and there is also an important religious split, as the north is primarily Muslim and the south is primarily Christian. After World War II, Britain experimented with various ways of handling this diversity. The plan eventually adopted was a decentralized system under which Nigeria was divided into three regions, each centered on one of the three main tribes (see Figure 2–3): (1) the northern region, based on the Hausa-Fulani tribe, (2) the western region, based on the Yorubas, and (3) the eastern region, based on the Ibos. These regions were administratively distinct, each having its own budget.

This arrangement continued in the initial democratic structure set up in 1960. The central government of the new state left many functions under the control of regional governments, in what is called a "federal" system. The situation was unstable, however, because tensions soon developed among the regions. The simple democratic procedures that were written into Nigeria's constitution favored the north, because it was the most populous region, and the north quickly established political control under the first prime minister, a northern Muslim named Abubakar Balewa.

However, the Ibos in the eastern region—a restless, economically active, and well-educated minority—felt stifled by the political domination of the north. Ibos all over Nigeria were disproportionately urban and held many technical and administrative positions. Three-quarters of Nigeria's diplomats were from the eastern region, as were about half the students who graduated from Nigerian universities in 1966.[14]

In 1966 a coup by Ibo officers toppled the democratic government and put an Ibo general at the head of the state. Six months later Muslim soldiers struck back and a

---

[14]Pauline H. Baker, "Nigeria: Lurching Toward Unity," *Wilson Quarterly 4* (Winter 1980): 76.

new government under Yakubu Gowon, a northerner but a Christian, was installed. At this point the eastern region seceded from Nigeria and proclaimed itself the state of Biafra. The federal government refused to accept Biafra's right to secede, and there followed a bloody civil war lasting 2 $1/2$ years, in which over a million people died. Eventually the Ibos were starved out and had to give up on secession. Gowon wisely followed a generous, conciliatory policy toward the defeated province and its leaders, one calculated to make it easy for them to rejoin the rest of the country.

Gowon had promised an eventual return to democracy, but he proved slow to deliver and was ousted in yet another military coup in 1975. He was replaced by General Olusegun Obasanjo, a Yoruba Christian who proceeded carefully to build the basis for a return to democracy. Elected local governments were established, and a new constitution was designed under which regional diversity would be respected in local affairs and no one region could dominate the central government. The state was divided into nineteen federal districts that, to some extent, broke down the old Hausa-Fulani, Yoruba, and Ibo regions. In order to be elected president, one had to receive not only at least one-third of the total popular vote but also at least one-fourth of the vote in two-thirds of the nineteen regions. Finally, power was divided between the president and a congress, so that regions that had not supported the president had a chance to defend themselves in the congress.

The first presidential election was held in 1979, and a northerner, Sheliu Shagari, was elected. He ruled for four years and was reelected in 1983, but his administration was marked by corruption and economic decay. Many Nigerians—most critically, the military—were dismayed by the greed of the new political class and their inability to overcome the regional/tribal/religious divisions of the country. Shagari's government was overthrown shortly after his reelection in 1983.

Since then, the country has been ruled almost continuously by the military. Generally the military has teased the public with promises of democracy, while continually delaying its implementation. General Ibrahim Babangida, for instance, who ruled from 1985 to 1993, spent years setting up a structure for elections (including banning all existing politicians from participation and setting up two new, statewide parties—a bizarre way to establish democracy!). When the elections were finally held, however, they were promptly annulled by the defense minister, General Sani Abacha, who took power himself. He promised democracy "in the future," established a committee to study democratization in a leisurely way, and in 1995 announced that he would step down three years later (1998) and hold democratic elections. Few Nigerians expect that he will yield power easily.

The generals have proved adept at corruption and at holding onto power, but at little else. General Babangida became a very wealthy man during his eight years in power, but the Nigerian economy is in deep distress. Oil revenues have declined because the government has no money to invest in development of the oil and gas fields. The country owes vast debts to foreign lenders. And as the generals print extra money for the government to spend, inflation rises.

Resistance to the generals is hampered by the religious/ethnic/regional division between the North and the South. Southerners believe that the Muslim North will never allow them to gain power. (Babangida and Abacha are both Northerners; Chief Moshood K. O. Abiola, the winner of the annulled 1993 election and who is now jailed, was from the South.) Northerners fear that since the South has the oil and most of the economic activity of the state, they will be left with nothing if they give up political power to the South as well.

### Example: State Building in the European Union[15]

The European Union (E.U.) is an association of fifteen states in western Europe that have agreed to coordinate much of their economic policy and some other policy areas; toward this end, they have set up a weak governmental structure that has some limited power over the governments of the member states. The Union is of particular interest to political scientists because it represents the most serious experiment to date in getting states to give up some of their sovereignty voluntarily.

There had been mutterings about the need to unify Europe throughout the nineteenth and early twentieth centuries, but the first real push to do so came after World War II. Many people thought that France and Germany, which had twice in the century fought disastrously against one another, should be bound together in such a way that war between them would be inconceivable. Also, the advantages of operating as a large economic unit, with a single free market open to all, were obvious to those who were trying to rebuild Europe after the war.

With encouragement and some pressure from the American side, what would grow into the European Union was established in 1956. A French administrator, Jean Monnet, was a key figure in this. He had led several European states through earlier cooperative efforts in coordinating their policies on coal, steel, and nuclear power to a point at which they were willing to merge much of their economic policymaking. Initially, only six states were members—West Germany, France, Italy, and the Low Countries. To Monnet's great disappointment, Great Britain refused at that time to join.

The main economic agreement among the initial members was that all trade would flow freely within their borders. That is, no member could place a tariff on imports of a product from another member in order to discourage local people from buying it. All the combined populations of the six member states were freely available as customers to any producer in any member state. Also, the member states soon coordinated their agricultural policy, giving up control of most agricultural policy within their borders to the governmental structure of the Union. It is the Union government that decides how high price supports will be for a given commodity, what will be charged for that commodity abroad, and so on. The Common Agricultural Policy was a breakthrough in regional integration, although it has proved in practice

---

[15]Until 1993, it was called the "European Community."

to be cumbersome and expensive, leading to large production surpluses and to high prices for consumers.

Currently the Union is in a state of ferment. In 1985 it decided to institute an entirely free internal market by 1992. This turned out to require hundreds of specific changes, some of them drastic, such as the establishment of something approaching common tax rates in all countries. Initially many observers thought that the resolution was a hollow gesture, but the prospect of real economic union seized the imagination of many people. The Union did accomplish most of the 1992 objectives, and a substantial amount of national independence was given up in the process.

In 1993, the member states tried to carry the process still farther with a new agreement, the Maastricht Treaty, which would have brought the states under a single currency. In effect, this meant that all member governments would have relinquished their independent financial policies, since to maintain a common currency would have required a unified central banking system. The most important parts of the treaty have proven impossible to implement, however, partly because of economic circumstances and partly because the prospect of giving up their familiar pounds, marks, and francs reawakened strong nationalist sentiments among the Europeans. For now, the treaty sits rather as a dead letter, and the Europeans seem to be focusing inward on the problems of their own states, rather than outward to build a stronger union. Still, the overall result of the past decade's efforts is a considerable degree of political and economic integration.

The original six members set up a governmental structure for the Union that stands more or less unchanged today. The two most important parts of the Union government are the Commission and the European Council, which make most of the rules and carry out executive functions. Two other parts are the Parliament and the Court of Justice. These have lesser powers but are still important.

The European Commission consists of seventeen appointed commissioners who head a bureaucracy of about 10,000 people. Commissioners are appointed by their home governments for a term of four years, but they must swear an oath to act on a European basis rather than in the interests of their home country. In practice the Commission has been the focal point of broad European interests, as opposed to national interests. In this it has been cheered on by its thousands of bureaucrats, whose lives and careers are obviously bound up in the Union. The Commission has consistently pushed for a blending of states in the Union and has frequently been opposed in this by one or more members states fearful of giving up too much sovereignty.

The Commission has a great deal of power. It dominates the setting of most of the Union budget ($85 billion in 1994) and makes many rules. As the only permanent part of the executive branch of the Union's government, it also takes the lead in initiating new proposals for policy.

The other part of the executive is the European Council, in which national interests are represented. It consists of the foreign ministers of the member states; these meet together several times a year to consider proposals from the Commission.[16]

---

[16]In addition, four times a year the Council consists of the prime ministers of the fifteen states. Important questions are saved for these "summit" meetings.

Any major policy proposal must be approved by the Council before it can go into effect. The Council votes on proposals, with large states getting extra votes. For many years there was an unwritten rule that any state could veto a proposal if the proposal affected what the state considered to be a "vital national interest." This practice has been canceled, however, as part of the 1993 package of political reforms to achieve closer political union. Over the years the European Council, with its emphasis on states' governments and their needs, has tended to retard the blending of the Union, but it has probably also made possible such blending as has occurred. Without this haven for the individual interests of member states, the Union might have fallen part long ago.

The Union also has a parliament, but as yet it has not had great legislative power. Policies of the Commission and Council are debated and criticized in the parliament, but the parliament does not have the final say over most decisions. For instance, it has final authority over only about one-third of the Union's budget. A change made in 1979, however, added to the power of the European Parliament. Before 1979, members of the European Parliament were chosen by the parliaments of their home countries, but since then the members have been directly elected by voters in their countries. While this was not a change that directly gave the European Parliament any new powers, it indirectly did a great deal. The members of the European Parliament are now the only officials of the Union who are elected, who are there because some ordinary people wanted them to be there. This gives them an advantage in prestige and "standing" and has also attracted more able, vigorous members. (In the earlier period, membership in the European Parliament was sometimes a way for a country's parties to kick their more tired members upstairs.) Since 1979 the European Parliament has used this new vigor to push for a greater role in the Union's decisions, and recent years have been marked by considerable squabbling between this body and the Council and Commission.

The European Parliament gained somewhat greater powers after 1993, and it may eventually develop into a powerful body. The expanded power of the Union vis-à-vis member states, brought about by the recent expansion of its powers in economic and monetary policy, has led to a concern for the "democratic deficit"—the fact that national parliaments have less control now over their states' economies and that the E.U. itself, with its strong bureaucracy, has little democratic accountability. Expanding the power of the European Parliament, the only E.U. institution that is elected, would be a natural way to address this problem.

Finally, the European Court of Justice is a court of twelve justices serving six-year terms. It rules on disputes over the treaties that the states signed on joining the Union. Most cases that come before the Court involve trade problems, but it also decides disputes among the governing institutions of the Union and about the individual rights of citizens in the member states. Over the years, the Court has pretty well established itself as dominant over the states' governments, although it has had to tread cautiously in order to avoid stepping on any government's feet. From 1956 to 1983, the Court ruled in only forty or so cases involving individual rights, but some of these cases demonstrated an astonishing willingness on the part of member states to subordinate themselves to the Union's laws. Court decisions have included such

**TABLE 2–1**

EUROPEAN UNION COMPARED WITH THE UNITED STATES

|  | Total Population | Total Armed Forces (1993) | 1992 Total Gross Domestic Product (Billions of Dollars) | 1993 Defense Expenditures (Billions of Dollars) |
|---|---|---|---|---|
| U.S.A. | 257,143,800 | 1,729,700 | $5946 | $277.2 |
| E.U. | 347,161,700 | 2,046,700 | $6803 | $144.2 |

*Source: The Military Balance 1992–1993* (London: International Institute for Strategic Studies, 1993).

questions as whether British teachers could legally whip their students, how soldiers could be disciplined in the Netherlands, and the conditions under which people could be put in prison to await trial in West Germany. (For a more detailed discussion of the European Court of Justice, see Chapter 16.)

The original six members of the Union prospered economically after 1956, and gradually other states joined, until the Union reached its present size of fifteen states. Together, the members of the European Union have great strength. As seen in Table 2–1, the members of the Union combined have a population greater than that of the United States; they have more people under arms, and their combined gross domestic products are greater. If they could pursue a unified foreign policy and develop a full-scale strategic nuclear force, they would be a superpower similar to the United States.

As of this writing, the European Union is also faced with the prospect of becoming even larger. The E.U.'s economic buoyancy, combined with the collapse of communism in eastern Europe and the Soviet Union, has brought a large number of new applications for membership. Austria, Finland, and Sweden signed agreements to join the Union in 1994, and the Czech Republic, Hungary, Malta, Norway, Poland, and Turkey have applications pending. Such expansion will complicate the already difficult problem of governance, and the prospect offers yet another incentive to reform the Union's constitution.

How close is the European Union to being something like a state? Clearly the member states have given up a good deal of their sovereignty to the Union. The Union has independent taxing powers, collecting a sales tax of just over 1 percent to finance its operation. It sets its members' tariff and trade policies as well as their policies on agricultural price supports. The European Court of Justice has successfully imposed surprisingly political judgments on member states. On the other hand, military control is the real core of statehood; in that area, the Union has not developed any control over its members. Most—but not all—members of the Union are also members of the NATO alliance. But even NATO has not been very successful at coordinating its members' military policies. (It has been difficult for NATO even to establish a standard caliber for rifle bullets, so its members could exchange ammunition in time of war.) With the end of the Cold War, however, the United States has become more detached from European defense; in 1991, it started a gradual reduction of 50 percent of its troops stationed in Europe. With the United States lessening its commitment, there might now emerge more real military coordination among the Union members, but this is definitely not certain.

The European Union illustrates nicely the gray area in which it becomes difficult to distinguish clearly when a state is a state. But without a military core, it is still something less than a state.

## FURTHER READING

Badie, Bertrand, and Birnbaum, Pierre. *The Sociology of the State.* Chicago: University of Chicago Press, 1983.

Birch, Anthony H. *Nationalism and National Integration.* London: Unwin Hyman, 1989.

Deutsch, Karl. *Nationalism and Social Communication.* Cambridge, Mass.: MIT Press, 1953.

Evans, P. B.; Reuschmayer, D.; and Skocpol, Theda, eds. *Bringing the State Back In.* Cambridge, England: Cambridge University Press, 1985.

Hah, Chong-do, and Martin, Jeffrey, "Toward a Synthesis of Conflict and Integration Theories of Nationalism." *World Politics* 27 (April 1975): 361–386.

Herz, John H. *The Nation-State and the Crisis of World Politics.* New York: David McKay, 1976.

Hobsbawm, E. J. *Nations and Nationalism since 1780: Programme, Myth, Reality.* Cambridge: Cambridge University Press, 1990.

Jackman, Robert W. *Power Without Force: The Political Capacity of Nation-States.* Ann Arbor, Mich: University of Michigan Press, 1993.

Mandel, Ernest. *Late Capitalism.* London: NLB, 1975, Chapter 15.

Migdal, Joel. *Strong Societies and Weak States: State-Society Relations and State Capabilities in the Third World.* Princeton: Princeton University Press, 1988.

Nettl, J. P. "The State as a Conceptual Variable." *World Politics* 20 (July 1968): 559–592.

Skocpol, Theda. *States and Social Revolutions.* Cambridge, England: Cambridge University Press, 1979.

Skowronek, Stephen. *Building a New American State: The Expansion of National Administrative Capacities, 1877–1920.* Cambridge: Cambridge University Press, 1982.

Tilly, Charles, ed. *The Formation of National States in Western Europe.* Princeton, N.J.: Princeton University Press 1975.

Wallerstein, Immanuel. *The Capitalist World Economy.* Cambridge, England: Cambridge University Press, 1979.

# 3

# MODERN IDEOLOGIES
# AND POLITICAL
# PHILOSOPHY

Most people approach politics through an *ideology*—a set of related ideas that modify one another, an organized set of ideas. For instance, one person may believe that everyone is basically selfish, that politicians are all crooks, that a citizen owes nothing to the state, that it is all right to cheat on one's taxes, that gun control is a bad thing because it keeps us from protecting ourselves, and so on. This is an ideology—a set of ideas about politics, all of which are related to one another and that modify and support each other. The belief that everyone is basically selfish helps provide a justification for the need to carry a gun, the wish to cheat on taxes helps make one comfortable in the belief that the citizen owes nothing to the state, and so on. Another person may believe that individual freedom is terribly important, that government should regulate people as little as possible, that the United States should try to protect any people whose government is oppressing them, and that the U.S. government should not tell people whether or not they may carry guns. This is also ideology, an organized set of ideas that modify and support each other. In this second example, the high value placed on individual freedom supports both a wish to protect human rights around the world and a reluctance to have the government regulate the ownership of guns.

Ideologies are useful to people, both for their own personal ease and satisfaction and for their public political activities. From the *personal* point of view, an ideology helps us to make sense reasonably easily and quickly of the varied political questions that come to our attention. In any given week, the newspaper will raise questions about the control or deregulation of oil prices, the busing of schoolchildren to improve racial balance, the level of support for retired people in the social security system, the size of the military budget, federal acquisition of land for parks and wildlife refuges, and so forth. If we had to consider each of these issues anew, starting from scratch, we would have an awesome task. But if we approach each from the standpoint of a general ideology that we have developed over time, the job is much simpler. Most issues will turn out to be instances of more general principles that can quickly be settled by applying the principles.

The new issues may also modify our ideology, since an ideology is not graven in stone. For instance, devout Catholics who believe that the government should regulate people as little as possible may find themselves torn over the issue of legalized abortion and may modify some of their more general ideas about politics in light of the new issue. An ideology, then, is a continually developing, organized set of ideas about politics that helps us to make sense of the myriad of political questions that face us.[1]

An ideology also has *public* uses. In politics, we are normally concerned to convince others that a policy we favor is the right one. We usually have personal reasons for favoring the policy (we may want taxes to be cut because we are wealthy, oppose gun control because we like to collect guns, or favor national health insurance because we are poor), but these personal reasons are not usually good *public* reasons. People distrust a self-interested argument. Also, arguing for a policy by giving one's personal reasons for it would not win many allies; only those who are also rich could be convinced by the argument "I'm wealthy, therefore I want to see taxes cut." In political argument, we usually try to attract as many allies as possible to our position, and so personal reasons will not make good arguments. *Ideologies,* however, can serve this purpose very well. The wealthy person who argues, "Government spending and taxation hamper individual initiative," may appeal to a great many people who for various reasons favor individual initiative.

Ideologies are developed and maintained because of both their usefulness to individuals in responding to events and their utility in public political argument. This is not a conscious, cynical process in which we deliberately frame an ideology so as to enlist allies in some cause or another. Rather, we are all comfortable with ideology and generally, over time, work out ideologies that fit our particular needs. Too, ideologies are not simply the creation of those who hold them; they tend to take on a life of their own and guide their holders' political views in unanticipated ways. A business leader who feels that government should regulate as little as possible (for what we may think are obvious reasons) may find that this ideology also leads to positions—not particularly connected to self-interest—on the censorship of books in public libraries or the regulation of handguns.

An ideology is an organized set of ideas that helps us both to make sense out of politics for ourselves and to present arguments effectively in public. We obviously develop our ideologies in such a way that they fit our needs and predispositions, reflecting what we want; but they also take on a life of their own and *guide* our decisions.

## AMERICAN IDEOLOGIES

All of us have some sort of ideology, in the sense that our various ideas about politics bear some sort of relationship one to another. But not every ideology is equally neat and

---

[1]A review of the literature on ideology and an interesting approach are offered by Pamela Johnston Conover and Stanley Feldman, "Belief System Organization in the American Electorate," in *The Electorate Reconsidered*, ed. John Pierce and John L. Sullivan (Beverly Hills, Calif.: Sage, 1980).

tidy, nor is every ideology worked out in equally full detail. Americans' ideologies tend to be more loosely organized than those of other peoples. In fact, Americans tend to admit exceptions and inconsistencies into their ideologies rather cheerfully.

Two main ideologies are found among Americans: "American liberalism" and "American conservatism." The former is characterized in the following ways. Compared with American conservatism, it is:

• More concerned about inequality (between the poor and the well-off, between blacks and whites, between women and men).

• Less anxious to avoid using the power of the government to make conditions for people more equal. Thus, American liberals are more willing than American conservatives to see a larger government, supplied by higher taxes. And they are more willing to see the government intervene through such devices as forced integration of schools and a graduated income tax in order to alleviate inequalities.

• More concerned to maintain freedom of expression and the separation of church and state.

• Less concerned about the maintenance of morality, at least in the sense of prescribed rules of conduct, and opposed to the use of state power to ban the "victimless crimes" of prostitution, drug use, and gambling. Similarly, American liberalism opposes laws to ban abortion.

• More reluctant, at least in recent decades, to maintain a large military force and use military power abroad, although historically American liberals and conservatives have gone back and forth on this issue.

American conservatism represents the other side of all these comparisons.

American liberalism and American conservatism are not neat ideologies. It is hard to see, for instance, what logical connections exist among the various attitudes detailed above. In fact, it frequently happens that an American political figure is "liberal" on some of these issues and "conservative" on others. American labor unions, for example, have generally been quite concerned about issues of equality but have not been equally concerned about an issue like the separation of church and state.

As we shall see below, both American liberalism and American conservatism are variants of a more general and well worked out ideology known simply as *liberalism.* "American liberalism" and "American conservatism" are simply differing versions that have sprung up in a predominantly liberal society, to unite under the loose term "liberal" (American version) the weaker parts of society (the poor, those who were discriminated against, those whose moral values went against the dominant grain, those with unpopular ideas) against the stronger and more dominant parts, whose interests were represented by "conservatism" (American version). Both ideologies are thus hodgepodges, representing marriages of political convenience, and it is difficult to find internal coherence among the various parts of either one.

However, even though the American ideologies are untidy, they have still been of some influence. American labor leaders have probably been more concerned than they might otherwise have been with freedom of expression because of this issue's association with the redistribution of income in American liberalism. And Americans concerned about high taxes have probably picked up more concern than they might otherwise have had for questions of official morality because of the juxtaposition of these positions in American conservatism.

## LIBERALISM

The two American ideologies are actually variants of *liberalism,* one of the three great ideologies that developed in Europe in the eighteenth and nineteenth centuries. These ideologies—liberalism, conservatism, and socialism—have provided the framework for most political debate throughout the world since then.

To understand their development, we must remember that the medieval social order in Europe was one in which people were bound together in patterns of rather strict domination, with mutual responsibilities between those who were dominated and those who dominated them, between "top dogs" and "bottom dogs." Farmers often lived in a condition of near-slavery, subject to a local church official or a member of the nobility. A farmer paid heavy taxes to his local patron and had to provide him with specified periods of labor for road building, war, and so on. In many parts of Europe, the farmer was not allowed to leave his land and move elsewhere without the permission of his patron. Furthermore, farmers were required to offer the patron formal social respect and deference. In return, the patron was supposed to provide his farmers with protection and with help in times of illness or want. Such industry as existed was organized in guilds, which laid down strict rules as to how an item was to be manufactured, how many such items were to be produced, and what was to be charged for them. Trade in many items was subject to ancient rules: The king might have a monopoly on trade in a commodity such as salt, for instance, or a particular town might have the enduring right to receive all imports of some specific item. Jews were a pariah group, banned from many occupations and generally forbidden to own land. The church maintained a stern control over proper belief (a striking example of this occurred when, in 1616, the church forced the great astronomer Galileo to state, contrary to his true convictions, that he did not believe the earth orbited around the sun). To transport goods from one end of a country to another could be a complex affair, in which the carrier of the goods was required to pay taxes, fees, and tributes to various local personages at all stages of the journey. Politics was the province of the king, the nobility, and the church.

For our present purposes, two things are important about these arrangements: (1) People were bound to each other in complex and cumbersome systems of domination; and (2) the arrangements were static, difficult to change. Ownership of the land, feudal privileges, the rights of the church, the political role of the king and nobility, the power of the guilds—all were granted in perpetuity and could only evolve slowly over time.

Onto this setting—faintly in the fifteenth and sixteenth centuries, in crescendo through the seventeenth and eighteenth centuries, and with a deafening crash in the nineteenth century—came modern large-scale commerce and industry. The new commercial and industrial leaders chafed under the static restrictions of medieval society. In order to carry on large-scale trade and manufacture, it was often necessary to move commodities over great distances; laborers had to be gathered together at large factories, which often involved moving people from one end of the country to another;

canals and roads had to be built, which would run through many different patrons' domains; prices and the nature of goods often had to be adjusted to reflect changing needs and technology; science and invention had to be free to pursue truth wherever they found it, regardless of orthodoxy. All these requirements collided with the organization of preindustrial medieval society. The new and increasingly powerful commercial and industrial elite cast about for ways to make society more fluid and manageable. One helpful solution, as we saw in the preceding chapter, was the invention of the modern state. Another was the appearance of liberalism.

Liberalism was not introduced by the commercial and industrial leaders themselves. Rather, it was invented by intellectuals who were moved by the general artistic and scientific restlessness of the age. But it suited the new economic leaders, and they warmed to it. It gave them a view of politics that could make sense to them in light of their needs, and it allowed them to argue for their causes in ways that were less crass than simply saying, "We wish to limit the power of the nobility, the guilds, and the church because we want to make money."

Liberalism posits as the highest good of society *the ability of the members of that society to develop their individual capacities to the fullest extent.* That is, in a good society, all individuals should be able to develop their minds, musical talents, athletic abilities, or any other gift as much as possible. This requires, according to liberalism, that people be maximally responsible for their own actions, rather than having someone else do things for them or tell them what to do. It is only by acting and feeling the consequences of such action that we can develop our capacity to act.

This is the central assumption of liberalism, from which a number of consequences flow. For instance, in his essay *On Representative Government,* John Stuart Mill based his argument in favor of democratic government on liberal premises, as follows: The chief end of politics is to allow people to become responsible and mature. They can do this only if they take part in decisions affecting their own lives. Therefore, even though a wise and benevolent despot or monarch might actually make better decisions on behalf of the people than they could make for themselves, democracy would be better, since under it the people make their own decisions, mistakes and all. Therefore, some form of democracy is the best kind of government.

---

JOHN STUART MILL AND LIBERALISM

John Stuart Mill (1806–1873) was a major figure in liberal thought. His father, James Mill, himself an important figure in the history of British philosophy, educated young John himself, following an incredible regimen: John was reading Greek at age three, and by the time he reached maturity he probably knew more of science and literature than anyone else in Britain. He spent his adult years in a sinecure with the British East India company, which allowed him plenty of time to write. His main contribution to liberal thought was to reconcile, in a fairly tight logical system, individual freedom with the general good of society. Curiously for his time, John Stuart Mill was a strong feminist and advocated women's suffrage. Some have ascribed this to the influence of his wife, Harriet Taylor Mill, while others simply believe his logic pushed him to this conclusion.

By the same sorts of argument, the following elements follow from the basic liberal premise; together, they constitute the liberal ideology:

- Democracy of some sort is the proper form of government.
- People should have full intellectual freedom, including freedom of speech, freedom of religion, and freedom of the press. (They should have responsibility for their own values, so that they will develop the ability to judge values.)
- Government should remain minimal and should regulate people's lives very little. (As few decisions as possible should be made *for* people, so that they learn to make decision for themselves.)
- In particular, people should be free to regulate their own economic activity. (As above.)
- Power of one person over another is a bad thing; hence government should be organized so as to guard against abuses of power. (Again, one person should not make decisions for another.)

Liberalism flourished especially in Great Britain and her colonies, perhaps because Britain was the first country to industrialize. In Britain, liberal forces first gained control of the House of Commons and the cabinet in 1832; through the nineteenth century, political control of the country seesawed back and forth between liberals and conservatives. (See below for a discussion of conservatism.) In the United States, the new Constitution of 1789, with its precautions against a concentration of power in any one part of the government and its guarantees of various individual freedoms, clearly signified the ascendance of liberalism. On the continent of Europe, liberalism was a potent force throughout the nineteenth century, but it was nowhere as strong as in Britain and her former colonies. Most western European countries had liberal constitutions by the end of World War I, but by that time liberalism was fading quickly.

Note that with regard to the distinction between the "choice" and "power" perspectives, liberals will strongly favor a view of politics as choice. To liberals, power is simply a bad thing that should be limited as much as possible. Power allows some people to force choices on others, which flies directly in the face of liberal principles. To a liberal, politics should properly consist of public choices, in the making of which each person shares equally. And furthermore, as many choices as possible should be kept private. That is, the sphere of politics itself should be limited.

## THE CONSERVATIVE REACTION

When liberalism arose to challenge the existing social arrangements, the defenders of those arrangements needed an ideology to counteract the persuasive power of liberalism. Conservatism was developed in response to this need.

Conservatism in the European sense is unfamiliar to Americans, since it is quite different from American conservatism. Defenders of existing arrangements in Europe pointed out quite properly that liberalism is an individualistic doctrine; that is, liberalism looks on society as simply consisting of the individuals constituting it. To liberals, the whole of society equals the sum of its component parts, so that a society is happiest when the total of individuals' happiness is greatest. This is implied in the basic premise of liberalism, that the goodness of a society is to be judged by the extent to which its members individually are able to develop their capacities.

In opposition to this, conservatism holds that societies and other groups of people are *more* than just the sums of their parts, that a group of people creates greater happiness through its existence and maintenance as a group than its members could individually produce for themselves. Liberalism, conservatives say, is a lonely and selfish philosophy whose ultimate result would be a group of people resolved to better themselves with no regard for the people around them.

Conservatives regard it as important that their society should have order and structure and that this structure should be stable enough to let people know where they stand with regard to each other. Most important, an ordered group develops and maintains religion and standards of morality. People gain greater happiness as members of a family, members of a church, and members of society than they could possibly gain individually. This is what conservatives see as the highest good of society: *the maintenance of ordered community and of common values.*

In such a society, it is silly to try to keep one person from doing things for another or to keep one individual from exercising power over another. The whole point of "community" is that people are important as members, not as individuals. What matters is how they fit into the web of mutual responsibilities.

Since the structure of the community should be relatively stable and predictable so that all may easily fit into their place in it, there is nothing wrong with assigning power to people by even such arbitrary devices as heredity if those people can be expected to use their power wisely. Patterns of domination that have evolved gradually over time should not be changed casually, since what has grown slowly is at least familiar to us and must have had some virtue to have lasted so long. Conservatism is an ideology that accepts and welcomes power; conservatives believe that appropriate arrangements for power will ensure good treatment for everyone.

It is obvious why this philosophy based on ordered community was useful to the aristocracy, the established church, and others who were trying to maintain their positions against the liberal challenge. But ideologies take on a life of their own, and conservatism stresses another theme that might not otherwise have come so naturally to the defenders of the status quo: the responsibilities of power. Where liberalism is suspicious of power and seeks to limit it, conservatism sees power as binding and shaping its

---

EDMUND BURKE AND CONSERVATISM

Edmund Burke (1729–1797) is perhaps the most important figure in the development of conservative thought, at least in Britain. He was born and educated in Dublin, Ireland, the son of a lawyer. Although he was a professional politician and a great orator in the House of Commons, he was too intellectual and independent to rise to a major position in his party. As a philosopher, he was not abstract and did not deal in logical systems. Rather, he drew pragmatically from experience. What was already a well-developed conservative ideology was sharpened for him by what he saw as the excesses of the French Revolution.

holder in good ways. Conservatives do not see a powerful monarch or president as one who is in a position to treat people capriciously. Rather, they see such an official as one who is in a position of awesome responsibility, with generally very little choice as to courses of action. Conservatism stresses the responsibility of the powerful in a community to help the weak, a position opposed to the view of liberals that the weak should be given responsibility for their own affairs. Because of this side of conservatism, European conservatives have not been especially reluctant to help the poor or to develop the welfare state. In the late eighteenth century in Britain, under the conservative regime, there was already a system of guaranteed minimum income for anyone in Britain—a floor below which no one was to be allowed to fall. *Abolishing* this system was one of the first tasks of the liberals when they took power in 1832, To take another example, when Otto von Bismarck, the conservative chancellor of Germany from 1871 to 1890, introduced the world's first systems of unemployment insurance, workers' compensation, and social security, he had no apparent sense that he was doing something out of character.

We have noted that conservatism is unfamiliar to Americans. This is because, to the extent that the early immigrants had any ideas about politics at all, America was founded by liberals and populated largely by liberals. Most of the early settlers, after all, were trying to escape the rigidities of the old order in Europe. But also, our more fluid society has had few ordered systems of domination; conservatism, which is a defense of such systems, has therefore been largely irrelevant.[2]

In recent years, however, one of our few ordered systems of domination has come under liberal attack and something rather like conservatism has arisen as a defense. The feminist attack on men's domination of women has often been framed as a classic statement of liberal argument. Women should be free to take on all sorts of responsibility, according to feminists, so that they can develop their capacities to the fullest. Protective laws (limiting the hours women may work, barring them from certain dangerous jobs, protecting them from combat in the armed forces, and so on) are wrong because in being protected from unpleasantness people are made weak and dependent. Feminists do not want women put "on a pedestal."

Opponents of feminism have often responded in ways that are akin to conservatism. The traditional family is a good thing in its own right, they say, especially if children are involved. It is the family we should be thinking of, not the individuals who make it up. And families work better, children are raised better, everyone is in the end happier, if there is a clear structure of authority in the family rather than a situation in which each member is striving individually.

Conservatism was a strong force throughout Europe in the nineteenth and early twentieth centuries. With the massive changes brought by World War II and its aftermath, European conservatism changed. The nobility were generally destroyed or discredited, the church was in ferment, and most countries had introduced a sweeping expansion of taxation and social services, the "welfare state," in order to make people more equal. After the huge destruction of the war, it was not always clear that there was a social order for conservatism to defend.

---

[2]Louis Hartz, *The Liberal Tradition in America* (New York: Harcourt Brace, 1955).

But conservatism adapted fairly rapidly to these changed circumstances. Their traditional emphasis on the responsibility of the powerful to help the poor and weak, together with a willingness (in contrast to the position of liberals) to see power concentrated, made it fairly easy for conservatives to accept the welfare state. Also, conservatism welcomes active encouragement of religion by the state, whereas liberalism is suspicious of it; large numbers of Europeans after the war apparently felt a need for a stability of values offered by religion, although among the youngest recent generations religious practice has dropped off sharply. While liberalism has declined in Europe throughout the twentieth century, conservatism has lived on healthily. Its adherents have accepted the welfare state but urged that it be built in ways that are consistent with traditional moral values and that it should not lead to a leveling of society. In other words, conservatives feel that some structure should remain by which one part of society can lead the rest. In Britain, the Liberal party declined during the 1920s and 1930s, until it is weak today; but the Conservative party remained as the chief opponent of the new Labour party. When Labour introduced the welfare state in 1945, the Conservatives accepted it within a few years and went on to dominate British politics over the following decades. On the continent of Europe, after the war, Christian Democratic parties arose in many countries; these adhere to an established church but are flexible and pragmatic with regard to taxes and social programs. They have been especially strong in Italy and Germany, while a somewhat similar movement, the Gaullist movement, dominated French politics from 1958 to 1981. One can safely characterize the politics of most west European states since World War II as having consisted of a conflict between socialism (described in the next section) and a modified conservatism.

In the Third World, liberalism is generally weak (poor countries that are trying to develop their economies apparently find that they cannot afford to limit and restrain concentrations of power) and conservatism is rather strong. Traditional religious leaders and the aristocracy, as in Saudi Arabia and Iran, or new elites of business leaders, as in Japan or Brazil, can often maintain a strong political movement to keep the political leadership of the state in their hands. Frequently, the two groups join forces in a conservative movement.

There is often a strong element of direction from the military in such movements as well, as in the series of conservative regimes in South Korea from 1952 to 1987. While all military governments are by no means conservative, there is often an affinity between military leaders and conservative political parties. Military organization requires an ordered structure of command in which certain members of the military direct the activities of other members. This is rather similar to the conservative view of society as a whole and may help to make military leaders comfortable with conservatism.[3]

## THE SOCIALIST ALTERNATIVE

When liberalism first arose to challenge the established order, it drew considerable support from the "working class," the workers and their families who were beginning to congregate in the growing cities. Workers especially liked the assumption that all peo-

---

[3]However, see the more detailed discussion of military governments in Chapter 8.

ple were equal and should have an equal opportunity to develop their talents. And they liked the liberal doctrine of democracy, which would recognize them as having full and equal citizenship rights. In 1848 a wave of attempted revolutions by liberals swept across the continent of Europe; in most of these, skilled workers played a leading part, along with shopkeepers and other small businessmen. In Britain, the leaders of most labor unions were active in the Liberal party as late as 1900.

But through the latter part of the nineteenth century, the enthusiasm of the working class for liberalism weakened. Liberalism implied not only that people should be politically equal but that they should be regulated and helped by the government as little as possible. Workers were in a weak position socially and economically, and they often found that they would like help from the government in ways that were inconsistent with liberalism. Governmental protection against unemployment and sickness, governmental regulation of working hours and of safety in the factories, governmental prohibition of child labor—these and similar wishes of labor were inconsistent with liberal principles. Naturally, compromises and accommodations could be reached within the movement, and labor was not left totally out in the cold, but the fact remained that labor often found that it had to buck the basic philosophy of the movement of which it was a part. When a new ideology appeared that was more congenial to labor, workers moved to it fairly readily. This ideology was socialism.

Socialism retained the assumption of liberalism that all persons deserve equal treatment by the state and should have equal opportunities to develop themselves; but unlike liberalism it did not posit that people could develop individually, and it was not as suspicious as liberalism of the concentration of power and of positive action by the state. Karl Marx (1818–1883) was the greatest socialist writer, and socialism since Marx has been heavily influenced by his views. Marx thought that society consisted not of individuals but of *classes*. A class is a group of people who share the same relationship to the means of production and who therefore develop a distinctive view of themselves and of the world. Marx thought that the most important thing about us is our work, that this is what creates for us most of our view of the world; people who share similar work (a similar "relationship to the means of production") form the natural basis for a class. The aristocracy had been such a class, intellectuals were such a class, the industrialists were

---

KARL MARX AND SOCIALISM

Karl Marx (1818–1883) was raised at first in Bonn, Germany, and later in Berlin. After graduating from the university, Marx and his close friend Frederich Engels (1820–1895) worked as journalists. In 1848 they wrote the *Communist Manifesto* and, in the aftermath of unsuccessful revolutions in Germany in that year, were forced to flee Germany. They settled in London, where Engels's family had connections and Engels could take care of Marx. Marx did not return to Germany until shortly before his death. In London he worked as a correspondent for the *New York Tribune* and wrote his massive, major work, *Das Kapital*. Marx combined a sweeping view of history with an astonishing appetite for the minutiae of economics. At its most basic level, his theory of politics, as of all other human activity, was that it is determined solely by economic processes and can be understood by economic analysis.

such a class, and now a new class—the working class—was appearing in Europe. To Marx, people did not develop themselves individually—in a vacuum, as it were—but of and through the class to which they belonged. According to this view, individuals do not form their own values, their own ideas about politics, their own sense of their needs; rather they and the people they associate with form these things communally in ways that are difficult to specify. A person may contribute to these values and ideas, but so do all of the other members of his or her class. And each member draws much more from the class than he or she or any other single member contributes to it.

For Marx, then, the basic unit of concern was the class. As he saw it, the working class was oppressed; it was made to give up its members' labor to feed the rich capitalist class. But this was wrong, because the working class were numerically much larger than the capitalist class and their oppression bred great misery. Therefore the working class should take over control of the government and the government should take over all industry, so that the workers themselves, through their government, would control the industries in which they worked. This would ensure fair treatment for everyone.

The writings of Marx and other socialists derived their energy and moral force from the writers' awareness of the truly miserable conditions under which workers lived in the nineteenth century. Marx's friend and collaborator Friedrich Engels, in his study of the living conditions of English workers, quoted an Anglican priest's account in 1844 of conditions in his parish:

> It contains 1,400 houses, inhabited by 2,795 families, comprising a population of 12,000. The space within which this large amount of population are living is less than 400 yards square,

Karl Marx, architect of socialist ideology.
(UPI/Bettmann Newsphoto)

and it is no uncommon thing for a man and his wife, with four or five children, and sometimes the grandfather and grandmother, to be found living in a room from ten to twelve feet square, and which serves them for eating and working in. . . . There is not one father of a family in ten throughout the entire district that possesses any clothes but his working dress, and that too commonly in the worst tattered condition; and with many this wretched clothing form their only covering at night, with nothing better than a bag of straw or shavings to lie upon.[4]

Engels goes on to describe his own investigation of the living conditions of the working class in the city of Manchester:

One walks along a very rough path on the river bank, in between clothesposts and washing lines to reach a chaotic group of little, one-storied, one-roomed cabins. Most of them have earth floors, and working, living and sleeping all take place in the one room. In such a hole, barely six feet long and five feet wide, I saw two beds—and what beds and bedding!—which filled the room, except for the fireplace and the doorstep. Several of these huts, as far as I could see, were completely empty, although the door was open and the inhabitants were leaning against the door posts. In front of the doors filth and garbage abounded. I could not see the pavement, but from time to time, I felt it was there because my feet scraped it.[5]

Marx developed a theory of history arguing that a revolution of the working class was not only appropriate but inevitable. According to Marx's _dialectical_ theory, all history has consisted of a successive unfolding of domination by one group, leading to revolution against that group, followed by domination by a new group (the group that had led the successful revolution), leading to yet another revolution, and so on. Thus, Europe in the Middle Ages was dominated by the nobility, but there was an internal contradiction in their rule: They needed the services of bankers and traders but were barred by their social codes from undertaking this work themselves. Thus they created a new class, the capitalist class, which (as we have seen above) eventually overthrew them in the industrial revolution and with the coming of liberalism. The capitalist class now dominated Europe, said Marx, but there was an internal contradiction in their rule as well, which would eventually lead to their overthrow. The capitalists had had to create a new class, the working class, to serve their needs. But because capitalists are forced by their code to seek ever-greater profits, they would have to grind the working class nearer and nearer to starvation, until at last the situation would be intolerable and there would be a revolution. Note that this theory of politics is based almost solely on the use of power.

Marx thought that the process of history would have worked itself out with the victory of the working class, because now for the first time the dominant class would not be a minority but would include almost the whole population. His theory of history and revolution was powerfully attractive to workers. It told them that their unhappy plight was not their own fault as individuals but rather a condition imposed on all of them as a class by the working out of a broad historical process. Furthermore, it prophesied that they must, in the end, prevail over the capitalists because that is the way history works.

---

[4]Friedrich Engels, *The Condition of the Working Class in England*, tr. by W. O. Henderson and W. H. Chaloner (Oxford, England: Basil Blackwell, 1958), pp. 35 and 36.
[5]Ibid., p. 61.

Finally, it assured them that once they had prevailed a brave new world would be created in which the cycle of revolutions was no longer necessary. In the words of a favorite British working class hymn:

> I will not cease from mental fight,
> Nor shall my sword sleep in my hand,
> Till we have built Jerusalem
> In England's green and pleasant land.
> (originally from WILLIAM BLAKE'S *Milton*)

Socialism burst explosively on Europe. In 1850 there were only a few socialists on the continent. By the early 1900s the Social Democratic party was the largest party in Germany and was growing fast; socialism was growing just as rapidly in other western European countries.

## COMMUNISM AND SOCIALISM

In 1917, a key event occurred in the development of socialism when Lenin's Bolsheviks succeeded in seizing control of the Russian Empire and transforming it into a socialist state renamed the Union of Soviet Socialist Republics (U.S.S.R.). Marx and Engels had never fully settled whether they thought the working class should take control of the state peacefully through electoral victory or violently through revolution. Many socialists thought revolution was the only answer, while others believed deeply in democracy. Lenin's successful revolution galvanized those who wanted to take the route of revolution, and over the years after 1917 they tried to dominate the socialist movement. They argued that the one state that had now successfully become socialist, the U.S.S.R., should lead all socialists in the world. The attempt to commit socialism to a revolutionary strategy led to a split in the socialist movement in the 1920s. The revolutionists set themselves up as Communist parties, while the democratic socialists continued to call themselves Socialist or sometimes Democratic Socialist parties.

The split has endured, so that there are today two branches of socialism, although outside of a few places like Cuba, communism has been in broad retreat for the last few years. Communists have generally held to a revolutionary strategy, although with the passage of time they have grown a good deal less emphatic about it. Socialists have been much more willing to settle for a portion of power within an only partially socialist system, and they have generally worked within a democratic framework. Socialists have also been more willing than communists to settle for partial improvements for workers, rather than holding out for a total change.

In the period after World War II, most of eastern Europe was governed by communists, with military help from the U.S.S.R. By 1989 communism in eastern Europe and the Soviet Union had become more a bureaucratic sink than a shining ideology, and over the next two years these communist regimes all collapsed. The eastern European states now tend to look to democratic socialism, combined with free markets, as a model; the remnants of the Soviet Union have made stabs at economic change, but most have become preoccupied with working out ethnic and nationalistic conflicts. In western Europe, Socialists have participated strongly in government for many years, and Socialists took the lead in bringing the modern welfare state to Europe. Communism and socialism have both been strong forces in the Third World. China, Cuba, and Vietnam have more or less communist governments, while scores of Third World states have socialist governments.

## FASCISM

In the 1920s and 1930s there arose a political movement, fascism, which did not hang together well as ideology (the twentieth century, unlike the nineteenth century, did not emphasize the intellectual completeness of theories) but was rather more a style of politics and a popular movement. Adolf Hitler in Germany, Benito Mussolini in Italy, and Francisco Franco in Spain all established fascist regimes at this time. Fascists did not generally write elaborations of their theory, since among other things they despised intellectualism and ideology. Accordingly most analysts of fascism as an ideology have looked mainly at what fascists did. The essence of fascism seems to have been a rejection of most institutions of modern life, combined with a national rebirth focused on a charismatic, dictatorial leader. Fascists were all antisocialist, generally anticapitalist, and (at least in Hitler's and Mussolini's cases) hostile to the church. They tended to glorify instead a mythical war-based society of the past—for Mussolini the ancient Roman Empire, for Hitler the Teutonic knights of the Middle Ages and Wagner's dreamy stories about the old Germanic gods.

Their political style was opportunist. All used violence and terror to advance their movements. Somewhat paradoxically, since they despised modern institutions, they were also "up to date" and presented themselves as forward-looking. Hitler was the first German politician to campaign from an airplane, for instance, and the design of fascist propaganda and rallies was often done in the current, modern-looking "art deco" style.

Fascism appealed particularly to those who felt left out in the modern age. In Spain and Italy, these were mostly the traditional elites, who felt threatened both by modern industrial managers and by socialist workers. In Germany, the "left out" appear to have been mainly the middle class, small farmers, and shopkeepers. The uprooting of European civilization in the First World War helped prepare the ground as well, adding to the sense of loss among the disinherited of modern life.

The details of fascism actually varied a good deal from one place to another. The Nazi party of Germany attacked the existing social system, including the churches, more actively than most. It had a strong element of anti-Semitic racism that was not present in Italian or Spanish fascism and that ultimately led to the murder of millions of Jews. Spanish fascism identified with conservative church leadership and supported the church. Italian fascism was marked by an attempt to reorganize the economy into "corporations"—guilds of employers and workers in each industry. Such variations in fascist policy again underscore the fact that fascism was, and is, rather more a political style than a system of ideas.

The defeat of the fascist powers in World War II ended most organized fascism; but since then, when established sets of people have felt their positions threatened by modern change—especially by new racial or ethnic claims, or by immigration of new groups into the country—echoes of fascism have often been heard. The American Nazi party, anti-immigrant movements in Europe, and so on, often involve a dramatic leader, violence, and a denial of modern change in ways that show kinship with the old fascist movements.

## THE GREAT IDEOLOGIES IN THE LATE TWENTIETH CENTURY

With the long period of general peace in Europe and among other industrialized states since World War II, some of the edge has worn off the conflict among the great modern ideologies. As modern society has become more firmly established, the old grievances do not seem to move people as strongly as they once did. With the decline of religion (outside of Islamic regions) and with the poor economic performance of socialist states, there has been a resurgence of liberalism—but a liberalism modified by considerable governmental support for the weak.

Many leaders of parties, especially those which hold responsibility for the government of a state, have begun to modify their ideologies in light of practical experience. The most dramatic example of this is provided by the collapse of the Communist regimes of Eastern Europe and Russia. Many states of this region have become liberal democracies, and all have abandoned their old, ideologically based Communist systems.

Other leaders, too, show more and more a compromised blend of ideologies. Britain's Margaret Thatcher was for fifteen years the leader of the Conservative party, which among other things emphasizes close ties to the Anglican Church and the monarchy. But her personal ideology combined these conservative elements with a set of very liberal economic policies calling for a great shrinkage of the state's role in the economy, marked by the "privatization" (sale to private owners) of many government enterprises. On the other side of the spectrum, some socialists such as Premier Felipe Gonzalez of Spain have so blended their socialism with concerns for efficiency and stable economic growth that it is scarcely recognizable as a doctrine of conflict between classes. And Italy's former Communist Party, with even the word "Communist" now removed from its name, has emerged in the mid-1990s as the Democratic Party of the Left, a left-of-center, democratic party—and is one of the leading parties of post-Cold War Italy.

However, ideological conflict is not dead in the late twentieth century. In Europe, new "green" parties have raised a set of issues that established leaders, accustomed to the old ideologies, have found hard to absorb into their debates. These issues, labeled "postindustrial issues" by Ronald Inglehart, include feminism, protection of the environment, and open and spontaneous styles of life.[6] In part, they have been represented by totally new parties (among others, the Greens); in part they have found their way into established Socialist parties where they often represent a minority voice. In Socialist parties, the new mood has especially produced interest in direct participation by workers in the management of their industries.[7] At the other end of the spectrum, anti-

[6]Ronald Inglehart, *Culture Shift in Advanced Industrial Society* (Princeton, N.J.: Princeton University Press, 1990).

[7]See, for example, W. Rand Smith, "Toward 'Autogestion' in Socialist France? The Impact of Industrial Relations Reform," *West European Politics* 10 (no. 1, January 1987): 46–62.

immigrant parties, such as France's National Front, raise issues of race and nationalism that had been thought long dead since the Second World War. Outside of Europe, militant Islam, with its claims for a religious state, has raised the political temperature in many states of North Africa, the Mideast, and South Asia.

History, and the development of ideologies, does not stop. The great modern ideologies were a product of the tension between Europe's industrialization and the static institutions Europe had inherited from its feudal past. As that tension now recedes, other sources of ideological development have come to the fore, in a sometimes confusing mix of forces and tensions: the practical economic experiences of the Soviet Union and the United States; the increasing problem of degradation of the environment; the resurgence of militant Islam; the discovery of youth and women as classes, even though Marxist socialism saw classes as based solely on economic position; and the increasingly clear division of interests between rich states and poor states—the "North" and the "South."

## POLITICAL PHILOSOPHY THROUGH THE AGES

In this chapter we have followed the development of modern ideologies, approximately since the eighteenth century. But great minds throughout the ages have been concerned with the question of how politics should properly be conducted. Let us conclude the chapter by sketching briefly the development of political philosophy up to the modern period.

The Greeks were the first great political philosophers, especially the Greeks of Athens a few centuries before the birth of Christ. They were especially concerned with the nature of justice and with the question of what sort of constitution would produce the best political community. Plato (428–347 B.C.) was the greatest of the Athenian philosophers. In *The Republic*, he describes a utopian political community in which good, gifted people are selected as infants to be the leaders ("guardians") and are carefully trained (their reading censored, their minds honed by the study of mathematics) so that they will be able to rule wisely and autocratically. His was an ideal world, not likely to be accomplished in fact. It is reminiscent of modern conservatism.

While Plato sought for the ideal, Aristotle (384–322 B.C.), another great Athenian, restricted himself more to observations of the world around him. Aristotle thought that if people could be trusted to rule unselfishly, the very best constitution was one in which a single person ruled; the next best was aristocracy, the rule of the few; and the least good was rule by a large number of people. In practice, however, people were selfish, and Aristotle argued that—since the perversion of the best leads to the worst—selfish rule by a single person was worse than selfish rule by a large number. So in the end he argued for something like democracy.

With their concerns about the proper role of citizens, about the nature of justice, and about what sort of constitution produces a good community and good people, the Greeks laid the foundation for all Western political philosophy that followed. During the Roman Empire relatively little was done in this area, the Romans tending simply to rely on what the Greeks had already done. With the coming of the Christian church in the first centuries after Christ, however, a new period of activity began. The develop-

---

ANALYTIC POLITICAL PHILOSOPHY

Much work in the study of political philosophy is of the sort presented in this chapter—a history of the development of political ideas, with critical commentary on them. An alternative way of approaching the study draws its inspiration from the modern school of "analytic philosophy," which concerns itself especially with the meaning of words.

This approach, called "analytic political philosophy," does not primarily concern itself with the history of political ideas or with critical argument about them at a general level. Rather, its practitioners feel that they can contribute most to our understanding of politics by clarifying the language we use when we talk about politics. Certainly, a problem of muddled language lies behind many political arguments. The United States calls itself a "democracy," and so did the Soviet Union throughout the post-War period until its recent dissolution. The two meant quite different things by the word, but this was often forgotten in red-faced arguments along the lines of "We're a democracy!" "Are not!" "Are!" "Aren't!"

Some questions commonly dealt with by analytic political philosophers are, What is the state? (you already had a taste of the complexities of this question in Chapter 2) and, more important, What are our *obligations* to the state? What is the "public interest?" What should be considered "rights," as in "human rights"? What should be meant by "equality"? And so on.

One excellent example of work in the mode of analytic political philosophy is Hannah Pitkin's study, *The Concept of Representation*, in which the author examines all the varied ways in which, over the last several centuries, the word "representation" has been used, in order to make clear what *general, central* meaning it has.[1] A useful collection of analytic works is *Political Philosophy*, edited by Anthony Quinton.[2]

[1]Hannah Pitkin, *The Concept of Representation* (Berkeley: University of California Press, 1967).
[2]Anthony Quinton, ed., *Political Philosophy* (Oxford, England: Oxford University Press, 1967).

---

ment of a church that claimed allegiance from people all over Europe raised to the forefront the question of just what obligation people bore to their *earthly* rulers. If they were ruled by God in Christ, why should they do what their king told them to do? What should they do, for instance, if ordered by their king to do something that was a sin?

Much of the development of political philosophy for a thousand years or so centered on this question, and the answers shifted as the relative power of the church and of secular rulers waxed and waned. Early Christian writers, perhaps reflecting the weakness of the young church, claimed a rather modest role for the church in the affairs of this world. The greatest of these writers was Saint Augustine (354–430), who argued that government was made necessary by humanity's sinfulness and that only once we were without sin could we be ruled by God. To Augustine, government was a necessary evil (*made* necessary, in fact, by evil), which at least produced internal order for sinful humanity.

As the church grew in power, popes sought to assert more authority over secular rulers. By the Middle Ages, Saint Thomas Aquinas (1225–1274) was asserting that the church was responsible for people's spiritual well-being and rulers were responsible for their physical well-being; since the spiritual was more important than the physical, however, rulers must be guided by the church whenever the church held that spiritual needs were involved.

The church was not without opposition in this thrust, of course, especially as it weakened in later centuries. A curious and famous response to it was that of Niccoló Machiavelli (1469–1527), who wished to help kings resist the church and wrote *The Prince*, a primer of how to be successful king, to help them. In it he argued that a king should be ruthless and pragmatic, not swayed by sentiment or morality.

Toward the end of the Middle Ages, and as Europe entered the modern period, kings grew stronger and the church weakened. This became particularly clear during the Reformation, when the historic Catholic church was replaced in much of northern Europe by local Protestant churches established by local kings. The pendulum of political philosophy now swung back against the church, as in the writings of Martin Luther (1483–1546), who returned to Saint Augustine's doctrine that government is a necessity to which even faithful Christians should submit.

As kings now became more powerful, questions of political philosophy shifted to what obligations people in general bore to *them*. This question was brought to a head in the English Civil War (1647–1649), in which a diverse group of opponents to the king succeeded in deposing him and set up a republic that lasted for a bit over a decade. This successful challenge to royal authority focused attention on the question of the duties owed to kings and eventually led to the development of liberalism, discussed above.

One particularly important writer who participated in this debate was Thomas Hobbes (1588–1679), author of *Leviathan*, a strangely modern defense of authority. (Hobbes does not specify whether that authority must be vested in a king.) His argument is as follows: All people are selfish; in the absence of authority they will turn on each other, and life will be "solitary, poor, nasty, brutish, and short." To avoid this, people voluntarily band together into states and contract to give their rights to a sovereign, who will rule autocratically to provide a peace and order for all. Hobbes's theory was intended primarily to justify the rule of kings, but it could be used to justify any sort of dictatorship. Of their free wills, by a cooperative decision, the people set up a power to dominate them for the common good.

With the questioning of royal authority at this time, the stage was set for the development of liberalism and of the other modern ideologies responding to liberalism; the bulk of this chapter has dealt with these ideologies.


## FURTHER READING

Arendt, Hannah, *The Origins of Totalitarianism*. New York: Harcourt Brace, 1951.

Berlin, Isaiah. "Does Political Theory Still Exist?" In *Philosophy, Politics, and Society*, 2nd series. Ed. P. Laslett and W. G. Runciman. Oxford, England: Basil Blackwell, 1962.

Bronowski, Jacob, and Mazlish, Bruce. *The Western Intellectual Tradition*. New York: Harper & Row, 1960.

Cassels, Alan. *Fascism*. Arlington Heights, Ill.: Harlan Davidson, 1985.

Conover, Pamela Johnston, and Feldman, Stanley. "Belief System Organization in the American Electorate: An Alternate Approach." In *The Electorate Reconsidered*. Ed. John C. Pierce and John L. Sullivan. Beverly Hills, Calif: Sage, 1980.

Converse, Philip E. "The Nature of Belief Systems in Mass Publics." In *Ideology and Discontent*. Ed. David E. Apter. New York: Free Press, 1964.

Dahl, Robert. *A Preface to Democratic Theory*. Chicago: University of Chicago Press, 1956.

Dahl, Robert. *Democracy and Its Critics*. New Haven: Yale University Press, 1989.

Ebenstein, William, and Fogelman, Edwin. *Today's Isms: Communism, Fascism, Capitalism, Socialism*. 9th ed. Englewood Cliffs, N.J.: Prentice-Hall, 1985.

Laqueur, Walter, ed. *Fascism: A Reader's Guide*. Berkeley: University of California Press, 1976.

Plamenatz, J. "The Uses of Political Theory." *Political Studies* 8 (1960): 37–47.

Rawls, John. *Political Liberalism*. New York: Columbia University Press, 1993.

———. *A Theory of Justice*. Cambridge, Mass.: Belknap, 1971.

Riker, William, *Liberalism against Populism*. San Francisco: Freeman, 1982.

Sibley, Mulford Q. *Political Ideas and Ideologies*. New York: Harper & Row, 1970.

Strauss, Leo. "What Is Political Philosophy?" *Journal of Politics* 19 (August 1957): 343–368.

Voegelin, Eric. *Order and History*. Baton Rouge: Louisiana State University Press, 1956.

Wolin, Sheldon S. *Politics and Vision*. Boston: Little, Brown, 1960.

# 4

# POLICIES OF THE STATE

In Chapter 2 we saw that the modern state is a relatively recent invention. It developed gradually over the last several centuries and is developing still, as people come to expect the state to take care of more and more aspects of their lives and as military operations—the special purview of the state—become more complex and expensive. In this chapter we shall survey some of the most important policies of modern states in order to consider the variety of things the state does today.

Figure 4–1 charts the growth of state activity since the nineteenth century for Great Britain, France, Sweden, and the United States.

The most interesting thing about the figure is that these four countries have developed in much the same way, though they have had quite different kinds of governments and their experiences during the twentieth century have varied a great deal. France was occupied by Germany from 1941 to 1945. Britain had a socialist government from 1945 to 1951 and intermittently after that. Sweden was ruled uninterruptedly by a socialist party from 1932 to 1976 and intermittently thereafter, and is well known for its wide-ranging welfare state. The United States, on the other hand, has never had a socialist government, though the New Deal after 1932 was strongly oriented toward reform and the expansion of social programs. France, Britain, and the United States participated in both World Wars, while Sweden was neutral in both. Despite these political and historical differences, the four countries show a rather similar expansion of state activity. During the latter part of the nineteenth century and into the early twentieth, all four devoted a stable and relatively small percentage of their wealth to the government. Government spending accounted for approximately 8 to 10 percent of all economic activity in Britain, Sweden, and the United States and for approximately 15 percent in France. Beginning about the time of World War I, however, governmental spending began to

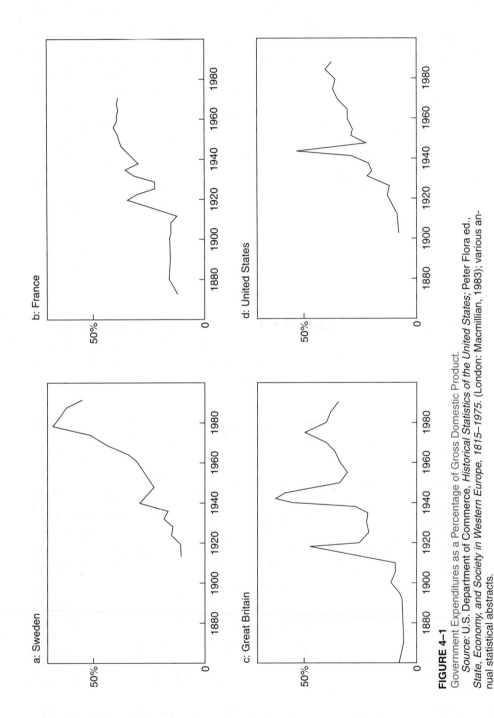

**FIGURE 4–1**

Government Expenditures as a Percentage of Gross Domestic Product.
*Source:* U.S. Department of Commerce, *Historical Statistics of the United States;* Peter Flora ed., *State, Economy, and Society in Western Europe, 1815–1975.* (London: Macmillian, 1983); various an-nual statistical abstracts.

take up more and more of the economy, until by 1971, it accounted for 34 percent (United States) to 49 percent (Sweden) of all economic activity.

The two great world wars appear to have contributed to this growth. Britain showed great jumps in the government's role in the economy at both wars, while France surged at the First World War and the United States surged at the Second World War. (France was defeated quite early in World War II, and the United States entered World War I only near the end of the war.) When the governments' roles subsided again after the wars, they generally did not return to the same levels as before. This pattern is most pronounced in the British case, but it is evident in the other two as well. The lasting expansion of government as a result of these wars is probably due not only to the actual expenditures in the wars but also to the fact that in the "total warfare" of the twentieth century, governments have become accustomed to controlling the lives of their people rather directly—rationing the goods they may buy, telling them what jobs they may work at, and so on. After the wars, the governments intervened actively in people's lives and acted this way on behalf of other causes as well.

Sweden was neutral during both wars, and so they did not have the same effect on her as they had on Britain, Italy, and the United States. But Sweden, too, left behind the stable, low level of expenditure that had characterized her in the earlier part of the period and, with a socialist government, began in the 1930s a steady increase in the government's share of the economy. By the 1960s, this had brought Sweden up to the same levels as the other three countries, and during the 1970s, Sweden surpassed all three.

A heavy governmental role in society appears to be typical of industrialized democracies late in the twentieth century. When we note that 35 percent of the U.S. gross national product consisted of governmental expenditures, this means that slightly over one-third of all purchasing of goods and services was done by the government.

There seems to be a strong pressure in industrialized democracies to expand the role of the state. This was well illustrated by Sweden in the late 1970s. In 1976 a nonsocialist government replaced the Socialists, who had been in power almost continuously since 1932. This new government had pledged to avoid expanding the role of government, but as Sweden entered a period of economic difficulty and businesses looked as though they might fail, the government felt it had to take over some of them and keep them going so as to prevent unemployment. Thus the *non*socialist government ended up nationalizing a number of industries, including the country's largest shipbuilding firm.

As a result of such pressures, to which all industrialized democracies seem to be subject, the industrialized democracies do not vary a great deal with regard to the degree of governmental involvement in society and the economy. In all of them the governmental role has expanded greatly during the twentieth century and is now very large. We do see some reaction to the great expansion in a modest downward movement in the charts for Britain under Margaret Thatcher in the 1980s and for Sweden after 1978, a point at which governmental expenditures had risen to two-thirds of the GDP. There obviously can come a point at which too much is too much. Still, the overall norm seems to be large governmental involvement. By about 1990, the four countries for which we have information in Figure 4–1 ranged from 36 percent of GDP (Britain) to 54 percent (Sweden).

In addition to this expansion of the government's role in the industrialized democracies, an even more marked expansion of this kind occurred with the establishment of communist governments in sixteen countries during the twentieth century. Most of these systems, however—at least, those in Europe—have now been engaged for the last few years in a massive move in the opposite direction, "privatizing" firms that had been owned and run by the state. This effort has dwarfed the rather small "privatization" movement that also occurred in many Western democracies. Conservative British Prime Minister Margaret Thatcher, for instance, privatized two dozen firms over a twelve-year period; Poland privatized over 3,000 in just a couple of years.

We cannot present figures to measure the role the state had in communist societies, as we did for industrialized democracies in Figure 4–1, because the state was so closely enmeshed in a communist economy that one could not clearly delineate where state spending ended and private spending began. It is enough for our purposes here to realize that in communist systems, the state played a dominant role. But it is also worth remembering that even in the communist systems the state did not control everything that happened, either in the economy or in other affairs. In all the communist systems there was some private economic activity. For instance, about 25 percent of agricultural production in the Soviet Union came from small plots (accounting for only 2 percent of the arable land!) that the peasants were allowed to farm for profit. And in Poland, almost all farms were privately owned. Apart from such exceptions, however, the fact remains that the coming of communism inevitably meant a massive expansion of the role of government.

If the industrialized democracies are all pretty similar with regard to the extent of governmental activity, the picture is different among states of the South. Here there is a wider range of governmental activity, and governmental involvement is generally lower than it is in the industrialized democracies. Table 4–1 gives a few examples.

As we have seen, the "South" is a bit of a catchall category, and the politics of the countries grouped in this category varies greatly. The extent of governmental activity in the economy varies just as greatly, and it is hard to come up with explanations for this.

**TABLE 4–1**

GOVERNMENTAL REVENUES AS A PERCENTAGE OF THE GROSS DOMESTIC PRODUCT
IN SELECTED STATES OF THE SOUTH

| Country | Government's percent of economic activity | Location | Governmental form |
|---|---|---|---|
| Zaire | 3% | Africa | dictatorship |
| Thailand | 19% | Asia | military-dominated partial democracy |
| Egypt | 36% | Middle East | one-party state |
| Israel | 40% | Middle East | democracy |
| Dominican Republic | 11% | South America | democracy |
| Paraguay | 14% | South America | recent democracy |
| India | 15% | Asia | democracy |

*Source:* International Monetary Fund, *Government Finance Statistics Yearbook,* 1994.

It is perhaps no surprise that Paraguay, which until the last few years was governed by a primitive military dictatorship, does not have an especially active government; but then why does the democratic Dominican Republic have a similarly low governmental profile?

Whereas the politics of industrialized democracies involves a rather standard set of pressures from business, interest groups, and the international community—which result in a similar level of governmental activity from one such country to the next—politics in the Third World is much more variable, less developed, and more fluid. Thus it is more difficult to generalize about politics of the South than about the politics of either industrialized democracies or communist systems.

## WHAT DO GOVERNMENTS DO?

We have seen that governments generally have gotten much larger in the twentieth century. What is it that these governments do? In general, their activities fall under four main headings, in order of the degree of governmental intervention: transfer of resources, subsidies with strings attached, regulation, and development and administration.

### 1. Transfer of Resources

A government often takes resources from some people and gives them to others without offering much direction as to what the transferred resources are to be used for. An American example of this is the social security system, which taxes employers and their workers, and gives the proceeds of the tax to retired people, the disabled, and the survivors of wage earners who have died young.

### 2. Subsidies with Strings Attached

As a somewhat more active form of intervention, the government may provide money to some of the people, but with the requirement that it be used in certain ways. The U.S. government voted a series of subsidies to Chrysler Corporation in the early 1980s, for instance, but with the requirement that Chrysler cut its costs, hold down wage increases, and so on. With its liberal tradition, the United States has been a bit reluctant to impose such state guidance, but in many other countries, the practice is quite pervasive. In the Scandinavian countries, for example, complex sets of purposive subsidies direct most aspects of the economy. Just to give one example, the Norwegian government—as part of a general campaign over the postwar period to keep the population from concentrating in the southeast, in the vicinity of Oslo—has provided a state subsidy on all milk produced in the western part of the country. This has had the two desired effects: (1) Milk prices have stayed low for the consumer; and (2) the dairy industry in the east was destroyed, helping to keep the population more evenly distributed. Note that such governmental intervention is not free; tax money is used to pay the subsidy, and many dairy farmers in the east suffered from the change.

'HOW D'YA LIKE THAT? MOSCOW SAYS TO FORGET ABOUT COMMUNISM - THEY WERE JUST KIDDING.'

Frequently, government subsidies occur not as direct payments but as *tax expenditures*, reductions in taxes for people who use their money in certain approved ways. In the United States, taxpayers have been encouraged by targeted reductions in their taxes to do such things as buy municipal bonds, invest in oil companies, and make their homes energy efficient.

### 3. Regulation

The government may also directly lay down rules telling people how to conduct their affairs. Traditional areas of regulation prohibit crimes such as murder, theft, or extortion. The twentieth century has seen an explosion of regulatory activity beyond this traditional sphere everywhere; many countries now regulate the way in which foods may be prepared or packaged, what sorts of things may be printed in books or newspapers, what type of access the handicapped must have to business premises, how many pollutants may be emitted into the air, and so on.

As regulatory activity has increased, regulations have rectified many abuses. In many countries today the air is cleaner, children are safer, food is more accurately labeled, workers are less vulnerable to injury—all because of government regulation. But regulation, too, is not free. It does not cost the government a great deal to set and administer regulations, but critics charge that the complicated mass of regulations that exists in many countries channels too much of the people's effort into keeping records, paying for lawyers and courts, and so on.

A rough measure of the growth of regulatory activity in recent decades in the United States is the number of pages in the annual *Federal Register*. This is a publication of the

**TABLE 4–2**
PAGES CONTAINED IN SELECTED
YEARS OF THE *FEDERAL REGISTER*

| | |
|---|---|
| 1936 | 2,355 |
| 1946 | 14,528 |
| 1956 | 10,528 |
| 1966 | 16,850 |
| 1975 | 60,221 |
| 1984 | 50,997 |
| 1990 | 53,618 |
| 1994 | 68,107 |

*Source:* Morris P. Fiorina, *Congress: Keystone of the Washington Establishment* (New Haven, Conn.: Yale University Press, 1977), p. 93; *The Federal Register* for 1984, 1990, 1994.

General Services Administration which updates rules and regulations set by the federal government. Table 4–2 presents the number of pages published in the *Federal Register* during selected years. Note especially the huge growth in regulatory activity from 1966 to 1975 and the slight reduction under the Reagan and Bush administrations in the 1980s.

### 4. Development and Administration

Finally, the government is not restricted to merely supervising how other people conduct their affairs but may step in and do the job itself. Defense and diplomacy are obvious areas where the government must do this, and education is another activity in which governments have felt that they must be active. (In the latter case, however, they have not generally felt the need to have a monopoly. In the United States, for instance, significant numbers of children are educated in private or parochial schools.)

There are other, more controversial areas in which some governments have chosen to develop and administer programs themselves. Especially notable here is nationalization, by which a government takes over one or another industry—the trains, the steel industry, auto manufacturing, or what have you—and runs it. The intent is that the industry should then be operated for the general public good rather than for private gain, but nationalized industries have generally not performed well. Critics charge, on the one hand, that nationalization makes the management of the industry cumbersome and inefficient and, on the other hand, that the civil servants who run the nationalized industries do not in fact do things all that differently than the old "selfish" managers did. Following a flurry of nationalization after socialist parties came to power (generally after World War II in Europe, or on the establishment of national independence in the states of the South), nationalization has gone rather out of vogue. In the late 1970s and early 1980s, however, many European countries felt that they had to nationalize numerous industries in order to keep them from going bankrupt and putting their employees out of work. This is generally a shortsighted policy, since it means that inefficient businesses

---

WHY ARE THE WORLD'S STATES EXPANDING?

Almost all states in the world today are expanding in the degree to which they intervene in their people's lives. Why this is so is a challenging puzzle for political scientists. David Cameron ("The Expansion of the Public Economy: A Comparative Analysis," *American Political Science Review 72* [December 1978]: 1243–1261) reviews five main explanations that have been advanced:

1   As people become more prosperous, they may want more and more done for them and are willing to pay for it. Thus, as industrialization makes people more prosperous, the state naturally grows.
2   As governments have become more clever at using "hidden taxes" such as excise taxes and payroll withholding of income taxes, they can get away with taxing people more heavily, and the state grows.
3   Electoral democracy results in a "bidding up" of the state's operations as parties compete to see which can promise more services to the voters.
4   Once governmental bureaucracies are established, they develop internal pressures for expansion. Inevitably, they succeed in slowly ratcheting upward the scope of their operations.
5   As world trade grows and states' economies become more and more subject to disruption by events in the international economy, their governments are less and less able to control what is happening in the state. The governments must then grow in order to compensate for the greater difficulty they find in functioning.

The jury is out, and will stay out for a long time, as to which among these explanations are valid. For examinations of evidence on the subject, see Cameron's article and also David Lowery and William D. Berry, "The Growth of Government in the United States," *American Journal of Political Science 27* (November 1983): 665–694.

Note, incidentally, that of the five proposed explanations, numbers 1 and 5 are based on the perspective of politics as choice, numbers 2 and 4 are based on the perspective of politics as power, and number 3 is ambiguous.

Note also the irony that this expansion coincides with growing challenges to the state (See pp. 34–35).

---

are kept in operation with the public absorbing their losses; but it is understandable that governments would not want to see large numbers of workers lose their jobs all at once.

Most countries have more of their industry nationalized than the United States does. Most countries of the South have significantly nationalized industries. And in western Europe, most countries have many more of their industries nationalized than does the United States. In France, for example, until recently the following industries were operated wholly or largely by the state: insurance, banking, automobile manufacturing, air transport, the railroads, natural gas, electricity, and coal. A number of these are now being "privatized"—sold to private ownership.

These, then, are the four main forms of governmental activity: transfer of resources, subsidies with strings attached, regulation, and the development and administration of programs. In the next chapter we shall look more closely at whether one or another of these forms of activity is preferable. For the remainder of the chapter, let us look a bit more closely at some selected areas of policy in order to see what sort of attention various governments have paid to them.

## DEFENSE POLICY

This is the one area of policy in which governments have almost without exception proceeded by developing and administering programs themselves and have insisted on holding a monopoly with regard to the policy. Private schools, private hospitals, and so on, are sometimes tolerated by governments, but this is practically never true of private armies!

As Table 4–3 shows, states vary a great deal in the effort they expend on defense. The industrialized democracies generally spend a few percent of their GNP on defense. Canada, the United States, and Britain all have volunteer armies, and none of the industrialized democracies in Table 4–3 spent more on defense than the United States did (5.3 percent of the gross national product in 1992). On the average, in 1987 all industrialized democracies (including those not appearing in Table 4–3) spent 2.9 percent of their gross national product on defense.[1]

Countries of the South vary tremendously in their military expenditures. Algeria, Columbia, Paraguay, Tanzania, and Madagascar show up as fairly low in Table 4–3, but Israel, Saudi Arabia, and North Korea are quite high. Some parts of the South have been the scene of continuing tensions in recent decades, with frequent threats of war, and countries in those regions may spend shocking sums on defense. North Korea, in particular, has ruined its economy by its massive military expenditures. In East Africa and the Middle East, many countries spend as much as 10 percent or more of their gross national product on defense. This is tragic, since defense spending neither feeds people nor furthers economic development. Outside of those "hot spot" regions, countries of the South, on the average, spent 3.3 percent of their gross national product on defense in 1986.[2]

The actual use to which this investment in the military is put varies a great deal from one country to another. The two superpowers, the United States and the U.S.S.R., invested substantially in nuclear weapons and missiles, although with the end of the Cold War they are cutting back considerably. Beyond this, the U.S.S.R. emphasized the development of a large land army, since it had long borders with potential enemies in China and Europe. The United States, with its peaceful borders, has emphasized more the development of its navy, so that it can keep in touch with its allies around the world and support them.

The military often play a special role in states of the South, simply because they are often the most "modern," best-organized group. They may figure importantly in the politics of the state, as we shall see in Chapter 8. But beyond this, they may serve as an important modernizing force. An organization through which thousands of young men

---

[1]International Institute for Strategic Studies, *The Military Balance, 1988–89* (London: Adlard & Son, 1989).
[2]Ibid.

**TABLE 4–3**
DEFENSE PREPARATIONS FOR SELECTED STATES

| | Military service | Percent of population in active military | Percent of GNP spent on defense |
|---|---|---|---|
| Russia | 18 months | 1.2 | 6.6 |
| Canada | Voluntary | 0.3 | 1.8 |
| France | 10 months | 0.7 | 3.2 |
| Germany | 12 months | 0.5 | 2.0 |
| Great Britain | Voluntary | 0.4 | 3.2 |
| United States | Voluntary | 0.6 | 4.6 |
| Israel | Men: 3 years | 3.4 | 9.8 |
| | Women: 21 months | | |
| Egypt | 3 years | 0.8 | 3.7 |
| Saudi Arabia | Voluntary | 0.8 | 13.1 |
| Algeria | 18 months | 0.4 | 2.6 |
| Colombia | 1–2 years | 0.4 | 2.0 |
| Paraguay | 12 months | 0.3 | 1.1 |
| South Korea | 26 months | 1.4 | 4.2 |
| North Korea | 3–10 years | 4.9 | 25.5 |
| Tanzania | 2 years | 0.2 | 3.2 |
| Madagascar | 18 months | 0.2 | 1.2 |
| Myanmar | Voluntary | 0.6 | 10.8 |

*Sources:* International Institute for Strategic Studies, *The Military Balance,* 1994–95 (London: Adlard & Son, 1995).

pass each year, in which they are taught disciplined methods of sanitation and organization, in which they learn how to use machinery, and so on—and from which they often return to their home villages—can be an important educational force as well as serving to defend the state.[3]

## EDUCATION

The most basic service that most governments are expected to offer their people is education. This is a prerequisite of economic development for the country as a whole, and it greatly expands the world of the individuals who are educated. Many nations of the South, whose populations were largely illiterate at the time independence was acquired, have had an uphill fight in bringing education to their peoples.

[3]See for example John J. Johnson, ed., *The Role of the Military in Underdeveloped Countries* (Princeton, N.J.: Princeton University Press, 1962).

**TABLE 4–4**

EDUCATIONAL EFFORT FOR SELECTED SCHOOLS

|  | Percent of GDP spent on education | Percent of eligible youth enrolled in high school* | Adult literacy rate (percent) |
|---|---|---|---|
| Russia | 8.2 | 94 | 98 |
| China | 1.7 | 54 | 78 |
| Canada | 7.6 | 107 | 97 |
| France | 5.7 | 102 | — |
| Great Britain | 5.2 | 86 | — |
| United States | 5.3 | 94 | 99 |
| Japan | 4.7 | 97 | — |
| Algeria | 5.7 | 59 | 57 |
| Costa Rica | 4.5 | 47 | 93 |
| Israel | 5.8 | 86 | 95 |
| Haiti | 1.8 | 22 | 53 |
| India | 3.9 | 49 | 52 |
| Madagascar | 1.5 | 15 | 80 |
| Botswana | 7.5 | 54 | 74 |
| Mexico | 5.2 | 56 | 88 |

*May exceed 100 percent because it is the "gross" percent: total enrollment (of all ages) divided by the population of the relevant age.

*Source:* UNESCO, *Statistical Yearbook,* 1993.

As Table 4–4 shows, most countries invest a substantial effort in this area of policy and most countries of the South, have already accomplished a good deal along these lines. Others have had to overcome great difficulties. One of these, Botswana, clearly exemplifies the problems faced by a poor state in attempting to educate its people. It takes almost 8 percent of Botswana's gross domestic product to provide sufficient education. Even at that, not many frills are possible; in 1990 (the most recent census), only 54 percent of youths between the ages of fourteen and seventeen were enrolled in school. However, 74 percent of adults can read, a dramatic improvement over the general illiteracy of the country at the time it attained independence.

## RESEARCH AND DEVELOPMENT

If states of the South must concentrate on spreading basic education throughout their populations, the more highly developed economies of the industrialized democracies and of communist systems depend on continuing technological development to give them a competitive edge in making "high-tech" goods (computers, electrical machinery,

Peruvian schoolchildren. (Paul Conklin)

aircraft, etc.) for export. In most of these developed economies, labor costs are too high to allow basic industries such as the manufacture of clothing or of simple plastic goods to be competitive internationally. States of the South can produce such goods much more cheaply. The special province of the developed economies is in the production of high-tech goods and services, where their scientific and technological capacities allow them to outperform everyone else.[4]

Table 4–5 shows how dependent the industrialized democracies, in particular, are on high-tech industry for their trade with other states. Even in the 1980s, half of all U.S. exports were high-tech goods. When we consider that about an additional 10 percent of U.S. exports were products of agriculture, we can see that the United States functions in the economic world primarily as a producer of foodstuffs and of high-tech goods.

In all countries, the technology that makes this sort of industry possible is provided partly by government-sponsored research, partly by research carried on directly by the industries involved, and partly by basic research conducted in universities and other in-stitutions of higher education. A good idea of the general level of such activity in a country may be gained by observing the number of scientists and engineers in the pop-ulation. This figure is displayed for several states in the second column of Table 4–5,

[4]This idea and its implications for economic policy are developed in Andrew Shonfield, *Modern Capital-ism* (Oxford, England: Oxford University Press, 1965). See also Robert Reich, *The Next American Frontier* (New York: Times Books, 1983).

**TABLE 4–5**

INVOLVEMENT OF SELECTED STATES IN RESEARCH & DEVELOPMENT

| | Percent of 1982 exports that were "high-tech" goods (machinery, electronic equipment, precision instruments weapons, etc.) | Number of scientists & engineers engaged in research & development (thousands) | Governmental spending on research & development as a percent of GNP |
|---|---|---|---|
| Canada (I)* | 38.9 | 65 | 1.5 |
| France (I) | 37.8 | 129 | 2.3 |
| Great Britain (I) | 44.0 | — | 2.2 |
| United States (I) | 48.9 | 949 | 2.8 |
| Japan (I) | 75.2 | 705 | 2.8 |
| Egypt (S) | 0.3 | 26 | 0.2 |
| Central African Republic (S) | 0.0 | 0 | 0.2 |
| Israel (S; I?) | 28.1 | 20 | 2.5 |
| Brazil (S) | 21.0 | 53 | 0.7 |
| South Korea (S; I?) | 37.4 | 87 | 1.8 |
| India (S) | 6.8 | 128 | 0.9 |

*I= industrialized democracy, S = South.
Sources: United Nations, Yearbook of International Trade Statistics, 1982; UNESCO, Statistical Yearbook, 1990, 1994.

which gives the number of scientists and engineers engaged in research and development.

## HEALTH AND SOCIAL WELFARE

Most modern states have accepted some responsibility for maintaining their people in reasonable health, in adequate housing, with financial security in their old age, and with some security against disability or disaster. Generally speaking, developed economies devote considerable resources to these purposes, while states of the South generally do not do as much. For the people of many poor states, daily life is a series of catastrophes, and it is all they can do to deal with those, much less prepare for future ones. Governments of the South must often use any surplus funds they have to develop systems of basic education or to build industrial plants for future economic growth. Finally, as we have already seen, many states of the South are burdened with large military budgets. All these circumstances put such strains on the economies of states of the South that so-

**TABLE 4–6**

SOCIAL WELFARE ACTIVITY BY SELECTED GOVERNMENTS

| | Percent of national budget spent on social security, welfare, and health | Percent of national budget spent on housing and community amenities |
|---|---|---|
| Canada (I)* | 44.8 | 1.7 |
| Sweden (I) | 48.0 | 5.8 |
| France (I) | 60.4 | 1.2 |
| Great Britain (I) | 43.6 | 2.9 |
| United States (I) | 46.2 | 2.6 |
| Bolivia (S) | 18.6 | 1.5 |
| Israel (S; I?) | 27.3 | 8.0 |
| Tunisia (S) | 20.9 | 4.4 |
| Philippines (S) | 6.7 | 1.7 |
| Madagascar (S) | 8.1 | — |
| South Korea (S; I?) | 11.1 | 0.8 |
| Syria (S) | 4.0 | 1.8 |

*I = industrialized democracy; S = South.
Source: International Monetary Fund, *Government Finance Statistics Yearbook, 1993.*

cial programs are put on a back burner. Israel is perhaps an extreme case of this because of its exposed military position, but it illustrates the point nicely, if with a bit of exaggeration. Military spending and interest payments on its debts and a development budget (for dams, irrigation, etc.) took 65 percent of the national budget for 1987–88. Israel devoted 24.9 percent out of the remaining 35 percent to social programs—actually evidence of a great devotion to social welfare, though the amount is small compared with what is spent in the developed economies.

This pattern is evident in the first column of Table 4–6, which lists the proportion of national budgets devoted to such items as health, recreation, unemployment insurance, pension systems, housing, and so on. These figures must be treated with caution, since spending by local governments is not included, and it is often difficult to tell exactly what the label on a budget item means. The broad pattern, however, is clear: The governments of developed economic systems make a considerable effort to ensure social welfare, whereas the governments of the South do not.

What sorts of things do governments do in order to promote social welfare? A vast number of programs have been used in one country or another for this purpose. To name a few: Governments may provide child-care centers for working parents, psychiatric counseling for emotionally troubled people, medical care for their citizens—as the British government does and as the United States does for poor people and for all people over age sixty-five; governments may build residential housing and offer it at inexpensive rates; governments may give grants of money to all families with children, to help them with the costs of child rearing (most European governments do this); governments may provide some sort of minimal national pension for people too old to work; and so on. There is a bewildering array of programs, and countries vary widely in the extent to which they give one or another kind of aid. The second column of Table 4–6 illustrates this diversity in one area of social welfare policy, the provision of residential housing. The activity of governments listed in the table varies from Israel, where the government spends 8 percent of its budget on housing, to South Korea, where housing commands only eight-tenths of one percent of the budget.

## REDISTRIBUTION OF INCOME

In all states of the world, incomes are distributed unequally; that is, some people make a good deal more money than others. Many governments make some effort to ease these differences in income by taking money from those who are better-off and redistributing it to those who are poorer.

Such efforts are of two types: (1) special subsidies and aids for the poor and (2) systems of "progressive taxation." A progressive tax is one that takes a greater percentage of income from a person who is relatively well-off and a smaller percentage from one who is not doing so well. Graduated income taxes are designed to be progressive, though they are often filled with loopholes that benefit the rich. This, of course, makes the tax less progressive. For instance, if an income tax is set up so that a person earning $5,000 a year pays no tax, a person earning $20,000 a years pays $2,000 (or 10 percent of that income), and a person earning $50,000 pays $10,000 (or 20 percent of that income), then the tax is progressive.

Not all taxes are progressive. Many are "regressive" in that they take a higher percentage of poor people's income than they do of the income of those who are better-off. The social security tax in the United States is an example. In 1996, workers in the United States had to pay 6.2 percent of their income, up to a maximum income of $62,700, to social security. Any income over this amount was untaxed; thus a person earning $10,000 a year paid 6.2 of that in social security taxes, whereas a person earning $90,000 a year paid only 4.3 percent.

In the United States over recent years, taking all sorts of levies into account, the progressive and regressive taxes have just about canceled one another out, so that people's relative incomes have been about the same before and after taxes.

Governments have not been very active in redistributing incomes, because those who have high incomes also usually have a good deal of political clout and are able to defend themselves vigorously. Table 4–7 displays income inequalities in a number of countries. In the table, the percentage of all income that goes to the poorest 20 percent is compared with the percentage of all income that goes to the richest 20 percent of the population. The greater this difference is, the more unequally incomes are distributed.

Three things are apparent in this table. First of all, states of the South are often burdened with considerably greater inequality of incomes than developed economies. It is paradoxical that in the midst of poverty, especially in Asian and Latin American states, there may be found a small group of people who are quite rich. Modern development— with its widespread education, mobility of populations, trade unions, and so on—alleviates inequality compared to countries with backward economies, where deep inequalities may be present.

**TABLE 4–7**
INCOME INEQUALITY IN SELECTED STATES

|  | Percent of national income earned by poorest 20% of population | Percent of national income earned by richest 20% of population | Difference |
|---|---|---|---|
| Hungary (E) | 10.9 | 34.4 | 23.5 |
| Canada (I) | 5.7 | 40.2 | 34.5 |
| Great Britain (I) | 4.6 | 44.3 | 39.7 |
| United States (I) | 4.7 | 41.9 | 37.2 |
| Sweden (I) | 8.0 | 36.9 | 28.9 |
| Israel (S; I?) | 6.0 | 39.6 | 23.6 |
| India (S) | 8.8 | 41.3 | 32.5 |
| Philippines (S) | 6.5 | 47.8 | 41.3 |
| Ivory Coast (S) | 6.8 | 44.1 | 37.3 |
| Brazil (S) | 2.1 | 67.5 | 65.4 |

E=East; I = industrialized democracy; S = South.
*Source:* World Bank, *World Development Report,* 1990.

The table also shows that if governments make an effort to do so, they can redistribute incomes somewhat. The formerly communist Hungary, at the top, is one of the least unequal states. Israel and Sweden have made special efforts to redistribute income; both have large and steeply progressive income taxes. And these two countries, along with Hungary, are the lease unequal countries in the table, although the differences between them and the other industrial states are rather small.

The clearest message of this table is that incomes are unequal in *all* systems. Even strenuous governmental efforts appear to have had relatively little effect.

## ECONOMIC DEVELOPMENT

This item has been left for last not because it is unimportant but because every other act of government we have considered depends on this one, and so it seems to fall logically at the conclusion. Except for actually keeping the boundaries of the state intact, there is probably nothing that citizens demand of their governments more urgently than this—that the economy grow so that people will be better-off from one year to the next.

The best way to measure the growth of economies is to compare the change in per capita real income from one year to the next, that is, the annual change in the people's average income adjusted to take the effects of inflation into account.

Figure 4–2 shows on a map of the world the average annual growth, 1960 to 1992, in per capita real income for each country.

One thing to note from the map is that this was a period of economic progress for most of the world. In 110 out of 131 countries, average per capita real income grew from 1960 to 1992. While the world generally did well, however, there was a good deal of variation from one state to another. How might we explain such variations?

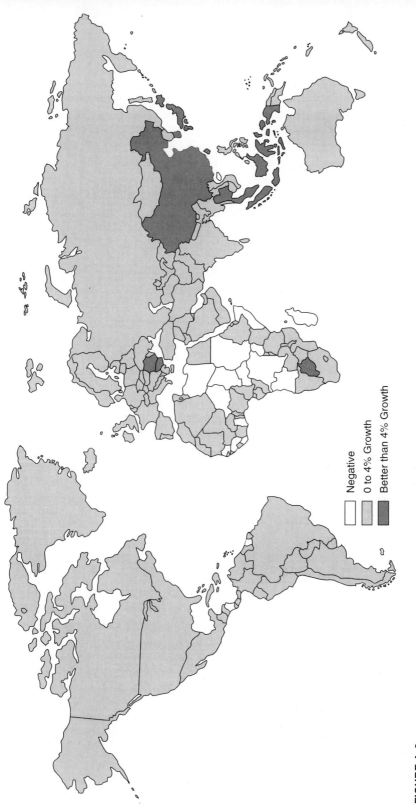

**FIGURE 4–2**
Growth in GDP per capita, 1960–1992.
*SOURCE:* United Nations Conference on Trade and Development, *Handbook of International Trade and Development Statistics, 1993.*

Negative
0 to 4% Growth
Better than 4% Growth

In what must be a frustrating aspect of this map from the standpoint of politicians, one is forced to the conclusion that politics—that is, what governments do—had rather little to do with how rapidly their states' economies grew at this time. Communist Bulgaria and Romania grew at a faster rate than democratic western Europe, but the non-communist eastern European states (Greece, Austria, Finland) grew rapidly as well, and conservative, noncommunist Japan was one of the great economic growth stories worldwide. The communist People's Republic of China and noncommunist Republic of China (Taiwan) grew at about the same rates.[5] And the oil-rich states of the Persian Gulf grew almost no matter what short of governments they had. Strategic position with regard to markets; availability of cheap, competent labor; the possession of natural resources—these, rather than political factors, seem to have dominated in determining economic growth.

On the other hand, wars or civil wars, which certainly constitute a "political factor," clearly hurt growth in a number of states that lost ground over the period: Nicaragua, Sudan, Mozambique, Afghanistan, and Kuwait. And a number of African countries that did especially badly appear to have suffered from agricultural pricing policies which drove many of their farmers out of business and thus damaged the base of their economics.[6] So although it is true that growth is not primarily determined by a state's broad political regime, it is nonetheless clear that political decisions can affect growth.

One sad fact is that the poorest states became still poorer over the period, at least "poorer" compared with the rest of the world. The average annual growth rate of these poorest states was less than one percent. And during this period of generally increasing prosperity around the world, per capita income *declined* in twenty-one states, all but one of which were poor to start with. On the other hand, most of the star performers (Malta, Hong Kong, South Korea, Singapore, and Botswana), which grew at rates over 6 percent annually over the whole thirty-one year period, all started from a poor base. Obviously the range of possible outcomes is greater for a poor country. Established industrial countries will not vary greatly in their performance. For poor countries, however, leadership and luck can make huge differences.

## THE PLACE OF POWER IN POLICY ANALYSIS

Since we have been looking in this chapter at policies, which are the product of the state, it is easy to lapse into an almost pure "choice" perspective. We are, after all, looking at a variety of choices that states have made, and it is easy to forget the interchanges of power lying behind the states' decisions.

This is indeed a common failing of specialists in the study of policy. Since they deal with the policies that states have adopted, it is easy for them to begin to treat states as unitary actors, as "black boxes" that produce policy. If they lose the habit of looking in-

---

[5]I must temper this argument, however, with regard to the communist states. Most of the undeniably strong growth of the east European states came early in the period, and for the past decade inefficiencies in their economies had been hampering them more and more; most are now in the process of switching over to market economies. The engine of economic growth in the People's Republic of China consists primarily of several provinces where the government has loosened socialist controls.

[6]Robert H. Bates, *Markets and States in Tropical Africa: The Political Basis of Agricultural Policies* (Berkeley: University of California Press, 1981).

side the black box to see why a particular policy came out, they may lose touch with reality in their analysis of policy. Good policy analysis will not only assess the objective merits of a policy but also take into account the political constraints under which the policy must work. For instance, any reasonable assessment of U.S. policy in banning the use of marijuana should take into account the difficulty of enforcing that law, the connivance of local governments with marijuana farmers, and so on. Once again, we see that even when our subject matter pulls us rather strongly toward one of the poles of power and choice, good analysis requires that we retain both perspectives to at least some extent.

### Example: Norway's Program to Encourage Norwegian-Language Publications

 As an example of how a state may address a problem through governmental policy, consider the plight of writers and publishers in Norway. Norway has a population of only about 4 million, roughly that of the state of Iowa. Few people outside of Norway can read Norwegian, and so an author who publishes a book written in Norwegian is limited to a relatively small potential market. By contrast, the potential worldwide market of an author writing in English is over 500 million, that of a Spanish author is about 250 million, and that of a Japanese author is over 100 million. How can a publishing house whose potential market is limited to just 4 million do enough business to survive? Left to its own devices, it would be forced to charge such high prices that no one could afford to buy its books. The Norwegian government—which, like most Scandinavian governments, is not shy about interposing itself in social choices in order to accomplish what it sees as worthy goals—has developed a complex set of policies to help publishers of materials written in Norwegian.

First of all, in Norway, the normal sales tax of 20 percent is not charged on books, which lowers their cost substantially (and artificially) compared with other things consumers may choose to spend their money on. In addition, the government buys the first 1,000 copies of every new Norwegian-language book of fiction, drama, or poetry and then donates them to public libraries. As a result, a publisher can be certain that sales on such books will never be less than 1,000 copies.

To lower the price of books further, the government also helps with the publisher's payment of royalties to authors. Norwegian authors receive a royalty of 20 percent of the sales price on each copy of their book, but the government contributes half of that to the publisher on the first 3,000 books sold and one-fourth of the royalty for the next 2,000 books. This means that the cost to the publishers is lower and that they can charge their customers lower prices.

There are additional special subsidies for types of books the government especially wishes to see published: classic Norwegian works, illustrated children's books, and books written in minority dialects.

Finally, all booksellers are required by law to keep any new Norwegian title in stock for three years after it appears, whether people wish to buy it or not, in order to give it a fair chance.

As you can see, the state intervenes directly and in very precise detail to encourage publication in the Norwegian language. In this way, it can help to keep the language alive and protect it from being displaced by neighboring languages such as German or English.

**TABLE 4–8**

THE WORLD'S MOST PROSPEROUS STATES, RANKED ON GROSS DOMESTIC PRODUCT PER CAPITA AND ON THE HUMAN DEVELOPMENT INDEX

| State | Gross domestic product per capita, rank | Human development index, rank | Difference in rank |
|---|---|---|---|
| United States | 1 | 2 | −1 |
| Switzerland | 2 | 13 | −11 |
| Qatar | 3 | 56 | −53 |
| United Arab Emirates | 4 | 45 | −41 |
| Luxembourg | 5 | 27 | −22 |
| Germany | 6 | 15 | −9 |
| Brunei | 7 | 41 | −34 |
| Canada | 8.5 | 1 | 7.5 |
| Japan | 8.5 | 3 | 5.5 |
| Hong Kong | 10 | 24 | −14 |
| France | 11 | 8 | 3 |
| Denmark | 12 | 16 | −4 |
| Austria | 13 | 14 | −1 |
| Belgium | 14 | 12 | 2 |
| Norway | 15 | 7 | 8 |
| Singapore | 16 | 35 | −19 |
| Sweden | 17 | 10 | 7 |
| Australia | 18 | 11 | 7 |
| Italy | 19 | 20 | −1 |
| Netherlands | 20 | 4 | 16 |
| Iceland | 21 | 6 | 15 |
| Bahamas | 22 | 26 | −4 |
| Great Britain | 23 | 18 | 5 |
| Finland | 24 | 5 | 19 |
| Cyprus | 25 | 23 | 2 |
| New Zealand | 26 | 17 | 9 |
| Israel | 27 | 21 | 6 |
| Bahrain | 28 | 44 | −16 |
| Spain | 29 | 9 | 20 |
| Ireland | 30 | 19 | 11 |
| Oman | 31 | 91 | −60 |
| Mauritius | 32 | 60 | −28 |
| Saudi Arabia | 33 | 76 | −43 |
| Portugal | 34 | 36 | −2 |
| Libya | 35 | 73 | −38 |
| Trinidad and Tobago | 36 | 39 | −3 |
| Barbados | 37 | 25 | 12 |
| South Korea | 38 | 31 | 7 |

*Source:* United Nations Development Programme, *Human Development Report, 1995.*

**Example: Economic Development Compared with "Human Development "**

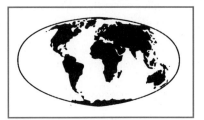

This chapter concluded with a brief review of how well the economies of the world's states developed over the last few decades—that is, whether and how much the gross domestic product per capita, the average economic production of the state's people, increased. This is obviously vital to people's well-being, but other things should also be taken into account—how equally the economic benefits are distributed, the state of the environment, the state of people's health, and so on. It is not enough just to ask whether the people of a state are prospering; rather, we must ask, how well are they living?

This is obviously hard to assess, because it involves so many diverse things, but a rough first stab has been taken in the "human development index" developed by the United Nations Development Programme (see Table 4–8).[7] The index combines indicators of gross domestic product per capita, life expectancy, and education into a single index; presumably this measures broad well-being better than gross domestic product alone, and it is interesting to examine how states compare with each other on the two measures.

Note that Switzerland, whose people have the second-highest incomes, ranks much lower when life expectancy and education are added into the equation. Champions at providing a good life given their level of prosperity are Spain, whose people are only the twenty-ninth richest but rank ninth on the human development index, and Finland (twenty-fourth, fifth). A number of industrialized Western states do well, including Norway, the Netherlands, Iceland, New Zealand, and Ireland. States that have high income based on a restricted product or service such as most Arab states (oil) or Singapore (commerce) tend to look the worst in these comparisons; in particular, many Arab oil-producers such as Qatar, Oman, Saudi Arabia, and Libya have accomplished little with great resources.

[7]United Nations Development Programme, *Human Development Report, 1995* (New York: Oxford University Press, 1995).

## FURTHER READING

### General Studies of Policy

Frieden, Jeffrey A. *Debt, Development and Democracy.* Princeton, N.J.: Princeton University Press, 1991.

Heclo, Hugh. *Modern Social Politics in Britain and Sweden.* New Haven, Conn.: Yale University Press, 1974.

Heidenheimer, Arnold J.; Heclo, Hugh; and Adams, Carolyn. *Comparative Public Policy.* 3rd ed. New York: St. Martin's, 1990.

### Studies of Particular Areas of Policy, Mostly American

Chubb, John E., and Moe, Terry M. *Politics, Markets, and America's Schools.* Washington, D.C.: Brookings Institution, 1990.

Coulter, Philip B. *Measuring Inequality*. Boulder, Colo.: Westview Press, 1989.

*Human Rights Watch World Report 1990*. New Haven: Yale University Press, 1991.

Jacobs, Lawrence R. *The Health of Nations: Public Opinion and the Making of American and British Health Policy*. Ithaca, N.Y.: Cornell University Press, 1993.

Lange, P., and Garrett, G. "The Politics of Growth: Strategic Interaction and Economic Performance in the Advanced Industrial Democracies, 1974–1980." *Journal of Politics* 47 (August 1985); 792–827.

Page, Benjamin I. *Who Gets What from Government*. Berkeley: University of California Press, 1983.

Peterson, Paul. *City Limits*. Chicago: University of Chicago Press, 1981.

Phillips, Kevin R. *The Politics of Rich and Poor: Wealth and the American Electorate in the Reagan Aftermath*. New York: Random House, 1990.

Piven, Frances Fox, and Cloward, Richard A. *Regulating the Poor*. New York: Pantheon, 1971.

Tinker, Irene, ed. *Persistent Inequalities: Women and World Development*. Oxford: Oxford University Press, 1990.

# 5

# POLITICAL CHOICES: THE PROBLEMS OF FAIRNESS AND EFFICIENCY[1]

Modes of Decision
- Incremental - a decision maker will only make a small change in any policy at any one time.
- Radical - decision maker will make a big change in policy.

In the preceding chapter we reviewed the varying things that governments do (or do not do) on behalf of their people. What are the considerations that lie behind these policies? What things must the leaders and their people think about in considering what the state should do? If you were the leader of a state, what sorts of policies would you opt for? On the "choice" side of "power and choice," what should a group of people choose to do?

There seem to be two broad characteristics that almost everyone wants to see in state policies: (1) The policies should be "fair"—that is, people in the state should be treated in the way they deserve; and (2) the policies should be "efficient," producing the greatest good at the least cost. As you might expect, the problem with these criteria is that both are multifaceted and hard to pin down. In addition, even these two broad criteria sometimes come into conflict, since what is most "fair" may not be most "efficient," and vice versa. Sorting out the various factors that make one policy "good" and another "bad" is more an art than a science, and people of goodwill may frequently come up with differing conclusions regarding a policy. In this chapter, we shall look at some of the things that go to make a policy "fair" or "efficient" and also, perhaps, come to see how complex the final evaluation of a policy must be.

## FAIRNESS AND THE PROBLEM OF JUSTICE

What do we mean by "fairness," by the notion that people should be treated "as they deserve"? One important element of fairness is our idea of *justice,* the idea that people should be treated *justly.* But what does this mean?

Does justice consist of treating everyone equally? Surely not, since we can think of

---

[1]Any author of an introductory book owes debts to many people, but in this chapter a special debt is owed to Charles Anderson, whose splendid book *Statecraft* (New York: Wiley, 1977) pursues similar themes in more detail and with greater elegance than we have done here.

many instances in which treating everyone equally would seem quite unjust. If you had worked especially hard on a paper but your instructor decided to give everyone in the class the same grade, this would seem unjust. You had worked hard while others sloughed off, yet all got the same reward. *Different members of the class had contributed different amounts, and justice would seem to require that they be rewarded accordingly.* A rather different consideration appears in the following example: Suppose six people were waiting on a corner on a cold, rainy day, and one of the six was suffering from asthma. Suppose further that a car came along that could take only one additional passenger. Equal treatment would require that the six draw lots to see who should get to go in the car. But would not justice require that the other five defer to the asthma victim, who was suffering more from the rain than they were? In this case, justice would seem to require that the person whose *needs* were greatest should get special treatment.

Should justice, then, be based solely on the weight of contributions or solely on need? Neither of these can provide a sufficient basis for justice, though obviously both are part of the picture.

There are many problems with the "weight of contributions." People's contributions are frequently as much a matter of luck as of virtue, and we are often a bit queasy when rewards are based solely on such "lucky" contributions. To continue with the example of grades, what if you worked very hard on your paper but a friend, who happened to have been born very intelligent, dashed off a brilliant piece in one evening while drinking beer and got a better grade than you did? You would probably have mixed feelings about the justice of the grades. Or, to follow the same line of thought, is it just that a ballplayer like Albert Belle should have been paid a very high salary because his shoulders and back were so constructed as to help him hit the long ball? Or, is it just that a worker living in West Virginia should have so few opportunities to find a job as compared with a worker living in Connecticut? Contribution alone, then, cannot provide a sufficient criterion for determining justice. Contribution may often involve elements of luck, so that we are uncertain how much it should be rewarded. And looking only at contributions would cause us to ignore questions of need; even if four of the six people on the rainy corner had managed to stop a cab (thus contributing more than the other two), we might think it "just" if one of them were excluded to make a place for the asthma victim.

Similar problems arise if need alone is used as a criterion for justice. Like "contribution," "need" is a tricky thing, and we are not always sure that it should be rewarded. If some members of an office staff are having a hard time economically because of bad luck (or bad judgment) in the houses they bought and the debts they've run up, should they get bigger raises than members of the staff who are not in trouble economically? Should parents get better pay because they have children to support? Would this be unjust to single people who are doing the same work as the parents are doing? And again, if need alone were used as a criterion, this would mean that contribution would have to be ignored. To return finally to the example of grades, how would you feel if the papers were graded solely on the instructor's assessment of each student's need for a "positive self-image"?

Justice, then, is a complex issue. It involves a number of things that are often in conflict and need to be balanced—the contributions people have made, their varying needs, and even some further sense that people should not be treated *too* unequally. Not only do

Fairness? On June 7, 1976, officials in a small town in Pennsylvania notified a Mr. Selby that he would have to tear down a backyard treehouse because he had not obtained a permit and the house exceeded the 40-foot height restriction. Mr. Selby ignored the notice, and the following month two police cars, a dump truck, and a power-line truck with a cherry picker returned to the tree house and demolished it. (Auth, by Tony Auth. Copyright 1976, Philadelphia Inquirer. Reprinted with permission of Universal Press Syndicate. All rights reserved.)

these things have to be balanced, but each of them is itself ambiguous and hard to pin down.

This does not mean that justice is an unworkable concept but simply that it is a difficult one. We all have a strong sense for the justice or injustice of certain things, and there is a good deal of agreement among us about these. If this were not so, the examples used above could not have been expected to mean roughly the same thing to each reader. It is when we judge a question of justice differently, though, that we must tackle the problem of working out our disagreement. Different people will weigh contribution, need, and the necessity of equality differently; and they will also disagree on precisely what sort of need or what sort of contribution exists, or on just what sorts of things need to be equal. Many might see no injustice in Albert Belle's high salary. One could argue that the amount of pleasure he gave millions of people merited this sort of pay, or one could see justice in the fact that an African American was well paid, or one could note the limited period during which Belle could play baseball, since he would need to retire in his thirties.

Justice is a complex question, but one on which we can talk productively. By bringing out and examining the differing ways people evaluate contribution, need, and the necessity for equality and by examining the differing weights people place on each, we may at least *clarify* disagreements about the justice of a policy.

## OTHER ASPECTS OF FAIRNESS

We entered into this long discussion of justice because justice is the primary component of "fairness"—the somewhat broader and vaguer term that designates one of this chapter's themes. We are concerned about how to judge when a policy is or is not "fair." Whether the policy is *just* is the most important part of this judgment, but it is not the only thing that enters in. Other things that may also make us see a policy as fair or unfair are *(1) whether governmental action is "arbitrary," (2) whether special basic rights are violated, and (3) whether special overriding social needs are present.*

### Arbitrary Policies and Due Process

Governmental action is *arbitrary* if decisions are made and communicated capriciously, that is, if the people affected by a decision do not know what to expect before the decision is made and do not learn on what grounds it was made. Decisions that single out particular individuals for punishment or reward are arbitrary decisions. For instance, highway patrols sometimes appear to be especially strict in enforcing speed limits and other regulations on "hot-looking" souped-up cars just because of the cars' appearance. This is arbitrary action. Librarians are acting arbitrarily when they allow people owing fines to escape without paying provided that they are "properly sorry about having been late." In some dictatorships such as Nazi Germany or Idi Amin's Uganda, a person could be executed simply because someone in the government bore a grudge against him or her. This was the worst sort of arbitrary terror.

Note that the question of arbitrariness is not exactly the same as the question of justice. A policy we regard as unjust might be reached by means we admit are not arbitrary. And arbitrary means might even produce results we considered just![2] Regardless of the justice of the result, however, arbitrariness lessens the fairness of a policy.

The notion of *due process* has evolved to help control arbitrary decision making. This is the idea that certain standard procedures must always be followed in making some policies, and that if those procedures were not followed in making a given policy, then the policy should be void. This prevents policymakers from acting arbitrarily, since they obviously want to see their policies stick. To keep from having their policies voided, they stay within the standard set of procedures in making policy.

This sort of standardization involves some costs in that it lessens governmental flexibility. Generally it is not set up for all areas of policymaking. Britain, the United States, and Canada especially emphasize due process in criminal trials, because historically those countries have been especially concerned to protect their citizens from unfair prosecution by the government. In criminal trials in English-speaking countries, due process generally consists of the following:

---

[2]This often produces uneasiness about legal processes in the United States and other countries with protections against arbitrary criminal investigation. If the police had stopped a "souped-up" car and found a bloody ax in the back seat, justice would require that the driver be investigated for murder. However, the initial search was arbitrary, and a court might well dismiss the evidence on the grounds that it had been obtained unfairly. Citizens frequently find it difficult to appreciate these distinctions.

**1** People may not be accused of crimes unless they could have learned of the existence and meaning of the law before they committed their acts.

**2** When people are accused of crimes, they are entitled to know what crimes are charged, they are entitled to know on what evidence the charges are based, and they are entitled to gather and present their own evidence to rebut the charges.

**3** Judges must be disinterested, unbiased, and attentive.

**4** Once a judgment has been made, some means for later reconsideration must be available.

**5** If any of these conditions has been violated in an American, Canadian, or British court except under certain special circumstances, the trial is ruled invalid.[3]

In other areas of policy, such as the setting of regulations, assignment of people to schools, levying of taxes, and so on, the general spirit of due process is still supposed to be followed—that is, policymaking is not to be arbitrary—but there are usually not such precise and strict rules to safeguard due process.

## Special Basic Rights

Another added factor that enters into considerations of fairness is the existence of certain basic rights whose violation is thought to be unfair in and of itself. Such rights have a special status in that only extraordinary circumstances would make it appropriate for policymakers to violate them for anyone. Although almost everyone would think that some such rights exist, it is not always possible to get people to agree on exactly which rights have this status. Three rights that have frequently been held to have the special status are:

**1** *The right to survive:* It can be argued that since death negates all other rights, the right not to be killed should be kept almost absolute. Opposition to capital punishment is often based on this idea, as is opposition to abortion.

**2** *The right of free speech:* It can be argued that since politics itself depends on the exchange of ideas, policymakers should be especially reluctant to regulate the expression of ideas, because decreasing the flow of ideas decreases politics itself.

**3** *The right to privacy:* It can be argued that if one's very personality is to exist, there must be some space that can be called one's own, where no one else may peek in, and that governments must if at all possible respect those boundaries. It is for this reason that in British, Canadian, and American law people may not be compelled to speak about themselves in court and wives or husbands may not be compelled to testify against their spouses.

Few people would hold any of these special rights to be *absolute.* Most people would agree that it would have been good if Hitler had been assassinated in 1942, even those

---

[3]To some extent this is an idealization of what happens. In fact, American courts, at least, are badly overworked and many shortcuts are tolerated to move the business through. For instance, in "plea bargaining," a deal is struck between the accused, the prosecutor, and the judge by which the accused pleads guilty to a lesser charge, the prosecutor's original charge is withdrawn, and the trial ends. Thus many of the theoretical protections listed above are avoided.

who believe strongly in the right to survive. Almost everyone recognizes that the special right of free speech must have some restrictions, as well; the classic example is that no one should have the right to yell "Fire!" in a crowded theater. Similarly, there must also be some ultimate limits to the right to privacy.

Thus "special rights" are not absolute. But to the extent that the idea of special rights is accepted, a society sets aside those rights as having a top priority, so that it would take something unusual for us to compromise them. Fairness, under these circumstances, may require that justice, or even due process, might have to be tempered in the interests of one or another special right. As one example of this, many people have opposed the establishment of a central, computerized data file of information about Americans because they are concerned about the potential abuses of people's right to privacy that could result if all official information about a person—military record, tax returns, criminal record, health information, record in school, and so on—were brought together and made easily accessible. Those opposing the file grant that justice might be better served if such a file existed, since tax fraud and other crimes would be easier to detect, but they think that the right to privacy is more important than these needs of justice.

### Overriding Social Needs

Finally, fairness in a broad sense may require that in order to be fair to most of the people, the state must be less fair to some people. That is, there may be overriding social needs which enter into considerations of fairness. The best example is the military draft. In many countries, young men (and at least in Israel, women) are required to serve a fixed period of time in the military, whether they wish to do so or not. The reasoning behind this is that the people of the state need to have a strong army, but it is difficult to get people to serve in an army of their own free will. Therefore some people must be compelled to do so for the greater general good. Similarly, affirmative action programs for employment in the United States often require that minorities and women should be given a slightly better than even break in hiring decisions (even though an even break would be the "just" decision) to help overcome historic patterns of unjust decisions going the opposite way. The argument is that society will benefit from an integrated work force and that at least modest levels of individual injustice during the transition period are not too great a price to pay.

Another example of this sort of consideration is seen during wars. When they are at war, most countries subordinate almost everything else to winning the war. Among the subordinated things is a concern for individual justice, due process, and special individual rights. Governments are often given extraordinary powers during wars, and they are not expected to be primarily concerned with fairness to individuals. Sometimes governments do things during war that they later regret. The internment of hundreds of thousands of Japanese-Americans in prison camps during World War II, simply because of their national origin, is a shameful piece of America's past that occurred under the stress of war.

Revolutionary governments often justify suspensions of due process and justice because of the great good that will eventually result from the revolution. Thousands of British sympathizers were driven into Canada at the end of the American Revolution, aristocrats and many others were beheaded during the French Revolution, and millions of farmers were executed or deported to forced-labor camps in the Soviet Union in the 1930s.

Each of the examples given here—the draft, affirmative action, wartime civil liberties, the needs of a revolution—in fact, any claim to an overriding social need, is based on an assumption that ends can justify means. This assumption should not be too easily accepted *or* too readily rejected. It would be wrong to read into the assumption an exaggerated claim that means can be ignored. Clearly, there are many means that cannot be justified by many ends. The internment of Japanese-Americans by the U.S. government during World War II did nothing to help the American war effort; even if it had helped in small ways, the enormity of the injustice would not have been worth it. That internment was unjustified. Similarly, even if many Soviet citizens had benefited from the Russian Revolution, the immense human suffering during that revolution and the limitation of free speech throughout the existence of the Soviet Union were unjustified.

But if we should not accept too easily the notion that ends can justify means, neither should we reject it totally. Some social ends, such as an integrated work force or secure national borders, may be worth modest degrees of individual injustice. *Some* ends can clearly justify *some* means—as anyone must agree who has ever told a "little white lie."

In the end, then, we see that "fairness" is a mix of several things: justice (which is itself a mix of concerns for contribution, need, and equality); governmental action that is not arbitrary; consideration of special rights; and the possibility of overriding social needs. It is because so many things are involved that people can honestly disagree on whether a policy is fair. At the same time, being aware of what goes into "fairness" can help us to understand and work out such disagreements.

## EFFICIENCY *gives state and people the greatest benefits.*

We have seen that one question for the policymaker is whether a policy is *fair,* both to individuals and to society as a whole. The other basic question is whether the policy is *efficient.* An efficient policy is *one that gives the state and the people of the state the greatest benefits at the least cost.* The trick in dealing with efficiency is that often neither the benefits nor the costs of a policy are easy to calculate.

First, many of the effects of a policy are difficult to measure and compare. They bring up the old problem of "apples and oranges" in its severest form. How can we compare the amount of recreational value gained by building a dam and the value of the protection against flooding that is gained by building it against the cost of pain and inconvenience of those who have to leave their homes to make way for it, the economic loss of farm production on the flooded lands, and the government's cost in constructing it? There is no common unit by which to measure recreational value, protection against flooding, pain and inconvenience, and agricultural loss, and so it is difficult to say whether in this case the gains are greater than the costs.

A second reason why the costs and benefits of a policy are not always clear is that policies always have a variety of effects, many of which one cannot anticipate when the policy is set up. These are often referred to as the *unanticipated consequences* of a policy.

As one example of such an unanticipated consequence, consider the following: A study of phosphate pollution of Lake Erie—which had at one time killed off almost all life in the lake—yielded the surprising finding that in the 1960s the level of phosphates in the lake had jumped sharply and had remained at that high level thereafter. It appeared that some massive new source of pollution had appeared on the scene at the time of the jump in phosphate levels, but no such new source could be found. On investigation it turned out that at the time of the jump, the state of Michigan had ordered Michigan steel mills to stop dumping waste acid into the lake. The acid had been combining with phosphates in the water to form a solid, which then dropped to the bottom of the lake. In other words, the acid had been cleaning phosphates out of the lake water; and when, in the name of *pollution control,* the source of acid was shut off, phosphate levels in the water shot up!

This is only one of the numerous incidental costs and benefits of stopping the dumping of acid into Lake Erie, many of which may not have been anticipated. As another example of the varied effects that a policy may have, consider the social security program of the United States. This is a fairly simple program. As of 1996, all employed workers except government employees paid a tax of 6.2 percent of their salary (up to a maximum salary of $62,700), and their employers paid a matching tax of the same amount.[4] From the proceeds of this tax, pensions are paid to people of age sixty-five and above who have retired; also, support payments are paid to disabled workers and to children of workers who have died young. The direct purpose of the program is to provide a national system of pensions and catastrophe insurance. Among the many *side* effects of the program, some good and some bad, are the following:

**1** People with low salaries are taxed relatively more heavily than people with high salaries (see Chapter 4). Thus, the distribution of incomes in the state is made less equal.

**2** Retired people have been made less dependent economically on their families. This has surely been a good thing for them, but it may also have helped to lessen the ties of the extended family, which are already weak in our highly mobile society.

**3** The age of retirement has been made more or less standard nationally.

**4** Because people are encouraged to retire at age sixty-five rather than at a later age, the overall production of goods and services has been reduced for the country and all the people are economically somewhat less well-off than they would otherwise be.

**5** But conversely, the policy has allowed many who wish to stop working at age sixty-five to do so without being forced by economic need to work on beyond that age.

**6** The payroll tax on employers takes a higher percentage of the payroll for low-pay employees than for high-pay employees. For example, the employer pays a tax of 6.2 percent of the salary of an employee who earns $30,000 a year but 4.3 percent of the salary of an employee who earns $90,000 a year. Thus the policy encourages industries like the electronics and computer industries, which have highly paid work forces, while it discriminates against industries like steel and automobile manufacturing, which em-

---

[4]An additional 1.45 percent tax on *all* wages, also matched by employers, supports medical care for persons over 65 years old.

ploy large numbers of workers at lower pay. This encourages the development of clean industries with a great deal of potential for export sales, but it also hurts the economically weak industrial areas of the northeastern United States.

As this example shows, even a fairly simple program like social security has many effects beyond those for which it was originally designed. Some of these were not anticipated by the designers and some have probably not yet even been noticed by scholars. Certainly the above list does not include all the consequences of the social security plan.

As a final example of the unintended consequences of policy, some studies have suggested that stiffer penalties for those caught driving while intoxicated may have led to an increase in hit-and-run accidents, as drunk drivers flee the scene of accidents in order to avoid the stiffened punishment for driving while intoxicated.

Any judgment as to the *efficiency* of a policy must take into account *all* its costs and benefits—insofar as we can guess what these are—not just the *intended* costs and benefits. It is often hard to put a price tag on these, as we have seen in the example of social security; we are usually comparing apples, oranges, bananas, and grapefruit. And many of the consequences may be difficult to foresee. As a result, it is just as much an art to judge the efficiency of a policy as to judge its fairness. There is nothing terrible in recognizing that policymaking is not an exact science; it is simply a good thing to realize that policy choices are neither simple nor direct.

## MODES OF DECISION: INCREMENTAL VS. RADICAL

How do policymakers react to the complex and difficult decisions they must make? One important way in which they may differ is in style. A decision maker may, to varying degrees, take an *incremental* or a *radical* approach to the making of policy.

A decision maker who operates more *incrementally* will make only a small change in policy at any one time, wait to see what the results of that change are, then make another small change, and so on. A person who is worried about all the uncertainty in devising policies—and about the possibility of making big, costly mistakes—will tend to be an incrementalist. As we have seen above, it is often very difficult to assess all the costs and benefits of a policy; therefore an incrementalist stance is certainly not unreasonable.

A *radical* decision maker, on the other hand, is more concerned about lost opportunities than about the possibility of costly errors. A radical is likely to feel that while the incrementalist is creeping up on a decision, a chance for a decisive breakthrough may be lost. Sometimes, says the radical, bold action may accomplish something that could never be done in small steps. A decision maker of relatively radical mood might hasten to buy up land for a state park all at once, before land prices rise to prohibitive heights, rather than announce a ten-year plan for gradual land acquisition.

Neither one of these styles is necessarily preferable. Partly, the choice is a matter of individual personality, as some people are more averse to risk than others. The incrementalist's caution in the face of uncertainty and complexity makes a lot of sense, and so does the radical's worry that opportunities may be lost through slow, cautious movement.

Some types of policy seem to lend themselves better to one style of decision making than to the other. Anything based on age and generational change is probably best handled incrementally, for instance, because we know well in advance what is coming and all change is rather slow. Closing of schools or the expansion of school systems in response to changes in the number of school-age children can be managed incrementally, because we know years in advance what we can expect simply from local birthrates.

Military policies, on the other hand, often require boldness because even the difference of an hour can change a situation totally, as armies change position, attacks are launched, and so on. History's great generals—Napoleon, Robert E. Lee, and others—have been gamblers. During World War II, Winston Churchill constantly complained that his generals were too cautious, as in this memo to the first sea lord:

> It is now three weeks since I vetoed the proposal to evacuate the Eastern Mediterranean and bring Admiral Cunningham's fleet to Gibraltar. I hope there will be no return to that project. Anyone can see the risk from an attack which we run in the Central Mediterranean. From time to time and for sufficient objects this risk will have to be faced. Warships are meant to go under fire.[5]

So one would not wish to say that one or the other of these stances is *the* right one. Which mix of the two is best depends on circumstances and on the character of the decision maker. What *is* true, though, is that modern politics tilts things heavily in favor of incrementalism. In fact, other than in revolutions themselves, radical policy changes are quite rare. Partly this is because in our complex and active societies a group will arise to protest vociferously against almost any change; such groups can usually force a compromise which is, in effect, an incremental change. The other reason for the predominance of incremental change is that officials and bureaucrats are rarely punished for a continuously unsatisfactory state of affairs, but they know that they *will* be punished for any dramatic failure. This makes for timid decisions.

## MODES OF DECISION: AUTHORITY VS. THE MARKET

Another very basic choice about policy is whether we want to rely more on *governmental authority* or on *market mechanisms* to carry it out. "Governmental authority" is just what it sounds like. Under governmental authority, policy is made by the government telling people what they may or may not do, how much they may spend on X, how much the country is to invest in Y, and so on. Many policies with which you are familiar are matters of governmental authority. The public school system, in which the government fixes a minimum number of years of education that each child must receive and sets up free public schools to provide that education, is an instance of policy provided by governmental authority. The system of highways and streets, in which the government decides where streets should run and then uses public money to build and maintain them, is another example. So is the nationalized coal industry of China, in which the government owns all coal mines and decides how much coal is to be mined, what sort of equipment is to be built, how much the miners are to be paid, and how much the coal will cost.

---

[5]Winston Churchill, *The Second World War,* vol. 2 (Boston: Houghton Mifflin, 1949), p. 443.

---

INCREMENTALISM: NORMATIVE AND EMPIRICAL ANALYSIS

Analysis in political science may be of either the normative sort or the empirical. Normative analysis deals with values: What should be? Empirical analysis deals with observation: What is? Incrementalism offers an interesting example of how a given thing may be dealt with either normatively or empirically.

In an influential normative book in the mid-1960s, Charles Lindblom argued that central direction of policy could not work but that a variety of decision makers, each operating incrementally, could produce good policies (*The Intelligence of Democracy* [New York: Free Press, 1965]). In this sense, incrementalism can be held up as a normative guide to how policies should be made.

But incrementalism has also functioned importantly as a descriptive category, to help empirical students of politics understand how politics actually happens. In their pioneer study of how governments design budgets, Davis, Dempster, and Wildavsky concluded that the budgetary decisions of the president and Congress could be described as simple incremental decisions. Agencies were rarely created or disbanded; rather, each year each agency received a budgetary increase of some small percent—an incremental way of designing the budget ("A Theory of the Budgetary Process," *American Political Science Review* 60 [September 1966]: 529–547). Here, then, "incrementalism" is not a *value* to be debated, but a descriptive category that is applied to U.S. budgetary politics.

---

Under a "market mechanism," the government leaves the choice as to what people are to do, what goods they are to receive, and so on, up to the people to choose for themselves, through their exchanges of goods and services with each other. Through the operation of supply and demand, if large numbers of people want G.I. Joe dolls and are willing to pay high prices for them, producers will make more G.I. Joe dolls. If no one wants to pay people well to care for children during the day, there will not be many child-care centers. Thus collective choices come to be made by millions of individual decisions about proper prices and what objects to purchase. The government depends on the *costs* of action, of goods, and so on, to restrain people in their choices so that they will end up choosing to do or buy only those things they most want (or can afford). In the coal industry of the United States, which is not nationalized, the choice as to how much coal is to be produced is a matter for a number of mine operators to decide on the basis of their operating costs; their decision is strongly affected by the choices of millions of customers as to how much coal they will buy at a given price. The policy decision—how much coal is to be produced—which in China is made directly by the government, is made in the United States by the interplay of a large number of individual decisions.

In a modification of the market mechanism, a government may leave a policy to be settled by the market but may intervene to structure the individual decisions that go to make up the market choice.[6] Almost every country, for instance, taxes liquor and tobacco products heavily so as to raise their prices and make it less likely that people will choose to consume such unhealthy substances rather than, say, meat and vegetables. The choice as to what to consume is still the customer's, but the government has taken

---

[6]See Chapter 4.

steps to help determine what that choice will be. By contrast, in banning the consumption of heroin, the U.S. government is relying on governmental authority rather than on a market mechanism to determine the level of consumption of a dangerous substance.

Whether authority or a market mechanism is a better way of making policy is a continual subject of debate. Is it better for the government to nationalize railroads, airlines, and such, and run them in the public interest? Or is it better to leave decisions on scheduling, allocation of investment, salaries, and so on, to be worked out by management, workers, and customers through their individual choices? In an energy shortage, should gasoline be rationed (with a set number of gallons allocated per family), or should the price be allowed to shoot up, so that those who do not need gasoline as much as others or who cannot afford it as readily will reduce their driving? Either policy would reduce consumption to meet the short supply, but they would have different side effects. *Both* types of policy—authority and the market—have considerable disadvantages.

**Problems with Authority-based Policy**    The two main problems with authority as a means of policy are that (1) authority does not generally get things to the people who will value them most—that is, it does not allocate optimally, and (2) authority-based

(Sidney Harris)

policy does not generally use resources as efficiently as they might be used. (Note that these are the twin problems of "fairness" and "efficiency" with which we introduced this chapter.)

Regarding the first of these problems, it stands to reason that if government officials make a choice on behalf of all the people, they cannot very well take into account the infinitely varying needs of those people. They might write a thousand exceptions and special conditions into their decision, but it would still be a clumsy instrument for deciding who is to get how much of what. Consider the example of gasoline rationing. If the government states that each family may receive 42 gallons of gasoline a month, should they not allow rural families more than that because of the long distances they must drive? But then, what about an urban resident who must drive to a job 20 miles away? Perhaps the government should allow less gas to those living near a bus line. How about people with weak hearts? Should they receive extra gasoline? How about people with small children? People who own a vacation house 40 miles out of town? This can go on forever, and even if the government writes terribly complicated rules, there will still be many people who do not receive gasoline in proportion to their desire and need for gasoline. As Lindblom has put it, authority systems have "strong thumbs, no fingers."[7]

The second main problem with policy made by authority is that it generally does not lead to a very efficient use of resources. When the government decides how much is to be invested in what ways in schools, highways, coal mining, or whatever, the government officials responsible do not *personally* gain much of anything from a wise decision or lose much of anything from an unwise one. Under a market arrangement, however, the people making such decisions save money directly from wise decisions and lose money directly from unwise ones. Even with the best intentions in the world, it is natural that, in systems of authority, decision makers should be more careless with resources than they would be under a market system. As a fairly extreme example of the sort of inefficiency that can result, the Soviet Union at one time allowed its farmers to manage small plots themselves and to sell their produce in competitive markets, though most Soviet agricultural products came from large government-managed collective farms. On the private plots, on the average, it took 4 pounds of feed grain to produce a pound of meat; on the collective farms, it took up to *13* pounds of feed grain to produce a pound of meat.[8]

**Problems with the Market**     Given these two very serious problems, why would anyone ever use authority? Why don't governments simply leave all decisions to market mechanisms? The reason is that market mechanisms themselves suffer from several serious defects; we shall consider three of them here.[9]

First, as we saw in Chapter 4, wealth and income are distributed unequally in all societies, with some people poor and others better-off. When decisions are left to the market, goods and opportunities flow to those who can afford them, and these will not necessarily be the people who need them most. If medical care is allocated by letting the price rise, for instance, poor people who needed surgery to avoid being crippled might have to do without, while richer people might be able to afford casual cosmetic surgery.

---

[7]Charles Lindblom, *Politics and Markets* (New York: Basic Books, 1977).
[8]*The Economist,* 7 February 1981, p. 14.
[9]For a more thorough discussion, see Lindblom, *Politics and Markets,* Chapter 6, n. 6.

Where a need is especially important, the government may step in to make certain that justice is done in a way that cannot be guaranteed by a market mechanism. This is part of the motivation behind systems of free public education, socialized medicine (such as the national medical care programs that serve people of all ages in Britain, Canada, and many European states, or Medicare, which serves those over age sixty-five in the United States), and the rationing of food during shortages.

A second problem with market mechanisms is that they are not very effective in producing *collective goods.* A "collective good" is something that benefits all members of the community and that no one can be prevented from using; every member of the community can enjoy the benefits of it whether that person has helped pay for it or not. Some examples of collective goods are national defense, medical research, weather forecasting, and public health programs to control the spread of disease. All members of the community benefit from such programs, whether or not they have helped pay for them. An army, for instance, cannot defend just those people who have helped pay for it; it defends a territory and unavoidably defends everyone in that territory. Left to the market, such collective goods would be terribly difficult to finance. Each individual could quite sensibly think, "If I don't pay my share, the army will still be there, and I'll get all the benefits of it; why should I pay?" As a result, no one would pay to finance the army, there would be no army, and all would lose out. Rather than let such paradoxical failures occur, governments often decide not to rely on the voluntary choices of a market mechanism. Instead, they force the people to pay taxes, and they use those taxes to provide the collective good that all (or most) desire.

A third problem with market mechanisms is that they do not take into account *externalities* of individual transactions. An "externality" exists when there are social costs or benefits beyond the individual costs and benefits between two individuals. For example, let us say that a couple contract with a trash company to dump refuse on their land. The trash company presumably has greater benefits than costs from the deal. For the landowners, the benefit is the money paid by the trash company; the cost is the odor and sight of the trash plus the fact that a portion of the land is occupied by the trash. Presumably the landowners are satisfied with the deal (the benefit outweighs the costs), or there would have been no deal. So, the trash company and the landowners are happy, and according to market practices the deal will be struck. But there is an externality here. All the landowners' neighbors, including a nursing home and a day-care center, must also suffer the sight and smell of the trash. They receive no benefits, and so there is a large *social cost* that should be taken into account but does not enter into market calculations. This is the problem of externalities, a problem in which governmental authority is often brought to bear to make certain that the broader social costs and benefits—as well as the narrower individual costs and benefits—are taken into account in transactions. The most obvious externalities are negative ones—pollution, the setting up of ugly structures, and so on. But there can also be *positive externalities,* in which there are positive social benefits that would not be taken into account in individual transactions and that government may step in to guarantee. Two examples are the preservation of historic buildings and the requirement that every member of society acquire a basic education. (The notion in the latter case is that society as a whole benefits from general literacy above and beyond the benefit any single individual gains from being literate.)

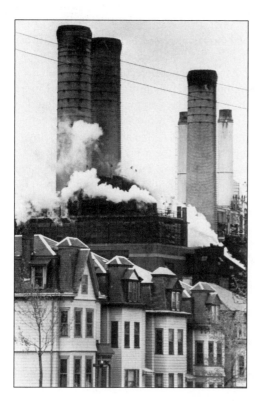

Factories and their neighbors in South Boston, Massachusetts. A strong example of "externalities." **(Ellis Herwig/The Picture Cube)**

Governmental authority and market mechanisms, then, are two general modes for the making of policy. There are problems with each, and so it is hard to argue an absolute case for one as opposed to the other; and personal preferences will play a role. Furthermore, it is clear that certain areas of policy lend themselves better to one mode than to the other. Defense is always provided by governmental authority, not by a market mechanism, probably because it is so difficult to provide collective goods through a market mechanism. Art and science seem to flourish best when left to a "marketplace of ideas" rather than being made to conform to decisions of governmental authority. Many other policy areas—industrial production, health care, and others—seem susceptible to either mode of decision; and examples of both modes from numerous countries can be found.

## CONCLUSION

At this point you may think the general message of this chapter is that policymaking is awfully complicated. This is understandable. We have seen that the question of "fairness" is complex and subjective, and that reckoning "efficiency" is similarly tricky— that it is difficult to count accurately the costs and benefits of a policy in order to choose the one that gives the greatest benefits at the least cost. It should by now be obvious that the making of policy is an art, not a science.

Unfortunately, a description of the complexity of policy decisions could lead some people to give up in discouragement. If it is difficult to decide what policy is most fair and most efficient, why bother to try? Carried too far, an appreciation of complexity can be paralyzing.

We must always carry on a difficult balancing act between recognizing that our decisions are fallible, and therefore require continual reexamination, and being able to act decisively on our best judgment at any given time. The fact that analysis is complex does not mean that "anything goes" or that one opinion is always as good as another. These questions are important enough to justify hardheaded analysis. It is the duty of those who recognize the complexity of decisions to hold themselves always ready to act in spite of their knowledge that their choices may be wrong. Otherwise, the only people to act would be those who did not understand the complexity of policy choices, and the world would be ruled by simpletons.

### Examples: Political Choice

Here are four examples of policy questions that have recently concerned governmental decision makers. In each instance the policy issue is stated; this is followed by some of the questions that those making a decision on the issue must consider:

1 *The problem of need-based scholarships:* Most systems for providing college scholarships are based on some definition of financial need, with scholarships generally being given only to those students who most need financial help in order to attend school.

Is need, rather than academic ability, the best basis on which to choose those students who are to be encouraged to attend college?

• Which way of choosing who gets aid is the more just?
• Which is the more efficient? Is the overall educational level of society increased more by giving financial aid to bright students or to needy students? Presumably the aid offers more leverage to needy students, since they all need the money in order to attend college, whereas many of the bright students would attend college in any case. But is a smaller number of bright students the more important addition?

Assuming we wish to use need as a basis, how do we determine "need"?

• Is need a function of parents' income? What, then, do we do about children of wealthy parents who are living independently of them and get no aid from them? Should they be punished for their parents' wealth? But if they are given aid, won't all students, in order to get aid, claim to be independent of their parents?
• Is need solely a matter of family income, or shouldn't we take a family's financial obligations into account? Doesn't it make more sense to give aid to someone whose parents must put eight children through school than to someone from a family of four with the same income? But in a possibly parallel situation, should a family that carries big mortgages on two large homes get preference simply because they don't have much money left to spend on college? (Many scholarship systems do count mortgage payments as contributing to need.) Does doing this merely reward

imprudence? Is there a difference between the case of the eight children and the case of the large mortgage?

• How should parents who are not married but are living together and supporting their children jointly be counted? Most systems allow just one of the parents to be counted as the "supporter," and if the one who earns less is so designated, the family will show up as more "needy" than most people would consider them to be. Is this fair to married couples? Does it discourage marriage? If it is not allowed, how can one address the problem of separated couples where one of the parents does not pay a fair share of support? In this case, the single responsible parent and children would appear as *less* needy than they really are. Whichever way you decide to define need in the case of unmarried parents, how can you police the system?

**2**  *The problem of water pollution:* Most states have laws to limit the pollutants that can be dumped into the water.

• How do we decide which pollutants to ban? Should we ban primarily those that are dangerous to human health? Those, such as phosphates or DDT, that have especially bad effects on fish, birds, and mammals? Those that discolor the water? Those that stink?

• Who is to bear the cost of cleaning up the water?

• Is it better to use a flat ban on pollution or to charge people and corporations a stiff fee for polluting? (This is an example of the choice between government authority and market mechanisms.) The main argument against the latter is that it puts the government in the position of saying that pollution is acceptable (or at least legal) as long as one can pay the fee. The main argument for it is that it adds flexibility to the law. Cleaning up pollution always carries costs and may lead to plant closings, higher prices for consumers, and other socially undesirable consequences. The fee system would allow some continued pollution where the cost of cleaning up would be prohibitive. Where the cost is not so high, people would choose to clean up rather than pay the fee. Thus, the system would be made more efficient, but at the expense of losing some of the moral and symbolic vigor of the law. Which is the better course?

**3**  *Children as a collective good:* A society needs to raise children to replace those who die, or else the society would disappear over a couple of generations. One could, therefore, think of the production of children as a collective good. Those who do not have children benefit from the child-raising labors of those who do; they enjoy a society of varied ages in which to live as they grow older, and a labor force of younger people is available to support them in their retirement. Should all not then share in the economic costs of raising the children? In the United States the cost of educating children is borne collectively through the system of public education, but all other costs of raising children are treated as private costs of the parents. In about half the world's states, however, the full society assumes some of the responsibility for all costs of child rearing, by giving direct grants to families with children. These grants are often pegged to the median income of workers in the country: 10 percent of the country's median income might be given to any family raising two children, for example.

• Should such aid go to all families with children, or only to poor families? Public education goes to all families, but should this be treated the same?

• How would it change society to define the raising of children as a collective effort, rather than a private effort of parents?

• Would this be a good way to address such problems as malnutrition, child abuse, and poor education?

• In a sense, this would mean the government was paying people to have children. Is this a wise policy, in a period of massive worldwide population growth?

**4** *The problem of gender-based pension payments:* Almost all insurance companies have varying insurance rates for low- and high-risk categories of people. Many companies give lower insurance rates to students who maintain a B average, for instance, on the assumption that those students drive better (or less often) than others and thus will have fewer accidents. Similarly, young drivers carry higher rates for auto insurance, nonsmokers have lower rates for life insurance with many companies, almost all companies give lower life insurance rates to women because women live longer than men, and so on. In the same spirit, until recently most insurance-based pension plans have paid women who retired at age seventy a lower monthly pension than men who retired at that age because, since women have a longer life expectancy, the companies can reasonably expect to make payments to the women for a greater length of time.

• Is it fair that a woman who has worked as hard as a man should not enjoy as comfortable a retirement as the man?

• On the other hand, if payments are made equal, a man who has worked just as hard as a woman can expect to draw out a smaller total amount of retirement income before he dies. Is this fair?

• If the system is changed to give equal payments, will men reinvest their retirement savings in other ways that allow them to draw out their retirement income in whatever way they wish? This could result in an insurance-based scheme with only female clients, thus defeating the purpose of the change.

• Why should gender be singled out as a basis for this distinction? People who live in Iowa live longer, on the average, than people from Rhode Island. If we're to be consistent, shouldn't Iowans draw a smaller pension than Rhode Islanders? How about people who exercise regularly, people who don't smoke, slender people, and so on?

## FURTHER READING

Anderson, Charles. *Statecraft.* New York: Wiley, 1977, especially Chapters 1–6.

Freeman, John R. *Politics and Markets: The Politics of Mixed Economies.* Ithaca, N.Y.: Cornell University Press, 1989.

Hardin, Garret. "The Tragedy of the Commons." *Science* 162 (13 December 1968): 1243–1248.

Heidenheimer, Arnold J., et al., eds. *Political Corruption: A Handbook.* 2nd ed. New Brunswick, N.J.: Transaction Books, 1988.

Hochschild, Jennifer. *What's Fair?: American Beliefs About Distributive Justice.* Cambridge, Mass.: Harvard University Press, 1981.

Levi, Margaret. *Of Rule and Revenue.* Berkeley: University of California Press, 1988.

Lindblom, Charles. *Politics and Markets.* New York: Basic Books, 1977.

Ostrom, Elinor. *Governing the Commons: The Evolution of Institutions for Collective Action.* Cambridge: Cambridge University Press, 1991.

Sabatier, Paul, and Mazmanian, Dan. "The Implementation of Public Policy: A Framework of Analysis." *Policy Studies Journal* 8 (special issue, no. 2, 1980): 538–559.

Schulman, Paul R. "Nonincremental Policy Making: Notes toward an Alternative Paradigm." *American Political Science Review* 69 (December 1975): 1354–1370.

Solomon, Robert C., and Murphy, Mark C., eds. *What Is Justice? Classic and Contemporary Readings.* Oxford: Oxford University Press, 1990.

Titmuss, Richard M. *The Gift Relationship: From Human Blood to Social Policy.* New York: Pantheon Books, 1971.

Wildavsky, Aaron B. *Speaking Truth to Power.* New Brunswick, N.J.: Transaction Books, 1987.

# PART THREE

# THE CITIZEN
# AND THE REGIME

# 6

# AUTHORITY AND LEGITIMACY: THE STATE AND THE CITIZEN

In the preceding section we looked at the state and at questions that go into the setting of state policies. But how does "the state"—which comprises many different people— choose a particular set of policies? What goes on within a state that determines the policies it will pursue? It is not a simple decision-making mechanism, since its complex organizational structure strongly influences the processes of political choice. In the next two parts—Chapters 6 through 8 and 9 through 16—we will look at those internal structures.

In this chapter we shall consider the relationship between the state and its citizens. Every state has some sort of government, which sets its policies. A "government," when you think about it, is an unusual body within the state. It is the only group of people entitled to make decisions that everyone in the state has a duty to accept and obey.[1] There are many groups of people who have power over others, in that they can force others to do what they wish; for example, General Motors may induce a local government to give it a special tax break in return for locating a plant in the town, or a union may force an employer to increase wages.[2] But the government has a different kind of power, which we call *authority*. (We discussed this also in the preceding chapter, as an alternative to market mechanisms for making public choices.)

If General Motors tries to convince a family to sell their house and the family refuses, that is all there is to it. The family may have made a wise or an unwise decision; but whether they sold or not, the decision was theirs to make, and either decision is socially acceptable. If the school bully tells another child to eat dirt and the child runs away or

[1]See Chapter 2, pp. 28–30.
[2]See Chapter 1 for a fuller discussion of power.

fights the bully, no one faults the child for not doing what the bully commanded. General Motors does not have authority to make someone sell a house, and the bully does not have authority to make anyone eat dirt.

▮ *Authority is power based on a general agreement (1) that a person or group has the right to issue certain sorts of commands and (2) that those commands should be obeyed.* If a person fails to obey authority, that failure is socially unacceptable, since the authority itself is based on a general acceptance of its exercise.▮

Various individuals or groups in a society have limited sorts of authority that extend over specific ranges of behavior. A parent has authority to tell children of a certain age when they should go to bed, with whom they should play, and so on; but as the child grows older, the range of activities over which a parent has authority dwindles until it finally disappears entirely. A teacher in a classroom has the authority to tell students how they should prepare for classes, but the teacher cannot tell them whom they may date or what political candidate to support. A General Motors supervisor has the authority to tell an assembly-line worker which bolts to tighten, but he or she cannot tell the worker how to spend coffee breaks; and when the worker resigns, the supervisor has no authority at all.

⟦A *government* is unique in society in that all of its power involves authority, and at least potentially, there is no limit to the range of activities over which it may exercise authority.⟧Most governments themselves impose some limits on their authority; for instance, the U.S. government, in its Constitution, rules out the exercise of authority over what religion people are to follow, what people are to say to each other, and so on. But these limitations are self-imposed and not necessarily "natural" to governments. Many governments around the world, at one time or another, have claimed authority to tell people what religion they should follow, what they should or should not say to one another, what sort of sexual activity they were permitted, what they might eat or drink, or what sorts of sports and recreation they could take part in. It is safe to say that there is no area of human activity over which some government or another has not at some time exercised authority.⟧"Government," then, is set apart from all other groups in society by the fact that all of its power is based on authority and that, at least potentially, there is no limit to the range of activities over which it may exercise authority.⟧

⟦Authority is a particularly efficient kind of power. It may be backed up ultimately by the threat of coercion (the police will haul you off and punish you physically if you do not do what those in authority tell you to do), or it may be backed up ultimately by persuasion (if you keep your well clean, as the government tells you to do, you will be sick less often). But if people simply do what the government tells them to do, without having to be coerced or persuaded, everything goes more smoothly and—at least from the government's point of view—more satisfactorily. In general, authority does not require the actual use of coercion or persuasion to any great extent. No one has to stand at street corners to *force* cars to stop at red lights, and no one has to stand there to *persuade* them to do so. One of the things that makes the modern state such an efficient form of political organization is the very fact that the state has *authority*, and thus can ensure that people will comply with its commands with a minimum of expensive and time-consuming coercion or persuasion.

People do obey the authority of the state. Because actions against authority are by definition "outlaw" behavior and therefore extraordinary, we can think of many vivid examples of refusals to obey authority—burglary, speeding on the highways, tax evasion, and so on. But the startling thing, when you think about it, is that few people steal things even when it would be safe to do so, most people drive at or near speed limit even though only a sprinkling of police are available to monitor what they are doing, and most people pay the taxes they owe.

It is authority that makes this system of commands and obedience work as smoothly as it does, and this makes the modern state appear to us to be the most natural form of political organization. But authority is not a simple thing that is either present or absent. Rather, it is a matter of degree. Remember that authority exists because it is "generally agreed on"; that is, most people believe it exists. There will probably never be a state in which every single person agrees on the existence and range of the state's authority. Often, when a state issues certain commands, a portion of the people do not accept its authority to do so. If enough people deny the authority of the state, the state has a problem. In the early twentieth century, the government of the United States attempted to command people not to drink alcohol. So many people denied the authority of the state in this area that enforcement proved impossible and the law was eventually abandoned. More seriously, in the 1860s the whole southern region of the United States denied that the national government had any authority over them at all. They set up their own new government instead, and it took a long and bloody Civil War to reestablish the authority of the U.S. government over them.

## LEGITIMACY AND AUTHORITY

The crux of the state then, and of its ability to function effectively, is the government's wide-ranging authority to organize the lives of its people. But paradoxically, this authority exists only because the people in general believe it to exist and to be appropriate. If authority were to fail, it might still be possible for a government to organize its people by coercion and persuasion, but at such great cost that this approach could probably not be sustained over the long haul. A pure tyranny, existing without the benefit of at least some degree of authority, could probably not last long. LEGITIMACY

Thus it is crucial to a government that large numbers of its people should believe that it has authority and that it properly *should* have that authority. We call the existence of this sort of feeling, to the extent that it does exist, the *legitimacy* of the government. Legitimacy, like authority itself, is a matter of degree. Not everyone in a state will necessarily always agree that its government is legitimate or that a given kind of governmental act is legitimate. Much of the violence of politics in Iran in the early 1980s, for instance, resulted from a failure to agree on what sort of government could be legitimate.

## SOURCES OF LEGITIMACY

How does a government achieve a reasonable degree of legitimacy? There are many ways by which the people's allegiance may be bound to a government so that it is generally considered legitimate:

## 1. Legitimacy by Results

First and foremost, a government may gain and retain legitimacy from its people by providing for them the things they most want: security against physical assault, security of their country's borders against invasion, pride in their nation, economic security, and so on. If the government can provide these things, its legitimacy will be greatly strengthened. If it cannot, its legitimacy is likely to be called into question.

A good case in point of "legitimacy by results" is the rule of Adolf Hitler in Germany in the 1930s. In 1933, Hitler took power legally, but through dubious maneuvers and with at most a bare majority of support. The most votes the Nazi party had received in a fully free election was 37 percent—enough to make it the largest party in the country but hardly a mandate for dictatorship. Once in power, Hitler could initially count on the free support of only about one-third of the Germans, and powerful forces were arrayed against him—the labor unions, the Catholic church, much of the army's general staff. What solidified Hitler's hold on Germany and gave him a degree of legitimacy by the end of the 1930s was the *results* of his early policies. He reduced unemployment by large-scale deficit spending; by some audacious bluffs, he outmaneuvered France and England and reestablished Germany as a great power; he built the autobahn system of superhighways; he even pioneered the Volkswagen "bug" automobile. In spite of his suppression of free speech, his oppression of Jews, and the vulgar behavior of his party comrades, these accomplishments brought him widespread and deep support from the German people. By the late 1930s it would probably have been impossible for anyone to seek to overthrow his rule. It was not until 1944, when he had obviously lost World

Adolf Hitler dedicating his latest project, the Volkswagen; Fallersleben, Germany, 1938. (The Bettmann Archive)

War II, that a group of generals were able to muster sufficient strength to try to depose him; and even then, the attempt failed.

## 2. Legitimacy by Habit

Once a government has been around for a while, people become accustomed generally to obeying its laws. People expect to operate under some government or other, and so whatever government is in place and has been obeyed in the past is likely to be regarded as legitimate—unless a particular crisis arises or some force (another state, perhaps) intervenes from outside. In other words, once a particular government has been in place for a while, so that the people have developed the habit of obeying it, it no longer has to perpetually justify its existence. Rather, the burden of proof lies with whoever would propose an alternative government. The existing government remains legitimate unless and until a compelling alternative comes along. We should not underestimate the importance of simple habit in maintaining governments in power.[3]

## 3. Legitimacy by Historical, Religious, or Ethnic Identity

Many governments enhance their legitimacy by the ties that exist between themselves and the people because of the government leaders' past accomplishments (their historic role) or because of the religious and/or ethnic similarity between the government leaders and the people.

This may be especially important in a new state, in which the government has not yet been in place long enough for the people to have developed the *habit* of treating it as legitimate and in which the many economic and social problems that plague most new states make it difficult for the government to achieve legitimacy by *results*.

Many governments of new states are able to buy time by virtue of the status they acquired in leading the state into independence in the first place. George Washington was revered as the "father of his country" after his success as commander of the Revolutionary Army. He and his associates enjoyed a couple of decades in which the people of the United States regarded them as their natural government, and this time allowed them to get the Constitution into place and to establish among the people the habit of obeying it. Similarly, the Labor party in Israel, the Congress party in India, the party of Julius Nyerere in Tanzania, and the National Liberation Front in Algeria all had a breathing space in which their governments were accepted, simply because they had led the independence movements which had established their states in the first place. Religious or ethnic ties may also be used by a government to enhance its legitimacy. In Iran, the regime of the Ayatollah Khomeini and his successors has used its ties to the dominant Shiite Muslim sect and has played on antagonisms between the Persian majority in the country and the Arab populations in the rest of the Mideast to strengthen its legitimacy. Simi-

---

[3]Also, a government that is in place is usually able to foster a supportive mythology. For some examples of this in the case of the United States, see Dan Nimmo and James Combs, *Subliminal Politics: Myths and Mythmakers in America* (Englewood Cliffs, N.J.: Prentice-Hall, 1980); and Barry Schwartz, *George Washington: The Making of an American Symbol* (New York: Free Press, 1982).

larly, the government of South Africa long used whites' fears of blacks to strengthen its legitimacy among the white population.

### 4. Legitimacy by Procedures

Finally, a state may strengthen the legitimacy of its government by following certain procedures in setting itself up—procedures in which many people have confidence, so that they will start off with a fund of trust for any government that has been established along these lines.

The best example of this is democracy—a state in which all the citizens participate in selecting their leaders and perhaps also in determining the state's policies. Typically, democratic governments are chosen by competitive elections in which all citizens vote to decide which of various alternative leadership teams are to govern. Because the resulting government has won broader support than any alternative, it gains a strong base of legitimacy. It is the government "of the people."

The *procedures* of democratic election are what give such a government a good part of its legitimacy. One may dislike particular leaders or think their policies unwise, but it is hard to argue with their right to govern as long as they have been selected by the proper procedures.

Democratic government is the preeminent example today of legitimacy by procedures—so preeminent, in fact, that democratic procedures are often imitated through staged elections in dictatorships. But at other times, other procedures have served as the basis for legitimacy; all that is important is that the procedure be generally accepted as appropriate. Until a few centuries ago, for instance, it was generally accepted that political leadership was most properly passed on by inheritance. One king ruled; when he died, his heir became the new king. This procedure was so important as a basis of legitimacy that great care was taken to lay out precise rules of inheritance; if no clear heir was available, the result was sometimes civil war.

Authority, then, through the legitimacy on which it is based, depends on the relation between the state and its citizens. A particularly interesting problem in authority and legitimacy is posed by modern democracy. A "democracy" is a state in which all fully qualified citizens vote at regular intervals to choose, among alternative candidates, the people who will be in charge of developing the state's policies. It is in one sense an odd sort of state, since the government has power over the citizens (it makes the laws), but the citizens also have power over the government (they can vote it out of office). What sort of relationship between state and citizens is best in a democracy?

### THE "DEMOCRATIC CITIZEN"

The one most special thing about the relationship between a democratic state and its citizens is that democracy requires citizens who will do more than simply obey and follow the government. In our discussion above, it was more or less sufficient, in order for authority to exist, that the people regard the actions of the government as legitimate. This would ensure obedience to the laws.

Some nondemocratic states go a step further and try to generate *enthusiastic* support for the government. Hitler—through his pageantry, his rallies, and his network of youth organizations, sports clubs, and so on—tried to generate enthusiastic support for nazism that would help him to build a powerful German military force more rapidly. The Soviet Union and other communist countries always tried similarly to build enthusiastic support through rallies, discussion groups, parades, and strenuous campaigning, even when their elections were restricted to a single party.

But democracy goes yet a step further than this. In a democracy, it is hoped not only that people will obey the laws and be enthusiastic citizens but that they will also and at the same time be *critical* citizens. Democratic citizens are expected to walk a difficult line along which they support enthusiastically the authority of their government leaders but, at the same time, are critical enough of those leaders that they might readily vote them out of office at the next election. This requires a complex and sophisticated view of politics. It is not easy to be a citizen of a democracy.

What characteristics would we look for in a "democratic citizen"?

*1. Tolerance.*   If varied groups are to support their opinions, it is necessary that the people in general have a reasonable tolerance for diversity. If people could be prevented from setting forth unpopular ideas, then the democracy would not function well. Thus, citizens must generally be at least minimally tolerant of different races, different social behaviors, different religions, and political beliefs that may depart sharply from their own. At the very least, most citizens in a democracy must be willing to allow these various groups to present their cases freely. If they are not, then there is a danger that the voters will not be allowed a full range of options from which to choose.

*2. Active Participation.*   Democracy requires that citizens do more than just obey the laws the government lays down. Since authority in a democracy is a two-way street, the citizens must take concrete political actions to exercise their authority over the government. At the very least, they should vote in elections. Better yet, they should maintain frequent contact with the government by writing to their representatives, serving on citizen committees, and so on. If the citizens do not do this, a state simply cannot be a democracy. Its government will have authority over its citizens, *but not vice versa.*

*3. High Level of Interest and Information.*   But it is not enough that citizens participate actively. If they do not know what is going on, they can be as active as they wish but they will have little effect on what the government does. Action based on no interest or understanding would simply be aimless, and one person's act would tend to cancel the other's out. If the citizens' active participation is to be constructive, democracy requires also that those citizens be well informed.

*4. Support for the State.*   Finally, while the three characteristics noted above are required, if the people are to maintain authority over the government, democracy requires also that the government maintain authority over the people. This is difficult, since the people are required to remain skeptical about the holders of government positions and must stand ready to vote them out of office if that is necessary. What is necessary, if this balancing trick is to work, is that citizens retain an abstract support for the state—and for the democratic procedures that place certain individuals into positions in the government—even while they remain skeptical about the particular individuals currently holding those positions.

"I'M HEDGEPATH, FROM THE C.I.A., AND I'D LIKE TO CONFIRM YOUR SUSPICIONS. WE ARE BOMBARDING YOUR HOME WITH NUCLEAR RADIATION."

(Sidney Harris)

## HOW WELL ARE THESE REQUIREMENTS MET?

As you see, it takes work to be a citizen in a democracy. How well do the citizens of modern democracies measure up? In particular, how do citizens of the United States measure up?

### 1. Tolerance

The citizens of most democracies will readily agree with abstract statements guaranteeing minorities the right to express their opinions freely. However, concrete applications of this principle may be another matter. First of all, there is often not much support for any kind of participation beyond "conventional" acts such as running for office and voting in elections. A survey of the Italian public in 1975 showed that only 75 percent approved of people participating in peaceful demonstrations and that only 36 percent would themselves be willing to participate in a demonstration; furthermore, only 49 percent approved of people signing petitions and only 27 percent would be willing to do so themselves.[4]

---

[4]Sartori and Marradi, cited by Giacomo Sani in Gabriel Almond and Sidney Verba, eds., *The Civic Culture Revisited* (Boston: Little, Brown, 1980), p. 312.

Second, people often think that even conventional political participation should be banned for those who they think are wrong or dangerous. In a 1987 study in the United States, people were asked to name the political group they liked the least. (For instance, one might ask them to choose among skinheads, militant gays, born-again Christians, secular humanists, the American Civil Liberties Union, the Ku Klux Klan, etc.) They were then asked several questions about what rights that group should have to participate in politics. Only 27 percent thought that members of the group they disliked should be allowed to serve as president if elected, only 18 percent thought that members of that group should be allowed to teach in the public schools, and only 32 percent thought that the group should not be outlawed. A related study in Israel in 1985 showed Israelis to be even less tolerant in these ways than Americans.[5]

## 2. Active Participation

At the very least, citizens in a democracy should vote regularly in elections. As we shall see in Chapter 10, even this cannot be taken for granted. However, it is also necessary, if the democracy is to function well, that good numbers of citizens go beyond voting to involve themselves in more demanding tasks such as writing or phoning officials, organizing neighborhood groups, working in political campaigns, and so on.

Table 6–1 presents the results of a survey of the American public, in which people were asked whether they participated in a variety of ways. In looking at this table, you

[5]John L. Sullivan, Pat Walsh, Michal Shamir, David G. Barnum, and James L. Gibson, "Why Politicians are More Tolerant: Selective Recruitment and Socialization Among Political Elites in Britain, Israel, New Zealand and the United States," *British Journal of Political Science 23* (January, 1993): p. 60.

**TABLE 6–1**

PERCENTAGE OF AMERICANS ENGAGING IN SEVEN DIFFERENT ACTS OF POLITICAL PARTICIPATION

| Type of political participation | Percent |
| --- | --- |
| Voted in the most recent presidential election | 70 |
| Worked in a campaign for the most recent election | 8 |
| Made a campaign contribution for the most recent election | 24 |
| Contacted a government official within the past year | 34 |
| Attended a protest, march, or demonstration within the past two years | 6 |
| Worked informally with others in the community to deal with some community issue or problem within the past year | 17 |
| Served in a voluntary capacity on a local governing board or attended meetings of such a board on a regular basis within the past two years | 3 |

*Source:* Sidney Verba, Kay Lehman Schlozman, Henry E. Brady, *Voice and Equality: Civic Voluntarism in American Politics* (Cambridge, Mass.: Harvard University Press, 1995), p. 51.

must bear in mind that people usually tell pollsters that they are more active than they truly are; actual turnout in the most recent presidential elections was 50.2 percent, for instance, although 70 percent of the people polled said that they had voted. Still, the figures here give a rough idea of the relative frequency with which people participated in these various ways.

Do the people depicted here participate a lot or a little? Political science is often the science of the half-filled glass. (Is it half full, or is it half empty?) Against a standard of what a democracy *should* be, these citizens obviously fall short. Only 17 percent of them (or fewer, if some were exaggerating) had worked with others to solve a local problem. On the other hand, against a standard of what we might feel we could realistically expect, these figures show considerable activity. To turn the earlier sentence around, fully 17 percent of the people polled had worked with others to solve a local problem.

By way of comparison, Table 6–2 presents similar information on Austria, India, Japan, and the United States. Overall, the citizens of these states seem to be about as active as U.S. citizens, although there are interesting variations from one state to another in the *ways* in which citizens participate. (Indian electoral participation, by the way, is surely undercounted here.)

### 3. High Level of Interest and Information

Of course, people who regularly turn out and vote in elections might know little or nothing about the candidates among whom they were choosing; in that case, they would contribute little to the working of democracy. How interested are citizens of democracies in what goes on politically, and how accurately informed are they? Voters in the United States are rather interested in politics, according to most studies. For instance, a poll of Americans in 1992 showed that 29 percent said they followed what was going on

**TABLE 6–2**

POLITICAL PARTICIPATION IN FOUR COUNTRIES: PERCENTAGES WHO SAY YES OR PERFORM ACT REGULARLY

| | Austria (Percent) | India (Percent) | Japan (Percent) | United States (Percent) |
|---|---|---|---|---|
| Vote in national election | 96 | 59 | 72 | 72 |
| Ever worked for a party | 10 | 25 | 25 | 26 |
| Attended political rallies | 27 | 14 | 50 | 19 |
| Member of a political club | 28 | 6 | 4 | 8 |
| Active member of an organization engaged in solving community problems | 9 | 7 | 11 | 14 |
| Contacted local official on a social problem | 5 | 4 | 11 | 14 |

*Source:* Adapted from Sidney Verba, Norman H. Nie, and Jae-on Kim, *Participation and Political Equality* (London: Cambridge University Press, 1978), p. 58.

**TABLE 6–3**

PERCENTAGE ACCURATELY STATING CANDIDATE'S POSITION

| | Issue | | | |
|---|---|---|---|---|
| | *Public works jobs* | *Defense spending* | *Welfare spending* | *Tax burden* |
| Ford | 35 | 57 | 43 | 22 |
| Carter | 54 | 29 | 22 | 40 |

*Source:* Adapted from Thomas E. Patterson, *The Mass Media Election* (New York: Praeger, 1980), p. 154. The percentages reported include a correction for guessing.

in government and public affairs most of the time, 35 percent said they followed it some of the time, 23 percent now and then, and 14 percent hardly at all.[6]

Of course, most people will exaggerate to a stranger how much they do something as virtuous as following public affairs. How well informed are these virtuous-sounding people? Not very. Only 29 percent of a national survey of American adults could name their representative in Congress, and only 30 percent could name both of the senators from their state.[7]

In a study of the 1976 presidential election in two U.S. cities, Thomas E. Patterson found that even by October surprisingly few voters could accurately state the positions of the two candidates, Gerald Ford and Jimmy Carter. As seen in Table 6–3, in only two of eight instances could more than half of the voters accurately state a candidate's position on an issue.

## 4. Support for the State

You will recall that what is needed here is a general abstract support for the state and for its democratic form of government, which can coexist with skepticism about the qualities of individual officeholders. Many democracies seem to be fairly successful at commanding this kind of respect from their people.

In a survey in 1959, Americans were asked, "Generally speaking, what are the things about this country that you are most proud of?" They could mention anything they wished to, including religious values, the wealth of the country, landscape, culture, and so on. Over 60 percent of the things mentioned were aspects of government and politics.[8] At about the same time, in a survey in 1958, 73 percent of those polled said that they trusted the government in Washington to do what was right either "most of the time" or "just about always."[9] As we shall see later in this chapter, there has been a

[6]University of Michigan, Center for Political Studies, 1992 National Election Study. Data made available by the Inter-University Consortium for Political and Social Research.

[7]Michael X. Delli Carpini and Scott Keeter, *What Americans Know About Politics and Why It Matters* (New Haven: Yale University Press, 1995).

[8]Gabriel Almond and Sidney Verba, *The Civic Culture* (Boston: Little, Brown, 1965), p. 102.

[9]University of Michigan, Center for Political Studies, 1958 National Election Study. Data made available by the Inter-University Consortium for Political and Social Research.

steady erosion since then of this sort of generalized confidence and support of their government by the American people. The point is, such support was maintained at a time
when, in the same study, Americans felt considerable skepticism about the *people* running the government. In 1958, 24 percent thought that "quite a lot" of the people running the government are crooked, 37 percent said that the people running the government did not usually know what they were doing, and 85 percent said that the people in
government wasted "some" or "a lot" of the money they paid in taxes. At about this time
also the American electorate repudiated their Republican President Eisenhower by giving the Democrats a landslide victory in the congressional election of 1958.

This balance between support for state institutions and skepticism about officials is
hard to maintain, and many shaky democracies are rarely able to achieve it. As we shall
see in examples below, one democracy, West Germany, had to build it up over a twenty-
year period; while another, the United States, may have to a large extent lost it.

## POLITICAL CULTURE

Political scientists have given the name *political culture* to the types of basic attitudes
we have addressed in this chapter. The political culture of a society consists of all attitudes and beliefs held communally by a people, which form the basis for their political
behavior. We have borrowed the term from anthropology, in which the term "culture" (a
people's whole interrelated set of beliefs and ways of thinking) forms a central organizing concept.

It is clear that political culture varies a good deal from one state to another and that it
is responsible for major differences in how politics is conducted. We can often detect
differences in culture by looking at popular behaviors and sayings. For instance, we
sense that the Japanese put a greater emphasis on consensus than do Americans, and
value conflict less than Americans, when we compare two popular sayings:

> The nail that sticks out will get pounded down. (Japan)

and

> The squeaking wheel gets the grease. (United States)

Basic differences such as those reflected in these sayings must surely have something to
do with the fact that compared with the United States, political decisions in Japan are
much more likely to be made on the basis of unanimous consent rather than by a vote
(with one side losing).

Political culture is obviously important, but it is difficult to evaluate concretely. It almost seems that such a big concept resists precision and invites fuzzy generalization. It
is too easy to lapse into stereotyping of peoples: lockstep, obedient, efficient Germans;
unflappable British; breezy, pragmatic Americans; hot-blooded Latins. While there is
often a germ of truth in such stereotypes, it is usually only a germ, lost in a gross over-
simplification. Even in the hands of careful scholars, the concept can lead away from
precision. The best work on political culture in recent decades (Gabriel Almond and
Sidney Verba, *The Civic Culture* [Boston: Little, Brown, 1965]) was criticized justly because it casually assumed that the ideal culture for democracy was one that, perhaps un-
surprisingly, looked very much like American culture.

But even with these difficulties, political culture is too important to ignore. A work that demonstrates the potential importance of cultural analysis is *Culture Shift* by Ronald Inglehart (see above, p. 60). Inglehart argues that prosperous, industrial societies are undergoing a shift in culture in which concerns for security are being replaced by concerns for self-expression, and he uses this shift to account for broad generational changes occurring across Europe.

One striking characteristic of political cultures is that they change very slowly. A good example of this is provided by Alexis de Tocqueville in *Democracy in America.*[10] De Tocqueville visited the United States in the early nineteenth century to examine the workings of U.S. democracy, but his description of the American approach to politics still is recognizable today—the emphasis on individuality and freedom, reliance on local politics and voluntary organizations, the restlessness and desire for progress. This despite the fact that the America he saw was an almost totally agricultural society, without modern means of communication, and without the quasi-imperial world role the U.S. has adopted since the Second World War. Our state and society have changed immensely since he wrote his book, but the underlying culture has remained recognizably the same.

## POLITICAL SOCIALIZATION

The values and assumptions people hold about politics are acquired in a process called *political socialization*, which simply means the learning of political values and factual assumptions about politics.[11] In principle, this can occur at any age and under any circumstances, but it tends to be concentrated at certain points of our lives.

The importance of political socialization is evident, if nothing else, in the fact that without it any political culture would disappear after one generation. All of the cultural underpinnings of politics, as well as many other more transient values, are learned by children and other new citizens through political socialization. It is political socialization that allowed the United States to absorb millions of Irish, Italians, Russians, Poles, Chinese, Vietnamese, and so many other peoples, and yet maintain political continuity while doing so.

Like most learning, political socialization apparently comes most easily and fully in childhood, and diminishes as we grow older. However, explicit and detailed information about politics tends not to be picked up much before the teen years. Children learn in their families many basic social attitudes, such as trust in people and attitudes to authority, that will be important in shaping their later response to politics. But most children have only rather primitive ideas about what government is and how politics works. These things are primarily learned in adolescence and early adulthood and, of course, continue to be learned throughout adult life. For example, Table 6–4 shows the percentage of Swedish youths of varying ages who were undecided as to which political party

---

[10]de Tocqueville, Alexis, *Democracy in America* (New York: Knopf, 1980).

[11]A good general review of political socialization is Pamela Johnston Conover, "Political Socialization: Where's the Politics?", in William Crotty, ed., *Political Science: Looking to the Future*, volume 3 (Evanston, Ill.: Northwestern University Press, 1991), pp. 125–152. See also Stanley W. Moore, et al., *The Child's Political World* (New York: Praeger, 1985); Orit Ichilov, *Political Socialization, Citizenship Education, and Democracy* (New York: Teachers College Press, 1990); and Roberta S. Sigel, *Political Learning in Adulthood* (Chicago: University of Chicago Press, 1989).

**TABLE 6–4**

DEVELOPMENT OF POLITICAL ORIENTATIONS
AMONG SWEDISH YOUTH

| Age | Percent undecided as to best party |
|---|---|
| 11–12 | 73 |
| 13–15 | 66 |
| 16–18 | 55 |
| 19–21 | 47 |
| 22–24 | 32 |
| 25–27 | 35 |

*Source:* Adapted from Herbert H. Hyman, *Political Socialization* (New York: The Free Press. 1959), p. 49. This is certainly an old example, but I have not found anything more recent that permits this comparison across ages.

was the best. Among eleven- to twelve-year-olds, 73 percent did not have a preference among the parties. This indecision declined to 35 percent by early adulthood.

One of the concerns of political scientists studying socialization is to assess the varying roles of different *agents of socialization.* We must learn about politics *from* someone, and the various sources of learning are what we call the agents of socialization. Different agents operate in different ways and affect different areas of our values and assumptions about politics. Obviously, we learn about politics from an infinite variety of agents, but a few particularly important ones are our families, schools, and peer groups.

From our parents we acquire a number of general social values that will apply to politics just as they do to other aspects of our lives. It is also thought that we may gain expectations about how politics should occur in the state by extension from the way politics (the making of family decisions by the use of power) is conducted in the family; an authoritarian family may prepare one for an authoritarian state and a democratic family for a democratic state.[12] More specific political values and assumptions do not develop as much through the family as we might suppose. As noted above, they tend to be acquired during adolescence, a period when most children are trying to establish an independent identity.

Schools are of particular interest to students of political socialization because this is an agent of socialization that the state controls, and through which the leaders of the state can attempt to mold the citizenry. In all states there is some degree of guided socialization through the schools. Schools in the United States try to develop informed, patriotic citizens both directly through civics classes and salutes to the flag and indirectly through class materials in history, literature, and other courses. Some states such as Cuba, China, and Nazi Germany have used the schools vigorously and directly to remake their citizens.

---

[12]This is a controversial position; many scholars think it oversimplifies a complex process of the development of values. A good presentation of the position is Harry Eckstein and Ted Robert Gurr, *Patterns of Authority* (New York: Wiley, 1975).

Peer groups are extremely influential in developing adolescents' tastes and their view of the world, but they vary considerably in their political impact. In most friendship groups of adolescents, politics does not figure importantly in the attention of the group. Where this is the case, the group will influence its members' choices in clothes or social behavior strongly but will leave their political identity to develop independently. However, youths who are already somewhat involved in politics may gravitate together as a friendship group, and when this happens, the group may have a profound impact on the political development of all its members.

### Example: Building Authority and Legitimacy in West Germany after World War II[13]

After the defeat of Germany in 1945, the Germans as a people were demoralized politically. They had bought a dream of greatness from Adolf Hitler, but he had brought them defeat and international disgrace. They were hated throughout Europe, their country had been cut up on the map, and their industries and farms were in ruins. Germans who were fifty years old in 1945 could not be blamed if, having been dazzled by politics, they now withdrew from it. They had grown up under the kaiser's monarchy and had seen it overthrown in disgrace at the end of World War I, when they were in their early twenties. They then lived through fifteen years of chaotic attempt at democracy which never really established its authority and legitimacy with the people and ended in Hitler's dictatorship. They were thirty-eight years old when Hitler came to power; in the next twelve years they saw Germany approach world conquest and then come close to total destruction. They could be pardoned if they were shy of politics after that.

In many ways, West Germany after 1945 gave political scientists much the same opportunity to observe an evolutionary development as a new volcanic island rising from the sea offers to biologists. When a new island is formed, biologists get a rare chance to observe which animals are the first to appear on it and see how long it takes a diverse flora and fauna to be established. Similarly, political scientists get few chances to see attitudes toward politics establish themselves among a people who initially have essentially no attitudes. West Germany after the war did provide such a case.

For many years, political observers asked themselves whether democratic behavior and attitudes could possibly develop among Germans. Some said that the people who had put Hitler into office just could not develop into democrats. Others thought that if Germany were lucky enough to have a period of peace and economic stability, democracy would be able to establish itself. But no one could hazard a guess as to how long the process would take.

As we can see in Tables 6–5, 6–6, and 6–7, the optimists were correct; in fact, the development of democratic support occurred steadily and fairly rapidly. As we see in Table 6–5, during the first twenty years, the democratic regime established itself as the best arrangement Germany had known—better than Hitler's dictatorship or the kaiser's monarchy.

[13]Now a part of Germany since the reunification of former West Germany and East Germany in 1991.

It was not simply that the country was economically well off either. The political institutions of democracy became more popular during this period. In 1959, in a survey similar to that mentioned earlier for the United States, Germans were asked what they were proud of about their country. Only 7 percent pointed to Germany's political institutions. In 1978 the question was repeated in a survey. By that time, 31 per-

**TABLE 6–5**
ATTITUDES TOWARD THE "PAST," 1951–1970

Q.: When in this century do you think Germany has been best off?

| | Year | | | |
|---|---|---|---|---|
| | 1951 (Percent) | 1959 (Percent) | 1963 (Percent) | 1970 (Percent) |
| Federal Republic (present) | 2 | 42 | 62 | 81 |
| Under Hitler before the war (1933–1939) | 42 | 18 | 10 | 5 |
| Under the kaiser, before World War I | 45 | 28 | 16 | 5 |

*Source:* Adapted from David Conradt, "Changing German Political Culture," in Gabriel Almond and Sidney Verba, eds., *The Civic Culture Revisited* (Boston: Little, Brown, 1980), p. 226.

**TABLE 6–6**
TRUST AND HOSTILITY AMONG GERMANS, 1948–1976

a. Percent "trusting most people"

| 1948 | 1959 | 1967 | 1973 | 1976 |
|---|---|---|---|---|
| 9% | 19% | 26% | 32% | 39% |

b. Percent thinking more people are evil minded than good minded

| 1949 | 1951 | 1953 | 1971 | 1976 |
|---|---|---|---|---|
| 46% | 43% | 34% | 17% | 16% |

*Source:* Adapted from David Conradt, "Changing German Political Culture," in Gabriel Almond and Sidney Verba, eds., *The Civic Culture Revisited* (Boston: Little, Brown, 1980), p. 226.

**TABLE 6–7**
FREQUENCY OF POLITICAL DISCUSSION, 1953–1972

| | 1953 (Percent) | 1959 (Percent) | 1961 (Percent) | 1965 (Percent) | 1969 (Percent) | 1972 (Percent) |
|---|---|---|---|---|---|---|
| Daily | 9 | 11 | 10 | 10 | 37 | 50 |
| Occasionally | 29 | 50 | 51 | 66 | 40 | 34 |
| Never | 63 | 39 | 39 | 25 | 23 | 16 |

*Source:* Kendall Baker, Russell Dalton, and Kai Hildebrandt, *Germany Transformed* (Cambridge, Mass.: Harvard University Press, 1981), p. 40.

cent of the things mentioned were aspects of government and politics. By 1988, the figure had grown to 51 percent.[14]

Support for democracy in the abstract also grew across the first two decades. In 1953, only a bit over 55 percent of the Germans stated in the abstract that democracy was the best form of government.[15] By 1976, 90 percent answered yes to the same question.[16]

The sort of social relations among people that are required if a loose system of authority is to work was also developing. In a society where people are hostile and suspicious of each other, democracy cannot work well. As we see in Table 6–6, trust grew steadily and social hostility decreased during this time.

Finally, it is necessary that the people begin to be active and interested citizens. As we see in Table 6–7, this also developed steadily.

West Germany did not necessarily become an ideal democracy, but it is interesting to see that there were established, over just a couple of decades, patterns of behavior and support similar to those of such democracies as the United States or Great Britain. No one would have predicted this with any confidence in 1950, and it was an eye-opener for political scientists.

### Example: Declining Democratic Legitimacy in the United States

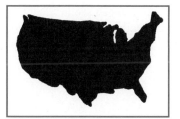

The story of the last few decades in the United States has been in some respects the opposite of what we have seen in Germany. Since about the mid-1960s, there has been a puzzling decline in people's confidence in officials and in the political system. It might not seem so strange that the political turmoil of the 1960s and the Watergate scandal of 1973 shook people's faith, but there appeared to be further erosion during the return to normality of the late 1970s and the 1980s.

Table 6–8 shows a generally downward trend in the percentage of Americans thinking that one can trust the government to do what is right most of the time or always and an upward trend in the percentage thinking that the government is run for the benefit of a few big interests and that quite a lot of people running the government are crooked. The steadiness of the trend across various events and various presidents makes it look as though it were not a response to particular disappointments, but political scientists are frankly at a loss to say just what *has* caused the decline.[17]

While this plunge in trust and legitimacy has been occurring, Americans have re-

[14]David Conradt, *The German Polity*, 5th ed. (New York: Longmann, 1993), p. 55.

[15]Kendall Baker, Russell Dalton, and Kai Hildebrandt, *Germany Transformed* (Cambridge, Mass.: Harvard University Press, 1981), p. 24.

[16]Conradt, "Changing German Political Culture," in Gabriel Almond and Sidney Verba, eds., *The Civic Culture Revisited* (Boston: Little, Brown, 1980), p. 234.

[17]Arthur Miller and Jack Citrin present an interesting interchange concerning the possible causes of the decline in "Political Issues and Trust in Government: 1964–70," *American Political Science Review* 68 (September 1974): 951–1001; see also Arthur H. Miller and Stephen A. Borrelli, "Confidence in Government during the 1980s," *American Politics Quarterly* 19 (April 1991): 147–173.

**TABLE 6–8**

DECLINE OF CONFIDENCE, 1958–1994

|  | 1958 | 1964 | 1968 | 1972 | 1976 | 1980 | 1984 | 1986 | 1988 | 1992 | 1994 |
|---|---|---|---|---|---|---|---|---|---|---|---|
| Percent who trust the government to do what is right "most of the time" or "always" | 73 | 76 | 61 | 53 | 33 | 25 | 45 | 39 | 41 | 26 | 21 |
| Percent thinking the government is run for a few big interests | — | 29 | 40 | 53 | 66 | 69 | 59 | — | 55 | 27 | 75 |
| Percent thinking "quite a lot" of government people are crooked | 24 | 29 | 25 | 36 | 42 | 46 | 33 | — | 34* | 41* | 50* |

*Source:* University of Michigan, Center for Political Studies, National Elections Studies. Data made available by the Inter-University Consortium for Political and Social Research.
*Slightly different question wording after 1988: "quite a few" crooked.

mained an attentive and reasonably active citizenry. As you can see in Figure 6–1, while turnout in elections has dropped somewhat, the decline is a fairly gentle one, from 59 percent of the electorate voting in the 1956 presidential election to 54 percent in 1992.

**FIGURE 6–1**

Percentage of Voting Age Population Voting, U.S.A.
*Source:* U.S. Bureau of the Census, *Statistical Abstract of the United States.*

The number of people performing the more substantial act of writing to officials rose steadily, from 17 percent in 1964 to 20 percent in 1968, 27 percent in 1972, and 28 percent in 1976, the last year for which we have comparable figures.[18]

Finally, the percentage who state that they follow what is going on in government and public affairs some or most of the time has remained virtually unchanged: 63 percent said that they did so in 1960 and 63 percent in 1994.[19]

The combination of a still fairly attentive citizenry who have dropped off sharply in their trust of the government is alarming and puzzling. It does not bode well for a continuation of stable, constructive democracy, and for this reason it is important that we find out the causes of the change. The person who does so will have made an important contribution to our understanding of democracy.

## FURTHER READING

Almond, Gabriel, and Verba, Sidney. *The Civic Culture*. Boston: Little, Brown, 1965.

————, eds. *The Civic Culture Revisited*, Boston: Little Brown, 1980.

"Authority." In *International Encyclopedia of the Social Sciences*.

Barber, Benjamin. *Strong Democracy*. Berkeley: University of California Press, 1984.

Conover, Pamela Johnston. "Political Socialization: Where's the Politics?", in William Crotty, ed., *Political Science: Looking to the Future*, volume 3 (Evanston, Ill.: Northwestern University Press, 1991), pp. 125–152.

Dahl, Robert. *Modern Political Analysis*. 4th ed. Englewood Cliffs, N.J.: Prentice-Hall, 1984.

Gellner, Ernest. *Culture, Identity, and Politics*. Cambridge, England: Cambridge University Press, 1987.

Graber, Doris. *Mass Media and American Politics*. Washington, D.C.: Congressional Quarterly Press, 1980.

Inglehart, Ronald. *Culture Shift in Advanced Industrial Society*. Princeton, N.J.: Princeton University Press, 1990.

Iyengar, Shanto, and Kinder, Donald R. *News That Matters: Television and American Opinion*. Chicago: University of Chicago Press, 1987.

Lane, Robert E. *Political Ideology: Why the American Common Man Believes What He Does*. New York: Free Press, 1962.

"Legitimacy." In *International Encyclopedia of the Social Sciences*.

McCloskey, Herbert. "Consensus and Ideology in American Politics." *American Political Science Review* 58 (June 1964): 361–382.

Patterson, Thomas E. *The Mass Media Election*. New York: Praeger, 1980.

————. *Out of Order: How the Decline of Political Parties and the Growing Power of the News Media Undermine the American Way of Electing Presidents*. New York: Knopf, 1994.

Rokeach, Milton. *The Open and Closed Mind: Investigations Into the Nature of Belief Systems and Personality Systems*. New York: Basic Books, 1960.

Sniderman, Paul. *Personality and Democratic Politics*. Berkeley: University of California Press, 1975.

[18]University of Michigan, Center for Political Studies, National Election Studies. Data made available by the Inter-University Consortium for Political and Social Research.

[19]Ibid.

Sullivan, John L.; Shamir, Michal; Walsh, Patrick; and Roberts, Nigel S. *Political Tolerance in Context: Support for Civil Liberties in the United States, Israel, and New Zealand.* Boulder, Colo.: Westview Press, 1985.
Verba, Sidney; Schlozman, Kay Lehman; and Brady, Henry E. *Voice and Equality: Civic Voluntarism in American Politics.* Cambridge, Mass.: Harvard University Press, 1995.

# 7

# DEMOCRACY AND ITS RECENT SURGE IN THE WORLD

A democracy is a state in which all fully qualified citizens vote at regular intervals to choose, among alternative candidates, the people who will be in charge of setting the state's policies. And since democracy is "government of the people," there is also a sense that the full population of citizens will be actively engaged between elections in debate over alternative policies and in the work of setting the policies; just how fully engaged they are varies across democracies, and whether they are sufficiently engaged has long been a matter of debate.[1]

Most of you are familiar with democratic government from your own experience, but in fact a relatively small number of the world's states are stable democracies. Democracy requires an implicit agreement by all the conflicting groups in a state to accept the possibility that they will lose out in the making of policy. In effect, it requires an agreement among labor unions, corporations, farm groups, environmentalists, vegetarians, motorcycle enthusiasts, and all other groups to take their chances on the outcome of a general process of policymaking in which the population as a whole gets the deciding voice. Each group accepts the fact that it must abide by the end result and hopes that it will be able to get enough of what it wants out of the process. This is the "democratic bargain."

When we look at it in this way, it is easy enough to see why democracy might be a fragile thing. All that is needed to make a democracy collapse is for one or more important groups to reject the results of the democratic bargain and to have access to enough power to overthrow the system. Many parts of the world are beset by problems of overpopulation, poverty, and chancy positions in world trade—problems so fierce that it becomes difficult for powerful groups to face policy defeats philosophically; the stakes are

[1]Examples of this debate include proposals for referendums, workplace democracy, and citizen caucuses.

just too high. And military forces or popular movements usually lie close at hand, willing and able to overthrow the system.

As one might suspect, under these circumstances only a small number of the world's states are stable democracies. Of the 122 states that have been independent for at least thirty years, only 29 have had an uninterrupted record of electoral democratic government during that time. Most of these are prosperous industrialized states whose people can afford to compromise on the "democratic lottery." However, it is worth noting that such poor, small states as Jamaica, Malta, Botswana, and Costa Rica have also had steady histories of democratic government.

## THE MOVE TO DEMOCRACY

The world's imagination was seized in 1989 when the Iron Curtain fell, and the Berlin Wall with it, and most of the communist states of eastern Europe suddenly threw off their old systems and established democracies. The drama of the failed coup in the Soviet Union in 1991 and the victory of the pro-democratic forces there had people glued to their television sets. But these dramatic changes were only part of a larger move toward democracy that has covered two decades and ranged across many parts of the world.

Southern Europe saw three shifts from right-wing dictatorships to democracy in the late 1970s: in Greece, Portugal, and Spain. A bit later a wave of democratization swept Latin America, as several states reestablished democracies after periods of military (mostly right-wing) dictatorship: Ecuador and Peru in 1978, Bolivia in 1982, Argentina in 1983, Uruguay in 1984, Brazil in 1985, and Chile in 1989.

Finally in 1989 and 1990, along with the wave of democratization in the formerly communist states of eastern Europe (East Germany, which has since merged with former West Germany; Poland; Czechoslovakia; Hungary; Bulgaria; Romania; and Yugoslavia) several states scattered around the world moved to democracy: Algeria over the period 1989–1991 (and at the same time Egypt, Jordan, and Tunisia moved closer to being democracies); Haiti in 1990; South Korea in 1987; Nepal in 1990; Nicaragua in 1990; Pakistan in 1988; and the Philippines in 1986. However, this was not a story of uniformly forward progress. After establishing democracy in Algeria, the military was afraid that the fundamentalist Islam party would be victorious, and it abruptly banned elections in 1992. In Haiti, the military ousted newly elected President Jean-Bertrand Aristide in a 1991 coup; he was only reinstated in 1994 after strong pressure from the United States and the temporary occupation of Haiti by United States troops. Democracy is very tenuous in most parts of the former Soviet Union.

Still, overall there has been a clear movement over two decades toward more democracy. Since the late 1970s, few if any states, and none with a large population, have moved in the other direction—away from democratic government (if it had been established for more than a year) to something else.

## POSSIBLE EXPLANATIONS

How may we explain this remarkable shift? Four possible reasons might be: fatigue of some authoritarian regimes, international pressures, people's desire for security against arbitrary abuse, and their desire for economic development.

(Auth, © 1989 Philadelphia Inquirer. Reprinted with permission of Universal Press Syndicate. All rights reserved.)

In a few cases, authoritarian systems had gotten "tired" and had lost popular support. In Spain and Portugal, long-term dictators had died, and their regimes had lost steam long before their deaths. In Argentina the military government had lost a war with Britain. Most dramatically, the exhaustion of the Soviet Union at maintaining its control of eastern Europe was a critical element in the wave of democratization in that region in 1989, and the corruption and senility of its Communist party led to the victory of democracy in the Soviet Union itself. This was evident in the Communists' botched coup in 1991.

Also, there has been international pressure on nondemocratic regimes to change. Spain, Portugal, and Greece came under pressure from their neighbors to become democratic, and the "carrot" of membership in the European Union was offered to them implicitly if they established democratic systems.[2] South Africans were under international trade and investment sanctions for several years to force them to give democratic rights to their black majority, and those sanctions led to democratic government in 1994. Though pressure for democracy in China has been repulsed since the Tiananmen Square massacre in 1989, concern for international reactions has softened slightly the suppression of the democratic movement there. Nicaragua's government held free elections under quasimilitary pressure from the United States, which promoted a civil war in the country to force a change in regime.

Probably more important than either international pressures or the weakness of the old regimes, however, are the remaining two factors: a desire for human rights and se-

[2]See Chapter 2, for the European Union.

curity against abuse and, especially in the communist states of eastern Europe, economic failure. A desire for security and dignity must have been high among the reasons for democratization in South America, where many of the military regimes had been brutally oppressive. In Argentina and Chile, thousands of people disappeared during the dictatorships and are presumed to have been tortured and killed. In the Philippines, the murder of Corazon Aquino's husband sparked the move for democracy. In East Germany, after the overthrow of the communist regime, it was learned that the secret police had maintained files on 6 million people, out of a total population of 16 million, and had employed hundreds of thousands of informants. In the formation of most democracies a simple yearning for dignity and security has always played a large part. This was true in the establishment of the first democracies in Europe and North American in the nineteenth century, and it is surely true today.

The fourth factor in the surge to democracy has been the economic stagnation of many authoritarian states, which contrasted with the dynamic prosperity of democracies such as Japan and (then West-) Germany. This has been particularly true of democratization in eastern Europe, where establishing democracy has been intermingled with the dismantling of inefficient socialist economies and the establishment of market economies. The connection between free markets, democracy, and prosperity is not all that clear, as we will see below; but in many democratizing states part of the thrust for democracy has come from a sense that the state had stagnated economically, that it was not "modern" (not up to date), and that democracy is part of being modern.

## THE END OF HISTORY?

While these have been exceedingly important changes, there is also a danger that we could read more into them than is there. One author, noting these events, has declared that capitalist democracy has won the great ideological debate of the nineteenth and twentieth centuries and that history, as we have known it, has now ended because there is nothing left to fight about.[3] Well, the end of history has been declared several times over the past century, but history does not stop.

First of all, just as we have now had a surge of democratization for the past twenty years, there have been other periods during the midcentury when the world saw surges of dictatorship. The 1920s were such a period, as Germany, Italy, Spain, and various eastern European states overthrew democracy; and in the 1950s and 1960s a wave of dictatorship spread over South America and Africa. It is possible that basic circumstances have changed—especially the diminished superpower rivalry of the Soviet Union and United States in the 1990s, which makes it less important for both sides to maintain client dictators—so that the current set of changes will prove long-lived. But it is also possible that we have simply been watching one long wave in a slow surge back and forth between democracy and authoritarianism.

One thing that should give us pause is that while in many states such as Spain, Por-

---

[3]Francis Fukuyama, "The End of History?" *The National Interest* 16 (Summer 1989): 3–19.

tugal, Greece, Argentina, Brazil, Poland, Czechoslovakia, and Hungary there is a broad base of support for the new democracy and a full understanding of the "democratic bargain," in others, democracy has been adopted primarily as an alternative to a hated earlier regime; and neither its implications nor its requirements were fully prepared for. In Haiti, for instance, the despicable Duvalier dictatorship was ousted in a democratic movement in 1986; but the Duvaliers had destroyed most alternative leadership, and so a stable democratic regime has not developed. The years since then have been marked by violence, strikes, military coups, and occasional chaos.

Romania is another country for which "democratization" may have been as much as anything else a banner under which to overthrow the oppressive Ceausescu dictatorship. Under the democratic government which was established after Ceausescu's fall, a cult of reverence developed for Ion Antonescu, the fascist dictator during Hitler's occupation who was executed in 1945 for having killed 250,000 Jews. In 1991 the Romanian parliament voted unanimously to honor Antonescu with a minute of silent tribute. Honors for Antonescu were supported by all major newspapers, and only President Ion Iliescu courageously opposed the Antonescu revival and its accompanying anti-Semitism.[4] One has to wonder about the depth of democratic commitment under these circumstances; and indeed it should not surprise us if Romania, which has had only fleeting experiences of democracy in its past history, failed to immediately settle into stable democratic habits after ousting Ceausescu in a spasm of popular uprising. At the very least, the Romanian future is unclear.

Aside from the fact that a broad base of support for democracy may be lacking in a number of the new democracies, another aspect of democratization that we should bear in mind is that democracy's openness often unleashes regional nationalist pressures that had been held in check by more oppressive regimes. Unless the state is strong and lucky, it may be pulled apart. Alternatively, the danger to the state may then prompt an anti-democratic reaction from the military, and we may end up back at dictatorship.

The new democracy in Spain, for instance, was immediately challenged by a terrorist movement for separation of the Basque region and weathered that challenge only with difficulty. In 1990 the new democratic system of Yugoslavia was immediately threatened with the secession of its two most prosperous provinces, Slovenia and Croatia, and a bloody war resulted. Finally, the Soviet Union, as it gradually became more democratic after 1986, saw violent national conflicts between Armenians and Azerbaidzhanis and between Uzbeks and Turks, and attempts by Georgia, Estonia, Latvia, Lithuania, and the Ukraine to secede. The upshot of the triumph of democracy in the failed coup of 1991 was the disintegration of the union and its division into a number of new, independent states.

None of the cautions in this section are meant to make you discount the importance of what has happened in the past couple of decades. We have seen great events. But it is a common weakness for social scientists, as for people in general, to assume that what is happening now will continue into the future. Understanding some of the complexities of democratization may help to guard us against this.

[4]*New York Times*, 19 June 1991, p. 10, "Rising Verbal Attacks Shake Romania's Jews."

Lenin's statue dumped near a cemetery after a failed August 1991 Soviet coup. (Andy Hernandez/Sipa Press)

## WHAT HAVE WE LEARNED?

Theories of political science have had difficulty encompassing the wave of democratization, probably because what is grouped as "democratization" actually consists of many different sorts of processes, in different parts of the world, where the push for democracy came from many different causes and motives. (I have tried to give you some sense of the variety of these processes of "democratization" above.) Accordingly, political scientist have not been able to come up with a single theory of democratization that is at all general. We have learned some things, however:

1. *The Importance of "Pacts."* Perhaps the best general treatment to date is a broad review by O'Donnell, Schmitter, and Whitehead (1986) of what were then the most recent cases of democratization, primarily in Latin America and southern Europe.[5] This study does not so much develop a theory as note and comment on similarities across cases.

One important conclusion the authors reach is that it is very important for successful democratization that the democratizers form "pacts" with those whom they are ousting to ensure a smooth transition and to lay a good base of support for the future democracy.

PACTS

[5]Guillermo O'Donnell and Philippe C. Schmitter, *Transitions from Authoritarian Rule: Tentative Conclusions about Uncertain Democracies* (Baltimore: Johns Hopkins University Press, 1986).

Such pacts might include, for instance, amnesty from prosecution for crimes committed under the dictatorship; symbolic affirmation of the old regime, as in the maintenance of a powerless or weak monarch; or guarantees of funding for the army. "Pacts" figured importantly in the Spanish case, described in detail below.

As always in looking at democratization, however, there are few universal truths. In the wave of democratization across eastern Europe in 1989, which occurred after the Whitehead et al. study, pacts were not nearly so important. Unlike Latin America, this was not a case of ousting a military associated with powerful domestic forces, which had to be dealt with gingerly. Rather, the force being ousted was primarily the Soviet army, and broad nationalist sentiment coincided with the democratic thrust.

2. *Sudden Changes.* Many of the recent shifts to democracy have taken observers by surprise. No one predicted in 1988, for instance, that by the end of 1989 many eastern European states would be democracies. One scholar has provided a good explanation for why these shifts might be sudden and difficult to predict.[6]

Under an authoritarian regime there are few rewards and many punishments for anyone coming out in favor of democracy. But this is a function of how likely it is that democracy will actually be established; if democracy in the end is actually established, there will be many rewards and no punishments for those who had come out in favor of it. The key factor here is that net rewards of coming out shift very suddenly as the probability of success shifts over from less than even to greater than even. This is depicted graphically in Figure 7–1. As the probability of success rises from zero to .2, .3, or .4, the net rewards for favoring democracy do not increase much. In fact, regimes may crack down more on opponents as their situation becomes slightly less secure than it had been. Suddenly, however, at some point the danger in favoring democracy appears to decrease. People find that when they demonstrate in the street, there are thousands of other people there, too many for the government to take on. Almost overnight, favoring democracy may shift from being a dangerous activity, restricted to the hard core, to an easy activity that may carry future rewards.[7]

3. *Democracy and Freedom.* Analyzing the thrusts for democracy has also *reminded* us of a truth, which is really an old truth rather than a new one: Democracy and individual freedom are certainly related, but they are not identical; while moving toward one generally means moving toward the other, there is not an automatic correspondence between them, and there may be occasional instances of marked disparity.

The fact that there is some connection between democracy and individual freedom should be apparent. Both democracy and a variety of individual freedoms derived originally from the same basic principles of liberalism.[8] And for purely practical reasons, democracy requires at least minimal levels of freedom of speech and freedom of association if the public bargaining that is the essence of democracy is to proceed at all.

---

[6]Adam Przeworski, "Some Problems in the Study of Transition to Democracy," in Guillermo O'Donnell, Philippe C. Schmitter, and Laurence Whitehead, eds., *Transitions from Authoritarian Rule: Comparative Perspectives* (Baltimore: Johns Hopkins University Press, 1986).

[7]I do not mean here that the process is automatic from this point on. China is an example where this point had been reached in 1989, thousands were flocking to the democratic banner, and the government responded with the Tiananmen Square massacre, thus moving the probability of success back to a lower level.

[8]As we saw in Chapter 3.

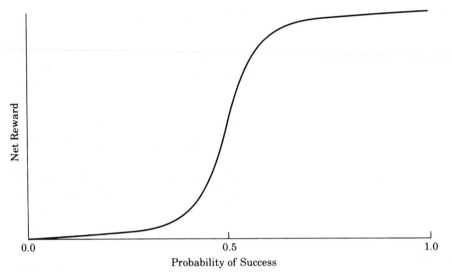

**FIGURE 7–1**
Probable reward for coming out in favor of democracy, as probability increases that democracy will in fact be established.

But a variety of other freedoms—such as freedom of religion, free markets (see below), freedom to travel where you will, freedom to consume alcohol, and so on—are not necessary companions of democracy, although we may find in practice that they usually go together.

A good example that freedom and democracy do not necessarily imply each other is Hong Kong, which as a British colony has never had democratic government but which has a very open society with many liberal freedoms—a free press, freedom of religion, freedom of speech and association, and so on. The United States also furnishes examples from its history in which, although we are a democracy, we have seen the level of freedoms rise and fall. The internment of Japanese-Americans during the Second World War, the system of legal racial segregation in many parts of the country through the first two-thirds of this century, the McCarthy period in which freedom of expression was limited—all demonstrate that there is not an automatic correspondence between democracy and freedom.

This question has arisen in the case of democratization because in a number of countries authoritarian systems have gradually become more liberal and open, often with no shift to democracy for some years. Democracy has then come—or not come—only as a last step. Thus it has been necessary, in analyzing the process of democratization, to separate the two processes. We might well conclude that democratization works best where it has been preceded by slow liberalization, which has provided time for opposition leadership to form, for organizations of representation to be established, and for working relationships to be established between the old regime and the forces for change. For example, in Brazil a process of *abertura*, or "opening," was begun by the military regime in 1974, under which discussion became more open, local governments became more independent, and political parties could form. It was not until 1985 that democracy was established.[9]

4. *Democracy and Capitalism*. The surge of democratization in eastern Europe had much to do with the failure of the communist economic systems to provide prosperity and flexible production of goods and services. Especially in the Soviet Union, what came first seems to have been a realization that the Soviet economic system was not competitive with the market systems of the West; steps toward democratization were largely just a part of the way Soviet leaders tried to adjust the overall system to improve their economic performance. Does a decision to adopt market mechanisms for the economy also imply a move to democracy?[10]

As in the case of freedom and democracy, we might expect that free markets and democracy would go together, since both are based on the aggregation of individual choices as a way to make collective decisions, and both reflect the basic liberal value of making individuals responsible for their choices.[11] Thus it is no surprise that most democracies of the world have market-based economies.

However, there have been plenty of nondemocratic states in the past that used market mechanisms for their economy. Hong Kong, again, is a good example. It operates with an open market economy, yet has never had democratic government. Many dictatorships and military governments in Africa rule states which essentially have market economies. And China, even as it was brutally putting down the movement for democracy, has allowed a considerable evolution of its economy away from communist planning and toward market mechanisms.

Thus there is no automatic connection between democracy and capitalism, and the eastern European states could in principle have made a shift in their economies without moving to democracy. Very likely, however, their rejection of the past and their desire for change and integration with the West were such that it seemed natural to become "Western" both in politics and in economy. Since a radical change in the economy would have been very difficult without a thorough change of leaders, a basic governmental change of *some* sort was probably necessary, whether or not it was a move to democracy.

### Example: Democratization in Spain

For a brief period in the 1930s, Spain had a democratic government; but the army, supported by Hitler and Mussolini, overthrew the government at the end of a long and bloody civil war in 1939 and established Francisco Franco as a fascist dictator. Franco ruled from 1939 until his death in 1975.

His dictatorship was ironfisted and authoritarian in the early years, but for the last decade or two of his rule

---

[9]For a discussion of why military regimes might choose to yield up power in this way, see Chapter 8.
[10]See Chapter 5 for "market mechanisms."
[11]See Charles Lindblom, *Politics and Markets* (New York: Basic Books, 1977), Chapter 12.

there was considerable liberalization in Spain. Labor unions, which were technically still illegal, were tolerated and bargained collectively for large numbers of workers. Public education, which had earlier been suppressed, blossomed: In 1957 there were only 120 high schools in Spain, one *fewer* than in the last year of the Republic, but in the next decade the number of students attending high school went up 1,000 percent. The Spanish economy, organized as a free market in contrast with the political structure, grew rapidly and diversified; the large landowners who formed the core of Franco's support became less and less central to the economy.

Thus when Franco died in 1975, the stage was set for change. However, everyone was very apprehensive. Against the promise of a more modern society in 1975 were set the bloody memories of the civil war of the 1930s, which had been characterized by shocking brutality and atrocities.

There seems general agreement that the transition was eased by unwritten agreements ("pacts") between the army and the democratic forces. The army apparently acquiesced in establishment of a democracy on three conditions:

**1**  The monarchy (which Franco had set up to succeed to power after his death) was to be retained.

**2**  The political right, rather than the army's old enemies on the left, were to lead the change.

**3**  The country's regions should be given no self-determination.

In 1976 King Juan Carlos and his conservative prime minister, Adolfo Suarez, put a democratic constitution before the people of Spain in a referendum. The referendum was important because it added the legitimacy of popular approval to the new democracy. The constitution, reflecting the King's wishes, established more of a democracy than the army had probably envisioned, one with a constitutional, mainly symbolic monarch.

Over the next few years the new democracy was plagued by disorganized party conflict in the parliament, together with a rising campaign of terrorism by Basque nationalists. The terrorists' targets were primarily officers of the police and the army, which added to the tension because those institutions were potentially dangerous if they became disenchanted with the new system. In 1981 there was a serious attempt to overthrow the regime. A group of soldiers seized the parliament when it was in session, with the entire cabinet present, and announced that they were taking over the state in the name of the King. However, they failed to cut off communications into and out of the palace; Juan Carlos telephoned all of the commanders of the army, some of whom were already preparing to set out for Madrid in support of the coup, and told them they would have to depose him if they wished to overthrow the democracy. The coup failed, and the political leadership were freed.

Afterward, Juan Carlos reportedly met with the parliamentary party leaders and told them they would have to work out better techniques of decision making and compromise, because he doubted he could thwart another coup if one were attempted. In the next several years Spanish democracy was solidified in several ways:

- In 1982 a moderate socialist, Felipe Gonzalez, became prime minister. His long, not very radical rule helped to calm fears of the "reds" and lay the civil war to rest.
- Considerable power of self-government was devolved onto the regions.
- Spain became a member of the European Community in 1986, integrating it into a democratic organization of democratic states.

Spain now appears to have successfully established a stable base for democracy.

### Example: Fragile Democratization in Peru

 In contrast to the (relatively) smooth progress of democratization in Spain, Peru illustrates the uncertain and fragile process by which democracy is often established.

Peru is a poor country on the west coast of Latin America—a poor country, but one with a vibrant cultural life and a long history of intellectual contributions; three of its universities are over three hundred years old. The country has long been torn by ethnic, economic, and regional conflicts. Approximately half of its people are Amerindians, mostly living in the impoverished interior of the country. Economic disparities between the interior and the more prosperous coast are indicated by the fact that infant mortality in the coastal region is just 46 per thousand births, but is 128 in the lower areas of the interior and 156 in the mountains.[12]

From the Second World War until 1978, except for a five-year interlude of democratic government from 1963 to 1968, Peru was ruled by various military groups, who replaced each other from time to time by seizing power in coups d'état (see below, p. 145). In 1977 General Francisco Morales Bermúdez announced a plan to restore civilian rule. A constitution-writing assembly was elected, the new constitution emerged in 1979, and a new president and Congress were elected in 1980.

From 1980 to the present there have been regular presidential and congressional elections every five years, so one might conclude that steady democracy had been established in the democratization of 1979. However, the experience of democracy since 1980 has not been all that smooth, and the outlook remains uncertain. In this, Peru is probably more typical of newly established democracies than is Spain.

Not long after the first election of the new democracy, a left-wing terrorist movement appeared in the interior that called itself *Sendero Luminoso,* the "Shining Path." It developed broad-based strength in the region, and drew down on itself an unprincipled retaliation from the military that was almost as destructive of society as *Sendero Luminoso* itself. At the height of the movement's activities in 1989, the government reported that 3,198 people had been killed in terrorist violence. At the same time, it was estimated that since 1982 approximately 3,000 people had been executed by the military, and another 3,000 had "disappeared" in military jails and were assumed to

---

[12]James D. Rudolph, *Peru: The Evolution of a Crisis* (Westport, Conn.: Praeger, 1992), p. 8.

be dead.[13] The government appointed Peace Commissions to investigate human rights abuses by the military, but both Commissions eventually resigned, stating that they could get no cooperation from the military.

The economy also did badly during the initial years of the democracy. Real incomes in the area around the capital city of Lima declined by 1990 to about one-third what they had been in 1980.[14] And by 1990, inflation was running at 7,650 percent a year. (If inflation were to run at that rate in the United States, a shirt that cost $10 at the beginning of a year would cost $765 by the end of the year!) Governmental economic policy had been crippled by opposition from both businesses and labor unions. The latter had launched several "general strikes" at various times, in which all unions go out on strike simultaneously, for maximum political impact.

In the 1990 election a little-known agronomist of Japanese descent, Alberto Fujimori, won on a pledge to fight inflation and corruption. He initiated an austerity plan for the economy—abolishing subsidies, breaking up monoplies, simplifying the tax system, and privatizing a number of publicly owned industries. In November 1991, Fujimori convinced the Congress to give him 150 days of emergency dictatorial power to deal with economic problems; he used this power to deregulate most forms of transport and to open up telecommunications, the postal services, the schools, and other services to private competition. He also gave the military added leeway in combating *Sendero Luminoso.*

His relations with Congress deteriorated as a result of these actions, and on April 5, 1992, Fujimori carried out what has been called an *autogolpe* ("self-coup"). He announced suspension of the 1979 constitution, had troops seize the Congress and all television and radio stations, and placed large numbers of labor leaders and leaders of Congress under house arrest. Tanks patrolled the streets of Lima.

A week later, when censorship was lifted, opposition leaders called on the people to take up arms against the president, a right which had been guaranteed in the 1979 constitution. But the *autogolpe* had been fairly popular, and there was no response to the opposition's call to arms. Fujimori presented his revised version of the 1979 constitution to the electorate in 1993, with new provisions allowing the president to run for reelection, and setting a death sentence for terrorist activity. The revised constitution was approved with 52% of the vote.

Over the next couple of years, Fujimori maintained generally good relations with the military. He and his courts protected military officers from charges of human rights abuse, transferring even well-documented cases of murder from civil courts to the military courts, for instance, where they received relatively mild sentences. The government gradually won the twin battles against inflation and against *Sendero Luminoso,* capturing *Sendero's* leader in 1994.

In the 1995 presidential election, Fujimori won in a landslide with 65% of the vote, and his party gained a majority in Congress.

The continuation of democracy in Peru is by no means a certainty, although Fuji-

---

[13]*Europa Yearbook 1995,* p. 2360.
[14]Susan C. Stokes, *Cultures in Conflict: Social Movements and the State in Peru* (Berkeley, Calif.: University of California Press, 1995), p. 46.

mori's successes in bringing stable prices and peace have helped to set the conditions for successful democracy. The main problem is not that Fujimori has in the past called out the tanks to get his way with Congress—though that is certainly a serious problem. Rather, the main problem is that even though he has successfully put down rebellion and gotten the economy into reasonable order, Peru still has intense lines of political animosity. The military remains highly political and is a lightning rod for angry passions on both sides, and Peru remains a poor country with huge disparities of income and education between half of the population living on the relatively prosperous coast and the other half, mostly Amerindian, living in the interior. Also, Fujimori himself is such a smart politician, ruling in such a personal style, that once he leaves office he is not likely to leave behind many skilled leaders, either in his own party or in the opposition. He has discouraged the development of any structure to dispense highly visible social services like school building, for instance, preferring to keep all of this in the president's office where he can use it to maximize photo opportunities.

So on the one hand, the outlook for democracy remains uncertain. On the other hand, the glass is half-full rather than half-empty: Peru has now had over fifteen years of democratic rule, even if that period has been punctuated by rebellion, by a military almost out of control, and by an armed coup led by the president. The seeds for legitimacy-by-result and legitimacy-by-habit appear to have been sown.

What might explain the differing experiences of democratization in Spain and Peru? There is probably no one answer to this question. Some possible factors include:

- Income and educational disparities are much greater in Peru than in Spain.
- Ethnic divisions in Peru split the population about 50–50, which is very hard to handle. In Spain, regional/linguistic splits distinguish smaller minorities of the population.
- The military in Spain look to role models in the rest of Europe who deliberately avoid involvement in politics. The NATO alliance structure draws the Spanish military away from domestic political concerns and more toward broader European security issues.
- Spain is a member of the European Union, a rather tightly integrated regional association that could exercise strong sanctions if Spanish democracy were under attack. Peru is a member of the Organization of American States, a much weaker organization. During Fujimori's coup, the Organization of American States could never bring itself to go any farther than passing resolutions.

## FURTHER READING

Bates, Robert H.; Przeworski, Adam; and Tarrow, Sidney. "Understanding Political Change in Eastern Europe." *PS* 24 (no. 1, March 1991): 12–27.

Fukuyama, Francis. "The End of History?" *The National Interest* 16 (Summer 1989): 3–19.

Hirschman, Albert O. "On Democracy in Latin America." *New York Review of Books* (10 April 1990).

Linz, Juan. "Transitions to Democracy." *Washington Quarterly* (Summer 1990): 143–164.

O'Donnell, Guillermo, and Schmitter, Philippe C. *Transitions from Authoritarian Rule: Tentative Conclusions about Uncertain Democracies*. Baltimore: Johns Hopkins University Press, 1986.

Pridham, Geoffrey and Vanhanen, Tatu, eds. *Democratization in Eastern Europe*. London: Routledge, 1994.

Przeworski, Adam. *Democracy and the Market*. Cambridge: Cambridge University Press, 1991.

———. *Sustainable Democracy*. Cambridge: Cambridge Univesity Press, 1995.

Sisk, Timothy. *Democratization in South Africa: The Elusive Social Contract*. Princeton, N.J.: Princeton University Press, 1995.

Smith, Hedrick. *The New Russians*. New York: Random House, 1990.

Wesson, Robert, ed. *Democracy: A Worldwide Survey*. New York: Praeger, 1987.

Williamson, John, ed. *Latin American Adjustment: How Much Has Happened?* Washington, D.C.: Institute for International Economics, 1990.

## What Have We Learned

1. Pacts
2. Sudden Changes
3. Democracy and Freedom
4. Democracy and capitalism

### Elements of Democracy

1. Rulers
2. Public realm
3. Citizens
4. Competition
5. Elections
6. Majority rule
7. Cooperation

Principles
1. Winners will not use their position to bar losers from taking part in the political process.
2. Losers will respect the right of winners to make binding decisions.

# 8

# AUTOCRATIC GOVERNMENT

We noted in the last chapter that the worldwide trend has been toward democracy for twenty years. But democracy is a fragile thing; of the 122 states that have been independent for at least thirty-five years, only 29 have had an uninterrupted record of electoral democratic government during that time. Autocratic government has its own fragilities, however. In this chapter we will (1) look at some of the major forms of autocratic government and (2) explore the sources of their fragility and success.

What is autocracy like? The autocratic alternatives to democracy are by no means of one piece. Consider this sampling:

• **The Union of Soviet Socialist Republics (1917–1991)**   From the Russian Revolution (1917) until a couple of years before the breakup of the Union in 1991, power in the Soviet state was lodged clearly with the Communist party. It was self-sustaining, recruiting new young members who could progress through it to build careers. Although Stalin's rise to power in the 1930s was bloody, after Stalin the party saw five peaceful, orderly transitions of leadership. As far as we know, decisions were made more or less collectively within the party, with strong leadership by the party head and a great deal of influence from such groups as the army. Ordinary people did not have a great deal of personal freedom but—compared with the bloody past—laws were at least predictable and dealings with the governmental apparatus were generally orderly.

• **Bolivia**   Transitions of power in Bolivia traditionally were frequent, and usually occurred by military coups. Bolivia has experienced 191 coups in her 170 years of independence. At the same time, there have been recurrent attempts to establish democratic government. For example, in 1973, the military group then in power announced a return to civilian government and set elections for 1974. After two attempted coups (which failed) the president, Colonel Hugo Banzer, announced that elections were postponed until 1980. Widespread strikes in 1976 led him to move the election date up to 1978. Elections were held then, but there were so many charges of fraud that the election was declared void. General Juan Asbun, the government-sponsored candidate, thereupon staged a successful coup and took over the government. He himself was deposed four months later by a left-wing officer, General David Aranciba. Elections were held in 1979 but led to a split result, another coup, and another election in 1980; but again a coup followed an inconclusive result. A civilian government was reestablished in 1982, with a promise to hold elections, a promise that was honored in 1985. The parliament elected in 1985 survived without overthrow until the election of 1989, which came off as scheduled. The period since 1985 has been marked by turmoil caused by the worldwide collapse of the price of tin and the rising influence of illegal cocaine manufacturers. Over this period there have been four changes of cabinets, and the nation underwent several hunger strikes by national leaders including the president; two general strikes by the trade unions; and a national strike by teachers, which three times prompted the government to impose a national state of siege. However, Bolivia has now had continuous democratic government since 1982.

• **Saudi Arabia**   Saudi Arabia has been an absolute monarchy for most of the twentieth century, with power lodged in the Saud family. This is a large, extended family that provides not only the king but also most of the council of ministers and other high government officials. It appears that while the king figures very importantly in the making of decisions, this is a genuinely collegial effort in which the council of ministers (including the king) discusses issues and decides on policies. The Saud family are conservative in religious matters and enforce strict Muslim standards of behavior, though they have been enthusiastic about economic modernization. Even the turmoil of the Gulf War left this system essentially unchanged.

• **Zaire**   Zaire became independent from Belgium in 1960 and immediately plunged into a civil war fomented by Belgian mining interests. After a chaotic period of civil war, coups, assassinations, and attempts to establish democracy, power was seized in 1965 by Colonel Joseph-Désiré Mobutu; he established a one-party state and has remained in power since then, as president and, at various times, chair of the single party and head of the armed forces. His rule has been characterized by charges of massive corruption and of widespread abuses of human rights; Mobutu has proved adept at maintaining his rule despite unrest by giving ground at critical moments, and retaking it when the opportunity arises. Since 1982 an organized opposition has existed, based mainly abroad but operating openly, when circumstances have permitted, in Zaire itself. In the 1990s, Mobutu has fended off strong opposition pressure and student riots. Meanwhile the country has sunk ever more deeply into social and economic disorganization.

These examples are roughly representative of autocratic systems as a whole. It is worth noting, first of all, that they are quite varied politically; they range from conservative Saudi Arabia to the bureaucratic Soviet Union to the personal dictatorship of Zaire. Second, note that many of the autocracies are not organized stably. Of these examples, Bolivia had an incredibly turbulent history before establishing its current democratic government. Most parts of what was once the Soviet Union are now moving toward democracy, or at least toward change. Few expect Mobutu to remain in power in

Zaire over the long haul; the main question is when and how he will be ousted. Saudi Arabia, on the other hand, appears to have a rather stable system.

## MILITARY GOVERNMENT

The most dramatic alternative to democratic government is *military government*, in which a group of officers use their troops to take over the governmental apparatus and run it themselves. This is called a "coup," from the French "coup d'état" (strike at the state). About one-tenth of the world's states are under military government.

Why is military government so common? A better question might be why it is not even more common. The military in any state control more armed power than anyone else. If they choose, as a group, to oust the existing government—or even if only a part of the military choose to do so and the rest decide to sit it out—there is no one who can stop them. Civilian governments must obviously depend for their safety on the military's satisfaction, disunity, or reluctance to take over the government. While each of these protective shields is evident in many military groups, it must not be so very unusual that all three would from time to time fail and that the military would break out in a coup. This is particularly likely in a new state, where a tradition of civilian government has not yet had time to take hold. It is not surprising that military coups occur with some frequency around the world.

In a few states, coups have become so routine that they have almost been institutionalized as the normal method of governmental change. In such cases, other political forces have come to be involved informally, much as they would under other arrangements. Key groups such as labor unions may be sought out by one or another military faction as potential allies, and—even though they do not themselves bear arms—their weight is felt.[1]

In Bolivia, for instance, factions of the armed forces in the past regularly depended on other political groups when they were attempting a coup. In 1978, a right-wing government was overthrown by the army, who were aided by left-wing allies in the unions and political parties. After an attempt at an election in 1979, a right-wing coup was tried, but it failed because its leaders were not able to get the support of Congress. And in 1982 yet another military group was forced out of office by a general strike led by the unions. In a bizarre way, coups under these circumstances become a system that involves a fairly wide range of people in the political process. Generally, however, they are more isolated events.

Military governments vary greatly in their political role. In Paraguay, General Alfredo Stroessner seized power in 1954, and secured his position with repression and torture until he was himself deposed by a military coup in 1989. It was estimated that in 1982 one-quarter of the Paraguayan people were in exile outside the country's borders.[2] In Nigeria, a series of military governments ruled from 1966 to 1978, and again from

---

[1]Martin C. Needler, "Political Development and Military Intervention in Latin America," *American Political Science Review* 60 (September 1966): 616–626.

[2]*Europa Yearbook 1983*, vol. 2, p. 1228.

---

ARE MILITARY COUPS CONTAGIOUS?

A number of observers have noticed that military coups cluster at certain times. Suddenly a rash of coups will break out in a region such as Latin American or southern Africa, and then coups will once again decrease. Statistical tests have shown that this is not coincidental. Coup makers apparently watch each other's success, and if they have seen a number of their neighbors succeed, they are likely to have fewer qualms about undertaking a coup themselves. Furthermore, if a number of coups have recently occurred in the neighborhood, this lessens the problems of legitimacy. If coups are a frequent thing in the region, initiating a coup will not seem as flagrantly illegitimate as if yours was the only army doing it.

Beyond considerations in any one state, then, coups appear to involve broad, wavelike regional processes. Statistical analysis to measure these processes has proven to be complex and challenging. A good example is Richard P. Y. Li and William R. Thompson, "The 'Coup Contagion' Hypothesis." *Journal of Conflict Resolution* 19 (March 1975): 63–88.

Actually, it is likely that regime changes of *any* sort operate in this way, at least in part. As we saw in Chapter 7, democratization occurred in waves at different times, in different parts of the world. Most east European states shifted to democracy between 1989 and 1991, for instance. And there is evidence that movements for democracy in one area are often influenced by movements in another.[3]

---

1983 to the present. During much of that time, there was considerable civilian support for the military regime. Although democracy was reestablished peacefully by general consent in 1978, the democratic regime fell once again to a military coup in 1983; since then a series of military rulers have talked about restoring democracy, with one general even going so far as to schedule—and then cancel—a presidential election, but democracy has not yet returned to the country. In the mid-1990s, the military rulers turned from the tradition of benign, if corrupt, autocracy and became vicious, hanging nine dissidents in November 1995. Greece was ruled by a right-wing group of officers from 1967 through 1973; this government maintained itself by harsh repressive measures. It broke up in 1974, and democracy was reestablished. In Turkey, the military have taken over the government three times since World War II—in 1960, 1971, and 1980—each time when Turkey's democratic government was verging on chaos. The Turkish takeovers have all been broadly supported and have been followed by a return to democracy after stability was restored.

Military governments vary widely in the one thing in which we might have expected that they would be similar: in their political direction. They are not all of the political right or of any other direction, even though we have a stereotype of the right-wing officers' coup. Some are clearly of the right or the left, but many are not identifiable as either. Which sort results depends on which group of officers leads the coup; there are many officers of the left in most countries, as well as of the right, especially if recruitment is not limited to the upper class. Studies that have compared fairly large numbers of military regimes with civilian regimes conclude, on the whole, that whether or not a

---

[3]See, for instance, Douglas Anglin, "Southern African Responses to Eastern European Developments," *Journal of Modern African Studies* 28 (No. 3, 1990): 431–456.

state has a military regime has little effect on the state's rate of economic development. That is, as a group, military governments are neither especially good at guiding their states' economies nor especially poor at doing so.[4]

These two aspects of coups—the fact that they sometimes become incorporated in the broader political process and that they have no clear political complexion, of the left or of the right—have made political scientists a bit cautious in assessing them. As one scholar has noted:

> I would still affirm the general correctness of the position I took on this question ten years ago [that military coups are a repressive move backwards, thwarting necessary social change]. However, subsequent events have suggested that I underestimated the extent to which apparently democratic political processes could in fact be manipulated by elite economic interests to its advantage. This means that interruption of those processes by military seizures of power could, at least in some cases, be a force for promoting development instead of retarding it.[5]

## WHY AREN'T THERE MORE MILITARY GOVERNMENTS?

Good or bad, though, it is still surprising that more countries are not governed by the military. There are not as many coups as we might expect, and most military govern-

[4]See especially Robert Jackman, "Politicians in Uniform," *American Political Science Review* 70 (December 1976): 1098–1109.

[5]Martin C. Needler, "The Logic of Conspiracy: The Latin American Military Coup as a Problem in the Social Sciences," *Studies in Comparative International Development* 13 (Fall 1978): 31.

"Good news. The 'Times' has upgraded us from a 'junta' to a military government.'" (Drawing by Joe Mirachi; © 1984, The New Yorker Magazine)

ments stay in power only a few years. This may be partly because most states take pains to imbue their military officers with inhibitions against political intervention. Adolf Hitler required all officers to swear oaths of personal allegiance to him, for instance; and in the training of its officers, the U.S. government assures in many ways that they will understand their proper role to be nonpolitical.

However, more important than such inhibitions are a series of important problems faced by military governments—problems that make officers somewhat reluctant to take and hold power. A uniquely serious one for them is that of *legitimacy*, which was discussed as a general problem of all governments in Chapter 6. Since a military government itself takes power through no regular process but simply seizes it, how can it claim that no other group should similarly displace it? A democratic government is legitimized by the electoral process that produced it, a monarchy is legitimized by the rules of succession on which it is based, a communist government is legitimized by Lenin's theory that the Communist party must lead the revolution. But no process of selection legitimizes the military government. Those who live by the sword shall die by the sword, they say, and a military government must always be concerned to justify its existence. To this end, many military governments add civilians to their governing apparatus or set future dates for a return to democracy. Others try to rally the people through wars and appeals to nationalism.

Another problem of most military governments is that while their leaders *may* be skilled politically, there is little in the profession to which they have been trained that makes this likely. Military organization is usually marked by a fairly orderly passage of commands from higher officers to lower officers, without a great deal of argument in between. This orderliness should not be exaggerated, but many military officers are clearly frustrated by the jabber of daily political requests and arguments with which they must deal once they have taken power.

Finally, many military governments are themselves fairly shaky alliances, united primarily by their opposition to the regime they have displaced and likely to fall apart as new issues that may divide their members arise.

As a result of these problems, military governments are actually rather fragile. Unless they set up the institutions to transform themselves into one-party states, there is a good chance that they will eventually yield to the establishment of democracy. If a military regime is internally divided or has problems generally in governing and if enough of the key figures concerned feel that the uncertainty of the outcome of democratic choice is preferable to the certainty of any other particular group being in control, the stage is set to introduce democracy—or reintroduce it, as the case may be.[6] In the last twenty years, fully twenty-two states have switched at least for a time from military government to democracy.[7]

---

[6]For an expansion of this argument, see Adam Przeworski, "Some Problems in the Study of the Transition to Democracy," in Guillermo O'Donnell, Philippe C. Schmitter, and Laurence Whitehead, eds., *Transitions from Authoritarian Rule: Prospects for Democracy.* (Baltimore: Johns Hopkins University Press, 1986), pp. 47–63.

[7]Argentina, Bangladesh, Bolivia, Brazil, Burkina Faso, Burundi, Chile, Ecuador, Fiji, Ghana, Honduras, Nigeria, Pakistan, Panama, Paraguay, Peru, the Philippines, Portugal, South Korea, Thailand, Turkey, and Uruguay.

## ONE-PARTY STATES

Most autocracies are not straight military governments, but *one-party states*. The one-party state is distinguished by the fact that the government is based on and supports a political party, which is the only party allowed in the state. One-party arrangements have often had their origins in military coups. For example, in Libya, Colonel Muammar Khadaffi seized power in a coup in 1969 and established the Arab-Socialist Union as the sole political party; its general congress, chaired by Khadaffi, is in effect the chief governing body of the state. Other one-party arrangements originated in national independence movements, which were then institutionalized as the single party. In Tanzania, for example, Julius Nyerere led the movement for independence, and his independence movement, the Tanganyika Africa National Union, won 70 of the 71 seats in the first election to the National Assembly. Four years later, a constitution was written that established it as the state's sole party.[8] A number of one-party states originated in socialist revolutions, either indigenous, as in the cases of Cuba, China, or the U.S.S.R.; or imposed by the U.S.S.R., as in the cases of (pre-1989) East Germany, Czechoslovakia, and other eastern European states.

What distinguishes these states from other autocratic systems, especially from straightforward military governments, is the existence of a reasonably large national political party that both bolsters the government and provides an institutional basis for it. Compared with military rule, the one-party state offers a more stable and responsive form of government. The military government is necessarily limited by the field of vision of the officers who hold power. There is little provision for dealing with broad factional conflict or for the intrusion of diverse opinions. And since the government itself came into being by irregular means, there exists no regular set of arrangements to provide for the replacement of old leaders by new. These are things that may be provided for by the single political party.

A national party is likely to embrace at least a reasonable range of the social groups in a state—labor leaders, industrialists, and intellectuals as well as military leaders. Not all of these may be equally happy with the party; however, they have little choice but to cooperate with it if asked. The party, on its side, needs to involve them if only to keep tabs on potential troublemakers. As a result, the single party as an organization is generally able to have a better feel for opinion in the countryside than a simple group of officers will have. It provides institutional links between the government and the population.

Second, the party can provide an arena in which varied political positions can develop into factions. In this way new conflicts may develop within an existing system rather than arising outside it and posing a threat to it.

Finally, the single party may provide a set of arrangements by which a transition of leadership can be accomplished. An example of this capacity was the fairly easy transition from Chernenko to Gorbachev in the Soviet Union after Chernenko's death in

---

[8]Although there is only one legal party, there are still many contests between *individuals* in elections. A majority of the seats in the National Assembly are filled by election, the rest being appointed. Defeats of individual incumbents in elections are common, though all candidates must come from the ruling party. In recent years Nyerere has urged democratization and the establishment of a multiparty system.

1985. During Chernenko's illness, there had obviously been some process at work by which the Communist party leadership decided who would take over from him.

The one-party state must be distinguished from a democracy with a dominant-party system.[9] A few democracies have party systems in which a single party has dominated government over a long period of time; Italy is a good example. From 1945 to 1994, without a single break, the Christian Democratic party received the largest vote of any party at each election, and except for a couple of years, it dominated all coalition cabinets during that period. (It finally fell from grace in 1993 due to its leaders' involvement in massive scandals.) What distinguished Italy from the one-party states during this period is that other parties were able to organize, and did so; it was also universally recognized that those other parties would gain office if enough people voted for them.

To sum up our treatment of one-party systems: This is the most frequently seen form of autocratic government. It may originate in all sorts of ways—military coups, movements for national independence, socialist revolutions, and many others. Distinctively, the one-party state has one (and only one) political party that is fostered by the government. This party adds to the government's capacities and helps to make these regimes more stable than straight military governments.

## "COURT" POLITICS

A characteristic of many autocracies—especially of monarchies and of personal dictatorships like that which the Duvalier family exercised in Haiti from 1957 to 1986, but also of many military governments and one-party states—is that a single person may hold almost all ultimate power in the system and that politics revolves around that single person. It must be emphasized that this is not true of all autocracies; many have plural institutionalized bodies for decision, as in the central committee of a communist state or the officers' councils that guide some military governments. But it is frequently the case. Extreme examples are the great power held by Hitler in Nazi Germany, Stroessner in Paraguay, Duvalier in Haiti, and the apparently undisputed preeminence of the Ayatollah Khomeini in Iran from 1977 to 1989.

Politics revolving heavily around one person in this way is called "court" politics, after the royal courts of the great European monarchs. Court politics is usually marked by:

• *Less emphasis on the rule of the law and more on the arbitrary whim of the ruler:* In a more plural system, politics is based on competing forces, which may need to agree on the relatively neutral devices of laws and legality to settle their disputes rather than confronting each other directly. In a system dominated by a single person, that person's wishes are likely to dominate over legal considerations.

• *Heavy competition by all other figures for access to the leader:* Access to the leader's ear may be a major factor in political outcomes. Lower officials may not dare to take vacations, for instance, for fear of missing such a chance.

• *Unusual importance of even apparently nonpolitical figures who necessarily have access to the leader by virtue of their other roles in the leader's life:* Doctors, hairdressers, and even childhood friends may all turn up as important political figures. Mar-

[9]See Chapter 11.

Muammar Khadaffi, leader of Libya.
(Reuters/Bettmann Newsphotos)

tin Bormann, Hitler's personal secretary, was probably the second most important political figure in Germany toward the end of the Third Reich; doctors, astrologers, and others also had some political influence.

• *Flattery, and attempts to shield the leader from unpleasant reality*[10]: A graphic illustration of court politics follows this chapter, in the excerpt from Albert Speer's *Inside the Third Reich.*

### "POWER AND CHOICE" AGAIN

To return to the theme of our text, these governments—especially the military governments—might appear to embody a rather pure strain of politics as power. After all, when political control depends on who has the guns, it is hard to deny that power is at work. On the other hand, it is a common mistake to think of autocratic governments simply as raw examples of power at work.

One-party governments often see themselves as pursuing communal objectives and develop organizational mechanisms for bringing a wide spectrum of opinion to bear on the government's decisions. Even military governments usually portray themselves as heeding the country's call, and there is often broad support among the people for a military coup. We shall deal with governments such as these more wisely if we remember that the picture is not all black or white but that politics in these states—as in democracies—consists of both power and choice.

---

[10]Actually, aspects of "court" politics (especially this and the preceding one) can be seen wherever great political power is held by a single person. The American presidency has sometimes shown signs of it.

## CONCLUSION

To sum up, the autocratic alternative is quite a diverse thing and not necessarily very stable. A number of autocratic states have set up institutions of politics, especially through a single party or through a monarchy, that provide for politics to be conducted over the long haul; straight military governments, however, have not. There is a good deal of flux among regimes, with rather few stable democratic regimes, even fewer stable autocratic regimes, and a great many states that are likely to shift among regimes of different sorts. We who live in a stable democracy tend to think of democracy as something that a state either has permanently or does not have at all. It is probably better thought of as a mode of government that is used by many states some of the time but to which relatively few states are permanently committed. Even ancient Athens, the birthplace of democracy, moved in and out of democratic government and dictatorship from time to time. Such a perspective helps us not only to view democracy as less than a permanent attribute of states but also to see the alternatives to democracy in the same way.

### Example: Civilian Participation in Nigeria's First Military Regime

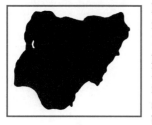

Professor Henry Bienen has studied the nature of the military government that ruled Nigeria from 1966 to 1974.[11] Although this regime included some civilian politicians, the military leaders always had the ultimate last word, a not uncommon pattern for military governments. Professor Bienen studied this regime from the standpoint of the civilians by interviewing a large number of politicians from the Western Province of Nigeria.

About a year after the 1966 coup, the military government brought a number of civilian politicians into the cabinet. At that time a civil war was raging in Nigeria, as the eastern provinces were trying to secede, and the military apparently thought they needed help to mobilize the population and to keep in touch with the grass roots. In the Western Province, General Adebayo, the governor, consulted with local party leaders before he appointed civilian commissioners to the provincial government. The military also set up advisory bodies called Leaders of Thought, in which military and civilian leaders met regularly on an informal basis.

The commissioners to whom Professor Bienen spoke disagreed as to how much real influence they had over the actions of the government, but in general they thought that while the military held ultimate control, the cabinet had considerable power over day-to-day decisions:

> Adebayo said the cabinet was purely advisory. We told him we have an executive council. A Governor in Council. The Secretary Odumosu (civil service head in the state) told him

---

[11]This presentation relies heavily on his study. Henry Bienen, "Military Rule and Political Process: Nigerian Examples," *Comparative Politics* 10 (January 1978): 205–225. See also Henry Bienen with Martin Fitton, "Soldiers, Politicians and Civil Servants," in K. Panter-Brick, ed., *Soldiers and Oil* (London: Cass, 1978), pp. 27–57.

we were right. The attorney general did the same thing. He ignored this often, particularly where the profit margin was involved. . . .

To some extent I would agree that commissioners did not have the old ministerial powers. Legally speaking we did, but not practically speaking. As a military regime [sic], the governor is the final authority. A commissioner is his advisor. In practice he of course cannot see to everything. He allows you to take decisions on consultation. He invariably approves. . . .

The cabinet was an executive body; that's a correct view. It was not just advisory. Only once or twice did Adebayo try to assert his position as military governor, and then he reconsidered and took the consensus advice. There were no votes.[12]

The bureaucracy apparently had greater leeway under the military regime than they had had under democracy, and there was a technical rather than political air to decision making. Of the political leaders who were interviewed, 60 percent thought that most of the bureaucracy would not welcome a return to democratic government, while only 10 percent thought that the bureaucracy would want such a return.[13]

If the governmental machinery operated somewhat more smoothly under military rule, this was offset by a lack of communication between the population and the government. It was to address exactly this problem that civilians were added to the government. In the Western Province, the government was severely pressed when widespread rioting by farmers broke out in 1968 and 1969. Farmers attacked the federal prison in daylight in September of 1969, freeing all its occupants; many police were ambushed or disappeared; tax collections nearly ceased. The military were caught unprepared for the level of grass-roots discontent because they had not had enough contact with the villages to sense what was building up. The civilians in the cabinet gained somewhat in power during this period, as the military leaders depended on them to help assess the farmers' discontent and rebuild a coalition of support for the regime.

How did the civilian politicians rate the military rulers? Though they were, for obvious reasons, predisposed to be critical of the military, they distinguished among the military government's strengths and weaknesses.

The greatest criticism of the military was that they failed to represent and take into account the various groups in the population.

Those cabinet members who felt that the [civilian] cabinet was politically strong, that its members had grass-roots support, did not see the military as having local links. Individual members mentioned many times how "little people" were afraid to go and see military officers, because to do so they had to pass a series of armed soldiers. Nigerian politicians were often outraged that although the officers and soldiers became rich they spent money only on themselves and their close relatives. The money did not trickle down.[14]

Of the politicians, 81 percent thought that the military had been less successful than civilians in representing the people.[15]

---

[12]Bienen, "Military Rule," p. 213.
[13]Bienen and Fitton, "Soldiers, Politicians," p. 42.
[14]Bienen, "Military Rule," p. 219.
[15]Ibid., p. 220.

On the other hand, the politicians generally credited the military with creating national unity more successfully than the civilians (by a margin of about 3 to 1) and with bringing stability (by a margin of 2 to 1). They split on whether the military had been more successful in promoting economic development than the civilians, and by about a 2 to 1 margin they thought the military had been less successful than civilian governments at developing health and educational services.

### Example: "Court" Politics in Nazi Germany

Albert Speer was the relatively nonpolitical coordinator of industrial production for Adolf Hitler during the latter part of World War II. He offers the following accounts of politics in Hitler's inner circle. These provide good examples of the peculiarities of the "court" politics described above.[16]

In the winter of 1942, during the Stalingrad crisis, Bormann, Keitel, and Lammers decided to close their own ring around Hitler more tightly. Henceforth, all orders to be signed by the Chief of State had to be cleared through these three men. This would supposedly prevent the unconsidered signing of degrees and therefore put a stop to the command confusion caused by this practice. Hitler was content so long as he retained the final decision. Henceforth, the divergent views of various branches of government would be "sifted" by this Committee of Three. In accepting this arrangement Hitler counted on objective presentation and a nonpartisan method of working.

The three-man committee divided up its jurisdictions. Keitel, who was to be in charge of all orders relating to the armed forces, came to grief right from the start, since the commanders in chief of the air force and the navy utterly refused to accept his authority. All changes in the powers of the ministers, all constitutional affairs, and all administrative questions were supposed to go through Lammers. As it turned out, however, he had to leave these decisions more and more to Bormann, since he himself had little access to Hitler; Bormann had reserved the field of domestic policy for himself. But he not only lacked the intelligence for these matters; he also had insufficient knowledge of the outside world. For more than eight years he had been little more than Hitler's shadow. He had never dared go on any lengthy business trips, or even to allow himself a vacation, for fear that his influence might diminish. From his own days as Hess's deputy, Bormann knew the perils of ambitious deputies. For Hitler was all too ready to treat the second men in an organization, as soon as they were presented to him, as members of his staff and to make assignments directly to them. This quirk accorded with his tendency to divide power wherever he encountered it. Moreover, he loved to see new faces, to try out new persons. In order to avoid raising up such a rival in his own household, many a minister took care not to appoint an intelligent and vigorous deputy.

The plan of these three men to surround Hitler, to filter his information and thus control his power, might have led to an abridgement of Hitler's one-man rule—had the Committee of Three consisted of men possessing initiative, imagination, and a sense of responsibility. But since they had been trained always to act in Hitler's name, they slavishly depended on

[16]Albert Speer, *Inside the Third Reich* (New York: Macmillan, 1970), pp. 300–306, 389–393.

the expressions of his will. What is more, Hitler soon stopped abiding by this regulation. It became a nuisance to him, and was, moreover, contrary to his temperament. But it is understandable that those who stood outside this ring resented its stranglehold.

In fact Bormann was now assuming a role which could be dangerous to the top functionaries. He alone, with Hitler's compliance, drew up the appointments calendar, which meant that he decided which civilian members of the government or party could see, or more important, could not see, the Fuehrer. By now, hardly any of the ministers, Reichsleiters, or Gauleiters could penetrate to Hitler. They all had to ask Bormann to present their program to him. Bormann was very efficient. Usually the official in question received an answer in writing within a few days, whereas in the past he would have had to wait for months. I was one of the exceptions to this rule. Since my sphere was military in nature, I had access to Hitler whenever I wished. Hitler's military adjutants were the ones who set up my appointments.

After my conferences with Hitler, it sometimes happened that the adjutant would announce Bormann, who would then come into the room carrying his files. In a few sentences he would report on the memoranda sent to him. He spoke monotonously and with seeming objectivity and would then advance his own solution. Usually Hitler merely nodded and spoke his terse, "Agreed." On the basis of this one word, or even a vague comment by Hitler, which was hardly meant as a directive, Bormann would often draft lengthy instructions. In this way ten or more important decisions were sometimes made within half an hour. De facto, Bormann was conducting the internal affairs of the Reich. A few months afterward, on April 12, 1943, Bormann obtained Hitler's signature to a seemingly unimportant piece of paper. He became "Secretary to the Fuehrer." Whereas previously his powers, strictly speaking, should have been restricted to party affairs, this new position now authorized him to act officially in any field he wished.


[Speer developed an infected knee and was hospitalized.]


Dr. Gebhardt, SS Group leader and well known as a knee specialist in the European world of sports, ran the Red Cross's Hohenlychen Hospital. It was situated on a lakeside in wooded country about sixty miles north of Berlin. Without knowing it, I had put myself into the hands of a doctor who was one of Heinrich Himmler's very few intimate friends. For more than two months I lived in a simply furnished sickroom in the private section of the hospital. My secretaries were quartered in other rooms in the building, and a direct telephone line to my Ministry was set up, for I wanted to keep on working.

Sickness on the part of a minister of the Third Reich involved some special difficulties. Only too often Hitler had explained the elimination of a prominent figure in the government or the party on grounds of ill health. People in political circles therefore picked up their ears if any of Hitler's close associates was reported "sick." Since, however, I was really sick, it seemed advisable to remain as active as possible. Moreover, I could not let go of my apparatus, for like Hitler I had no suitable deputy at my disposal. Though friends and associates did their best to give me the opportunity to rest, the conferences, telephone calls, and dictation conducted from my bed often did not stop before midnight.

My absence unleashed certain elements, as the following incident will illustrate. Almost as soon as I arrived at the hospital, my newly appointed personnel chief, Erwin Bohr, telephoned me, quite excited. There was a locked filing case in his office, he said. Dorsch had ordered this case transported at once to the Todt Organization headquarters. I instantly countermanded this, saying that it was to stay where it was. A few days later representatives of the Berlin Gauleiter's headquarters appeared, accompanied by several moving men. They had orders, Bohr informed me, to take the filing case with them, for it was party property along with its contents. Bohr no longer knew what to do. I managed to postpone this action by telephoning one of Goebbels's closest associates, Naumann. The filing case was sealed by the party officials—but the seal was placed only on its door. I then had it opened by unscrewing the back. The next day Bohr came to the hospital with a bundle of photocopied documents. They contained dossiers on a number of my time-honored assistants—adverse reports almost without exception. Most of the men were charged with attitudes hostile to the party; in some cases it was recommended that they be watched by the Gestapo. I also discovered that the party had a liaison man in my Ministry: Xavier Dorsch. The fact surprised me less than the person.

Since the autumn I had been trying to have one of the officials in my Ministry promoted. But the clique which had recently taken shape in the Ministry did not like him. My then personnel chief had resorted to all sorts of evasions, until I finally forced him to nominate my man for promotion. Shortly before my illness I had received a sharp, unfriendly rejection from Bormann. Now we found a draft of that sharp note among the documents in this secret file, composed, as it turned out, by Dorsch and Personnel Chief Haasemann (whom I had replaced by Bohr). Bormann's text followed it word for word.

From my sickbed I telephoned Goebbels. As Gauleiter of Berlin he was head of all the party representatives in the Berlin ministers. Goebbels agreed at once that my old assistant Gerhard Fränk was the man for this post in my Ministry. "An impossible state of affairs! Every minister is a party member nowadays. Either we have confidence in him or he must go!" Goebbels said. But I could not find out who the Gestapo's agents in my Ministry were.

The effort to maintain my position during my illness proved almost too much for me. I had to ask Bormann's state secretary, Gerhard Klopfer, to instruct the party functionaries to stay within their bounds. Above all I asked him to look out for the industrialists working for me and to see no obstacles were placed in their way. For I had no sooner fallen sick than the district [Gau] economic adviser of the party had begun making inroads into my system. I asked Funk and his assistant Otto Ohlendorf, whom he had borrowed from Himmler, to take a more affirmative attitude toward my principle of industrial self-responsibility and to back me against Bormann's district economic advisers.

Sauckel, too, had already taken advantage of my absence to "make a general appeal to the men involved in armaments for an ultimate commitment." Faced with these effronteries from all sides, I turned to Hitler to tell him of my woes and ask his help. My letters—twenty-three typewritten pages that took me four days—were a sign of the funk I was in. I protested against Sauckel's arrogation of power and against the thrusts of Bormann's district economic advisers, and I asked Hitler for a statement of my unconditional authority in all questions that fell within my jurisdiction. Basically, I was asking for the very thing I had unsuccessfully demanded in such drastic language at the conference in Posen, to the indignation of the Gauleiters. I further wrote that our total production could be carried out rationally only if the "many offices which give directions, criticism, and advice to the plant managements" were concentrated in my hands.

Four days later I appealed to Hitler again, with a candor that really was no longer in keeping with our present relationship. I informed him about the camarilla in my Ministry which was undermining my program. I said there was treachery afoot; that a certain small clique of Todt's former assistants, led by Dorsch, had broken faith with me. I therefore considered myself forced, I wrote, to replace Dorsch by a man who had my confidence.

This last letter, with its news that I was dismissing one of Hitler's favorites without asking him beforehand, was particularly imprudent. For I was violating one of the rules of the regime: that personnel matters must be broached to Hitler at the right moment and by skillful insinuation. Instead, I had bluntly come at him with charges of disloyalty and questionable character in one of his men. That I also sent Bormann a copy of my letter was either foolish or challenging. In doing this I was running counter to all I knew about the nature of Hitler's intriguing entourage. I was probably acting out a certain attitude of defiance, forced upon me by my isolated position.

My illness had removed me too far from the true focus of power: Hitler. He reacted neither negatively nor positively to all my suggestions, demands, and complaints. I was addressing the empty air; he sent me no answer. I was no longer counted as Hitler's favorite minister and one of his possible successors—a few whispered words by Bormann and a few weeks of illness had put me out of the running. This was partly due to Hitler's peculiarity, often noted by everyone around him, of simply writing off anyone who vanished from his sight for a considerable time. If the person in question reappeared in his entourage after a while, the picture might or might not change. It disillusioned me and snapped some of my ties of personal feeling toward Hitler. But most of the time I was neither angry nor in despair over my new situation. Physically weakened as I was, I felt only weariness and resignation.

## FURTHER READING

Collier, David, ed. *The New Authoritarianism in Latin America.* Princeton, N.J.: Princeton University Press, 1979.

Duverger, Maurice. *Political Parties.* New York: Wiley, 1954, especially pp. 255–280.

Finer, S. E. *The Man on Horseback: The Role of the Military in Politics.* New York: Praeger, 1962.

Huntington, Samuel P. *The Soldier and the State.* Cambridge, Mass.: Harvard University Press, 1957.

————, and Moore, Clement. *Authoritarian Politics in Modern Society.* New York: Basic Books, 1970.

Jackman, Robert. "Politicians in Uniform." *American Political Science Review* 70 (December 1976): 1098–1109.

Jackson, Robert H., and Rosberg, Carl G. *Personal Rule in Black Africa.* Berkeley: University of California Press, 1982.

Johnson, John J., ed. *The Role of the Military in Underdeveloped Countries.* Princeton, N.J.: Princeton University Press, 1962.

Linz, Juan J., and Stepan, Alfred. *The Breakdown of Democratic Regimes.* Baltimore: Johns Hopkins University Press, 1978.

Needler, Martin C. "The Logic of Conspiracy: The Latin American Military Coup as a Problem in the Social Sciences." *Studies in Comparative International Development* 13 (Fall 1978): 28–40.

Neumann, Franz. *Behemoth: The Structure and Practice of National Socialism, 1933–1944.* New York: Oxford University Press, 1944.

Nordlinger, Eric A. *Soldiers in Politics.* Englewood Cliffs, N.J.: Prentice-Hall, 1976.

O'Donnell, Guillermo; Schmitter, Philippe; and Whitehead, Laurence. *Transitions from Authoritarian Rule: Prospects for Democracy.* Baltimore: Johns Hopkins University Press, 1986.

Perlmutter, Amos. *The Military and Politics in Modern Times.* New Haven, Conn.: Yale University Press, 1977.

Rouiquie, Alain. *The Military and the State in Latin America.* Berkeley: University of California Press, 1987.

Sartori, Giovanni. *Parties and Party Systems.* Cambridge, England: Cambridge University Press, 1976, especially Chapter 7.

Skidmore, Thomas E. *The Politics of Military Rule in Brazil, 1964–1984.* Oxford: Oxford University Press, 1988.

# PART FOUR

# THE APPARATUS
# OF GOVERNANCE

# 9

# CONSTITUTIONS AND THE DESIGN OF GOVERNMENT

Every state—in fact, every political organization, club, or other group—has a constitution, or set of rules by which power is distributed among the members. Obviously no group of people engaged in politics could exist without rules of this kind.

We speak of such unwritten rules as a "constitution with a small 'c,'" meaning simply the generally understood rules by which power is distributed in any political group—rules that have come to be accepted informally, over time.

Most organizations and states, however, also have a formal set of central rules that outline the basic ways in which they conduct their affairs. The Constitution of the United States (note the *capital* "C") is such a document, as are Canada's Constitution Act of 1982, the Basic Law of Germany, and the Constitution of the Netherlands. Typically, such a document tells who is to carry out the major functions of politics (proposing, deciding on, and implementing laws); how the people holding those positions are to be chosen; who is to be in charge during an emergency; and by what procedures the constitution itself may be changed. Often there is also a section, such as the Bill of Rights in the U.S. Constitution, that sets out certain basic rights of the citizen or basic aims of the state. Thus, a constitution may state that all citizens are guaranteed the right of freedom of speech (U.S.A.) or that the state guarantees full employment (France) or that the state is socialist (China).

No state can put *all* the rules governing the distribution of power into its formal constitution: Much must always be left to informal arrangements or to other documents. In the United States, the Constitution lays out a basic structure for politics. But the "constitution with a small 'c'" includes a great deal more than just the Constitution. It includes the understanding that the U.S. Supreme Court may overturn an act of Congress—a rule not written into the Constitution but only developed later under the strong Chief Justice John Marshall. Furthermore, it includes the tradition that presidents take a leading role in the making of foreign policy, and it includes much else besides. All these things are rules governing the distribution of power, which are not part of the Constitution but *are* part of our constitution.

There is often some disparity between the formal rules of the Constitution and actual political power. In the United States, a reading of the Constitution would lead one to think that the members of the electoral college had great power, since they are elected to meet and select a president; in fact, however, the practice and expectation have developed that the members of the electoral college simply ratify the vote of the citizens of their states, so that in practice it has essentially no political power at all. As another example of the frequent disparity between formal political power and actual power, consider the fact that no constitutions in Europe or North America mention the great political power of newspapers and television networks other than in passing.

## VARIATIONS IN FORMALITY

Constitutions vary as to how much is set out formally in a central document and how much has gradually developed outside of it. Generally speaking, older constitutions put less into a central document; newer ones, more. Two of the oldest political bodies in the world, Great Britain and the Catholic church, have no central written constitution at all. Rather, the rules of politics for each are embodied in a variety of documents, traditions, and accepted practices. Each has a constitution (with a small "c"); people are aware of it and cite it frequently in British or church politics, but they are not referring to any single document when they do.

The United States is a relatively old state, and the original U.S. Constitution was approximately 4,300 words long; approximately 2,900 words have since been added in amendments. Germany is a new state, and its Basic Law, written in 1949, is approximately 19,700 words long; this includes numerous amendments. France's most recent constitution, published in 1958 and amended only slightly since then, is about 9,100 words long. Perhaps constitutions that have been written in more recent years are longer because their writers are aware of the greater size and importance of the state today and have taken greater pains to protect the state's power from difficulties that might arise. A large part of Germany's Basic Law is devoted to who is to govern during emergencies, though this is unusual. The one thing that is generally true of recent constitutions is that they are *specific* and complicated.

## THE VIRTUE OF VAGUENESS

Such specificity is by no means always an advantage. Napoleon once said that a constitution should be short and obscure. If rules are stated very specifically, it becomes difficult to adapt a constitution to unforeseen or changing circumstances. Just as French generals in the period from 1919 to 1933 devised a marvelous fortification (the Maginot line) that would have served well for the trench warfare of World War I but was useless against the changed strategies of World War II, writers of constitutions often include in their design solutions to the problems with which *they* have become familiar. If these solutions are precise and inflexible, they are likely to produce new problems later on. Republican lawmakers in the United States were upset by the fact that Franklin Delano Roosevelt (a Democrat) had served more than the customary two terms as president. After his death, they wrote a stern amendment into the Constitution, limiting presidents to two terms of service. A few years later they were faced with Dwight Eisenhower, a popular Republican candidate whom they would have loved to nominate for a third term but who was now constitutionally barred from running again.

Similarly, the writers of the Basic Law of Germany were preoccupied, after the war, with the fact that Hitler had been able to take over the democratic government of Germany peacefully and more or less legally in 1933 and transform it into a dictatorship. In dozens of ways, they tried to make their new constitution "Hitlerproof." One of the many devices they added was a restriction on the ability of the parliament to unseat the chancellor and his cabinet. This power of parliament was hemmed about by numerous conditions, which led to an unpleasant comic opera when in 1972 the socialist-led government of Willy Brandt had lost so much support in the parliament that it could not even pass the national budget. Brandt and his cabinet wished to step down and call for a new election, since, under the circumstances, they could not govern effectively. But for six months no one could think of a way by which this could be arranged, under Germany's complicated constitutional provisions, without the embarrassment of the socialists formally voting themselves out of office (which they were not willing to do). The point is that the authors' precise and detailed constitutional tinkering with the Basic Law, designed to "win the last war," led to unforeseen difficulties in governing Germany.

Another example of misplaced specificity in writing constitutions comes from a regional political science association in the United States. This group publishes a scholarly journal, the editor of which is changed every three years. At one time, it was suggested that the term of the editor might be lengthened to four years, since it cost the association a few thousand dollars each time the editor was changed and the journal's operations had to be moved from one campus to another. This was not a big issue, but everyone agreed that the change would be a good idea since it would save some money and inconvenience. On looking at the association's Constitution, however, it was found that the change could not be made easily. This document, instead of sensibly stating that the editor should serve a term "to be determined by the association's council," plainly said that "the editor shall serve a term of three years. . . ." Since an amendment to the Constitution, tedious and difficult to arrange, would have been required in order to change the editor's term, the idea was dropped. One would think that the political scientists who wrote this document would have known better!

## OTHER PRINCIPLES OF CONSTITUTIONAL DESIGN

Let us now assume that you are in a position to help design or amend a state's constitution. Are there any additional principles that might help guide you? Beyond the general principle that you should not try to be too specific, a few additional rules of thumb you might consider are as follows: (1) The constitution should preferably not break drastically with long-standing traditions of government, (2) the constitution should be relatively easy to change, and (3) "incentive compatibility" should be built in as much as possible, so that the holders of power will find it personally advantageous to do what society as a whole needs from them. Let us consider each of these in some detail.

### The Importance of Long-standing Traditions

If a set of rules is to work, it must not be too far out of line with what most people in the state wish to do. One famous instance of a rule that did not work because it deviated too far from the people's wishes was the prohibition of liquor in the United States in the 1920s. In 1919, a constitutional amendment forbidding the possession or consumption of alcoholic beverages in the United States was passed. While many people had obviously supported this amendment (else it would not have been passed), many opposed it. The law was openly disobeyed, and criminals like Al Capone flourished on the illegal traffic in liquor. Eventually the state gave up, and in 1933 the Constitution was amended to make alcoholic beverages legal once again.

It is not enough, either, just to set up rules that the people are willing to obey only reluctantly; something more is needed than bare acquiescence. As we saw in Chapter 6, it is important that a state have a reservoir of goodwill and positive support from its people to carry it over the occasional rough times. A good constitution will not only be one that people are *willing* to obey but also one that comes close enough to their preconceptions that they will be able to identify enthusiastically with the system. Many historians think it is unfortunate that, when Germany lost World War I, the monarchy to which its people were accustomed was destroyed. The democratic constitution of 1919 did not provide for the sort of personal, emotional attachment that the monarch had always provided. Instead, the first president of the new system was a quiet man, the son of a lowly saddle maker, with no dash or glamour. Hitler was later able to exploit the people's hunger for an exciting focus of patriotic devotion. How much better if the constitution of 1919 could have made a less dramatic break with the past by including a powerless but handsomely dressed monarch. This of itself would not have solved all of Germany's problems, but it might have helped.

This is not to say that a constitution cannot depart at all from what the people expect. Many revolutionary states—such as China, in 1949, for example—have imposed new systems of government and society that transformed their people's expectations. There has always been a great deal of tension associated with this, however, and such states have had to keep tight control of things, causing much human suffering, in order to ensure the state's stability. There is inevitably a price to be paid in instituting rules for which the people are not prepared; but in some instances this price might be worth paying.

### The Importance of Amendability

If a new constitution must come reasonably close to reflecting the people's expectations, it must also be open to revision or amendment in response to changing needs over time. It is always a temptation, when writing a formal document, to "protect" it by making it difficult to change.

The U.S. Constitution, for example, was designed to be difficult to change. As a result, in the approximately two hundred years that it has been in force, only sixteen amendments beyond the original Bill of Rights have been added. Such inflexibility could have been dangerous, since the conditions of U.S. politics must obviously have changed immensely over two or more centuries. Fortunately, a new device for adaptation appeared when the Supreme Court took onto itself the power to interpret the Constitution with a certain amount of discretion. The Constitution itself was sufficiently "obscure," in Napoleon's sense, that the Court could adapt it with reasonable ease to change circumstances. In 1954, for instance, the Court ruled that, in light of modern sociological theory, "separate but equal" schools for blacks and whites could not be taken to provide the equal protection under the laws that the Constitution guarantees. The Court ruled in this way despite the fact that in earlier decisions, without the benefit of such theory, it had ruled that segregated school systems *were* constitutional.[1] Allowing nine judges who are appointed for life the discretion to adapt the Constitution may not be the best or the most democratic way to proceed, but it has at least provided a flexibility that the authors of the Constitution were not originally wise enough to build in.

In many states provisions for adapting the constitution are much simpler. Often, a simple majority in the parliament is sufficient.

### The Importance of Incentive Compatibility

In any political system, it is important that people in positions of power have personal incentives to do what society as a whole needs from them. That is, holders of power should find that they are personally rewarded when they do what society needs done and personally punished when they do not.

We may safely assume that when people find that what is good for them personally conflicts with what is good for the state, they will usually choose what is good for themselves. This is not to say that people are extremely selfish. Because the state and the individual are so different in size, it is easy for the individual to conclude that the damage to the state will be tiny compared with the benefit to him or her. As a result, people can usually make the "selfish" choice without feeling that they are doing much damage to the state. If a little cheating on my income tax can save me $300, what does that matter to a national budget of billions upon billions of dollars?

The problem, of course, is that if large numbers of people find themselves in a similar position, the result can be very serious indeed. Precisely this problem occurs in constitutions. The constitution—the set of rules determining who has what kinds of political power—places individuals in positions in which they will make certain choices that society needs to have made. Presidents and members of a congress or parliament are expected to make laws for the state, public health officials are expected to watch out for epidemics, judges are expected to settle legal disputes fairly, police officers are expected to keep order, members of town councils are expected to set rules within their towns, and so on.

But it is not enough simply to *say* what a person is to do in one of these positions. If

[1]Brown v. Board of Education, 347 U.S. 483 (1954).

"THE HECK WITH THE CONSTITUTION—
I'M GOING TO SHOUT 'FIRE'."

(Sidney Harris)

costs and benefits are not set up so as to encourage officials to act in the intended manner, there is a good chance that they will act in ways that suit their personal interests rather than those of society.

For instance, the U.S. Congress was set up to make rules for the country as a whole. However, members of Congress are rewarded or punished not by the country as a whole but by the voters of their districts. It is a well-known problem of American democracy that, if the two conflict, members of Congress will generally pursue the needs of their districts rather than those of the country as a whole. If the United States had stronger political parties, which could develop national programs and punish members of the Congress who did not support their party's program, then the personal incentives to members of the Congress would be different and we might expect to see them support national interests even when these conflicted with their own districts' interests. As we will see in Chapter 11, many states do have political parties of this sort, and there we do not find that members of the parliament place local needs over national ones.

As another example, consider the role of civil servants. Society needs to have civil servants develop programs creatively and administer them to the public efficiently, that is, at as low a cost as possible. However, in almost all countries civil servants are personally rewarded most highly if they are cautious about innovation (in this way they will avoid ever making a dramatic mistake) and always spend all the money that had been allocated to them (if they show that they can do the job for less money, they're likely to be given less money the next year). These rewards push civil servants toward uncreative, inefficient administration of programs.

Other examples could be drawn to show the importance of designing incentive structures so as to reward people for doing what the constitution intends them to do rather than for something else. It should be stressed that this is necessary *not* because holders of public office are especially greedy or cynical or selfish. Rather, just like the income tax cheater, they are faced with differences in scale such that very important things for them personally (security in their jobs, advancement) are balanced against almost trivial losses to the state. (What does it really matter if I vote for an inefficient project for my district? It is tiny compared with the overall budget. Is it really that important to the United States that my office—the transcribing division of the Southwest Regional Advisory Branch of the Weedgit Marketing and Regulatory Board—function at top form?) Just as with the problem of tax evasion, the problem here is that from the point of view of the single official, little damage is done to the state; but because there are thousands of officials like this, their combined impact may be grave indeed. We can expect most of these individuals to do what they are actually rewarded for doing, not necessarily what they are meant to do. Therefore we must try to design our constitution so that rewards follow for what officials are meant to do.

## THE GEOGRAPHIC CONCENTRATION OF POWER

In later chapters we will look at a variety of questions on one aspect or another of constitutional design: how officials should be chosen, how laws should be passed, what the best way of administering policies is, and so on. But one very general question of constitutional design deserves treatment in this chapter.

That is the question of how much political power should be concentrated in the central government and how much should be distributed among the governments of cities, of "states" (as in the United "States"), or of regions. Some constitutions place almost all political power in the central government, with very little independent decision making left to localities or regions. Others create a relatively weak central government, with many political decisions being made at lower levels. And a variety of arrangements that fall between the two are possible.

What makes this a particularly important question is that all over the world, hot conflicts frequently rage between central governments and local groups. This is the single greatest cause of political conflict today—a more incendiary one, for instance, than the perennial conflict between "haves" and "have-nots" or any of the newer conflicts such as those associated with feminism or with protection of the environment. In Spain, separatists for several years waged an intermittent campaign of terror on behalf of their claims for a separate Basque state or at least for a greater degree of local independence in making political decisions. Since 1982 Canada has been involved in a divisive constitutional crisis over the relationship between Quebec and the rest of the country. In Britain, a Scottish nationalist party has from time to time been able to sweep most of the Scottish seats in the parliament with its claim for greater independence for Scotland. India is divided into many districts speaking different languages; these districts operate fairly independently of the central government, and disputes over language policies and job preferences for those speaking different languages are always hot political items. Until 1991 the Soviet Union consisted of fifteen governmental units called "republics" (one of which was Russia); many of these had their own languages, and there were frequent conflicts among them. In the end the Union had to be dismantled, with each of the republics declaring independence. In another part of the world, many parts of Africa have had intense center-region conflicts; civil wars have been fought in Nigeria, Ethiopia, the Sudan, and Zaire between the central government and one or more regions that wished to break away. In the Mideast, Kurdish regions of Syria, Iraq, and Iran have been a source of political tension for those countries for many years. As one last example, remember that the one time that politics in the United States heated up into civil war was 1865, in a dispute between the central government and the southern part of the country.

## "FEDERAL" AND "UNITARY" STATES

The question of central versus local control is a hot item of politics; how is it dealt with constitutionally? First of all, there is a formal distinction between states that are "unitary" and those that are "federal." We shall look first at this formal distinction (a characteristic of constitutions with a capital "C") and then consider less formally (and more realistically) the division of power between central governments and their local or regional units.

A *unitary state* is one in which no other governmental body but the central government has any areas of policy that are exclusively under its control. In a unitary state, local and regional political bodies may potentially be overruled by the central government in any political decision they make. In a *federal state*, by contrast, local governmental authorities of some sort are set up by the constitution (usually for regions of the state, as in the "states" of the United States or the "republics" of the Soviet Union), and these authorities are given certain political decisions over which they have a legal monopoly of control.[2] In a *federation*, then—a federal state—two governments both control the same group of people but with regard to different political questions.

Germany is an example of a federation. The regional governments, called Länder, have total control of education, television, and radio; the central government has total control of defense, diplomacy, currency and monetary policy, the postal service, railroads and air transport, and copyrights; the central government and Länder share responsibility for all other areas of policy.

A federal system has often been the result of a compromise by which reluctant members were induced to join together in a state; this is how the United States was originally formed, for instance. Generally, federal systems exist where there was some difficulty in uniting the state or where the state is so large or so culturally diverse that it is thought

---

[2]William Riker, *Federalism: Origin, Operation, Significance* (Boston: Little, Brown, 1964). Chapter 1.

there may be problems holding it together. Small states are less likely to be federal systems than large ones simply because problems like these are more likely to have cropped up in large states with diverse populations.

As of 1995, a total of 18 states were federal systems while 172 were unitary. From this it might appear that the question of federalism is unimportant, since so few states are federal systems. However, the federal states tend to be the larger ones. Though these 18 states represented only 9 percent of the world's states, they contained 36 percent of the world's people and covered 41 percent of the world's land area. The 18 states are indicated in Figure 9–1.

## THE DISTINCTION BETWEEN "UNITARY" AND "CENTRALIZED" STATES

A formal definition like that given above usually needs to be supplemented by an understanding of informal arrangements. We stated there that in a federal system, separate governmental units coexist on the same territory, each with its own constitutionally set areas of policy. In a unitary system, by contrast, the central government is given the authority to make all policies, although it may deputize other governmental structures to act on its behalf. From this, we can see that in at least a *formal* sense, political power is more *centralized* (concentrated more on a central authority) in unitary systems than in federal ones.

However, politics is filled with surprises, and as usual there are many informal arrangements that modify the centralizing tendency of the unitary state and the opposite tendency of the federal state. First of all, actual control of money counts at least as much in politics as the formal authority to make decisions. "Who pays the piper, calls the tune," as they say. Table 9–1 shows the percentage of all governmental revenues collected and controlled by central, regional, or local governments in a variety of federal and unitary systems. While the central government controls more of the money in almost all unitary systems than in any of the federal systems, there is considerable variation within each category, and some overlap across the two. Japan's central government draws only 44 percent of governmental revenues, well under the 71 percent drawn by Australia's central government, the most centralized of the federal systems displayed here. Clearly, if we look at the control of cash, there is considerable variation in degrees of government centralization that goes beyond the constitutional distinction between "federal" and "unitary."

In other ways, less easily measured than revenues, states vary in their degree of centralization. France and Britain, for example, look fairly similar on Table 9–1. Both are unitary states, and the central government of France draws 78 percent of all revenues while the central government of Great Britain draws 81 percent. But *how* authority and revenues are used is as important as *whether* they are used. In Britain, the central government has traditionally kept only a loose control over local governments' actions and expenditures. For instance, the choice of whether to shift to the modern "comprehensive" high school was left entirely to localities. Or, as another example, consider that the British central government faced a serious difficulty several years ago in writing its budget: It had to provide money to local governments to pay their work force, but it did not

**FIGURE 9–1**
Federal systems (shaded areas) of the world.

**TABLE 9–1**
PERCENTAGE OF REVENUE COLLECTED BY DIFFERENT LEVELS OF GOVERNMENT

|  | Central government | "States" or regions | Local governments |
|---|---|---|---|
| FEDERAL SYSTEMS | | | |
| Australia | 71 | 24 | 4 |
| U.S.A. | 56 | 24 | 19 |
| Canada | 46 | 41 | 12 |
| Germany | 42 | 35 | 23 |
| Switzerland | 32 | 45 | 24 |
| UNITARY SYSTEMS | | | |
| Netherlands | 95 | 1 | 3 |
| Israel | 92 | 1 | 8 |
| Great Britain | 81 | — | 19 |
| France | 78 | 10 | 12 |
| Sweden | 60 | — | 40 |
| Japan | 44 | 28 | 28 |

*Source:* Annual statistical yearbooks for each country

know in advance how big the raises granted by local authorities to their civil servants would be. In effect, local authorities had control over the writing of a significant chunk of the national budget.

In France, on the other hand, power was for centuries lodged firmly in Paris. A minister of education in the late nineteenth century is said to have demonstrated this to a visitor, when, checking his watch, he looked up and said, "My friend, at this moment every third-grade pupil in France is reciting 'The Blue Bird.' " Power in France has become somewhat less centralized in the decades since then; but it was still true until recently that for almost any major decision—whether to build a new town hall or school, for instance—cities had to gain the approval of the government of Paris. In 1981 President Mitterand instituted a number of decentralizing reforms, devolving many functions on new regional and departmental councils, but the system remains on balance a centralized one.[3]

To sum up, the degree of centralization in politics is greatly influenced by the formal constitutional choice between federalism and a unitary arrangement, but it is also strongly affected by all sorts of less formal arrangements.

## HOW MUCH CENTRALIZATION IS GOOD?

Obviously, any country has to strike some balance between centralized and decentralized politics. With totally decentralized politics, the state would cease to exist; it would be broken up into many small independent states. And even short of this, strong decen-

[3]See Vivien A. Schmidt, *Democratizing France: The Political and Administrative History of Decentralization* (Cambridge: Cambridge University Press, 1991).

tralization might lead to uncoordinated policies and confusion. But great centralization, on the other hand, especially in a state that is at all large or geographically varied, would make for inflexible and insensitive government.

How much centralization is good will vary from state to state and with the circumstances the state faces. Generally, large and diverse states find it necessary to be less centralized than other states in order to meet varying local needs flexibly. Or if a given state is faced with an emergency, as in time of war, it may feel that all power must be pulled together centrally so that it will be able to concentrate its resources on the single goal of meeting the emergency. (Most decentralized systems do, in fact, give their central governments extraordinary temporary power during war.) There is no single level of centralization of politics that one should necessarily prescribe for all states at all times.

It is interesting to note, though, that at least the industrialized states of the world have shown signs over the last few decades of converging toward a fairly similar degree of centralization. Apparently the circumstances in which these states find themselves are sufficiently similar that a common level of centralization has seemed appropriate to the leaders of each.

Thus a centralized state like France has attempted over the last decade to decrease the centralization of power. The government of President Mitterand sharply decreased the powers of the "prefects," civil servants who had used to be responsible for keeping Paris in control of what local governments were doing. On the other hand, in the decentralized United States, the last thirty years—despite recent attempts to reverse the trend—have been marked by an extension of power by the central government over the states and localities. This has been accomplished by aid grants from the central government to the state or local government that carry with them some control over how the money is to be spent. As one example of this, the central government today has the power to order school districts to supply certain services to handicapped students. This would have been unthinkable thirty years ago.

We cannot give a simple answer to the question of how much centralization of government is good. But we can note that all around the world, complex industrialized states are indicating by their own choices that they are most comfortable with a considerable but limited degree of centralization. The main exceptions are states like Canada, where deep ethnic conflicts have boiled up to threaten the state itself, and a radical decentralization may be the best solution.

### "CONSTITUTIONALISM"

A somewhat different question from the *nature* of constitution is the question of "constitutionalism": Given that each state has a constitution, how faithful is a state to its constitution? That is, how fully do the leaders of the state honor the rules of politics in the state? "Constitutionalism" is the doctrine that states should be faithful to their constitutions because the rules so provided are all that can protect the citizens from arbitrary decisions by powerful people. There is also a notion in "constitutionalism" that constitutions themselves should be designed fairly, rather than to give undue advantage to one particular group.

Constitutionalism is strong in Britain, the United States, Canada, Australia, and New

Zealand. In the United States, for example, the Supreme Court, which is rather insulated from political pressure, has the power to overturn any act of government if it finds that the act is unconstitutional. The Court has been particularly active in guarding the Bill of Rights, a list of personal freedoms from governmental action that is written into the Constitution. Britain, Australia, Canada, and New Zealand do not have a supreme court to enforce the formal constitution, but in all of them there is a long tradition of impartial obedience to the rules of politics and to the protection of individuals from arbitrary official action. Even in these five countries, however, constitutionalism is only *relatively* strong. It is not, and probably can never be, an absolute. Especially in times of national emergency, the governments of these countries have sometimes felt that it was necessary for them temporarily to suspend rights that they would ordinarily honor. Great Britain, for instance, held no elections for the duration of World War II, even though an election had been due in 1940; Churchill and the other party leaders thought that an election would be an unnecessary distraction during wartime, and they were critical of the United States for going ahead and holding its presidential election in 1944. Similarly, President Roosevelt ordered the internment of most Japanese-Americans during the war on the grounds that they were security risks. The president would never have had the power to do this in peacetime.

A country in which traditions of constitutionalism are a bit weaker is France. While individual rights are generally secure there, leaders' faithfulness to the rules of politics is a more fragile thing than in the United States, Canada, or Britain. In the last century, France has had four different constitutions, and it has had a total of nine different systems for holding elections. Election laws, in particular, are manipulated so as to benefit the party in power. Also, it is generally understood that the party in power will manipulate news reports on public television and radio to enhance its election chances, and French embassies abroad have often tried to manipulate absentee voting so as to help the party in power. Finally, aside from these cynical manipulations of the rules of electoral politics, three times in this century French military leaders have given up on democratic rules altogether and have tried to seize power; twice they have been successful.

If France is a bit weak in its constitutionalism, though, many states are far, far weaker than France. The majority of the world's people live in systems that give them only small protections against arbitrary power. In China from 1966 to 1976, over a million people were killed in the Cultural Revolution, which the state's leader, Mao Tsetung, initiated in order to restore the Communist party to its original revolutionary zeal. A similar disregard for individuals was shown in the 1989 suppression of the student movement at Tiananmen Square. In *The Gulag Archipelago*, Alexander Solzhenitsyn described the network of concentration camps in the Soviet Union under Stalin; in these, several million Soviet citizens were arbitrarily confined, often without trial.[4] In the late 1970s under a right-wing military regime, several thousand Argentinians "disappeared" when they were seized by the state police; they were never tried and were not seen again.

---

[4]Alexander Solzhenitsyn, *The Gulag Archipelago, 1918–1956* (New York: Harper & Row, 1974).

### Example: Constitutional Government in Great Britain

 Great Britain is an unusual example of constitutional government in that there is no written constitution—no single document that claims to set out the central principles of the organization of power.

What does the British constitution consist of? Some of it is made up of statute, or acts that Parliament has passed. Much of it also consists of court precedent, decisions that have been made by judges in cases of constitutional significance. And finally, some important parts of it simply consist of practice—behavior that has arisen in the day-to-day conduct of government and that is not written down anywhere. In all of this, Parliament is ultimately supreme, because a new statute passed by it would override decisions by any court and would, of course, override any practices that had grown up. In the absence of contrary action by the Parliament, however, court decisions or practices stand. And much of the British constitution consists exactly of this: Court precedent and practices that the Parliament has not chosen to change by statute.

The Magna Carta is one of the earliest parts of the British constitution. In 1215 an unpopular king (John) was forced by rebellious barons to sign a document limiting the king's authority over them in a number of ways. This document was later read into statute in 1295. Other important statutes have settled the system for determining who succeeds to the crown when a king or queen dies (Act of Settlement of 1701) and have laid out the powers of the two houses of Parliament (Parliament Acts of 1911 and 1949). Many smaller matters are also dealt with in statutes.

Court precedents have also contributed importantly to the constitution. For instance, the powers of the queen are largely determined by a long series of precedents from court cases over the centuries. And the definitions of individual rights—which in the United States are written into the Constitution as the Bill of Rights—evolved over centuries of court decisions in Britain.

Finally, and this is probably the most puzzling thing of all to non-British readers, important parts of the constitution are not written down in any document whatever but simply exist in practice. They are "what one does." For instance, the prime minister and cabinet are probably the most powerful single part of the process of government in Britain. All but a few of the bills considered by Parliament have been initiated by the cabinet, and the cabinet controls closely what happens in the Parliament. (You will see more about this in Chapter 13.) But nowhere in any statute or in the decision of any court is the cabinet set up or its powers defined. The only law that mentions the cabinet even indirectly is one setting the salaries of cabinet ministers.[5] All the rules governing the cabinet's behavior and defining its powers have arisen in practice and remain as unwritten understandings.

One might well ask how a constitution like this gets enforced. How do we make sure that people play by the rules if not all of the rules are even written down? For instance, the fact that the prime minister is dominant within the cabinet and can ask

---

[5]Ministers of the Crown Act 1937, from S. B. Chrines, *English Constitutional History* (London: Oxford University Press, 1947), p. 21.

members to resign or to exchange posts is simply a matter of practice. What would happen if a prime minister fired a cabinet minister, but the cabinet minister did not leave? Or as another example, an important aspect of the British constitution is that a British monarch will always sign into law a bill passed by the Parliament. Without the signature, the bill does not become a law, and so in principle the monarch has the right to veto acts of Parliament. In practice, however, this is not done. What would happen if a monarch were to try to exercise the right?

The British themselves puzzle over how a system like this can work. The authors of a British textbook write:

Why have countries found it necessary to draw up [formal constitutions]? Three reasons can be advanced. First, they are needed when nations make a fresh start with their institu-

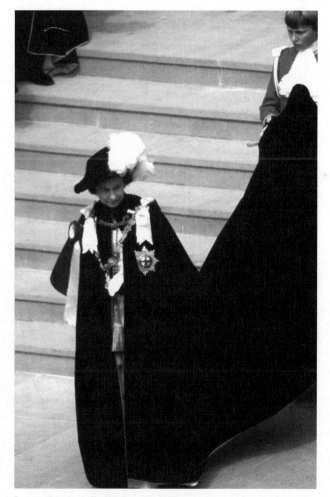

Queen Elizabeth II, the ceremonial head of state of the United Kingdom. (Tim Graham/Sygma)

tions, as when India, Pakistan, Ceylon, etc. gained their independence after World War II. Secondly, the country may contain groups of people distinct from each other through race, religion or language. In order to incorporate all people within the nation, each group must be given some guarantee that its identity will be maintained. Thirdly, in large countries, people in different parts may have particular interests and needs which they feel cannot be adequately provided for by a government in a remote capital. Here some form of federalism is likely, the division of powers between federal and state authorities being laid down in a written constitution. None of these considerations applies to Britain.[6]

This does not ring true, however. Certainly, Britain has been subject to major stresses, especially the breaking away of Ireland in the early twentieth century and the continuing troubles in Northern Ireland today. It is not plausible that the British have simply been so peaceful that they have not needed a set of rules to govern them. In the end, one must conclude that the system depends on the goodwill of those who are involved in it. They must *want* to have the system work and see this as in their interest; otherwise it would not work. It may be that the very existence of an unwritten constitution pushes people to behave cooperatively. Where there is a formal set of rules, clever people may feel challenged to find loopholes. But where there is only a set of practices based on certain commonsense principles, clever people will find it necessary always to cite those central commonsense principles and to tailor their arguments and their behavior to them.

For good or bad, an "unwritten" constitution is not something a state can just decide to start up at any time. It must be received from the past, and so it is unlikely that a state could deliberately imitate Britain and set up an unwritten constitution! However, we may draw the lesson from Britain that it is well to leave some aspects of our constitution to custom, if that is practical, rather than trying to write everything down.

### Example: Constitutional Government in Russia

 One of the many challenges facing the new Russian government since the breakup of the Soviet Union in 1991 and the subsequent collapse of the Communist regime, has been establishing a new constitutional order for the state. Russia did not bring from the Soviet period much of a tradition of constitutionalism. Constitutions were never seen in the Soviet Union as a solid foundation for government, which should regulate the government's actions. Rather, they were seen as ratifications of whatever power relationships were currently in place. From the Soviet revolution of 1917 until the breakup of the Union in 1991, the Soviet Union had four different constitutions. These were seen more as descriptions of how the government

---

[6]J. Harvey and L. Bather, *The British Constitution*, 3rd ed. (London: Macmillan, 1974), p. 510.

operated than as guides to how government should operate; when power relations shifted, a new constitution was written to reflect the new situation.

Not only were constitutions seen as readily exchangeable, they also were seen as only minimally binding even while they were in place. Great disparities between the constitutional description and actual political reality were tolerated. For instance, the Constitution of 1977 gave each of the fifteen republics of the Soviet Union (units like Russia, Ukraine, the three Baltic republics of Latvia, Lithuania, and Estonia) the right to secede from the Union; in fact, however, the Republics were kept under tight control through the army and party structures. Similarly, the Constitution assigned to the Soviet parliament the supreme power to pass laws. However, in fact, the parliament met only twice a year for a few days, during which time it heard long reports from the Central Committee of the Communist party and ratified the reports unanimously with a show of hands. Obviously, constitutionalism was almost nil in the Soviet Union.

In truth, the Soviet constitution (with a small "c"—*not* the formal Constitution) could have been summarized simply by noting that the Communist party was supreme in running the country. Regardless of the formal governmental structure, the party maintained its control in a practical sense by carefully placing party members in key positions in the armed forces, universities, bureaucracies, and the government.

With the collapse of Communist rule, Russia's leaders needed to design a governmental structure to replace it. President Boris Yeltsin presented a draft constitution in November 1993, and the Constitution was ratified in a referendum a month later. However, this was a document clearly designed to benefit Yeltsin (it gives the president massive power), and it is not certain that it will last beyond his presidency. The uncertainty is not helped by the fact that in the turbulent period of 1991 to 1993, when Yeltsin was locked in a conflict with the old parliament, *everyone* had played fast and loose with the then-valid constitution. This period of extraconstitutional jockeying culminated in Yeltsin sending troops to destroy the Parliament Building.

Under the new Constitution, citizens elect a president and a Federal Assembly that consists of two chambers. The president has immediate control of all parts of the government that use weapons—the armed forces, the police, and what is left of the old secret police and intelligence networks. This is particularly important given the amount of armed confrontation in politics in the recent past. Other operations of the state, such as economic policy, health policy, education, and so on, are administered under a prime minister appointed by the president, but who must also work closely with the Federal Assembly and who can be voted out of office by the Federal Assembly.

The Federal Assembly has the sole power to pass laws for Russia, and unlike the old Soviet parliaments, this power is actually used and may bring the Federal Assembly into conflict with Yeltsin. The result of the December 1993 elections was that Yeltsin's opponents (mainly the remains of the old Communist Party, on one hand, and a new ultranationalist right-wing movement organized by Vladimir Zhirinovsky on the other) controlled both houses of the Federal Assembly. A dramatic example of their willingness to challenge Yeltsin was a law passed early in their first session to free the leaders of the 1991 coup attempt, all of whom were among Yeltsin's most bitter enemies. (In general the president has a number of constitutional devices to prevent bills passing without his approval, so for most legislation, unless the president and the National Assembly agree, nothing will be done. In this case, though, the National Assembly took advantage of a provision that gives it the sole power to give pardons for crimes.)

Russia, like the Soviet Union of which it used to be a part, is a federal system, with 89 separate federal units.[7] The federal arrangements still leave a great deal of power to the central government. All legislation passed by the parliaments of the federal units, for instance, must be approved by a head of administration appointed by the president. And the president may suspend any administrative act of a federal unit.

A Constitutional Court is included in the Constitution, with the power to decide on the constitutionality of laws and resolve jurisdictional disputes among various parts of the governmental structure. The Constitution also guarantees certain legal protections for citizens, such as a right to trial by jury and a guarantee that judges will be independent of the state. However, the general tradition of constitutionalism is so weak in Russia, and the political turmoil and disregard of rules from 1991 to 1993 is so fresh in people's experience, that we must wait to see how this part of the Constitution will work out. As of late 1995, for instance, it still was the case that many judges made $160 a month, less than half the pay of a secretary, and were dominated by the often politically powerful prosecutors. And Russia had only 20,000 independent lawyers for a population of 148,000,000 people. This compared with 800,000 lawyers in the United States.[8]

## FURTHER READING

Bakvis, Herman, and Chandler, William M. *Federalism and the Role of the State.* Toronto: University of Toronto Press, 1987.

"Constitutions and Constitutionalism." In *International Encyclopedia of the Social Sciences.*

Duchacek, Ivo D. *The Territorial Dimensions of Politics Within, Among and Across Nations.* Boulder, Colo.: Westview Press, 1986.

Finer, S. E., ed. *Five Constitutions.* Baltimore: Penguin, 1979.

Friedrich, Carl. *Limited Government: A Comparison.* Englewood Cliffs, N.J.: Prentice-Hall, 1974.

Goldwin, Robert A.; Kaufman, Art; and Schambra, William A., eds. *Forging Unity Out of Diversity: The Approaches of Eight Nations.* Washington, D.C.: American Enterprise Institute, 1989.

Harvey, Jack, and Bather, L. *The British Constitution.* 3rd ed. London: Macmillan, 1974.

Jennings, W. Ivor. *The British Constitution.* 3rd ed. Cambridge, England: Cambridge University Press, 1950.

Riker, William. *Federalism: Origin, Operation, Significance.* Boston: Little, Brown, 1964.

Schlesinger, Joseph. *Ambition and Politics: Political Careers in the United States.* Chicago: Rand McNally, 1966 (especially with regard to incentive compatibility).

Tribe, Lawrence H., and Dorf, Michael C. *On Reading the Constitution.* Cambridge, Mass.: Harvard University Press, 1991.

Wheare, K. D. *Federal Government.* 4th ed. London: Oxford University Press, 1963.

[7]The basis for "federal units" varies a good deal. The cities of Moscow and St. Petersburg are themselves federal units, for instance; other federal units are ethnically distinct regions such as the Tatar territory; and others are more general geographic divisions of Russia.

[8]"Russian Law: Groping Ahead." *The Economist* Sept. 2, 1995: 42–48.

# 10

# ELECTIONS

In the long swing of history, elections with broad mass participation are rather new. Such elections originated with democratic government, which means that they came along at the end of the eighteenth century and the beginning of the nineteenth. Today elections are widespread around the world, even though most of the world's states are not democracies. Many nondemocratic states, such as the pre-1989 Soviet Union, have held them regularly. Why are elections so much in vogue?

Part of the answer, of course, is that "democracy" is a word that purrs with respectability. Even states that are not democratic wish to appear democratic, and holding elections is one of the easiest ways to follow some of the *forms* of democracy even if the state is not in fact democratic.

But a second reason is that elections can serve more purposes for the state than merely the democratic one of allowing the mass of people to help in the selection of leaders and policies. Elections were invented in order to make democracy possible; but once invented, they turned out to have further uses as well. This is an interesting aspect of political institutions that we shall encounter frequently in later chapters. Institutions may be devised to serve a particular purpose, but once they are in existence, they may be adaptable to a variety of purposes.

In this case, the thing that recommends elections to the leaders of autocratic states is that they can serve *two* main purposes: (1) *the purely democratic purpose of allowing the mass of people to have some direct say in the choice of leaders and policies, and* (2) *the more or less universal purpose of allowing the state to mobilize its people and to build up their support for the state by acting it out and participating in the process of government.*

## ELECTIONS AS A MEANS OF BUILDING SUPPORT

Let us consider the second of these first. To take one example of an autocratic state in which elections figured importantly, consider the Soviet Union before 1989. (Since 1989 most parts of what had been the Soviet Union, including Russia, have moved toward open electoral democracy.) One can make a good case that mass political participation among Soviet citizens was always as great as it was among citizens of the United States.

To quote a study from the 1970s:

> Campaign activities draw upon the efforts of millions of Soviet citizens, just as they do Americans. Soviet national election campaigns last about two months, and the campaigning is extremely intensive. The party leadership mobilizes millions of "agitators" and "propagandists," as well as ordinary citizens, to publicize the election, explain the issues and programs which the party considers important, and ensure that the entire population goes to the polls. The weeks preceding the election see the formation of countless study circles, discussion groups, campaign meetings, door-to-door canvassing, rallies, demonstrations and speeches.[1]

Similar comparisons could have been made in other areas of political activity, beyond elections per se. For example, about one person out of five in the United States has ever contacted a local government official about some issue or problem. Soviet citizens seem to have been about as active in this sphere as Americans, though comparable measures of activity are not available. One study notes that "in the first four months of 1962 some 11,803 citizen demands poured into the offices of the Kirov raion of Moscow. In the first half of 1963 officials of a single raion in Leningrad received over 15,000 letters and visits from the populace involving demands of various sorts."[2] On another front, a recent study found that 8 percent of all Americans belong to some sort of political organization. By way of comparison, about 10 percent of all Soviet adults were members of the Communist party through most of the postwar period.

In elections specifically, a similar comparison can be made. While only about 50 to 60 percent of all Americans vote regularly in presidential elections, about 99 percent of all Soviet citizens generally voted in their national elections. There was great social pressure to vote in Soviet elections, and turnout was high:

> The network of agitators is fully activated during the ten days preceding the election. Agitators must visit each voter in the precinct, explaining the virtues and qualifications of the sole candidate. The mass media publicize the biography of each candidate to the larger soviets and urge a resounding vote of confidence for the regime. The candidate spends no money campaigning but holds meetings with voters. . . . Refusal to vote is regarded as an unpatriotic act. Even the sick are expected to vote and ballot boxes are brought to the bedsides of hospital patients. Voting occurs on ships that are at sea on election day if there are at least twenty-five voters aboard; the votes are added to those cast in the ship's home port. Passengers on long-distance trains vote in special precincts while in transit.[3]

---

[1] Richard D. Little, "Mass Political Participation in the U.S. and the U.S.S.R.: A Conceptual Analysis," *Comparative Political Studies* 8 (January 1976): 439.

[2] James Oliver, "Citizen Demands in the Soviet System," *American Political Science Review* 63 (June 1969): 467. Cited in Little, "Mass Political Participation," n. 1.

[3] John S. Reshetar, Jr., *The Soviet Polity*, 2nd ed. (New York: Harper & Row, 1978) p. 196.

Rene Preval, a candidate in the 1995 presidential election in Haiti, greets supporters.

The election took up a great deal of time and cost a lot of money. Over 2 million candidates were elected each time—better than one out of every hundred adults—and they invested a great deal of time and energy in the campaign. Millions more were engaged in agitation, in serving on electoral commissions, and so on. It was an expensive business.

And yet, until the democratic reforms of 1989, there was never any suspense over the outcomes. Only a single candidate was nominated for each position. Voters could vote *against* that candidate by crossing out the name, and if a majority of those voting did this, the candidate was not elected. But that happened only rarely. Of the 2,200,000 candidates for election to local soviets in 1977, only 61 were dumped in this way, and almost all of these were from small villages.[4] Clearly the purpose of all this electoral activity was not to choose who would govern the Soviet Union, but it must have had *some* purpose else the authorities would not have invested so much in it.

The most reasonable guess is that the main purpose of elections in the Soviet Union was to renew the people's enthusiasm and support for the regime. Elections provided a recurring opportunity for the newspapers to pour out praise for the leaders of the state and for citizens, through their actions, to feel that they were a part of it. As all behavioral therapists know, a good way to ingrain a particular point of view in a person's consciousness is to have the person act it out. This would be reason enough for the Soviet Union to have put its population "through their paces" at regular intervals.

[4]Ibid., n. 3, p. 197.

**TABLE 10–1**

PERCENTAGE AGREEING THAT ORDINARY PEOPLE HAVE LITTLE "SAY" IN GOVERNMENT

|  | Voters | 1968 Nonvoters | Total |
|---|---|---|---|
| Before the election | 71 | 83 | 74 |
| After the election | 37 | 58 | 42 |
| Change | −34 | −25 | −32 |

|  | Voters | 1972 Nonvoters | Total |
|---|---|---|---|
| Before the election | 34 | 58 | 40 |
| After the election | 29 | 54 | 36 |
| Change | −5 | −4 | −4 |

*Source:* Recalculated from Benjamin Ginsberg, *The Consequences of Consent: Elections, Citizen Control, and Popular Acquiescence* (Reading, Mass.: Addison-Wesley, 1982), pp. 167 and 170.

The Soviet Union was not unusual among autocratic states in investing a great deal of time and energy in elections. Nazi Germany's election extravaganzas were famous, and approximately 99 percent of the German people regularly proclaimed their loyalty to Adolf Hitler in this way. In modern times, such states as Guatemala, Egypt, Romania, Algeria, Chile, both North and South Korea, Paraguay, Hungary, Czechoslovakia, Cuba, the Ivory Coast, and many others have staged elaborate elections of which the outcome was never in doubt. The obvious reason for such elections is to strengthen the people's attachment to the state.

While we do not normally think of elections in democracies as functioning to build support for the system, it can be shown that they serve this purpose just as much in democracies as in autocracies. A 1982 study of presidential elections in America highlighted this fact quite well.[5] At both the 1968 and 1972 presidential elections, a sample of American adults were asked both before and after the election whether they agreed or disagreed with the statement "People like me don't have any say about what the government does." Before the 1968 election, most people, whether or not they ended up voting in the election, agreed with the statement, as can be seen in Table 10–1. The electorate in 1968 was quite disillusioned and had lost a great deal of its faith in the nation's leaders. Conflict over civil rights and American involvement in the Vietnam War had soured people on politics, and the American public had just seen the Democratic nominating convention in Chicago torn apart by demonstrations and by the reaction of the police to the demonstrations. Of those who voted in that election, 71 percent initially agreed that ordinary people do not have any say in government, as did 83 percent of those who ended up not voting. But over the campaign and the election, this outlook changed considerably. After the election, only 37 percent of those who had voted agreed with the cynical view of government, for a drop of 34 percentage points. Among those

[5]Benjamin Ginsberg, *The Consequences of Consent: Elections, Citizen Control, and Popular Acquiescence* (Reading, Mass.: Addison-Wesley, 1982), pp. 166–170.

who did not vote but who experienced the period of campaigning and election, the figure also dropped, but by somewhat less—25 percentage points.

The circumstances in 1972 were different, but there again the election apparently served to reassure the public about the political system. The pre-election public in 1972, in contrast to that of 1968, was not turned off to politics. The incumbent Nixon administration was popular (Nixon would get 61 percent of the vote), and the Vietnam trauma had passed. Only 34 percent of those who would eventually vote and 58 percent of those who would not initially agreed with the cynical view of government. The campaign was not one to inspire confidence in the system. It was marked by the forced withdrawal of Thomas Eagleton as the Democrats' vice-presidential nominee because it became known that he had a history of mental illness; by a great deal of personal vituperation between the candidates; and by rumors of corruption and "dirty tricks" that would later produce the painful Watergate scandal.

In spite of this, the campaign period and election of 1972 produced small moves toward greater support of the system, even among an electorate who were already rather supportive before the election. After the election, 5 percent fewer voters, and 4 percent fewer nonvoters, agreed with the cynical view.

In Chapter 6 we examined the state's need to maintain sufficient support among its citizens that its authority would continue undiminished. For democracies and autocracies alike, elections apparently furnish a potent tool to help ensure this popular base of support. At regular intervals, people's acceptance of the system is reinforced as citizens act out their identification with the state and its leaders.

## ELECTIONS AS A MEANS OF SELECTING LEADERS AND POLICIES

But in many countries, elections are obviously meant to do more than simply bolster support for the regime. They may also be the means by which leaders and (sometimes) actual policies are chosen by the people. For this to be the case, an election must involve a *choice between candidates* or a *choice whether or not a particular policy is to be followed.* In democratic states, elections are set up in this way. And in some states that are not ultimately democratic, elections are allowed to function in this way at least at the local level.

In democracies, the choice of political leaders at all levels is made by competitive elections. In addition, some democracies provide for the *referendum*, a device by which the voters choose directly through their ballots whether or not a particular proposal will become law. Controlled referendums are also sometimes used in autocracies to exhibit and stimulate support in the same way as other elections do. The referendum is discussed in a later section of this chapter.

## ELECTORAL SYSTEMS

If elections are to be used to choose political leaders, there must be some rule for translating people's votes into a particular selection of leaders. This is not as simple a matter as one might think. For instance, one might state simply that the candidate who gets the most votes will win the election and take office. But what of the people who voted for a losing candidate: Should their votes simply count for nothing? And what if there were a dozen candidates and the one who got the greatest number of votes had only about 20 percent of the vote: Would we want that person to take office? Because of these and similar problems, there is no single obvious way to translate the votes cast by the electorate into the people who will take office. States need to design rules determining what person wins office as a result of any particular result in the voting; these rules are called the *electoral system* of the state.

Obviously rulers of states could, if they wished, write many detailed differences into their electoral systems. At one or another time and place, for instance, a party has been required to win at least 5 percent of the vote to get a seat in the legislature, owners of businesses have been given double votes in order to increase their weight in the electoral choice, some seats in a legislature have been reserved for members of one or another race, and votes have been counted separately and weighed differently for rich people and poor people. The possibilities are limited only by the imagination of those in charge of the state.

In general, however, two broad types of electoral system are used in almost all democracies today: *single-member-district plurality* systems and *proportional representation systems*. For convenience, they will be referred to from this point on by their initials, SMDP and PR.

## SMDP and PR Systems

In the SMDP system, the state is divided into a set of districts, usually having roughly equal populations. One representative is elected from each district to be a member of the legislative body of the state; and whoever gets a plurality of the votes wins the seat. (A "plurality" is the largest number of votes cast for any candidate; note that if there are many candidates running, the plurality may be less than a majority of all votes cast.) Hence the name: A *single member* is elected from each *district* by a *plurality* of votes.

This arrangement is familiar to U.S. and Canadian students, since both countries use versions of the SMDP system. In Canada, the members of Parliament are elected by the SMDP system. In the United States, members of the House of Representatives are elected by an SMDP system and members of the Senate by a variant of SMDP. (There are two senators from each state of the United States, but they are elected in separate years by a plurality so that, in effect, the senatorial electoral system is SMDP.)

Britain is an SMDP system, and these systems are in fact more or less limited, worldwide, to Britain and such of her former colonies as the United States, Canada, India, and New Zealand.

Most electoral democracies of the world use versions of proportional representation (PR). PR is really very simple. Though various formulas and methods are used to calculate the proportional result, the basic principle of PR is that political parties' representation in the legislative body is set roughly proportional to their strength in the electorate. That is, if the Fundamentalist Neopejorative Party got 18 percent of the votes cast in the election, it would get roughly 18 percent of the seats in the legislative body; if it got 30 percent of the votes, it would get roughly 30 percent of the seats.

This may not seem an unreasonable result, but PR was invented precisely because

SMDP generally does *not* give such a proportional result. Instead, SMDP generally favors large parties and hurts small ones. This is because a small party, if its voters are spread at all evenly geographically, will have only a small number of voters in each district and may, in fact, not have enough in any one district to achieve a plurality and win there. This is illustrated in Figure 10–1. The hypothetical country of Aksala is divided into twenty districts, each having 50,000 voters. In its most recent election, the Prudential Improvidence party polled 450,000 votes, or 45 percent of the total; the Protection of Artificats party polled 350,000 votes, or 35 percent of the total; and the Revolutionary Inaction party came in third with a still substantial poll of 200,000, or 20 percent of the votes. As you can see from the map, the PIP won 14 seats with its 450,000 votes, the PAP won 5 seats with its 350,000 votes, and the poor RIP got only 1 seat for its 200,000 votes. That is, 45 percent of the vote got 70 percent of the seats, 35 percent of the vote got only 25 percent of the seats, and 20 percent of the vote got only 5 percent of the seats.

RIP received a lot of votes—20 percent of the total—but these votes were spread around so that RIP received 15 percent in one district, 25 percent in another, 30 percent in another, 8 percent in another, and so on. Only in district number 3 did RIP's share of the vote top the shares of PIP and PAP, so that it won.

This is a fairly typical result of SMDP. Although the example is made up, it was not deliberately constructed to produce this result beyond stating the initial condition that the three parties were of those sizes and had a more or less even distribution of their voters across the country. Most "real life" examples of SMDP fit the same pattern. In the British election of 1992, for instance, the Liberal-Social Democratic Alliance polled 18 percent of the votes but won only 3 percent of the seats in the House of Commons.

In their early elections, most European states used electoral systems similar to SMDP. It was at the urging of small or new parties that felt unfairly discriminated against that most states changed to PR systems in the early part of the twentieth century.

**FIGURE 10–1**
A hypothetical SMDP result.

PIP victory

PAP victory

RIP victory

Why, you may ask, do any states retain SMDP as an electoral system when it is so un-fair? The reason is that there is a practical benefit to the distortion in favor of large par-ties, which many observers think compensates for the unfairness to smaller parties. Since small parties are disadvantaged by SMDP, there is a tendency for them to disap-pear or to merge together over time; as a result, SMDP electoral systems tend to en-courage the emergence of two large parties rather than a variety of smaller parties.[6] With only one major exception—Canada—SMDP systems have only two major parties, which generally makes it easier to govern the state. With only one possible exception— Germany—PR systems have more than two major parties, which may make it difficult to govern the state. (We will discuss the relative merits of having just two parties in Chapter 11.)

The trade-off between the two systems is generally one of fairness to minorities and small parties, on the one hand, versus simplifying the party system by weeding out small parties, on the other. Two other issues that may enter into a choice between the two electoral systems are these:

• Electoral participation is likely to be higher under PR than under SMDP. Under SMDP, voters who are in the minority in their district (a Republican in Boston, a Con-servative in Quebec City, a Democrat in San Diego) may feel that there is no sense even in voting, since their candidates cannot win in any case.

• SMDP provides all legislators with a tie to a particular locality, with a particular set of constituents, while most PR systems do not make this kind of connection.

*Two Conditions for the SMDP Bias.* The bias of SMDP in favor of large parties is a function of two conditions: *First, if a small party has most of its strength concentrated in just a few districts, it may not be hurt at all by the SMDP system,* because it may have enough strength in those few districts to win there. Consider if a Southwestern Auton-omy party had appeared in Aksala and had polled 60,000 votes in the four southwestern districts. Depending on how its votes were spread among the four districts, it might well have won in one or two of them. (It would have averaged 30 percent of the vote in the four districts, and the rest of the vote would have been spread among three parties.)

Again, there are plenty of "real-life" examples of this exception to the rule of SMDP bias. One is the Plaid Cymru, a Welsh nationalists party, which in April 1992 polled only one half of one percent of the vote nationally but, by concentrating that vote in Wales, won 4 of the 651 seats in the House of Commons. Another good example is Canada itself, which as noted above is the major exception to the rule that SMDP elec-toral systems tend to limit a country to two major parties. Five major parties are active in Canadian politics, but each of them has a distinct regional identity, so that there is no selective pressure on them from the SMDP system.

*Second, the smaller the number of districts, the more likely it is that small parties will be hurt by SMDP.* If the state is divided into a small number of large districts, there

---

[6]The standard statement on the effects of electoral systems is Maurice Duverger, *Political Parties* (New York: Wiley, 1954). See also Douglas Rae, *The Political Consequences of Electoral Laws*, rev. ed. (New Haven, Conn.: Yale University Press, 1971); Rein Taagepera and Matthew S. Shugart, *Seats and Votes: The Effects and Determinants of Electoral Systems* (New Haven: Yale University Press, 1989).

PIP victory

PAP victory

RIP victory

13–16

17–20

1–4

5–8

9–12

**FIGURE 10–2**
A hypothetical election by SMDP,
with Aksala divided into only five
districts.

is less chance that a small party will happen to have enough votes to win in a particular district.

This is illustrated in Figure 10–2, in which the districts of Aksala from Figure 10–1 have been grouped by fours, so that there are now just five larger districts. Under this arrangement, the largest party (PIP) expands its share of the seats from 70 to 80 percent, the PAP drops from 25 to 20 percent, and the "small" RIP (with 20 percent of the vote) disappears.

To carry this to an extreme, if there were only one seat in the legislative body, the whole country would represent a single-member district, with a plurality winning. In this case the ultimate distortion would occur, with the candidate of the PIP winning 100 percent of the "seats" (i.e., the one seat), even though PIP had gained only 45 percent of the total vote.

This last extreme possibility is mentioned because it does, in fact, occur in the real world. If a state has a president who is popularly elected by all the voters, the election functions, in effect, as a legislative election with one seat under SMDP. (Most democracies do not have a powerful president, but some do—the United States, France, Mexico, and others. Presidential government is discussed at length in Chapter 14.) Where there is a presidency, small parties are driven out of contention, and there is very strong pressure indeed for the system to evolve into one with two large parties. A notable example of this is France, which in 1962 shifted to a popularly elected presidency. Since that time small parties have been gradually declining, until today there are four parties arranged by pairs in loose alliance into a bloc of the Left and a bloc of the Right, plus a fifth party off on its own dimension of opposition to immigrants. The conclusion is unavoidable that the institution of the presidency has forced France's quarrelsome parties to coalesce into something like two large parties.

To summarize the point of this section dealing with electoral systems: *The SMDP system tends to drive out small parties and ultimately to produce an arrangement consisting of two large parties. This effect is less strong if the parties have geographic con-*

*centration of voters and may disappear altogether, as in the case of Canada, if the parties' strengths are very concentrated by region. The effect is heightened by reducing the number of districts and is especially strong when the state is simply a single district, as in presidential elections.*

## REFERENDUMS

Generally, democracies restrict their citizens' involvement in the affairs of state to participation in elections, where they may express their choice among potential political leaders. State policies are then set by the elected leaders, without any direct input from the voters. Some democracies, however, allow voters under some circumstances to choose directly, in an election, whether a given policy should be followed. Such an electoral choice is called a *referendum*. The United States does not have any provision for national referendums, but many localities and states do provide for them. California is particularly noted for their use, as in the famous "Proposition 13" referendum in which the state's voters chose to limit property taxes in California communities to 1 percent of the value of the property. Outside the United States, a few democracies provide for the regular use of national referendums. France and Switzerland are two examples, the latter relying on them rather heavily.

Beyond these few instances, many democracies that would not accept the regular use of referendums *do* use them for decisions of great gravity, where it is felt that all the people should be involved in the decision, if only by voting. Spain, for instance, when it initiated its new democratic constitution in 1978, held a referendum so that the constitution could be ratified by the people. Similarly, when the powers of the European Union were to be expanded in the 1993 Maastricht Treaty, France, Ireland, and Denmark all held referendums to allow their people to decide whether they should sign the treaty. (France and Ireland voted "yes"; the Danes voted "no," but the treaty was rewritten to accommodate them and on a second try they voted "yes.")

Why are democracies so reluctant to give "power to the people" by using the referendum to make laws? The main objection is that a proposed law cannot get the sort of careful consideration and detailed examination in an election campaign that it would get in a legislature or parliament. Voters typically do not have the time or resources to inform themselves about the intricacies of a bill. In a sense, that is "what they hire politicians for." Especially when many bills are voted on in a single campaign, as in California, where twenty or more may appear on a single ballot, only one or two will have been widely discussed among the voters. The other bills will be decided by chance factors such as how enticingly they are worded or where they appear on the ballot, or by the small number of people who may stand to gain from them in special ways and therefore take a special interest in them.

## ELECTORAL PARTICIPATION

Let us now shift from elections and electoral systems, per se, to examine how voters act in elections. We shall confine our attention here to voters in democratic elections.

First of all, it is evident that not all of those who are entitled to vote do vote. In the 1992 American presidential election, for instance, only 55 percent of those who were eligible to vote did so; in most elections for local office, the turnout is even less than this.

There is great variation from one place to another, and among different sorts of people in any one place, as to how active people are in elections. At roughly the same time that 55 percent of eligible Americans voted in the 1992 presidential election, the following percentages of the eligible electorate voted in a variety of European elections: Great Britain, 75 percent; Netherlands, 80 percent; Germany, 78 percent; Italy, 87 percent; Sweden, 87 percent. It is generally true, as in these cases, that European democracies exhibit higher levels of electoral participation than the United States. But even within the United States, electoral turnout varies a good deal by geography. In 1992, Hawaii had the lowest turnout among the 50 states, with only 41 percent; the highest, 72 percent, was Maine's.

Beyond geographic variation, certain types of people seem especially likely to vote. Table 10–2 lists various sorts of people who seem especially likely or especially unlikely to vote.

What is it that leads some people to vote more regularly than others? Partly it seems to be a matter of cultural traditions. The high electoral turnout of a state like Minnesota, for instance, seems likely to be a result of the general tradition of constructive citizenship that was strong among the Scandinavian immigrants who made up a large part of Minnesota's early population.

Partly it is a function of practical, almost mundane questions—whether polling day is on a working day (as in the United States), which is less convenient than a Sunday; or whether registration to vote is a cumbersome procedure or an easy one. (In some countries, registration is automatically done by the local authorities and requires no specific action by the person being registered.)

Partly it is a function of the difficulty of making political decisions. This may help explain why well-educated people are more likely to vote than people with less education; those with less education presumably find politics more puzzling and confusing than those who are better educated. This problem surely helps to explain why voting turnout is generally low in referendums, which demand more from a voter than simply choosing a party or a candidate.

**TABLE 10–2**
WHO IS LIKELY OR UNLIKELY TO VOTE?

| Groups unusually high in participation | Groups unusually low in participation |
|---|---|
| Suburban residents | Young people |
| Well-educated people | Women (except in Europe and North America) |
| Well-off people | Blacks (U.S.A.) |
| Farmers (U.S.A.) | Blue-collar workers (U.S.A.) |
| Blue-collar workers (Europe) | |

Finally, it is partly a function of the political circumstances under which the election is held. A close election generally stimulates greater turnout than one that promises to be a walkaway for one side. National elections, because of the great stakes of war and peace that are involved, generally get a higher turnout than they probably deserve as compared with local elections. As noted above, elections conducted under a PR electoral system generally get higher participation than those under SMDP, because under PR no one need worry about "wasting" a vote on a candidate who has no chance to win. And finally, blue-collar workers in Europe participate more faithfully than those in the United States partly because unions in Europe are more active than American unions in mobilizing their voters. And in all European states—unlike the United States—there are explicitly working-class socialist parties that draw blue-collar workers into political activity.

## THE PARADOX OF PARTICIPATION

We might also flip the question of participation around, and instead of asking "Why doesn't everyone vote?" ask "Why are all these people voting?" Looked at in one way, it is irrational to take the trouble to vote. Seeing how unlikely it would be for a single vote to decide a U.S. presidential election, one might consider it hardly worthwhile to spend a half hour and 8 cents worth of gasoline to get to the polling place. (The odds must be less than one in a trillion that the other 80 million voters would split exactly even, so that one vote could decide the outcome.) We met the cynic of Skinner's *Walden Two* earlier:

> The chance that one man's vote will decide the issue in a national election is less than the chance that he will be killed on his way to the polls. We pay no attention to chances of that magnitude in our daily affairs. We should call a man a fool who bought a sweepstakes ticket with similar odds against him.[7]

This is what we call the "paradox of participation."[8] It is paradoxical because, if things are considered from this perspective, *no one who is sensible should vote.* If the result of the election is virtually certain to be the same whether you vote or not, why should you take the time and go to the expense? To put it in the concrete terms alluded to in the quotation from Skinner, over the years more people are hit by trucks and killed on the way to the polls than change the results of national elections by their single votes. On the average and over the long run, voting is apparently a dangerous and unproductive act.

Paradoxes generally have solutions, and we can try two possible solutions here. First, this paradox obviously holds only for voters taken one at a time. If a large group of voters chose to sit out an election, it is quite possible that their absence could change the outcome. In fact, most politicians spend more time and effort in their campaigns in trying to make sure that the right people get to the polls than in trying to change the

---

[7]B. F. Skinner, *Walden Two* (New York: Macmillan, 1948), p. 221.

[8]William H. Riker and Peter C. Ordeshook, *An Introduction to Positive Political Theory* (Englewood Cliffs, N.J.: Prentice-Hall, 1973), pp. 45–68, esp. pp. 57–58.

minds of people who are planning to vote for their opponents.[9] Politicians certainly recognize the importance of turnout rates in determining elections. Thus, the paradox of participation is a paradox only for voters taken individually. This might resolve the problem for us except that a voter's decision whether or not to vote is taken individually. That is, groups do not decide whether to vote, *voters* decide whether to vote. So the paradox remains.

A second way of addressing the issue is to note that it looks at voting solely as an act to provide benefits or costs to the individual voting. The paradox arises only if we think that voters vote solely because of their wish to exercise their own power in making the government's policies. While it is true that this is the democratic justification for holding elections, we must realize that it casts voting as essentially a *selfish* act in which voters participate only in order to increase their own individual political power. Yet we saw at the beginning of this chapter that in many countries, high electoral turnout occurs even though the voters have no choice of candidates. Clearly voters in those countries are voting for some reason other than to exercise their individual political power, be-

---

WHAT IS THE BEST LEVEL OF PARTICIPATION?

A major argument among political scientists in the 1960s and 1970s turned on this question: Is more participation always better, or is there some optimal level of participation that is lower than 100 percent? Among others suggesting that more was not always better, Gabriel Almond and Sidney Verba expressed the opinion, in *The Civic Culture* (Boston: Little, Brown, 1965), that the ideal citizen participated up to a point but then sat back and trusted government officials to take things from there. This guaranteed an attentive citizenry, but one that would also give its government trust and support. Seymour M. Lipset also fueled the distrust of excessive participation by his finding, in *Political Man* (Garden City, N.Y.: Doubleday, 1960), that the high turnout in the German elections of 1932 and 1933 had had a great deal to do with Adolf Hitler's victories.

Of the several responses, that of E. E. Schattschneider—*The Semisovereign People* (New York: Holt, Rinehart and Winston, 1960)—suggested that nonparticipants were like a time bomb waiting to disrupt the system. Since they were not building patterns of support for the existing system by participating, they could, if they suddenly flooded in as the German voters for Hitler did, cause dangerous results. Schattschneider concluded that we should try to get everyone to participate as much as possible. Carole Pateman, in *Participation and Democratic Theory* (Cambridge, England: Cambridge University Press, 1970), drew an argument straight from classical liberal theory. A main purpose of participation was to help people improve themselves by exercising their judgment and by informing themselves of what was going on. Whether or not instability results, more participation is in and of itself a good thing; the more there is, the better.

The argument seems to have been resolved for now in favor of the defenders of participation. Today, one does not often hear arguments against full and extensive participation. But this argument has been going on sporadically since the time of the ancient Greeks. We may anticipate that it will come up again.

---

[9]But see W. Phillips Shively, "From Differential Abstention to Conversion: A Change in Electoral Change, 1864–1988," *American Journal of Political Science* 36 (May 1992): 309–330.

cause *their* votes represent no individual political power whatever. They are voting out of a desire to do their duty, out of a love of country, and often because of a good deal of social pressure from those around them. In other words, voting for them may be more of a communal act than an individual one.

There is no reason to think that these communal aspects of voting are absent in a democracy. This would certainly help to explain what is otherwise unexplainable—the fact that millions of people vote in elections even though it can easily be demonstrated that voting is of no individual benefit to them. This seems an attractive resolution to the paradox partly because it elevates our discussion of voting above selfish calculations of individual costs and benefits. Love of country is a noble sentiment, and if electoral participation is based partly on it, all the better for elections.

## THE BASES OF INDIVIDUALS' ELECTORAL CHOICES

For whatever reason, then, a great many people vote in elections. How do they choose which party or candidate to vote for? Any number of things may serve as the basis for voting choice in one country or another.

We can distinguish usefully between short-term factors in voting choice and long-term factors. Short-term factors are things about a particular election that may lead a person to vote one way or another. The general state of the economy usually operates in this way, for instance. If times are bad, a number of people will vote against whoever is in office as a way of showing their unhappiness. Edward Tufte has calculated that a 2 percent increase in real disposable income, compared with a 2 percent loss, should make a difference of about 2.5 percent of the vote for the president's party in midterm congressional elections in the United States; this would generally mean that about twenty to thirty more seats would go to the president's party in the good year.[10]

Other short-term factors may include the particular appeal (or lack of same) of a candidate. This appears to be particularly the case in the United States and Canada, where the personalities of possible presidents and prime ministers sway large number of voters. In most European countries, on the other hand, the voters seem to weigh primarily the various political parties as whole organizations, with less emphasis on the personal characteristics of a party's leading candidate. In 1979, for instance, polls in Britain showed that Margaret Thatcher, the Conservative candidate for prime minister, was less admired and respected personally than James Callaghan, the candidate of the Labour party. But the British electorate did not hesitate to defeat Labour soundly and put the Conservatives—and Mrs. Thatcher—in power. In general, as will be seen in the next chapter, political parties in the United States and Canada are weak organizations compared with those in most countries; as a result, individual candidates in American or Canadian elections carry more personal weight. In countries with strong parties, the focus of the electorate is more on the parties, per se, and individual candidates do not count for as much.

---

[10]Edward R. Tufte, *Political Control of the Economy* (Princeton, N.J.: Princeton University Press, 1978), p. 112.

"HOW BINDING ARE CAMPAIGN PROMISES MADE ONLY IN PRIMARIES?"

(Sidney Harris)

Short-term factors such as a particular candidacy, the state of the economy, or an international crisis can be potent in deciding an election. But most elections most of the time are determined largely by things that do not change much or that change only very gradually.

One such long-term factor is the identification of some people with a particular political party. We all know some older person who has been a Democrat (or a Republican or a Conservative or a Liberal or a Labour voter or whatever) "since I was a young child." To such a voter, a particular candidacy or the state of the economy makes less difference than to other voters. Most of the time this person is going to vote by party no matter what is going on. Political scientists call this sort of continuing tie *party identification*.[11] It adds a good deal of stability and predictability over time to election results. We will discuss party identification in more detail in the next chapter.

Another long-term factor that adds stability over time is the commitment of various

---

[11]Angus Campbell, Philip Converse, Warren E. Miller, and Donald Stokes. *The American Voter* (New York: Wiley, 1960), Chapters 6 and 7.

**TABLE 10–3**

SOCIAL BASES OF SUPPORT FOR THE SOCIAL DEMOCRATIC PARTY OF WEST GERMANY, 1953-1972

|  | 1953 | 1957 | 1965 | 1969 | 1972 |
|---|---|---|---|---|---|
| *Percent voting socialist of:* |  |  |  |  |  |
| Working class | 58 | 60 | 57 | 58 | 70 |
| Middle class | 28 | 23 | 31 | 46 | 53 |
| Those who never attend church | 63 | 64 | 64 | 77 | 74 |
| Those who occasionally attend church | 48 | 39 | 48 | 45 | 61 |
| Those who frequently attend church | 17 | 19 | 17 | 32 | 28 |

*Source:* Calculated from Kendall Baker, Russell Dalton, and Kai Hildebrandt, *Germany Transformed* (Cambridge, Mass.: Harvard University Press, 1981).

social groups to one or another party. As we see in Table 10–3, the basic commitment of the working class and the less religious to the Social Democratic party of West Germany was fairly stable from 1953 to 1972; the flip side of this is that the middle class and the religious were rather consistent in *not* supporting the Social Democratic party.

We have noted that long-term factors are things that do not change or that *change slowly*. In this table we see that the effect of religion did not change over the twenty years, since the difference between those who are religious and those who are not stayed about the same. But notice the gradual change in the effect of social class. The difference between the two classes was considerably greater at the beginning of the twenty-year period than at the end. In 1953, there was a 30-percentage-point spread between the two classes, but this had narrowed to a 17-point spread by 1972.

In other countries and at other times, the following social differences have functioned importantly as bases for voting distinctions:

• Region (The "solid Democratic South" of the United States from the 1870s to the 1960s is an example, or the regional basis of all Canadian parties.)

• Language (The Swedish People's party of Finland is an example.)

• Farming (Many countries have had Agrarian parties; Norway and Sweden are two examples.)

• Country of origin (Irish and Italian voters in the United States tend to be Democrats; German and Anglo-Saxon voters tend to be Republicans.)

• Race (Blacks tend strongly to vote Democratic in the United States; the politics of Guyana has been almost totally determined by conflicts between blacks and East Indians.)

• Gender (Women in many countries favor conservative parties, although this may be an indirect effect of religion rather than a direct effect of differences between men and women; in recent years, by contrast, a "gender gap" has opened in the United States and several European countries, with *men* voting more conservatively than women.)

• Age (In 1990, for instance, 10.2 percent of Germans aged eighteen to twenty-five voted for the Green Party, while only 0.1 percent of those over sixty did so.)

## Example: Proportional Representation Elections in Israel

The Knesset (Israel's parliament, with 120 seats) is elected every four years by an unusually simple and direct form of proportional representation. Parties submit lists of candidates (in ranked order) to the electoral commission. Any party that receives 1.5 percent or more of the vote nationally gets at least one seat in the Knesset, and each party's number of seats is proportional to how large a proportion of the vote it received. Compared with most countries, this is a very simple and straightforward PR system. The accounting is done across the state as a whole, rather than separately for different regions of the state. And the "threshold" of 1.5 percent is low enough to be quite generous to small parties; in Germany, for instance, a party receives no representation unless it has received at least 5 percent of the vote.

To put a list on the ballot, the party must submit a petition containing a few thousand signatures, and pay a fairly small deposit (usually a couple of thousand dollars). In 1992, 25 lists were on the ballot.

Voters then simply choose a list, and vote for it. Persons on the list enter the Knesset according to their rank in the list; for instance, the Labour Party qualified for 44 seats in the Knesset in 1992, so the first 44 names on the list became Knesset members. If a seat is vacated before the next election, the next person on the list simply steps in.

Obviously, where candidates rank on a party's list is utterly important. Parties put their key leaders at the top of their lists, to make sure that they are elected, but beyond that, groups and factions compete to get "their" people placed high. Who does the placing varies by party. In the two largest parties, Labour and Likud, the party "center" (a gathering of 1000 to 3000 leaders of the party, broadly representative of its constituent parts) does the ordering. In Labour, a variety of rules are followed to guarantee at least some representation of various important groups. Slots among the top thirty or so positions on the list are guaranteed to: representatives of each of the fifteen national districts of the party organization (this guarantees geographic spread); the kibbutz movement; women; youth; poor neighborhoods; and Arabs. Likud's list construction is more of a free-for-all, in which various factions of the party jostle for position. And aside from the allotted slots, Labour's nomination process is likewise a big political fight.[12]

Like most proportional representation systems, the Israeli system distributes "surplus" votes in a way that gives a slight edge to larger parties. "Surplus" votes occur when a party gets less than 1.5 percent of the vote, so that its votes do not count towards any party's share, or when rounding off in assigning Knesset seats to parties leaves some votes unused. In 1992, these leftovers gave Labour (with 34.8 percent of the vote) 36.7 percent of the seats in the Knesset, and gave Likud (24.9 percent of the vote) 26.7 percent of the seats. This is obviously only a minor advantage, however.

[12]Gideon Doron and Giora Goldberg, "No Big Deal: Democratization of the Nominating Process," in Asher Arian and Michal Shamir, eds., *The Elections in Israel—1988* (Boulder, Colo.: Westview Press, 1990).

The bottom line is that the Israeli system of PR is unusually straightforward and faithful to proportionality.

As a result, typically a lot of parties get into the Knesset. In 1992, the result was:

| | Votes | Seats |
|---|---|---|
| Labour (a left-of-center party) | 34.8% | 44 |
| Likud (a right-of-center party) | 24.9% | 32 |
| Meretz (alliance of the Civil Rights and Peace Movement, "Change" Movement, and United Workers Party) | 9.2% | 12 |
| Tzomet (personal following of Rafael Eitan) | 8.9% | 8 |
| National Religious party | 5.0% | 6 |
| Shas (a religious party) | 5.0% | 6 |
| United Torah Judaism | 3.4% | 4 |
| Democratic Front for Peace and Equality | 2.4% | 3 |
| Moledet (ultra-Zionist party) | 2.3% | 3 |
| Arab Democratic Party | 1.6% | 2 |
| Others | 2.5% | — |

Such a diverse party system could produce unstable government, as it might prove difficult to combine enough different parties to make up a working majority in the parliament (especially when, as in Israel, they are deeply divided on policies). This has not proved the case in Israel, possibly because the country's constant exposure to external danger has forced the parties to cooperate in spite of their inclinations. However, one major result of the dispersion of the parties is evident from the above. It is almost impossible to form a governing majority without including at least one of the religious parties; this has given them a good deal of leverage, by which they have commanded patronage and policy concessions way out of proportion to their electoral strength.

### Example: Elections in Nigeria

Nigeria has had elected democratic government for only nine of its more than thirty-five years of independence—from 1960 to 1966, and again from 1979 to 1983. After thirteen years of military government, the current military rulers are still making noises—but not very convincingly—about reinstating democracy.

Even aside from the military's propensity to throw out the results, electoral politics is difficult for any country like Nigeria. First of all, it tends to bring out sectarian conflicts between tribes and regions of different religions, which always threaten to tear the state apart. Nigeria fought a bloody regional civil war from 1966 to 1969, and in recent decades thousands of people have died in Christian-Moslem riots.

Second, Nigeria is a large, spread-out country. The difficult logistics of an election, together with the passions of hostility that an election awakens, leave the process open to violence and fraud. At the time of its last election in 1983, Nigeria was a country of 80 million or so people, spread over a large area with often primitive communications. The elections were held in five weekly installments. First the president was elected; then, a week later, governors of the states; a week later, the senate was elected; then the house of representatives; and finally the state assemblies. The first task facing the government in setting up the election was to draw up a roll of eligible voters. Throughout the country, 158,000 voting stations were established, and men and women were asked to go to the stations to register themselves for the election. The problem of security that this involved is indicated by the fact that with 90,000 policemen in Nigeria, there were nearly twice as many voting stations as there were law enforcement personnel.

The two main concerns of most observers were violence and the possibility of rigged results. Violence did break out; scores of people were killed, and the last three waves of elections had to be canceled in two states because of rioting. But all in all, the violence did not reach levels that made it impossible to respect the elections. Fraud, or the suspicion of it, was a far greater problem. The published roll of registered voters was particularly suspect, because it listed 65 million people. In a country of approximately 80 million, there simply could not be that many adults, and it was thought that many fraudulent entries had been made. When the incumbent President Shagari won more strongly than anyone had expected and his party succeeded surprisingly well in the further elections, the other parties cried foul. There were plenty of examples of fraud for them to point at. The village of Modakeke, for instance, cast 170,000 votes for Shagari, about 500 votes per household.[13]

Shortly after the election the government was overthrown by the military; charges of electoral fraud were among the stated reasons for the coup, although more important reasons were probably the management of the economy and a general sense of widespread economic corruption. The new military leader, General Ibrahim Babangida tried between 1987 and 1992 to set up a new basis for democratic government. His plan for doing this was odd, even bizarre.

Under the plan all former politicians, all university staff, and members of his own government (including himself) were banned from party activity. All former political parties, in fact, were banned. His initial plan was to allow only two parties, to be organized by "grass-roots" movements. Thirteen potential parties applied for licensing, but he rejected them all, on the grounds that too many former leaders had sneaked into the organizations and that they carried forward the old regional conflicts he was trying to overcome.

Instead, he and his staff organized two new grass-roots parties, complete with almost identical election programs. This might seem an odd way to start up a democracy; but in fact, in the local elections of 1990, the two parties' strengths were spread pretty well across regions, which was what Babangida had hoped to accomplish. In the midst of the presidential election in 1992, however, Babangida suddenly halted the election and banned both parties, charging them with electoral corruption. The

---

[13]*The Economist*, 20 August 1983, p. 38.

military are still in power in Nigeria, with Babangida now replaced by another general, Sami Abacha.

## FURTHER READING

Barnes, Samuel H.; Kaase, Max; and Allerbeck, Klause. *Political Action: Mass Participation in Five Western Democracies*. Beverly Hills, Calif.: Sage, 1979.

Campbell, Angus; Converse, Philip; Miller, Warren; and Stokes, Donald. *The American Voter*. New York: Wiley, 1960.

Cronin, Thomas. *Direct Democracy: The Politics of Initiative, Referendum and Recall*. Cambridge, Mass.: Harvard University Press, 1989.

Duverger, Maurice. *Political Parties*. New York: Wiley, 1954.

Flanigan, William H., and Zingale, Nancy H. *Political Behavior of the American Electorate*. 8th ed. Washington, D.C.: Congressional Quarterly Press, 1994.

Huntington, Samuel P., and Nelson, Joan M. *No Easy Choice: Political Participation in Developing Countries*. Cambridge, Mass.: Harvard University Press, 1976.

Iyengar, Shanto, and Kinder, Donald R. *News That Matters: Television and American Opinion*. Chicago: University of Chicago Press, 1987.

Lewis-Beck, Michael S. *Economics and Elections*. Ann Arbor: University of Michigan Press, 1988.

Patterson, Thomas E. *Out of Order: How the Decline of Political Parties and the Growing Power of the News Media Undermine the American Way of Electing Presidents*. New York: Knopf, 1994.

Pierce, John C., and Sullivan, John L., eds. *The Electorate Reconsidered*. Beverly Hills, Calif.: Sage, 1980.

Powell, G. Bingham, Jr. "American Voter Turnout in Comparative Perspective." *American Political Science Review* 80 (March 1986): 17–44.

Rae, Douglas. *Political Consequences of Electoral Laws*. rev. ed. New Haven, Conn.: Yale University Press, 1971.

Riker, William H., and Ordeshook, Peter C. *An Introduction to Positive Political Theory*. Englewood Cliffs, N.J.: Prentice-Hall, 1973.

Rosenstone, Steven J., and Hansen, John Mark. *Mobilization, Participation and Democracy in America*. New York: Macmillan, 1993.

Sorauf, Frank J. *Inside Campaign Finance*. New Haven: Yale University Press, 1992.

Taagepera, Rein, and Shugart, Matthew S. *Seats and Votes: The Effects and Determinants of Electoral Systems*. New Haven, Conn.: Yale University Press, 1989.

Teixeira, Roy A. *The Disappearing American Voter*. Washington: Brookings Institution, 1992.

# 11

# PARTIES:
# A LINKING AND LEADING
# MECHANISM IN POLITICS

In preceding chapters we have talked a good deal about "political parties." The political party crops up in all aspects of politics. It is an invention that first developed in the nineteenth century in response to the appearance of elections involving large numbers of voters. Politicians developed the political party at that time as a device to help themselves and like-minded friends get elected, but the party proved to have many others uses as well and went on to become a ubiquitous feature of modern politics.

We shall explore this theme below, but first let us deal with questions of definition.

## THE POLITICAL PARTY

*A political party is a group of officials or would-be officials who are linked with a sizable group of citizens into an organization; a chief object of this organization is to ensure that its officials attain power or are maintained in power.*

The latter part of this definition distinguishes the political party from the "interest group," which is discussed in the next chapter. In most countries there are many interest groups—such as the American Medical Association, the American Dairy Farmers' Organization, the Natural Gas Supply Association, Friends of the Earth, and so on—who band together to try by way of lobbying, campaign contributions, and other tactics to make sure that the government's policies will be in tune with their wishes. Interest groups are distinguished from political parties in that the former simply try to influence which policies are chosen without actually taking power or setting policies; parties, on the other hand, have as their central purpose the acquisition of power and the direction of policy.

Note that there is nothing about the above definition that says political parties are restricted to democracies and to electoral activity. Revolutionary parties may be organized not to win elections but to seize control of the government by force; totalitarian parties—such as the Nazi party of Germany in the 1930s—may oversee the machinery of a nondemocratic state.

Finally, note that a party joins people together in a more or less formally organized structure. U.S. political parties surely fall at an extreme in the looseness of their organization, but in most countries the parties are clearly delineated, with formal membership that sets those who are "in the party" apart from the rest. For instance, the Conservative party of Britain has about 1 million dues-paying members. The Communist party of China has about 48 million members, who must pass a probationary period before they are accepted for full membership.

*The party's nature as a structure, tying together a large group of officials and citizens, provides an avenue by which one part may control or communicate with another. It is this that has made it such a versatile tool of modern politics.* We shall explore this in more detail below.

## ORIGINS OF THE MODERN PARTY

Although the party has turned out to be useful for a variety of tasks that require control or communication, it was first invented for more limited and self-serving purposes. Long before the coming of electoral democracy, the state had had a varied structure of public officials—mayors, members of parliament, ministers for defense, and so on. Before democracy arrived, people attained these offices in a variety of ways: by being born into them, by buying the office (much as we might today purchase a fried-chicken franchise), by bribery, by appointment.

Once democracy was introduced, however, many of these positions were filled by election. This was different from all the old ways of choosing officials in one important respect: In all the old ways, the person who wished to have the office dealt with a single king or perhaps with a few people who could be bribed; under democracy, the would-be official had to seek the votes of a thousand or more people.

It did not take long for politicians in the new democracies to see that some sort of club or organization that bound them together with large numbers of voters would help them to attain and hold office. Furthermore, large national clubs binding together a whole set of officials with voters throughout the country could function more effectively than a local club built around a single official. With a nationwide organization, voters were not "lost" to the club as they moved from one place to another; a popular official could go from place to place, helping to convince the voters to choose other candidates of the organization; and there would be enough money to hire professional staff who could help with the job of organizing thousands upon thousands of voters. Thus the political party was born.

The first modern electoral democracy was the United States of America, and it was here that the first parties developed. By the 1820s there were well-organized parties, and the Democratic party, which can trace its roots back to that time, is the oldest political party in the world.

In Britain, 1867 marks the first year in which there was a reasonably widespread extension of the vote. As of that year, 10 percent of the population was entitled to vote. Directly as a result of this expansion of the electorate, the first modern party organization

Britain had known was established in the city of Birmingham:

> [In 1867] the Registration Societies, the Reform or Liberal Associations which had sprung up since 1832, were groups of subscribers, of amateurs, and were in the hands of traditional leaders incapable of getting at the masses who had just been brought on the political stage by the extension of the franchise. Birmingham received 30,000 new electors. The [Liberals] believed that to ensure the victory, the party organization ought to reach all these voters, to make them feel that they were about to fight *pro aris et focis*, that the Liberal party was their own party, the party of each one of them. To meet these views, one of the Radical leaders, Mr. W. Harris, architect, man of letters, and secretary of the Birmingham Liberal Association, proposed a plan of organization according to which all the Liberals of the locality were to meet in every ward, and elect representatives to manage the affairs of the party.[1]

In fact, the possibility that an expanded suffrage would lead to the development of political parties was one of the arguments raised by some members of Parliament against expanding the suffrage in 1867:

> . . . with a widely enlarged suffrage the candidate would find himself less and less able to come face to face with his constituency, and would be compelled in consequence . . . to rely more and more on the aid of the election agent, and, as in America, of that of committees and canvassers whose mouthpiece and delegate he would have to make himself.[2]

In the United States, suffrage had been expanded earlier than in Britain, and it was in the United States, in the first decade of the nineteenth century, that the first modern parties had appeared. Similarly, all over Europe, whenever a reasonably large and varied electorate was established with the coming of democracy, the political party appeared.

Like elections themselves, political parties have been widely copied and are now found in many countries that are not electoral democracies. The Communist parties of the eastern European states were obvious examples of this, but many another autocratic state has had a political party that functioned importantly in its politics. Egypt, for instance, is governed by the National Democratic party, Guinea by the Democratic Party of Guinea, Kenya by the African National Union, Syria by the Ba'ath party. Many more examples could be noted, for many regimes that do not require parties in order to win elections have found that the modern political party—with the links it creates between masses of people and a set of political leaders—is useful to them. One of the wonders of modern politics is that this invention, which was originally devised in order that some officeholders could keep their jobs, has proved adaptable to all sorts of other purposes. The political party has become a "miracle glue" of sorts for politics. Whenever one group of people is to be controlled by another group or even just kept in contact with them, the party has turned out to be a useful tool.

Let us look at some of the ways in which the political party has been used to do these things. Parties provide all of the following: a basis for the mobilization of masses of citizens; a means of recruiting and socializing political leaders; structured political identity, at both the mass and elite levels; and a method of control within a government structure. Let us look at each of these in turn.

---

[1]M. Ostrogorski, *Democracy and the Organization of Political Parties,* vol 1 (Garden City, N.Y.: Doubleday, 1964), p. 80.
[2]Ibid., p. 78.

## POLITICAL PARTIES AND THE MOBILIZATION OF THE MASSES

We argued in Chapter 10 that one of the main effects of holding elections was to involve the masses of ordinary citizens in acting out their support for the state and, by so doing, strengthening that support. In order for this to happen, millions of voters must be stimulated to go out and actually take the trouble to vote. Governments themselves cannot easily get people out to the polls, so how to reap this particular advantage of elections poses a bit of a problem. The problem is particularly great where only one slate of candidates is allowed, so that there is no suspense whatever about the outcome of the election. How can the voters be mobilized to get out and vote under these circumstances? A political party is a handy instrument with which to stir up the electorate and get them to the polls. It is controlled by its leaders, who are at the same time the rulers of the state; and it may have a membership that extends down into every village, so it is strategically placed to turn out large numbers of people.

In the United States, political parties make great efforts to get out the vote. They do this not to bolster support for the regime, although that is a side effect, but to help themselves win elections. In the Soviet Union the Communist party had no such motive for stirring up the electorate, but its leaders were anxious to generate a good show of support, and so the party did much the same things as American parties do at election time.

Aside from elections, political parties may serve to mobilize the people for special purposes or to meet crises. When President Anwar Sadat of Egypt was assassinated in 1981 and was succeeded by Vice President Mubarak, over a million people joined a demonstration in Cairo to show their support for Mubarak. The demonstration was partly organized by the government apparatus itself but also, in large part, by the ruling National Democratic Party. When the regime of Charles de Gaulle was threatened in France by a general strike in 1969, the turning point at which his opposition was defeated came when his Union of Democrats for the Republic party organized a massive demonstration in Paris for which hundreds of thousands of supporters were bused in from the countryside.

A party may also mobilize masses of people *against* a regime. Many of today's political parties in states of the south—the Congress party in India, for example, or the National Front for Liberation in Algeria—were initially organized in order to carry out a campaign to overthrow a colonial ruler like Britain or France. And when German armies occupied much of Europe during World War II, it was the churches and the political parties that provided the basis for a resistance movement because these were the only structures binding large and widespread groups of people together in ways that made coordinated resistance possible. Today the most important focus of opposition to many regimes lies with political parties.

## POLITICAL PARTIES AND THE RECRUITMENT AND SOCIALIZATION OF LEADERS

Another use to which parties have lent themselves, beyond what they were originally designed for, is the recruitment and socialization of leaders. Somebody has to do this in any society, and where there are political parties, they are an obvious choice for the

Menaka Gandhi addressing a party rally, India. (Baldev/Sygma)

task. What other organization could better seek out promising young people, give them experience at relatively small jobs, and gradually move those who do well to more important jobs, all the while imbuing them with the values that the political leadership wishes to encourage?

In Britain, for instance, an ambitious young woman who was interested in entering politics might work for a while at lesser tasks for one of the major parties, such as the Conservative party. Before too long, if she were interested in standing for Parliament, she might be nominated from a district. To get the nomination, she would have to convince the local selection committee of the Conservative party in that district that she was their best nominee. As a beginner, she would probably be selected in a hopeless district, where no Conservative had much of a chance; but once she had proved that she could campaign well in one or two lost causes, she might get the nomination from a decent district, win, and enter the House. In the House, she would continue to be molded and guided by the party. If she were the sort that party leaders like—witty in debate, hard working, and above all a faithful party voter—she might advance into positions of real responsibility, such as party spokesperson on defense or on health. Eventually, she might aim so high as to be prime minister. To be selected for this position, she would have to win an internal election at which all the Conservative members of Parliament vote to choose their leader. Throughout this career, her advancement would have been primarily due to her support from her party organization, and she would have risen to the top only because she was the sort of person her party wanted and because, in each position she held, she had learned from the rest of the party how to behave in the ways they preferred. This is essentially the only way to make a political career in Great Britain.

In the United States, too, parties are important as devices for the recruitment and so-cialization of leaders. However, parties in the United States are weaker organizationally than those in Britain, and so they do not hold the same monopoly in this regard that British parties do. Most political leaders have worked their way into place through the apparatus of either the Democratic or Republican party, starting at fairly lowly posi-tions. However, primary elections at which a candidate can appeal directly to the voters for nomination, rather than relying on party leaders, can allow a popular celebrity such as the astronaut John Glenn or basketball star Bill Bradley to enter directly into politics at a high level. (The existence of primary elections, which take the selection of candi-dates out of the hands of party leaders, is often considered the single most important cause of American parties' organizational weakness.) Furthermore, people who have distinguished themselves at some other career are often appointed to a president's cabi-net directly without any prior political career and thus without any screening by a party. When John Kennedy appointed his brother Robert as attorney and when Richard Nixon appointed Harvard professor Henry Kissinger to be secretary of state, no party was in-volved.

In a one-party state such as Yugoslavia was before 1990, the single party may serve as the major avenue to any sort of political or economic advancement. The Yugoslav Communist party actually restricted its membership in order to keep out opportunists who would join simply in order to advance themselves. By strict entrance requirements and by purges, the party was limited to a membership comprising just about 5 percent of Yugoslavia's population. Party leaders had good cause to be concerned about the prob-lem of opportunism. Since all factory directors, all important public officials, and most leaders of institutions such as universities were required to be Communists, there was ample reason for ambitious young people to seek membership no matter what their po-litical beliefs.

## POLITICAL PARTIES AS A SOURCE OF POLITICAL IDENTITY

Another unforeseen effect of political parties was the extent to which parties, once one was associated with them, would become an important part of one's identity. Party is probably not the first thing a person would mention when asked "What are you?" A more likely reply would be "I am a Presbyterian," "I am a woman," "I am a student," "I am a Canadian," and so on. But along the way, if you keep prompting, you may well be given the name of the political party with which that person feels associated. As we saw in Chapter 10, this source of identity is called *party identification*.[3] For those who be-come quite active, the political party may become a vital and central personal concern.

---

[3]The concept of "party identification" was first developed fully in Angus Campbell, et al., *The American Voter* (New York: Wiley, 1960), Chapters 6 and 7. For a review, see W. Phillips Shively, "The Nature of Party Identification: A Review of Recent Developments," in John C. Pierce and John L. Sullivan, eds., *The Elec-torate Reconsidered* (Beverly Hills, Calif.: Sage, 1980).

"WHAT I DON'T UNDERSTAND IS HOW, IN A FEW YEARS, WE'LL BECOME CONSERVATIVE REPUBLICANS."

(Sidney Harris)

What would John Kennedy or Lyndon Johnson have been without the Democratic party? Or Willy Brandt of West Germany without the Social Democratic party? Or Yeltsin of Russia without the Communist party (both initially as a source of identity and then as a foil)?

One important thing about party as a source of identity is that it can provide continuity in a political world that is otherwise quite fluid. Candidates come and go, wars start and end, political issues arise and fade and are replaced by others, but parties may go on and on and on. The two major parties of the United States are over a century old; the single main party of Mexico is about seventy years old, as was the Communist party of the Soviet Union at the time of its collapse; Britain's Conservative party is over a century old, and its Labour party is over a half-century old.

By furnishing individuals and politically active people with a lasting political identity, the party can give them a source of political community throughout their lives. Parties may provide an even longer-range continuity in politics than that of a single lifetime if party connections are passed on from parents to children of if local party organizations continue their activity across generations. An ironic instance of the way in which

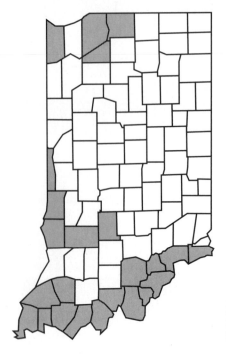

**FIGURE 11–1**
Indiana counties that are 40 percent or more
Democratic, 1992.

parties can create this sort of continuity is provided by the state of Indiana.[4] Ever since
the Civil War, there has been a political split between the southern part of the state and
the northern part. There was a good deal of sympathy for the Confederacy in the 1860s
in southern Indiana; this translated into support for the Democratic party, which was
more sympathetic to the Confederacy at that time. In northern Indiana, abolitionist and
Union sentiment ran strong, and this led northern voters to support the Republican party.
One hundred thirty years later, this pattern still holds! As may be seen in Figure 11–1,
most of the counties in which the Democratic candidate Bill Clinton received 40 percent
or more of the vote in 1992 fell in the southern fourth of the state. North of this area,
Clinton got as much as 40 percent of the vote in only a few counties, which is to say that
Republican George Bush and Independent Ross Perot, between them, got over 60 percent of the vote almost everywhere in northern Indiana.

This distribution of support bears little relation to what we normally think of as the
basis for Democratic and Republican voting. Figure 11–2 shows the counties in Indiana
in which over 30 percent of the labor force consists of workers in manufacturing industries. Such workers are commonly thought to be the mainstay of the Democratic party,
yet a comparison of the two maps show that whether or not a county is heavily industrial
has little to do with whether or not it is strongly Democratic. In fact, there is a slightly

[4]This case was first presented by V. O. Key, Jr., and Frank Munger in Eugene Burdick and Arthur J. Brod-
beck, eds., *American Voting Behavior* (Glencoe, Ill.: Free Press, 1959), Chapter 15. Their analysis has been
updated here.

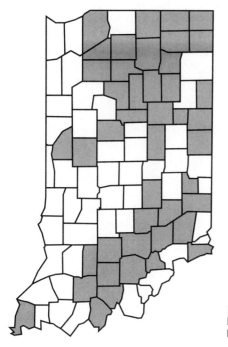

**FIGURE 11–2**
Indiana counties with over 30 percent of the labor force employed in manufacturing, 1990.

negative relationship between the two: While 33 percent of the counties that are "nonindustrial" in Figure 11–2 are heavily Democratic in Figure 11–1, only 18 percent of the "industrial" counties are heavily Democratic.

The basic north-south split in the state has been a political fact of life continually since the 1860s. The chief determinant of the geographic distribution of party support is not the economy and not the distribution of industry but events that occurred and were pretty well disposed of 130 years ago. The ability of parties—through their organizational structure and through their grip on people's consciousness—to establish stable lines of conflict is impressive. In this case, the results border on the ludicrous, since it must make little sense that Indiana elections in 1992 were determined by who took what position on slavery and secession in 1860.

## POLITICAL PARTIES AS A CHANNEL OF CONTROL

A final unforeseen effect of political parties was to provide some political leaders with a new channel through which to exert control over other leaders. This has been an important factor in politics in the twentieth century.

Remember that a party is an organization that binds a sizable group of political leaders together with a sizable number of ordinary citizens. It is the only sort of organization that regularly does this. Since it spreads so widely both within the set of political leaders and out into the mass of people, it offers an excellent channel for power through which political leaders can control the actions either of other political leaders or of the citizens.

As a channel for controlling other political leaders, the party is important in all sorts of states. The leaders of a party have many punishments and rewards at their disposal—nomination for various offices, support in passing favored legislation, and so on. Perhaps the greatest carrot or stick most of the time is the chance to advance to more powerful positions within the party. Leaders use these inducements deliberately to force obedience on lesser party figures in legislative votes, campaign activity, and so on. Sam Rayburn, who was for many years the leader of the Democratic party in the U.S. House of Representatives, used to caution new members, "To get ahead, get along." That is, to advance within the House hierarchy, obey orders. In the British House of Commons, the party organizations expect such pure obedience in voting that the life of ordinary members is in some ways rather dull, since they are generally just following orders in how they vote.

As we shall see in Chapter 13, this channel of control is crucial in making the parliamentary governments of western Europe and other parts of the world work. But party functions as a channel for power in all sorts of other systems as well. In one-party states the party may provide a means by which the apparatus of the state, especially in touchy areas such as the armed forces, is kept under the control of the party leaders. As much as possible, only party members were allowed to serve as high-ranking officers in the armies of the communist countries, for instance, and their advancement was strongly affected by their standing in the party.

Parties may also be used as a channel for power by which the leaders of the state control the mass of citizens. This is more common in authoritarian states than in democracies, where direct control of citizens is supposed to be the exception rather than the rule. For example, one particular problem for authoritarian systems is the control of intellectual activity, which might pose a threat to the leaders of the state if it proceeded freely. By placing party members in leadership positions in writers' organizations, universities, professional associations, and the media, the leaders of the state can help to ensure their control over what the citizenry thinks and says. This has particularly been the practice in communist systems, although military dictatorships, the fascist regimes of the 1930s, and other authoritarian regimes have practiced it as well.

## PARTY ORGANIZATION

Political parties in the United States are unusual in their organizational structure inasmuch as they are very loose and informal. Any other organization in the country—a savings bank, a bird-watchers' club, a church—would have some sort of formal membership, for which one applies and in return receives a membership card of some sort. Political parties in the United States do not require this of their "members"; in fact, it is often difficult for people to be sure whether or not they are members of a party or indeed which party they are members of. Political scientists have some difficulty specifying just what group of people they are describing when they speak of the "Republican party." Do they mean only the elected Republican officials in Congress and elsewhere? Do they mean the people who run the party's offices? Do they mean just the people who work for Republicans in election campaigns? Do they mean those who are "registered" as Republicans (even if they regularly vote Democratic)? Do they mean those who sympathize with the Republicans? Since there is no formal organization defining those who "belong" and those who do not, anyone is free to define the set as desired.[5]

In other states, however, parties are set up in a more normal way as formal organizations; if one wishes to be a member of the party, one applies for membership, pays some sort of dues, and is formally enrolled with a membership card. As explicit, well-defined organizations, these parties have *organizational structure*, which may greatly affect their political role.

The Conservative party of Great Britain offers a fairly typical example of organizational structure. As we see in Figure 11–3, the party consists of several parts. The key position is occupied by the leader of the party, who is a Conservative member of the House of Commons, elected by the other Conservative members of the House. If the Conservative party is in power, the leader serves as prime minister for Britain; the present leader of the Conservative party is John Major.[6]

Notice that one-way arrows (indicating power) go out from the leader to all other units with which the leader interacts except the members of the House. With regard to the latter, power is a two-way street—the members may unseat the leader, and this has occurred several times in the twentieth century; but the leader directs the business of the Conservative party in the House.

Other parts of the party serve as a supporting structure for the leader and the party's members in the House. There are about 1 million dues-paying party members organized into constituency associations. These determine local party policy—including the important question of who will be the party's candidate from that district—but they have little say otherwise in national party policies. Their only influence in this regard is to send delegates to the party's Annual Conference, from which, as seen in Figure 11–3, *no* arrows of power go anywhere. Issues are discussed at the Conference and resolutions passed; these are not binding on anyone, although the party's leaders may treat them as important symptoms of discontent that must be taken seriously.

The National Association is not elected but consists of about three thousand members of Parliament, prospective candidates, party officials, representatives of the constituency associations, and others. It meets annually, and elects an executive committee of 150, which meets several times a year. These bodies consider the direction of the party, organizational questions, and so on, but the fact that they meet so infrequently indicates that what they do is not terribly important.

The Central Office is a large and well-financed party bureaucracy that hires regional and local party agents, conducts research on policy, and publishes propaganda. The Central Office is closely controlled by the leader, who directly appoints most of its top officials.

Thus the Conservative party has a complex structure, which is dominated by the members of the House of Commons through their leader. Other parts of the structure are important to the members of the House as a support group, but except for the important power over nominations held by local constituency associations, they have little power

---

[5]For a more detailed analysis of this problem, see Frank J. Sorauf and Paul A. Beck, *Party Politics in American*, 6th ed. (Glenview, Ill.: Scott, Foresman, 1988), Chapter 1.

[6]This arrangement is discussed in more detail in Chapter 13.

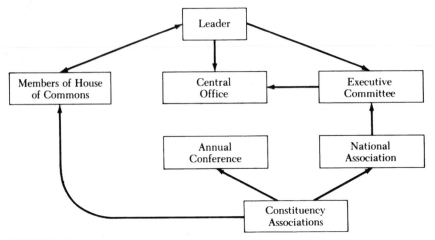

**FIGURE 11–3**
Organizational structure of Great Britain's Conservative party.

over the party's policies. This is not to say that the outside structure is unimportant; if nothing else, the dues paid by its members are the major source of party finance.

Most parties outside the United States have organizational structures more or less similar to this.[7] They may vary in the degree of power given to the outside structure. (The Labour party of Britain, for instance, gives more real power to its Annual Conference than does the Conservative party.) Or, they may vary in how tightly control is exercised. In communist parties, "lower" units in power generally have to toe the line much more precisely than in noncommunist parties; this allows the leader to direct party policies more completely and more efficiently than leaders of other parties can.

## PARTY FINANCE

Parties get the money with which to finance their activities from a variety of sources. In the United States, parties generally do not have much money, since most of it is raised directly by candidates from individual contributors and from organized interest groups.

Outside of the United States, *parties* generally raise the money and determine its use themselves.[8] It may come from many kinds of sources:

• *Public finance:* Most states pay a portion of their parties' campaign expenses from public funds. It is always difficult to decide how much money to give to which parties, and established parties generally benefit disproportionately.

---

[7]See Leon D. Epstein, *Political Parties in Western Democracies* (New Brunswick, N.J.: Transaction, 1979).

[8]A general review of party finance is Herbert Alexander and Rei Shiratori, Comparative Political Finance Among the Democracies (Boulder, Colo.: Westview Press, 1994.)

## MICHELS' "IRON LAW OF OLIGARCHY"

In *Political Parties* (first published in 1915), Robert Michels argues that a political party can never be faithful to the program and constituency for which it was originally founded. In order for the party to vie successfully for power, he wrote, it is necessary that it be organized through a specialized division of labor in which certain people become full-time leaders. Once this has happened, however, the leadership group inevitably develops a set of values and perspectives that is different from the original aims of the party. The leaders deal daily with the enemy, sitting with them in parliament, bargaining with them; the party may develop its own stake in the status quo (many European parties, for instance, own banks, newspapers, and other business enterprises) that makes its leaders cautious about rocking the boat; and finally, it is in the leaders' interests for the party to grow as large as possible, and the easiest way to effect this is to moderate the party's positions so as to bring in new groups who had previously not been willing to support it. In short, a political party is caught in a dilemma: It may refuse to develop central leadership, in which case it will probably not attain power; or it may develop central leadership, but at the cost of losing its soul.

*Political Parties* is perhaps the most influential social scientific work of the twentieth century. Michels's theme has been picked up time and again to explain why parties disappoint their followers. It was popular among east European critics of their communist regimes. It provided the theme of George Orwell's novel *Animal Farm*. The Green parties of several west European states (radical environmental protection parties) have taken it to heart, with the West German Greens rotating their leadership at short intervals so that they will not develop a "leadership class."

Whether one regrets Michels's conclusion depends to some extent on whether or not one likes radical parties. But however you feel about the question, it is worth noting two factors that put it in a slightly different light:

1   All the factors that Michels sees at work (contact with the enemy, development of a stake in society, etc.) are things that occur over time. If a movement is successful very quickly, we might expect to see Michels disproved. The Bolshevik seizure of power in Russia in 1917 and the Nazi seizure of power in Germany from 1930 to 1933 are two such cases, and both parties followed their original programs fairly closely. On the other hand, large communist parties have been attempting, since 1945, to gain power in France and Italy, but without success, and both have moderated their positions considerably; in fact, the Italian party dropped the title "Communist" in 1991. This suggests that for the opponents of a radical movement, "buying time" is not a trivial strategy but can systematically help to change the movement.

2   We should also note that even if Michels is right, all is not lost from the radical standpoint. It may be true that every radical party gradually becomes more moderate, yet we might also see party systems in which, over long periods of time, there were always radical parties present, since new parties would replace older parties. This apparent paradox depends on whether we look at things from the viewpoint of the individual party or of the party system. A similar paradox exists with regard to our own lives. We might note that everyone is constantly growing older and conclude, in the style of Michels, that "youth is impossible to maintain." This is true for any individual person, but it is not true for society because new young persons are continually being born to replace their elders.

- *Individual memberships:* These may provide a good deal of income to a party, especially one with a large membership. Socialist and Communist parties have been particularly successful in this; in some countries, members pay a percentage of their income as dues to the party.
- *Bribes and kickbacks:* Especially where a single party is associated with a dictatorship, the closeness of the party to government allows it to organize corruption on its own behalf. In 1993, the Liberal Democratic Party of Japan, which had ruled without interruption for so long that it closely approximated one-party government, became embroiled in a huge scandal involving kickbacks of millions of dollars from construction contractors.
- *Interest-group donations:* Business and labor groups, and a few others, may subsidize favored parties heavily.
- *Profits from business enterprise:* Many parties own their own newspapers, banks, and other service firms, which they operate for the benefit of their members. Usually these cost money rather than make it, but some may be profitable.
- *Subsidies from foreign countries:* The United States, the Soviet Union, Libya, China, Israel, France, Japan, and other states have, at times, subsidized parties in other countries to further their own policies.

## POLITICAL PARTY SYSTEMS

So far we have addressed the questions of what a political party does, how it is structured, and so on. All these questions have involved a single political party, looked at by itself. Another important set of questions revolves around the *pattern* formed by all the political parties in a state. We speak of a "party system" as the set of all parties. Political scientists generally distinguish such systems primarily by the number and relative size of the parties.[9]

A *one-party system* is one in which only a single political party is allowed to be active. The former communist states of eastern Europe; Egypt, Tanzania, and many other new states of the South; and the right-wing dictatorships of Nazi Germany or Franco's Spain are all examples of the one-party system. In such systems, the government and the party are closely identified, since the government generally enforces the rule that other parties are not allowed to be active. The party may closely control the governmental apparatus, as was the case in communist states, or the party may simply have been created by those in charge of government. The party in a one-party system concentrates heavily on the tasks of mobilization, communication, and control. It cannot serve well as an alternative source of political ideas because it is so closely tied to those who are already running the state.

A *dominant-party system* is similar to the one-party system in that a single party

---

[9]For good discussions of each of the party systems discussed below, see Maurice Duverger, *Political Parties* (New York: Wiley, 1954); and Giovanni Sartori, *Party and Party Systems* (Cambridge, England: Cambridge University Press, 1964).

holds power all the time, but it differs from the one-party system in that other political parties are allowed to function openly and with reasonable effectiveness.[10]

A good example of a dominant-party system is that of Mexico. This system is now under serious challenge and looks unlikely to continue for more than a few more years, but the way it has worked for seventy years is that a single party, the Party of the Institutionalized Revolution (PRI), has won every presidential election, usually with 60 to 70 percent of the vote. It has been well understood in Mexico that serious politics occurs only within the PRI. Because of this party's long dominance of politics, the whole governmental structure from the civil service on up has had intimate ties to it, and the party has had an identification with the system (which it dominates) of the sort that we observe also in one-party states. Thus the PRI was concerned over recent years about raising electoral turnout not because it thought it would be more likely to win a high-turnout election—it would win in any case—but because the system that it dominated needed high electoral participation in order to build citizen support for the regime. In many ways, then, a dominant-party system is like a one-party system. But the tolerance of other parties in the system does lead to important differences. For one thing, the existence of alternative parties provides a base for criticism of the government and guarantees that there will be more open debate about politics than in a one-party system. Alternative points of view must inevitably be openly present in a dominant-party system. For instance, the largest opposition party in Mexico has for many years been the National Action party, a party of the middle class that has been opposed to the PRI's emphasis on labor and the poor. In 1982, for the first time, a group of socialist parties to the left of the PRI figured significantly in a presidential election, gaining about 10 percent of the vote. In the 1988 election the candidate of the Left almost beat the PRI candidate—would have beaten him, most observers believe, but for fraudulent counting of the votes. The 1994 election was more genuinely competitive—and the PRI did not win automatically. By the next election, in 2000, most observers expect a wide open election.

A frequent pattern associated with dominant-party systems in states of the South is for the independence movement and its leaders to form a political party once independence has been achieved. They will have generally been more or less united in the movement for independence, and so it is easy for them to come together in a single party. Furthermore, the problems facing a new state are so awesome that its leaders often agree that it would be better if the state were spared internal disagreement for some time. However, once the dominant party that results from this has ruled for a few decades, it may well begin to lose its dominance. Corruption may set in with a group of entrenched officials; the state, now better established, can more easily afford internal disagreements; and the issues of independence fade while new issues that may divide the old ruling group arise.

In addition to Mexico, two examples of this pattern are provided by India and Israel.

---

[10]See Alan Arian and Samuel Barnes, "The Dominant Party System: A Neglected Model of Democratic Stability," *Journal of Politics* 36 (August 1974): 592–614. Also Ariel Levite and Sidney Tarrow, "Legitimation of Excluded Parties in Dominant Party Systems: A Comparison of Israel and Italy," *Comparative Politics* 15 (April 1983): 295–327.

For three decades after attaining independence in 1947, India was dominated by the Congress party, which represented Mohandas K. Gandhi's independence movement. Elections during this period were sure to provide a Congress majority in Parliament, and all important political maneuvers occurred within the Congress party. In 1977, however, Congress slipped below 50 percent of the vote and a coalition of many small, opposed parties came into power. Since then Congress has held power most of the time, but its dominance has not been assured in the way it was in the decades after independence.

Israel provides another example. After the state of Israel was established in 1948, the Labour party (which was formed by the mainly European leaders of the Zionist movement) held virtually unchallenged power until 1977. It was a great surprise to everyone when, in that year, a coalition of opposition parties called Likud, led by Menachem Begin, defeated Labour at the polls. In this case the usual problems of a party that had been in power too long were magnified by demographic change. In the 1950s and 1960s there had been massive immigration into Israel of Jews from other parts of the Mideast, and by 1977 the country was split about evenly between voters of European origin and those of non-European origin. The almost exclusively European-led Labour party had drifted badly out of touch with about half of the electorate.

The point of these examples is that, while a dominant-party system is similar in important ways to a one-party system, the availability of other active parties does guarantee that there will be fairly open discussion and debate, and it also provides for possible long-term flexibility and adjustment in the system.

A third variant is the *two-party system.* This is typified by the fact that no one party can count on always holding power but that only two parties can normally expect to have a chance at doing so. In a two-party system, the two major parties will typically receive over 90 percent of the votes cast, but neither party will very often receive more than 55 or 60 percent of the vote. A prime example is the U.S. party system, in which only the Republican and Democratic parties are normally serious contenders for power. Note that a two-party system does not necessarily *have* only two parties; a dozen or so parties run regularly in a U.S. presidential election, including the Vegetarians, the Prohibitionists, the Libertarians, and the Socialist Workers' party. But only the two major parties usually have any expectation of winning. Other examples of two-party or nearly two-party systems are those of Great Britain and Austria.

In contrast to a dominant-party system, a two-party system offers somewhat more regular variety and choices in policies and candidates. At the same time, a single party generally wins an election cleanly and is able to govern by itself without forming a coalition with other parties. Thus two-party systems are typified by a certain amount of choice combined with fairly stable and straightforward governance.

The final type of party system dealt with here is the *multiparty system.* This system consists of more than two major parties. A good example is Norway, whose Parliament, after the election of 1993, consisted of representatives from the following parties:

| | |
|---|---|
| Labour Party | 67 seats |
| Centre (agrarian) Party | 32 seats |
| Conservative party | 28 seats |
| Christian People's Party | 13 seats |

| | |
|---|---|
| Left Socialists | 13 seats |
| Progress (antitax) Party | 10 seats |
| Liberal Party | 1 seat |
| Red Electoral Alliance | 1 seat |

Since there are 165 seats, 83 are required to control the Parliament, and no one party had enough seats to rule by itself. In this case, no group of parties with 83 or more seats among them was willing to form a coalition. Instead, the Labour Party governed alone with their 67 seats; other parties agreed to support them on certain bills, while remaining out of the government. Such a cabinet is called a "minority government."

Most democratic systems are multiparty systems. The one factor that seems strongly to determine whether a given state will have a two-party or a multiparty system is its electoral system. If a state uses a form of plurality electoral system, it will almost surely have a two-party system. If it uses a proportional representation system, it will almost surely have a multiparty system. The reason for this should be clear from the discussion in Chapter 10. Under a plurality system, large parties have such an advantage that small parties are driven out, until only two major parties are left.

Compared with a two-party system, a multiparty system offers the voter a wider range of choice. Not only are there *more* choices, but the parties are able to be more distinctive than they could be in a two-party system. In a two-party system, since a party must command half or more of all votes cast in the election to succeed, there is great pressure on parties to appeal simultaneously to many different groups. A party may not stake out a clear appeal to farmers, for instance, because it might alienate its supporters in the cities; it cannot appeal clearly to the East because it might lose votes in the West, and so on. Parties in a multiparty system do not have this problem. Since the formation of a coalition is likely in any case, a party does not *have* to be huge to get some share of the power. In the Norwegian example given above, the Labour party represents the special interests of the labor unions, fishing crews, and various other groups; it is a bit bland. The Conservative party represents especially the urban middle class, who want taxes kept down and do not want moralistic constraints imposed by the state. The Christian People's party represents devout Lutheranism and favors prohibition of liquor, religious instruction in the schools, and a ban on abortion. The Centre party represents especially the interests of farmers. The Left Socialists have a variety of programs but are most noted for their opposition to Norwegian membership in NATO. The Progress party is a right-wing party sharply opposed to the welfare state and to immigration. What a "smorgasbord," compared with any existing two-party system! The voter simply has a greater range of choice in multiparty systems than in two-party systems.

However, there is a balancing advantage to the two-party system. Since most of the time multiparty systems require a coalition government to operate smoothly, a government cannot be set up unless two or more parties agree to cooperate by forming a coalition. Now this may be fine. Sweden, Norway, Finland, Germany, and other countries have been ruled by stable coalitions of one sort or another through most of their postwar history. But if the need for a coalition coincides with a great deal of animosity among the political parties, there may be trouble. Under this combination of circumstances, it may be difficult to put together a coalition of parties in the first place; or if one is formed, it may be torn apart by mutual mistrust before it has lasted very long. A prime example of this problem is Italy, which has been governed by fifty-five different coalitions since 1945.

## CONCLUSION

The disjunction between politics as choice and politics as power has led to some distortion in our view of political parties in a democracy. In general, we have viewed the party much as what Michels wishes it could be—an instrument that expresses politically the unified choice of its members. We have viewed parties as unitary actors and have thought of them, from the standpoint of their members, predominantly in terms of choice. We have not thought of a party as consisting of various groups that may be at odds with each other and that exercise power over one another.

But more often than not, a chief function of a party is to serve as a conduit by which one part may exercise power over another. It is this that has made the party almost as important to nondemocracies as to democracies, and we have seen that it is also an important function of democratic parties.

Our emphasis on the party as a vehicle for expressing choice has often helped make us insensitive to its importance as a channel for the use of power. Once again, both power and choice are necessary to a full understanding of politics.

### Example: The Communist Party of the Soviet Union (1917–1991)

The Soviet Communist party originated in the revolutionary socialist movements of the late nineteenth century. In 1917, drained after three years of fighting World War I, the Russian monarchy collapsed; and in the ensuing confusion, the Communist party seized power and established the Soviet system. This party was intimately tied into the state apparatus that it controlled. Until 1990, for instance, article 6 of the Soviet Constitution stated, "The leading and guiding force of Soviet society and the nucleus of its political system, of all state organizations and public organizations, is the Communist Party of the Soviet Union."

By placing party officials in key positions in the army, the bureaucracy, universities and schools, factories, and so on, and by controlling the legislative and executive portions of the government, the party determined public choices in the Soviet Union.

This was the situation until the late 1980s. In the early 1990s, as part of the general collapse of the Soviet system, the party lost its preeminent position and disbanded. However, a number of party leaders have regained a portion of their old power—ruling some of the new states of the former Soviet Union, and leading the opposition in others, including Russia. Even though it no longer holds power, indeed no longer exists, the Communist Party of the Soviet Union is still well worth studying as the most important example in this century of a party ruling a one-party state.

The Communist party was a disciplined organization. One did not join it casually:

To be eligible for party membership, an applicant must be eighteen or older, have a good personal record, and know the basics of Marxism-Leninism. Every applicant is required to secure written recommendations from several members who have belonged to the party for at least five years. The application is then considered at a meeting of the entire primary organization, with the applicant present and obliged to answer questions pertaining to his or her political beliefs, private life, personal ambitions, and familiarity with Marxism-Leninism. A favorable decision by the primary organization must be approved by the appropriate upper-level party office. During the first year, the new member, or "candidate," is on probation and may not vote. All members pay monthly dues, ranging from a token fee required from students and pensioners (ten cents per month), to 3 percent of the salary of high-ranking officials. Members are expected to attend periodic meetings of their primary organization, take an active part in various political campaigns, and set an example for nonmembers in work, study, and general conduct. Party members are also expected to do volunteer work in various community projects.[11]

As of about 1990, approximately 19 million Soviet citizens, or 10 percent of the adult population, were members of the party. In return for their service to the party, they received good jobs and various privileges, and might be able to work their way up to positions of power. Those who joined the party submitted to the discipline of what was called "democratic centralism." Under this rule, all lower levels of the party were unconditionally subordinate to higher levels. Absolute obedience was required, and disobedience was punishable by expulsion. This once meant arrest and exile, and later generally meant that one was fired from his or her job and blacklisted for future employment. Such discipline was the "central" part of "democratic centralism." The "democratic" side required that as decisions were in the process of being made, there should be wide discussion of them at lower levels, with communication of the sense of these discussions all the way up to the central level. It was a participatory but tightly disciplined way of organizing the party.

At the national level of organization, the lowest of the important organs of power was the party's Central Committee. It consisted of 200 to 300 members plus perhaps half as many nonvoting probationary members. The Central Committee met a few times a year. It did not actively make major governmental decisions—it could hardly do so, meeting so infrequently—but as the "crème de la crème" of Soviet politics, it might function importantly in times of crisis. When a new leader of the Soviet Union had to be chosen, for instance, the Central Committee presumably played an important role. It elected members to the two highest levels of the party, the Politburo and the Secretariat; in fact, however, the Central Committee merely ratified the nominations it had received from the previous members of the Politburo and Secretariat.

---

[11] Vadim Medish, *The Soviet Union*, 2nd ed. (Englewood Cliffs, N.J.: Prentice-Hall, 1984), p. 87.

The Politburo was the party's most important body. It was small (fourteen members in 1981) and included all the chief leaders of the Soviet Union. It met frequently and dealt with all the important decisions of the state. How it functioned varied with the power and personality of the party's general secretary, who presided over the Politburo. Stalin presumably was able to dictate to the rest of the Politburo. Later general secretaries, Andropov and Chernenko, were not in as strong a position within the party, and Politburo proceedings were presumably more lively. Mikhail Gorbachev, the last general secretary of the party and a leader of reform, had greater power in the Politburo than his predecessors because he was able to appoint allies to several new positions in it.

The party Secretariat was nearly as important as the Politburo. Its membership overlapped with that of the Politburo, and the party's general secretary presided over it as well as over the Politburo. While the Politburo dealt with all important decisions of the state and many specific party issues as well, the Secretariat was more specialized. It dealt with all the internal affairs of the party—appointments, rules, relations with communist parties in other countries, and so on.

To sum up, the Communist Party of the Soviet Union was a large and demanding organization that had intertwined itself with the apparatus of the state to a point at which it was difficult to distinguish the two. We could describe the formal organization of the party, but—because so much depended on informal political processes within the Politburo, Secretariat, and Central Committee—that still left us with large areas of ignorance about how decisions were made.

After seventy years of almost total domination of Soviet politics, the party found itself in the late 1980s under fire from reformers emboldened by Mikhail Gorbachev's program of *glasnost* ("opening"). It was fully and finally discredited when it attempted a coup d'état in 1991 to turn back Gorbachev's reforms, but in fact the coup was more its last gasp than the cause of its fall. It had been decisively weakened a year before.

At the 28th Congress of the Communist party in February 1990, Gorbachev had pushed through a reform program in which the party voted to abolish its monopoly of power as guaranteed in Article 6 of the Constitution. It was now possible for multiple parties to organize; and although initial efforts to do so were chaotic (150 separate parties formed just in the small state of Georgia), the party could no longer count on election.

The party had also lost much of its old control over government operations. After the 28th Congress, the once-powerful Politburo was allowed to meet only once a month, and it was not allowed to discuss government policy. Boris Yeltsin, the president of Russia (at that time the Soviet Union's largest republic), had banned Communists from meeting and maintaining organizations in factories and government offices in Russia shortly before the 1991 coup. (Indeed, this may have precipitated the coup attempt.)

Finally, the party's popular base had crumbled. From 1989 to 1991, more than 3 million members left the party, including such prominent figures as the president of Russia, the mayors of Leningrad and Moscow, and Eduard Shevardnaze, former foreign minister and Gorbachev's close ally; public opinion polls, which had in late

1989 showed 70 percent support for the Communist party, by late 1990 showed only 20 percent support.[12] Essentially, the party had experienced meltdown.

### Example: Mexico's Dominant Party System

 Since 1929, when a decade of bloody violence was ended by its establishment in power, the PRI (Partido Revolucionario Institucional) has had uninterrupted control of Mexican politics.[13] Mexico has in a formal sense been a democracy, but with practically no real political competition. Until the 1988 election (see the discussion below), no PRI presidential candidate had ever received less than 60 percent of the vote, only a handful of members of the Chamber of Deputies had other than PRI affiliation, and no candidate of another party had ever been elected as governor of a state. The only well-organized opposition party before 1988 was the PAN, a right-of-center, business-oriented party with its greatest strength in the northern provinces bordering the United States; the PAN, however, could normally muster only 10 to 20 percent of the vote.

The PRI maintained its ascendancy in a number of ways. It held to the symbols of revolution, with a formal structure representing the three revolutionary "sectors": organized labor, small farmers, and the civil service unions. But in fact, its leadership was largely from the middle class, and it grew over the years to represent the interests of an interlocked structure of monopolies—trade unions, producers' associations, etc.—in close cooperation with the government and bureaucracy. This gave the party a genuinely broad base of support, although not necessarily as broad as the election results showed; furthermore, since the PRI was the "only game in town," it attracted much of the ambitious young talent for political leadership. The PRI also benefited, from about 1940 to 1980, from forty years of strong economic growth.

However, in recent years the increasingly well educated Mexican population has become more and more disillusioned with the PRI and the system of monopoly power it represents. Although the PRI has enjoyed genuinely broad support, it has also used considerable election fraud to maintain its lock on power. "Michel Basañez, a former senior PRI official and now one of Mexico's best pollsters, had the most accurate pre-election poll in 1988 because he corrected his data to include a 7% estimate of fraud"[14] (i.e., he took what people told him as their voting intentions and added 7 percent as his estimate of what the PRI would add fraudulently). Corruption has also been a serious problem; in 1982 it especially flared up when the outgoing

---

[12]*New York Times*, 4 July 1991, p. 1 "Gorbachev Says Hard-Liners Risk Communist Demise"; *Economist*, 20–25 October 1990, p. 19, "Survey."

[13]Just how violent this period was can be seen in that about 1 million people, or 1 out of every 15 Mexicans, died violently from about 1910 until order was established. The trauma of this violence may help to explain the staying power of the PRI afterward.

[14]Robert A. Pastor, "Post-Revolutionary Mexico: The Salinas Opening," *Journal of Interamerican Studies and World Affairs* 32 (Fall 1990): 10.

administration was found to have stolen as much as $3 billion from the treasury. A good indication of general alienation from the PRI was the declining participation in its elections, from 77 percent in 1964 to 65 percent in 1970, and 62 percent in 1976. Participation turned back upward in 1982 and 1988, when stirrings of reform made the elections more significant.

The 1988 election was a great watershed event. The PAN was joined in opposition by a new left-wing party, the Party of Democratic Revolution (PRD), led by Cuauhtenoc Cárdenas, a popular figure on the left wing of the PRI who broke with the party. Amid financial depression, and with widespread dissatisfaction with the PRI, the PRI presidential candidate Carlos Salinas won with only 50.4 percent of the vote (and this almost surely included some fraudulent component), against 31 percent for Cardenas and 17 percent for the PAN's candidate.[15] The PRI won only 260 of the 499 seats in the Chamber of Deputies.

The PRI had, however, responded to the temper of the times by nominating in Salinas a strong reform candidate. While Salinas concentrated especially on opening up the economy, he also worked to make elections somewhat more open and democratic and to reform the organization of the PRI.

The end of Salinas' term in 1994 saw a flurry of reforms—audited lists of voters, the use of international observers at polling booths, changes in the way the PRI's candidates were nominated. This was a time of great unrest in Mexico. The PRI presidential candidate, Luis Donald Colosio, was assassinated in the midst of the campaign, probably at the direction of the PRI old guard. And leftist guerrillas seized the national imagination (both pro and con) with a campaign in the impoverished state of Chiapas. But in a fairly clean election the new PRI candidate, Ernesto Zedillo, won convincingly with 50 percent of the vote against 27 percent for PAN and 17 percent for the PRD.

Since taking office, even while coping with a disastrous tailspin in the nation's economy, Zedillo has pressed forward with reforms. He appointed a member of PAN to be his attorney general, and he has promised that he will break with the old tradition of naming his own successor. In state elections the two other parties have been allowed to take office. PAN now holds four governorships and over a hundred seats in the Congress.

The outlook for PRI is still quite uncertain. It is internally divided between reformers and the so-called "dinosaurs." And as reform proceeds it is likely that more and more of the old PRI corruption will be unearthed, in the police and elsewhere. But there is at least a chance that the PRI, if it can prove sufficiently adaptable, will be able to pull off the rare trick of opening up a dominant party system while still remaining a popular favorite.

## FURTHER READING

Burnham, Walter Dean. *Critical Elections and the Mainsprings of American Politics*. New York: Norton, 1970.

---

[15]The PAN candidate had proved so effective on television that he was barred from appearances on the government-run television station. See Howard Wiarda, "Mexico: The Unravelling of a Corporatist Regime?" *Journal of Interamerican Studies and World Affairs* 30 (Winter 1988–89): 7.

Dalton, Russell J., et al., eds. *Electoral Change in Advanced Industrial Democracies: Realignment or Dealignment?* Princeton, N.J.: Princeton University Press, 1984.

Downs, Anthony. *An Economic Theory of Democracy.* New York: Harper & Row, 1957.

Duverger, Maurice. *Political Parties.* London: Methuen, 1954.

Epstein, Leon. *Political Parties in the American Mold.* Madison: University of Wisconsin Press, 1986.

Hendel, Samuel. *The Soviet Crucible.* Boston: Duxbury, 1980.

Janda, Kenneth. *A Conceptual Framework for the Comparative Analysis of Political Parties.* Beverly Hills, Calif.: Sage, 1970.

———. *Political Parties: A Cross-National Survey.* New York: Free Press, 1980.

LaPalombara, Joseph, and Weiner, Myron. *Political Parties and Political Development.* Princeton, N.J.: Princeton University Press, 1966.

Lipset, Seymour Martin, and Rokkan, Stein. *Party Systems and Voter Alignments.* New York: Free Press, 1967.

Loewenberg, Gerhard. "The Remaking of the German Party System." *Polity* 1 (Fall 1968): 86–113.

Maisel, L. Sandy, ed. *The Parties Respond: Changes in the American Party System,* 2nd ed. Boulder, Colo.: Westview, 1994.

McCormick, Richard L., ed. *Political Parties and the Modern State.* New Brunswick, N.J.: Rutgers University Press, 1984.

Przeworski, Adam, and Sprague, John. *Paper Stones: A History of Electoral Socialism.* Chicago: University of Chicago Press, 1986.

Rogowski, Ronald. "Political Cleavages and Changing Exposure to Trade." *American Political Science Review* 81 (December 1987): 1121–1137.

Rose, Richard. *Do Parties Make a Difference?* Chatham, N.J.: Chatham House, 1980.

Sartori, Giovanni. *Parties and Party Systems.* Cambridge, England: Cambridge University Press, 1976.

Schlesinger, Joseph A. *Political Parties and the Winning of Office.* Ann Arbor: University of Michigan Press, 1991.

Sorauf, Frank, and Beck, Paul Allen. *Party Politics in America.* 7th ed. New York: HarperCollins, 1992.

# 12

---

# STRUCTURED CONFLICT:
# INTEREST GROUPS
# AND POLITICS

---

In the last chapter we distinguished the political party from the interest group. The former is associated with the process of leadership selection and the organization of government, while the latter is concerned primarily with trying to affect what those in power do. *The interest group is an organized group of citizens one of whose goals is to ensure that the state follows certain policies.*

All sorts of organized groups may function as interest groups. Some are organized solely to lobby governmental officials on behalf of one or another cause. The Sierra Club, a U.S. organization that lobbies for the preservation of wilderness areas, is an example of such an organization. Other groups may be organized primarily for other purposes but take on lobbying and other ways of influencing policy as an important task. Examples of such groups are labor unions, which are primarily organized in order to bargain with an employer but are also usually active politically. Still others focus on other goals but give some attention to politics. An example would be a university, whose first concern is to educate students and conduct research but which may maintain one or two people to lobby the government on bills that concern it.

There are a great many interest groups in a modern state, so many that we generally do not have a good idea of their numbers. There is available a reasonably good census of interest groups in Norway as of the early 1970s; this is presented in Table 12–1. Note how many of these were economic interest groups; this is fairly typical.

Over a thousand interest groups twenty-five years ago in the small country of Norway! And these are only the nationwide organizations; all sorts of local groups are not included. No one really knows how many different interest groups a large and diverse country like the United States has, but there must be many thousands.[1]

---

[1] As of July 1987, 4,211 national political action committees registered with the Federal Election Commission. And beyond this there were many local interest groups as well as interest groups that did not organize political action committees to give money to candidates. Edward Zuckerman, *Almanac of Federal PACs: 1988* (Washington, D.C.: Amward Publications, 1988), p. viii.

**TABLE 12–1**
NORWEGIAN INTEREST GROUPS, BY TYPE

| Category | Number of organizations | |
|---|---|---|
| Economic | 540 | |
|   Services, industry, finance, etc. | | 478 |
|   Agriculture, forestry, fishing | | 62 |
| Employers and unions | 274 | |
| Noneconomic organizations | 388 | |
|   Cultural | | 119 |
|   Sports, hobbies | | 94 |
|   Humanitarian, social | | 97 |
|   Religious | | 52 |
|   Political | | 25 |
| Total | 1,202 | |

*Source:* Robert Kvavik, *Interest Groups in Norwegian Politics*
(Oslo, Norway: Universitetsforlaget, 1976), p. 42.

Interest groups are not confined to democracies or open societies. All states have interest groups. Some do not permit a wide diversity of formally organized, politically active groups to exist, since this would seem threatening to their governments. However, even in such states, organizations set up for other purposes—the army, universities, natural history clubs, scientific associations, sports clubs, factories—exert political influence to help mold government policies.

In the Soviet Union, for instance, before 1988 only six "social organizations" were officially sanctioned—inventors', athletes', lifesaving, and stamp-collecting clubs; the Red Cross; and an organization for the preservation of historical and cultural monuments—and these were closely monitored.[2] Other social or political organizations outside the Communist party, such as certain religious groups and groups of intellectual dissidents, were harassed and were often either disbanded or forced underground. But at the same time it was well understood that conflict among functionally important groups such as the army, the secret police, the scientific establishment, the industrial bureaucracy—each trying to defend its turf—was a main driving force of Soviet politics, right up to the highest national levels.

## INTEREST GROUPS AND REPRESENTATION

Interest groups are probably the main vehicle in most states for representing public opinion and bringing it to bear in an organized (and therefore effective) way on the governmental authorities. Political parties cannot do this very well, since they are involved in trying to acquire governmental power for themselves. This quest for power forces parties to incorporate many compromises in their programs in order to appeal to the broadest spectrum of support. If the state is a democracy, this may take the form of an

[2]John S. Reshetar Jr., *The Soviet Polity*, 2nd ed. (New York: Harper & Row, 1978), p. 224.

"CHARGE!"

(Reprinted with permission of United Features Syndicate)

attempt to appeal to a wide range of voters; if the state is not a democracy, it may mean trying to have such a broad appeal that neither the army, the air force, the navy, urban workers, the church, nor any other major group will try to overthrow them. Whatever the case, a political party, by virtue of its most basic goal, cannot serve to articulate and represent people's wishes; it has a different task: to blend various wishes into a larger coalition. The party seeks to make differences fuzzy, but each interest group is free to present its group's wishes clearly and precisely. The task of representing the people's desires, then, falls on the interest group. How well do interest groups do this?

Generally speaking, interest groups do accomplish this fairly well. Otherwise they would not be the workhorses of political advocacy that they are. However, there are three important barriers that keep interest groups from functioning as well in this area as we might wish:

1. First, *not all interests are equally well organized.* Groups whose members have enough leisure to be active in politics are likely to enlist more of their potential clientele than other groups. Similarly, we will see high enrollment from among interests whose members are concentrated in particular localities, rather than spread out; have a basic economic stake in the outcome of politics (a labor union whose members depend on the price of coal for their jobs will organize more thoroughly than a consumer group which might stand to save its members a few percent on their cost of living); are well educated; and so on. Table 12–2, for example, lists enrollment percentages for labor organizations in several different occupational groups.

As a result of such disparities, some interest groups can speak strongly and confidently as representatives of their interest, and they are listened to with respect. Other interest groups, who formally represent only a small percentage of their potential clien-

**TABLE 12–2**

PERCENTAGE OF ELIGIBLE EMPLOYEES WHO
ARE ENROLLED IN LABOR ORGANIZATIONS,
BY INDUSTRY AND GENDER,
UNITED STATES

| | |
|---|---|
| Type of Industry | |
| Agriculture (wage and salary workers) | 2 |
| Mining | 15 |
| Construction | 20 |
| Manufacturing | 20 |
| Transportation and public utilities | 31 |
| Wholesale and retail trade | 6 |
| Finance, insurance, real estate | 2 |
| Services | 6 |
| Government | 38 |
| | |
| Gender | |
| Women | 13 |
| Men | 18 |

*Source:* U.S. Department of Commerce, Bureau of the
Census, *Statistical Abstract of the United States 1994,*
p. 439.

tele, must speak with a somewhat timid voice. The overall system of interest groups, as a result, does not represent all interests equally well. Those that are easy to organize bulk larger in the system, and their voices are heard more loudly than they should "deserve" on the basis of their numbers.

2. *Similarly, some groups command a disproportionate voice in the interest-group system because they have special advantages.* Consider the following examples:

• In almost all Western countries, business groups have influence beyond what one would expect based on the size of their memberships. They gain added influence for several reasons: they have a great deal of money to spend on politics; they have a good deal of expertise in advertising and organization, which can be used to political benefit; and the well-being of the country is so closely tied to their own well-being that they must be listened to with respect.

• In many states whose governments are shaky, large landowners as a group gain exaggerated political influence because of their ties to the army, which may be expected to intervene politically on their behalf.

• In Israel over the past decade, rather small groups of fundamentalist Jewish sects have wielded influence all out of proportion to their numbers because the Labour and Likud parties have been so evenly matched in elections that the small religious parties have held the balance of power.

• In almost all countries with much coastline, the fishing industry has had disproportionate influence because its members are concentrated in what are often key locations politically and because they are willing to go to great lengths to protect their livelihood and their traditional way of life. (It is for this reason, for instance, that it has been

Migrant farm workers, Imperial Valley, California. Moving frequently, working long hours, lacking education and political skills, such workers find it difficult to organize themselves for political action. (Peter Menzel/Stock, Boston)

so difficult for other countries to get Japan to stop the hunting of whales, even though only a few thousand members of Japan's huge labor force are involved in the whaling industry.)

Such examples could be added to, on and on. Partly because not all interests are equally well organized and also because some have special advantages such as these, the sum total of interest-group representation may give quite a distorted picture of the interests in a country.

3. *Finally, most interest groups are not organized very democratically; their leaders are not closely responsive to the members' wishes.* The leaders of an interest group are usually able to build a base of support within the administrative structure of the group and among its members, which makes it difficult to unseat them. Even where the members of the group elect the leader each year—as is true of most labor unions, for instance—an "inside" group usually dominates the election, so that the same person is elected year after year.[3] And many interest groups—such as universities, armies, and factories—are not even set up in such a way as to allow periodic elections.

Since the internal structure of interest groups is not very democratic, there is a real

---

[3]Seymour Martin Lipset, Martin A. Trow, and James S. Coleman explored an exception to this rule in *Union Democracy* (Garden City, N.Y.: Doubleday, 1962).

danger that their leaders may gradually drift apart from the ordinary members and follow their own political line. Democratic accountability to the membership could prevent
this, but in its absence there is little to keep it from happening.

We might expect that the free market would provide a control over this. That is, if the
leaders drifted too far away from the ordinary members, the latter would be able to "vote
with their feet" and join a competing group. For example, there are many different con-
servation societies, and so we might expect that if some members of, say, Friends of the
Earth did not like their leaders' positions, they would drop their membership and join
some other group, such as the National Wildlife Association.

The trouble with this solution is that a group's political positions are often *not* major
factors determining an individual's continued membership in the group; this is especially true of economic interest groups. For most union members, the important thing is
how skillful their union is in negotiating a good contract with their employer. Another
important consideration is the package of extra benefits the union can provide—low-
cost group insurance, educational and entertainment programs, low-cost package vacations, and so on. For most members, the union's political activity is a weak runner-up
among the things that matter to them.[4]

A survey of several business and agricultural associations asked members whether
they would stay in their association if it stopped its political activity altogether but continued to offer them the other benefits they enjoyed. As seen in Table 12–3, a majority of
each group said that the association's other benefits were important enough to them that
they would continue their membership even if the group did nothing in politics.

These side benefits, which the leaders of groups may manipulate in order to maintain
membership in the group, are called *selective incentives*. (They give members an *incentive* for being in the group; they are *selective* in that they may be targeted selectively to
members of the group.) If the selective incentives available through an organization are
sufficiently attractive, they can provide the leaders of the organization with a great deal
of leeway in their choice of political positions. Leaders of labor unions have been able to
take political positions varying from rather conservative Republican (the Teamsters'
Union in the United States) to communist (many French and Italian unions), and their

---

[4]Mancur Olson, *The Logic of Collective Action* (Cambridge, Mass.: Harvard University Press, 1965).

**TABLE 12–3**

PERCENTAGE OF MEMBERS WHO WOULD   STAY
IN THE ASSOCIATION IF IT DID NOT
LOBBY AT ALL

| | |
|---|---|
| Minnesota Farm Bureau | 77 |
| Minnesota Farmers' Union | 63 |
| Minnesota Retail Federation | 57 |
| Minnesota-Dakotas Hardware Association | 70 |
| Printing Industries of the Twin Cities | 94 |

*Source:* Terry M. Moe, *The Organization of Interests*
(Chicago: University of Chicago Press, 1980), p. 210.

members have not objected strongly as long as their wage settlements and other benefits were good.[5]

Interest groups, then, are not on the whole democratically organized, and their leaders may depart considerably from the members' views. Add to this our two earlier points (that the groups themselves may be rather unrepresentative of the population as a whole, because some kinds of people participate more in groups than others; and that some groups, because of strategic advantage, are able to have more impact than they would deserve simply on the basis of their numbers), and we can see that the overall result of lobbying and other political activity on the part of interest-group leaders may be quite unrepresentative of the wishes of the people.

As a few examples of how the interest-group system may distort public opinion, consider the following:

• In Israel, in deference to small fundamentalist groups, the national airline El Al does not fly on the Sabbath even though it is expensive to have the planes sit idle and most Israelis would prefer to have Sabbath flights.

• In the United States, a majority of those sampled in public opinion polls favor the regulation of handguns, but the National Rifle Association has effectively blocked such laws in most localities.

• In countries with state-run television networks, programming is almost always more "educational" (and dull) than the people would prefer. Leaders of cultural associations are in part responsible for this.

## TYPES OF INTEREST GROUPS

We can classify interest groups in all sorts of ways. One of the most frequently used classifications has the added advantage, for this text, of underscoring our point that all sorts of organizations may function as interest groups.[6]

### 1. Anomic Groups

These are groups with no formal organizational structure and no obvious leaders that come together only temporarily and with the loosest of coordination to their efforts. Typically they are the result of turmoil and excitement, and their actions are often violent. Examples of anomic interest groups include lynch mobs, the black urban riots in the United States in 1968, and the student rioters who almost brought down the French government in 1968. When the Canadian premier crossed Canada in a luxurious private railroad car at the height of the recession of 1982, his car was pelted with eggs, bricks, and stones in many towns. The people throwing them functioned as an anomic interest group. Though such groups are not formally organized, they may have a significant political effect.

---

[5]An added factor that may hold members in groups and that certainly operates in the case of many labor unions is *coercion*. "Closed shop" contracts often require that a worker must be a member of the union in order to hold a job.

[6]This classification is most fully developed in Gabriel Almond and James S. Coleman, eds., *The Politics of the Developing Areas* (Princeton, N.J.: Princeton University Press, 1960).

THE LOGIC OF COLLECTIVE ACTION

One of the more interesting works of abstract theory in the social sciences is Mancur Olson's *Logic of Collective Action* (Cambridge, Mass.: Harvard University Press, 1965), which is particularly applicable to the study of interest groups. Olson notes that organized groups will be plagued by the problem of collective goods. (You will recall from Chapter 5 that a collective good is one that no member of the group can be prevented from enjoying.) Even if a business owner does not join the local chamber of commerce, for example, he or she will still benefit from its lobbying activities with the state government.

To Olson, this means that the potential members of the group will each be inclined to save their dues money and not join the group, since they can enjoy the benefits of the group's activity whether or not they join. What is rational for the individual may be tragic for the group, however, since if every potential member did what was rational, there would be no interest group at all and no benefits for anyone.

Olson notes four possibilities that help to explain how one might be able to organize groups in spite of the problem of collective goods:

1 If a group is *sufficiently small*, it may be easier to organize. Each member's contribution is then not trivially small, and so all potential members can see that there will be less of the collective good available if they withhold their contribution to the group.

2 The group may offer *selective incentives*, such as life insurance programs or travel packages, that can be withheld from those who do not enter the group.

3 The group may be able to *coerce* members to join whether they wish to or not. The closed shop is an example of this in labor relations. In "neocorporatist" systems (see pages 238–239), the government may require that the group be formed so that it can help to carry out the government's policies.

4 If one member of the group bulks very large relative to the others, then that member may see that the collective good would be impossible to attain without its participation. Therefore that member may join and carry things forward even though smaller members who do not join get a free ride. The largest department store in town, for instance, can hardly avoid joining the chamber of commerce. For a slightly different "group," this helps to explain why the United States figures so importantly in the NATO alliance and provides its smaller allies with a partially free ride.

## 2. Nonassociational Groups

In a sense, this type contradicts our definition of "interest group" as an organized group of citizens one of whose goals is to ensure that the state follows certain policies. The nonassociational interest group is not organized in any formal way. It consists of some category or another of people who are treated by others *as if* they were representatives of an interest, even though they have not organized themselves formally to act as representatives. It is hard to find examples of nonassociational interest groups in the modern state, where most interests are represented by formally organized groups. In less developed states, the government will often seek out the views of, say, village elders on whether a dam should be built in their region or on some similar question of policy. The elders are not organized in a group to represent their region, but the government *treats* them as if they were.

Perhaps the best example of nonassociational interest groups in the modern state is provided by public opinion polling. In the poll, a randomly selected sample of a thousand or so people of some type—blacks, farmers, high school students, Catholics, or whatever—are asked questions about political issues and their responses are reported publicly. The thousand or so high school students are not organized formally in any way; in fact, they do not know each other or have any way of knowing who else has been contacted by the poll. But what they say is taken by everyone as if it represented the views of high school students as a whole.

### 3. Institutional Groups

These groups are set up primarily for purposes other than political activity and would certainly exist even if they did not deal with politics at all; they become politically active only in order to defend their own interests in the state's policy decisions. Many examples of this sort of group have been cited above: an army, which is set up to defend the state, may become active, even dominant, in the politics of the state in order to further the common interests of its members; a university, which is set up to educate students and conduct research, may hire lobbyists to procure financial support from the government; and so on.

Institutional interest groups are found in great numbers in all states, but they are of special importance to the politics of closed systems like China, where "associational" interest groups are by and large not allowed.

### 4. Associational Groups

These are groups that regard political activity as one of their primary purposes. An associational interest group may have some other primary purposes as well; labor unions, for example, exist to bargain with employers as well as to lobby the government, and the National Audubon Society of the United States exists to acquire and maintain its own wildlife refuges as well as to lobby for governmental protection of wildlife. But for all associational interest groups, political activity is *one* of the purposes for which the group was originally set up. This is the typical interest group with which we opened our chapter; it is what most people generally have in mind when they speak of "interest groups."

A major distinction among associational interest groups is between *economic* interest groups (also sometimes called "sectoral"), and *non-economic* groups. Economic groups form up around a shared economic interest (an association of small manufacturers, for instance, or a truckers' association). Non-economic groups form up around a shared idea, and obviously there can be quite a variety of such groups. They may form up to support an ethnic group (the National Association for the Advancement of Colored Peoples, for instance), to support a foreign policy position, to support a position on the environment, to support religious values, or whatever.

Non-economic associational interest groups seem much more important in the politics of the United States than in most other states of the world. This is probably because: (1) our parties are weaker and less unified on policy than most other states' parties, and thus are not well equipped to lead in a debate over ideas; and (2) our two-party system

(Reprinted by permission of Tribune Media Services)

does not provide room for small, specialized parties such as Israel's religious parties, which are able to seek directly a portion of the governmental power through participation in coalitions. Instead, those seeking to pursue an ideological goal in the United States must usually operate indirectly through an interest group to *influence* those who have attained power.

In contrast to the non-economic associational groups, economic groups probably vary less in their role from one state to another. The economy is such a central part of society that economic interest groups have a natural entrée to government everywhere. Thus their presence, and their activities, are probably less variable than is true of non-economic interest groups. Some states like the United States and Sweden have very active feminist groups, for instance—although in Sweden this interest is channeled somewhat more through political parties—while in others like Japan there is almost no feminist presence. But virtually every state has a politically active manufacturers' association.

## TACTICS OF INTEREST GROUPS

The tactics an interest group will use are determined by the sources of its power and by the opportunities that the political system offers for the use of power.[7] An interest group with many members but little money will concentrate on tactics that take advantage of numbers rather than money, while a group with few members but plenty of money will

---

[7]For a good review of this point, see Norman J. Ornstein and Shirley Elder, *Interest Groups, Lobbying and Policymaking* (Washington, D.C.: Congressional Quarterly Press, 1978), Chapter 3.

follow different tactics. And groups that have similar sources of power but find themselves faced with different sorts of political structures may also be expected to follow different tactics. In their political activity, U.S. labor unions, for instance, emphasize electoral activity and campaign contributions to public officials. For Solidarity, the labor union that transformed the politics of Poland in the 1970s and 1980s in spite of suppression by the Communist government, these focuses of political activity were not available, and so it concentrated instead on sit-ins and mass demonstrations.

Let us look specifically at several tactics available to interest groups in a democracy. What leads a group to choose one or more of these?

## 1. Control of Information and Expertise

Sometimes the members of an interest group control specialized information that is important to the government—information which may, in fact, be required if the group itself is to be controlled by the government. Doctors, for example, are the only people with the necessary expertise to judge medical policy and the quality of medical treatment. Scientists are the only ones sufficiently skilled technically to judge a variety of questions. Oil corporations know more about the oil business than anyone else. In all these cases a government that wishes to make policy relevant to an interest group must depend on the members of the group for the necessary information and expertise. This gives the group a great deal of power, because the resulting interpretation of things is likely to be slanted a good deal toward the group's prejudices. It does not require that anyone operate dishonestly. Everyone always has a certain slant on things, and if the members of an interest group are the only ones giving the government analysis and interpretation, their slant is inevitably going to enter in.

This tactic requires that relevant information and technical skills be scarce. Labor unions, religious groups, or hobby organizations generally cannot make good use of the tactic, because the skills and information they have are widely available. A dramatic example of power based on the control of information appeared during the Arab states' oil embargo of the United States in 1977, when it turned out that the only source for information on how much oil was in transit to the United States was the oil companies themselves. The government had no independent source for this information.

## 2. Electoral Activity

This tactic is especially suitable for groups with a large number of members who are at least moderately committed. Such a group may raise money from among its members to contribute to candidates, provide campaign workers to candidates, and deliver its own members' votes for candidates—all in an effort to ensure that people favorably disposed to the group end up in office. If the members of the group are not sufficiently committed to it to choose their vote on the basis of its recommendations, this tactic is of little use; an automobile club, for instance, would not generally be able to deliver its members' votes. Groups that have used this tactic successfully include labor unions, large religious organizations, and ethnic groups. Some other special organizations such as the National

Rifle Association in the United States or the wine growers of France have also been successful in this way.

## 3. Use of Economic Power

An interest group of economic importance to the state may influence the state by threatening to disrupt its economic contribution. Strategically placed unions, such as those of railroad or postal workers, have often been able to enlist the government's help by threatening a strike that would be catastrophically disruptive to the state. At some times, as in France in 1968 or Germany in the 1920s, a *general strike* in which all unions stop working at the same time has been used to try to force an unpopular government out of office. Businesses often threaten communities by telling them that if they don't give them tax advantages or other considerations, they will move their operations elsewhere. Professional sports franchises have been particularly skillful at this kind of threat, forcing communities to provide them with subsidies, build stadiums to house them, and so on. The civil rights movement of the 1960s in the United States gained great impetus when an unknown preacher named Martin Luther King organized a boycott of the city bus system of Montgomery, Alabama, to force the city to allow blacks to sit anywhere they wished on the buses. Similarly, economic boycotts of white businesses were an effective tool for blacks in South Africa in the late 1980s.

This tactic requires that a large economic stake be maneuverable. That is, the group must be able to turn on or turn off a large enough part of the economy to threaten dire results. This can be accomplished either by a single large corporation, for which it is usually fairly easy, or by a large number of people who, though they are not individually that important to the economy, are willing to coordinate economic disruption (a strike or boycott) so that their combined impact is important. Mass action like this is usually difficult to accomplish, because it requires a large number of people to make an economic sacrifice by stopping work, finding an alternative to riding buses, or whatever. It requires a large and unusually devoted membership.

## 4. Public Information Campaigns

A group that does not necessarily have a large mass base but which has substantial access to the media may try to change policy by the most indirect of means—by changing the minds of the entire population in the hope that this, in turn, will influence government policy. Institutional interest groups frequently use this tactic, since many other tactics are barred to them. The U.S. Air Force has at times helped to encourage comic strips such as Steve Canyon, which put the Air Force in a good light. Government agencies in all states use "public service advertisements"—giving health advice, moral admonition, and so on—to keep themselves in the public eye as well as to accomplish the direct goal of the advertisements.

This tactic is also useful for an interest with enough money to buy advertising time, especially if other tactics do not look very promising. In the 1970s, American corporations were faced with a new environmental movement that was difficult to combat. How could a group argue effectively for dirty air? An expensive and skillfully executed ad campaign on the theme "businesses don't cause pollution, people cause pollution" helped them to shift the terms of national debate.

## 5. Violence and Disruption

An interest group may also try to dramatize its case by violent or disruptive activity, or it may try by violence and disruption to convince the leaders of the state that they will pay a high price in turmoil by not yielding to the group's demands. Disruptive but non-violent protest may be an effective way for an interest group to bring attention to its cause, especially if it has few resources other than a dedicated mass following.[8] But violence is also a frequently used tool. Sometimes it occurs spontaneously in "anomic" interest group activity, as in the urban riots of 1968. Sometimes it is tightly organized, as in campaigns of assassination and kidnapping by terrorist organizations like Italy's Red Brigade.

Terrorism is usually not a very effective technique, as it is simply likely to cost the disruptive group what public sympathy it has and to call forth strenuous efforts at control by the authorities. A group with a decent chance of accomplishing its goals by other means is not likely to use violence as a tactic. However, there are two circumstances under which groups may resort to it:

- For a small group of extremely committed people, terrorism is an obviously useful tactic. One must remember that a truly small group (say, fifty to a hundred people) is not likely to be able to bring about major political changes in any case. If no other tactics would succeed anyway, terrorist violence offers them a long-shot possibility. Even a very few people may attract a great deal of attention by way of bank robberies, murders, and kidnappings. They would have little chance of parlaying this attention into the accomplishment of their political goals, but if they were totally committed, they might try despite the odds.
- The second case in which terrorism might be an effective tactic appears when one region is united in its opposition to the rest of a state and wishes to separate from it or at least to change its legal relationship to the government. A separatist group under these conditions can launch violent attacks on the rest of the state without losing the sympathy of the only "public" that counts for them, the people in their part of the state. In fact, the violence is likely to bring down harsher regulation and police activity in their region, which will serve to strengthen local support for the separatist cause. Many separatist movements—the Irish Republican Army in Britain, the Basque separatists in Spain, Moslem separatists in the Philippines—have used this tactic with success.

## 6. Litigation

Here an interest group attempts to affect policy by working within the court system. The historic reversal of segregated schooling in the United States was begun in this

[8]See Michael Lipsky, "Protest as a Political Resource," *American Political Science Review* 62 (December 1968): 1144–1158.

way when in 1954 the National Association for the Advancement of Colored People (NAACP) sponsored a constitutional test of segregation in the courts. A black student, with the help of the NAACP, sued her school board to admit her to the white school, and she won.

Through court cases, an interest group may hope to change the interpretation of a law or, in some countries, even get it thrown out altogether as unconstitutional. Also, court procedures can be so slow and expensive that the mere threat of tying a governmental agency up in court may get the agency to compromise.

However, litigation is generally a strategy based on weakness. For a group to be successful at litigation, it must depend on the way the law was initially written—something over which it has little control if litigation is its main tactic. And it must depend on finding a sympathetic court, which is also rather chancy. The great appeal of litigation is that it does not require large numbers (all one really has to have is a lawyer) or enormous economic power. Thus it appeals particularly to small weak groups. Groups that have in recent years depended fairly heavily on litigation in the United States include environmentalists, the handicapped, and groups favoring abortion rights. These are relatively weak groups that have usually been on the defensive.[9]

The history of the civil rights movement in the United States provides varied examples of how circumstances determine strategy. In the 1940s and 1950s the movement for civil rights for blacks was relatively weak. The majority of blacks were still barred from voting in the South, blacks were poor and did not have a great deal of money to contribute, and the movement did not have many white allies, either in public office or outside it. The chief civil rights organization at this time was the NAACP, and its chief tactic was litigation. It achieved several important successes in court, among other things overturning segregated schooling in the South and outlawing the exclusion of black voters from primary elections.

With the increase in support for civil rights in the 1960s and partly as a result of these successes, more money and resources became available to the movement. Blacks had become bolder politically; many more were willing to march in demonstrations to help draw attention to their cause, and they began to acquire significant white allies. At this time new, rival organizations wishing to use different tactics appeared. The Congress on Racial Equality (CORE) and Martin Luther King's Southern Christian Leadership Conference (SCLC) were two new organizations that emphasized, as ways of attracting sympathy and forcing segregationists to yield, the use of economic power and the provocation of segregationists into violence. (Note the clever twist on the use of violence as a tactic—here white officials were goaded into violence so that they would lose public sympathy.) Massive demonstrations, requiring large numbers of dedicated black and white participants, were held. Violence of their own was never a part of these leaders' strategy; but the provocation of white violence was useful, and the anomic black ur-

---

[9]See for example Susan M. Olson, *Clients and Lawyers: Securing the Rights of Disabled Persons* (Westport, Conn.: Greenwood Press, 1984). In 1989 the abortion rights movement strengthened a good deal in a popular reaction to an unfavorable court decision, and with its increased strength it began to shift its attention from litigation to electoral activity.

ban riots of 1965–1968, which occurred spontaneously, were used by civil rights leaders as evidence for their claims that blacks had to be treated more fairly.

At this time electoral activity was not especially emphasized, first, because during the 1960s many southern blacks could not vote or were just acquiring the vote and, second, because demonstrations and disruption were proving to be such powerful tools. By the 1970s and 1980s, however, demonstrations began to be less effective. The public was more used to them and thus less impressed by them, and police and public officials had learned not to respond in the picturesquely violent ways that demonstrators had once counted on. At the same time, the electoral importance of blacks had grown. The black percentage of the electorate in many northern cities had reached a point at which blacks could often determine the outcome of mayoral and other elections. In the South, thanks to the gains of the 1960s, most blacks were free to vote and could determine many elections. In the 1970s and 1980s, accordingly, the activity of all black civil rights groups shifted to emphasize more their importance in elections.

We can see in this evolution of the tactics of the civil rights movement a good illustration of our general principle, that interest groups will pick those tactics that best fit the group's resources and the political opportunities offered by those resources.

## PATTERNS OF INTEREST-GROUP ACTIVITY

Up to this point we have talked about interest groups primarily from the point of view of the individual group. However, we must also look at the pattern of all group activity in a state. In looking at political parties, we found that the overall pattern formed by the system of parties was important to the state's politics; similarly, we will see that the overall pattern of interest-group activity is also important. Interest-group systems vary in (at least) two important ways.

### 1. Degree of Organization

In some countries, people are heavily organized by groups; in others, they are not heavily organized at all. Most states of the South are only weakly organized. Institutional interest groups such as the church and the army bulk much larger in the politics of these states than they would otherwise, simply because interest groups of other sorts are weak.

Among industrialized states, there is also great variation. In some, such as the former Soviet Union, the formation of groups is suppressed, and here again institutional interest groups gain in importance by default. But even among open societies, there is a good deal of variation. The Scandinavian countries are probably more thoroughly organized than any others in the world. For example, 89 percent of all Swedish workers are members of trade unions, compared with 36 percent for Great Britain and 16 percent for the United States.[10] The percentage of people belonging to political organizations is about twice as high in Norway as in the United States.[11]

---

[10]Britain, 1989; Sweden, 1992; USA, 1992. Source: United Kingdom, Central Statistical Office, *Annual Abstract of Statistics 1994;* Sweden, Statistiska Centralbyrån, *Statistisk Årbok '94;* United States, Department of Commerce, *Statistical Abstract of the United States 1993.*

[11]Robert B. Kvavik, *Interest Groups in Norwegian Politics* (Oslo: Universitetsforlaget, 1976), p. 46.

## 2. Degree of Direct Involvement of Interest Groups in Government and Administration

We saw earlier in this chapter that government officials must often depend on interest groups for information and expertise. The way in which governments may tap into this varies from casual arrangements, in which officials occasionally call up interest-group representatives or look up a figure in the group's publication, to quite formal arrangements in which interest-group representatives may sit by right on administrative committees of the government. Under the latter sort of arrangement, which is fairly common in northern Europe, it may be hard to draw the line between interest groups and government.

Two important types of interest-group systems can be identified by variations on these two dimensions. These are *pluralism* and *neocorporatism*. They are important concepts for understanding how interest groups operate in democratic systems.[12]

### PLURALISM

"Pluralism" is a system in which all interests organize and compete freely and no one group is able to dominate things. The government is open to pressure from the interest groups, and politics consists largely of the competition among these interest groups to see that the policies they favor are adopted by the government.[13] In terms of our two dimensions above, pluralism is high on the scale of "organization" and low on "direct involvement of interest groups in government"; that is, interest groups are well organized but are quite distinct from the government. There is no state that is perfectly "pluralist"; the term is an abstraction. But the United States approaches the type more closely than most and is often used as a chief example of pluralism at work.

Those who favor a pluralist system of politics point out that with numerous groups operating, there is a good deal of spontaneity to things. It is relatively easy for new ideas to appear from the grass roots, and there is a good deal of flexibility. Furthermore, because the government is simultaneously influenced by many competing groups, negotiation and compromise should be the order of the day. Politics should typically be pragmatic and nonradical.

Pluralist writers see pluralism as an ideal way to reach the common ground of society. All the various interests in society pull in their varying directions, and the government responds to their pressure by ending up at a kind of equilibrium point where the pressures all balance. With a minimum of distortion, the most desired mix of policy is reached.

Critics, however, point out that in any real state—as distinct from the idealized abstraction—the set of interest groups cannot represent the people of the state very well, because not all interests are equally able to "organize and compete freely." This was discussed at the beginning of this chapter in the section "Interest Groups and Representation." If the criticism is true, then a pluralist system might have all the advantages cited

---

[12]Here, as in our discussion of interest-group tactics earlier in this chapter, we shall focus attention on democracies.

[13]The chief source is David Truman, *The Governmental Process* (New York: Knopf, 1951). See also "Pluralism" in *The International Encyclopedia of the Social Sciences*.

by those who favor it, yet we would still have to be suspicious of it because policies based on "pluralist" deliberations could be expected to slant systematically in favor of those groups that can operate effectively and against those that cannot.

## NEOCORPORATISM

"Neocorporatism" is another abstraction. It is a system in which all interests are organized and the government deals directly with all affected interests at all stages in the making and administration of policy. Unlike pluralism, under neocorporatism the government does not merely respond to the interest groups' pressure but actively involves the groups themselves in the job of governing.[14] In terms of our two dimensions above, neocorporatism is high on the scales of both "organization" and "direct involvement of interest groups."

Not only does the government draw interest groups into the governmental process in neocorporatism, but parts of the government may also act rather like interest groups. This is not so much a matter of "institutional interest groups" lobbying for their own perquisites and budgets, as it is active engagement in political debate on behalf of certain policies. Parts of the bureaucratic apparatus may take on a greater role of representing popular constituencies and initiating policy demands than is common under pluralism. They are in effect "self-starters" who try to mobilize popular support for their positions. An example is the founding of the European Common Market in 1956; the campaign for unification was spearheaded not by party leaders but by civil servants. From both sides, then, the boundary between government and interest groups becomes much more fuzzy in a neocorporatist system.

The Scandinavian states approach the neocorporatist model more closely than any others. For instance, in Sweden:

- The government is constitutionally required to send copies of any bill it is drafting to all affected interest groups and to solicit their responses at all stages of the legislative process.
- The drafting of any important bill is preceded by discussions in a special royal commission set up to consider the bill. Representatives of all affected interest groups sit on such a commission.
- Once the bill is passed, its administration will often be turned over to the affected group. For instance, governmental policies on the price of eggs are administered by the egg-growers' cooperative marketing board rather than by a governmental agency.
- Generally, policies are set in a spirit of cooperation and compromise. There is a reluctance to push any affected group to the wall.

Those who admire neocorporatism point to the cooperative attitude brought forth by such a system. In fact, for such a system to work at all, there *must* be a cooperative

---

[14]A good presentation of the model is Martin O. Heisler and Robert B. Kvavik, "Patterns of European Politics: The 'European Polity' Model," in Martin O. Heisler, ed., *Politics in Europe* (New York: David McKay, 1974), pp. 27–90.

spirit, and putting the system in place may therefore help to call forth the required cooperation.

Also, neocorporatism eases the problem of unequal organization of groups, which flaws pluralism. Simply because groups must be well organized in order to take part in governing, it becomes more important to interests that they organize their members, and they tend to so do. Indeed, the government sometimes writes a law in such a way that its administration requires the creation of a group that does not yet exist; when this situation has arisen, the government has simply organized the group itself![15]

On the other hand, the neocorporatist system is a fragile one, since it depends so much on cooperation and everyone's willingness to avoid rocking the boat. Since neocorporatism sets up an officially sanctioned set of actors in the system, each with rights to a piece of the pie, no group can go for the jugular of another without endangering the whole system.

This suggests a second important problem in neocorporatism. Because it defines a set of groups with claims on the state and routinizes the process by which the state consults with them, the neocorporatist system tends to petrify the existing line of conflict as of the time it was established. In effect, the government "licenses" an existing set of interest groups. We can expect that lines of conflict will change over time, as old conflicts fade out and new ones arise. It is difficult for the neocorporatist system, with its intricate organizational structure of established and "entitled" interest groups, to adjust to such change. As an example of this problem, one of the more difficult challenges faced by Swedish politics in the last couple of decades was to find a way of providing political expression to the new concern over the advisability of nuclear power and protection of the environment.

In this section we have considered what one might call "cooperative" neocorporatism of the sort typified by politics in the Scandinavian states. Neocorporatism of this sort arises from the desires of the government and the interests to develop consensus and minimize conflict in policymaking. Another form of neocorporatism was found especially in Latin America (Brazil in the 1970s and Perón's Argentina) as well as in Mussolini's dictatorship of Italy. This system is imposed on the interests by the state in order to keep them under its control. Though both types of government are "corporatist" in that the government deals directly with groups, the nature of politics is obviously very different in each.

## POWER AND CHOICE

Of "power and choice," pluralist writers certainly emphasize a "choice" perspective. The public choice—policy—is seen as a balanced outcome of the different pressures of organized interests, almost like a physical equilibrium, and the government is treated rather as an unexamined "black box." Power relations within the government, and espe-

---

[15]This illustrates what is probably the most basic difference between the pluralist and neocorporatist models. Under pluralism, it is assumed that the state apparatus simply responds to the system of interest groups. Under neocorporatism, the state is taken to have a good deal of autonomy; to some extent, it creates the system of interest groups and determines how it operates.

cially the difference in power of various interest groups, tend to be played down in this abstraction.

One might expect that the main alternative abstraction, neocorporatism, would take an opposed side of this great divide, but oddly it, too, embodies more of a "choice" than a "power" perspective—at least in the "cooperative" form we have looked at here. (Where corporatism is analyzed as a tool by which authoritarian governments construct their control of society, the emphasis is obviously more on a "power" perspective.) In its "cooperative" form, neocorporatism is seen as a system in which, as in pluralism, the interests of society in a rather natural way come together to produce their most-preferred mix of policies. The main difference between the two abstractions is in the role accorded government in the process: Under pluralism, the government is a passive receiver of pressures from interests; under neocorporatism, it is seen as a stimulator and shaper of those pressures, and the government itself blends with the system of interest groups. In both abstractions, the production of policy is portrayed as the natural outcome of a process designed to produce public choices. An interesting exercise would be to design an alternative abstraction of interest-group activities in democracies that is based more on a "power" perspective.

### Example: Interest Groups in France

France is a system that probably falls somewhere between the pluralist and neocorporatist models of politics. It also shows interesting peculiarities of its own, especially in a certain looseness and unpredictability of structure. French interest groups are rather fragmented, and compared with groups in other states, they are relatively more likely to engage in provocative violence.

In general, French interest groups have fairly low enrollments from their potential members. Labor unions enroll only about 10 percent of their potential membership, and other sorts of groups have similarly low enrollments.

Furthermore, the organized groups themselves are deeply divided. Frequently several different organizations compete for the same membership, which in other countries would be united behind a single organization. Workers, for instance, are organized in four major, separate unions: the CGT (a communist union with 37 percent of the total union strength), the CFDT (an independent-minded, generally socialist union with 23 percent of the organized workers), Force Ouvrier (a reformist union independent of parties with 15 percent of the organized workers), and the Catholic Confederation (with 4 percent). Independent unions account for the rest.[16] Farmers' interests, which figure importantly in French politics, are divided among no fewer than 500 rural defense organizations at the national level.[17]

French politics at all levels is punctuated by sporadic, intense activity against a general background of cynical disengagement, and this holds as true of interest

---

[16]France, Ministry of the Economy, INSEE, *Données Sociales 1989*, p. 195.
[17]Henry Ehrmann, *Politics in France*, 4th ed. (Boston: Little, Brown, 1983), p. 187.

groups as it does of other aspects of politics. This is most notable in the periodic national crises that engulf France. The most recent of these occurred in May 1968, when a dispute between the students and administration of a provincial university flared up into a national confrontation between students on the one hand and administrators and police on the other. It was marked by the occupation of campuses and pitched battles in the streets. Stimulated by the violence and seeing that the government was floundering in its response to the students, workers all over France went on strike to push their own demands for wage increases and greater control over working conditions. At its height, the strike probably involved half of all employees in France, and it effectively closed the economy down. It was not a tactical move by the union leaders, most of whom opposed the strike, but a spontaneous response by the workers. The combination of battles with the students and paralysis of the economy almost brought the entire system of government down.

It is not only in general crises that groups engage in confrontation. In the events of May 1968, violence and strikes were the result of anomic group activity, but the leaders of organized groups also use violent confrontation from time to time as a deliberate tactic. Farm groups occasionally attract considerable attention by barricading highways or overturning trucks carrying produce they do not wish to see marketed. Over the past decade, for instance, there have been numerous violent incidents involving agricultural imports from Spain. Other groups from which we might not ordinarily expect violence also occasionally tap into it in France. French shopkeepers have engaged in confrontational politics under the leadership of several groups, organizing tax strikes, kidnapping officials, and battling with police.

The incidence of violence on the part of French interest groups should not be taken to suggest that this is the tactic most frequently used by French groups. It is of interest to us because it occurs more frequently in France than in other industrialized states, but most of the time French interest groups spend their energy in less spectacular pursuits—meeting with bureaucrats and elected officials, dealing with potential parties, engaging in court actions, and so on.

In their relations with the government, French interest groups are in some instances bound to the government by formal ties of intimacy of the sort we associate with neocorporatism. But more often interest group and government maintain the sort of distance we expect under pluralism. The agricultural sector comes closest to the neocorporatist model. Not all agricultural interest groups are tied intimately to the government, but one group, the Federation Nationale des Syndicats d'Exploitants Agricoles (FNSEA), has become something like the "official" agricultural group for the government. The FNSEA claims to represent about 55 percent of the French farmers, which is low for a group that is to play a quasiofficial role in the neocorporatist mode, but it is quite respectable by French standards. During the 1970s, the government turned a number of administrative duties over to the FNSEA, including most of the educational and training tasks carried out in other countries by agricultural extension agents. In most areas the government recognized the FNSEA as the sole representative of farming interests.[18]

[18]John T. S. Keeler, cited in Ehrmann, *Politics in France*, pp. 188–189.

**TABLE 12–4**
REPORTED FREQUENCY OF INTEREST-GROUP ACTIONS

|  | Often (Percent) | From time to time (Percent) | Rarely or never (Percent) |
|---|---|---|---|
| Parliamentary lobbying | 32 | 59 | 8 |
| Participation in government committees | 55 | 31 | 14 |
| Formal meetings with government officials | 54 | 32 | 15 |
| Public relations campaigns | 33 | 44 | 23 |
| Informal meetings with government officials | 47 | 29 | 24 |
| Action in the Economic and Social Council | 26 | 26 | 48 |
| Influencing parties and their leaders | 10 | 37 | 53 |
| Demonstrations, strikes, direct action | 13 | 20 | 67 |
| Blocking or sabotaging policy decisions | 10 | 22 | 68 |
| Legal action | 8 | 20 | 72 |

*Source:* Frank L. Wilson, "French Interest Groups: Pluralist or Neocorporatist?" *American Political Science Review* 77 (December 1983): 895–910.

But on the whole, interest groups are not this close to the government. In a 1979 survey, 44 percent of the group leaders reported that they met with government officials only "sometimes," "rarely," or "never," and only 21 percent reported that they did so "almost daily."[19] When one considers that the job of the interest-group leader is after all to influence government policy, this suggests that modest distance is maintained. Similarly, when asked what their most effective means of action was, only 18 percent named participation in government committees or contacts with civil servants. Table 12–4 lists the percentage of interest-group leaders who stated that their groups used specified tactics "often" or "from time to time." It gives a good overall profile of the activity of French interest groups.

### Example: Interest Groups in Japan: Attenuated Neocorporatism

The Japanese system of interest groups is a strongly neocorporatist system. However, it is one that is sharply attenuated, by European standards; labor does not play the important role in the system that we usually see in neocorporatism, and many non-economic groups that we often see in Europe and North America are missing.

The bureaucracy is the key to the Japanese system. The higher civil service in Japan is an elite that is almost autonomous in making policy. It is a well-respected elite, drawing the very best university graduates and trading on the general public scorn for politicians to maintain its independence. Until the early 1980s, the Japanese system was a three-way arrangement among the bureaucracy,

---

[19]The following survey results are drawn from Frank L. Wilson, "French Interest Groups: Pluralist or Neocorporatist?" *American Political Science Review* 77 (December 1983): 895–910.

big business interest groups, and the Liberal Democratic Party, or LDP. Agricultural groups, which were critical to maintaining the LDP in power, played a supporting role in return for subsidies and agricultural trade protection. Business interests gave the LDP the huge amounts of money on which Japanese electoral politics was based ($2.6 billion in 1989), and the LDP cooperated as the bureaucracy and the business interests set up most public policies.[20]

The LDP was the dominant party in a "dominant party system" (see pages 212–214), but since the 1980s it has been losing its dominant position. Public disgust with the system of corruption and "big-money politics" has led to the rise of reform movements, and voters have proved willing to consider alternatives to the LDP, so the party corner of the LDP-business-bureaucracy triangle is now undergoing change. The role of the bureaucracy appears unchanged, however, and may in fact be strengthened because no clear party leadership has yet emerged to take the place of the old LDP hegemony. Interest groups and the bureaucracy mingle closely. As is so often the case in neocorporatist systems, government advisory committees heavily weighted to the bureaucracy and interest groups are quite important in policy-making. And bureaucrats often take high-level positions in the interest groups when they retire from the civil service.

One reason for the dominance of economic interest groups in Japan (at least business groups and agriculture) is that paradoxically, although Japanese society is very oriented to social groups—one's family or factory or association demands intense loyalty and support—the Japanese are rather apathetic about politics and groups formed around political issues. There are few environmental or consumer-oriented groups in Japan, and there is essentially no feminist movement. There are rather important ideological groups on the right, which are anti-labor, honor the Emperor, and refuse to apologize for Japan's role in World War II. As of late 1988, it was estimated that these groups had something over 125,000 members.[21] The left is not as well organized; it is represented primarily by the National Teacher's Union, which is aggressively of the left.

Thus economic groups fill most of the political space: business groups, agricultural groups, and labor. And of these, only the first two figure importantly; until now, labor has been almost excluded from the political process.

There are a large number of business groups in Japan, but one group, the Japanese Federation of Economic Organizations, is generally accepted as speaking on behalf of "business." It actually represents primarily large businesses; its members make up only 1 percent of Japanese firms, but account for 40 percent of all sales.[22] In addition, there are many trade organizations, often for quite specific activities, such as an association for manufacturers of tea services, or an association of manufacturers of pens. And beyond these organizations, much business policy is made by a business leader directly approaching a bureaucrat.

---

[20]Ronald J. Hrebenar and Akira Nakamura, "Japan: Associational Politics in a Group-Oriented Society," in Clive S. Thomas, *First World Interest Groups: A Comparative Perspective* (Westport, Conn.: Greenwood Press, 1993), p. 212.

[21]*Ibid.*, p. 207

[22]*Ibid.*, p. 204.

Agriculture's peak organizations are based on the Agricultural Cooperatives. These are organizations of farmers that have the right to be the sole marketers of rice; they also distribute some services on behalf of the government. As a result, farmers have little choice but to be members of their cooperative; Japanese society is so group-oriented, however, that this does not appear to be viewed as an imposition. The cooperatives have about 8 million members, but their political power is greater even than this would suggest. The old electoral system, now undergoing change in the present mood of reform, gave rural areas undue representation. And the farmers have also proved to be politically flexible. In 1989, for instance, they shifted many of their members' votes to the Socialist party to punish the LDP for being too open to free trade; this was a major reason for the LDP's loss of the upper house of parliament, and it demonstrated to everyone that the Agricultural Cooperatives could not be taken for granted. The power of the agricultural groups is one of the main reasons for Japanese-American tensions over trade; political leaders are very reluctant to open up the Japanese market to American agriculture products.

T. J. Pempel has dubbed the Japanese system "corporatism without labor."[23] Most Japanese workers are organized in company unions, not industry-wide unions, and these organizations tend to be less politically active and more compliant, and to look to their companies' interests. The main exception is the public employees' unions, such as the National Teachers' Union. But these unions have been marginalized in Japan's generally conservative society because they are quite far to the left on almost all issues. Labor is also split into two main organizations, one based mainly on company unions and the other based on the public employees' unions. As a result, political leadership in Japan has been able to safely ignore labor on most issues.

Change is in the wind in Japan, however. Scandals have publicized the reliance of parties, especially the LDP, on large illegal contributions of cash. (One recent scandal involved a bribe so large that the firm's secretary had to use a supermarket cart to carry the cash across a parking lot.) The electoral system has been changed, and reformers claim that they will change the system of campaign finance. The two labor organizations combined in a cooperative political movement in 1989, to some effect. So this may be a system in transition. On the other hand, the Japanese culture still reveres scholarly "nonpolitical" authority such as that of the bureaucrats. And Japan still sees much of its post-war prosperity as having been accomplished by an alliance between government and business. So it is not clear just where things will end up.

## FURTHER READING

Ball, A., and Millard, F. *Pressure Politics in Industrial Societies*. Atlantic Highlands, N.J.: Humanities Press International, 1987.

Bauer, Raymond A.; de Sola Pool, Ithiel; and Dexter, Lewis A. *American Business and Public Policy*. New York: Atherton, 1963.

[23]T. J. Pempel and Keiichi Tsunekawa, "Corporatism Without Labor? The Japanese Anomaly," in Philippe Schmitter and Gerhard Lehmbruch, eds., *Trends Toward Corporatist Intermediation* (Beverly Hills, Calif.: Sage, 1979).

Berger, Suzanne, ed. *Organizing Interests in Western Europe: Pluralism, Corporatism, and the Transformation of Politics.* Cambridge, England: Cambridge University Press, 1981.

Goodman, David S. G., ed. *Groups and Politics in the People's Republic of China.* Armonk, N.Y.: M. E. Sharpe, 1984.

Lehmbruch, Gerhard, and Schmitter, Philippe C., eds. *Patterns of Corporatist Policy-Making.* Beverly Hills, Calif.: Sage, 1982.

Loomis, Burdett A., and Cigler, Allan J., eds. *Interest Group Politics.* Washington, D.C.: Congressional Quarterly, Inc., 1983.

Mansbridge, Jane J. *Why We Lost the ERA.* Chicago: University of Chicago Press, 1986.

Moe, Terry. *The Organization of Interests.* Chicago: University of Chicago Press, 1980.

O'Donnell, Guillermo. *Modernization and Bureaucratic Authoritarianism: Studies in South American Politics.* Berkeley: Institute of International Studies, University of California Press, 1973.

Olson, Mancur. *The Logic of Collective Action.* Cambridge, Mass.: Harvard University Press, 1965.

———. *The Rise and Decline of Nations: Economic Growth, Stagflation and Social Rigidities.* New Haven: Yale University Press, 1982.

Ornstein, Norman J., and Elder, Shirley. *Interest Groups, Lobbying and Policymaking.* Washington, D.C.: Congressional Quarterly Press, 1978.

Salisbury, Robert. "An Exchange Theory of Interest Groups." *Midwest Journal of Political Science* 13 (February 1969): 1–32.

Schlozman, Kay Lehman, and Tierney, John T. *Organized Interests and American Democracy.* New York: Harper & Row, 1986.

Scott, James C. *Weapons of the Weak: Everyday Forms of Peasant Resistance.* New Haven: Yale University Press, 1985.

Skilling, H. Gordon, and Griffiths, Franklyn, eds. *Interest Groups in Soviet Politics.* Princeton, N.J.: Princeton University Press, 1971.

Thomas, Clive S. *First World Interest Groups: A Comparative Perspective.* Westport, Conn.: Greenwood Press, 1993.

Truman, David B. *The Governmental Process.* 2nd ed. New York: Knopf, 1971.

Walker, Jack L., Jr. *Mobilizing Interest Groups in America.* Ann Arbor: University of Michigan Press, 1991.

Wilson, Frank L. "French Interest Groups: Pluralist or Neocorporatist?" *American Political Science Review* 77 (December 1983): 895–910.

Wilson, James Q. *Political Organizations.* New York: Basic Books, 1973.

# 13

---

# NATIONAL
# DECISION-MAKING
# INSTITUTIONS:
# PARLIAMENTARY
# GOVERNMENT

---

In this and the following chapter we shall examine formal arrangements for governing democracies. This chapter will deal with "parliamentary" government, while Chapter 14 will deal with "presidential" government. Parliamentary government is conceptually the simpler of the two and is the form found in most democracies. It will seem unusual to many American readers, however, since the United States is one of the handful of democracies that operates with a presidential system.

The basic principles of a pure parliamentary system are as follows:

**1** A parliament of representatives is elected by the citizens of the state. It normally consists of anything from two hundred or so to several hundred representatives. The parliament is the only elected body in the state. Bills passed by the parliament are the law, and no one can overrule them.

**2** The executive power of the state (managing the bureaucracy, conducting relations with other states, etc.) is lodged with a *cabinet* of women and men who are selected by the parliament to conduct the affairs of the state. Most or all members of the cabinet are usually members of the parliament who take on executive responsibilities in addition to their legislative chores.

**3** The cabinet retains executive power only as long as it has the "confidence" of the parliament, that is, only as long as it can command a majority of the votes. At any time, a majority vote in the parliament may unseat a cabinet and cause a new set of people to be selected as a cabinet. This is referred to as the "government falling." Or, if no vote is actually taken to unseat the cabinet but the cabinet finds that it is unable to put together majorities to pass its important bills, it is expected that the cabinet will resign.

**4** Just as the parliament holds the cabinet in jeopardy, the leader of the cabinet (called variously "premier," "prime minister," "chancellor," etc.) normally has the right to have the parliament disbanded, forcing a new election that will lead to a new distribution of power.

This, in a nutshell, is parliamentary government. We shall examine some finer points and some variations below, but these four principles are basic. It is a simpler form than presidential government because it does not allow for any separation of powers. The parliament, and the cabinet that operates only by the support of the parliament, hold all the state's governmental political power.

With this simple concentration of power, political decisions should in principle be made clearly and directly, with a minimum of delay. The cabinet and the parliament should always be in agreement on important issues—if they were not, presumably the cabinet would fall—and their will cannot be blocked by a court or any other body.

Such a system has two special advantages and disadvantages.

### Advantages

1. Because power is unified, the government can respond fairly directly to changed circumstances. For example, parliamentary systems were more successful than fragmented systems such as the United States at developing national energy policies in response to the shortages of oil in the 1970s. In a parliamentary system, all it takes to make a law is a majority of the votes in the parliament, and so it is a rather straightforward thing for the party or parties in power to develop a policy and write it into law. In more fragmented systems like that of the United States, many barriers are raised that can slow down or halt the passage of a law. The president may veto the law, the Supreme Court may rule it unconstitutional, states may have proper jurisdiction over it, and so on.

2. A second advantage to a parliamentary system is that the lines of responsibility for policymaking are clear. Elections should mean more, because voters can know exactly whom to blame for their current situation: the party or parties in power. Parties can be held pretty well to their election promises once they are in office, because then there is nothing to prevent them from accomplishing what they had said they would do. In a more fragmented system like that of the United States, this is not so. There are so many independent centers of power that an unhappy policy cannot be blamed on any one of them. The president can say that Congress did it, Congress can point to the Supreme Court, and so on. President Harry Truman was famous for his desk-top slogan, "The buck stops here"; but in 1948 he campaigned across the country on the theme that the "do-nothing" Congress, which was controlled by the Republican party, was to blame for his not having accomplished his goals as president. Elections simply can mean more with regard to public policy in a parliamentary system than in a more fragmented system because once election results are in, the party or parties that have won control of the parliament have no excuse for not enacting the policies they had promised.

### Disadvantages

1. In a parliamentary system there are few protections for a minority that feels it is being wronged. In a presidential system, a minority may hope that even if it has lost its

fight in the legislature, it may retrieve things with the president, or vice versa. As a result, the support of a bare majority is generally not enough to get a law enacted.

This may be seen as either an advantage or a disadvantage. It is, in fact, the flip side of the advantage noted above, that in a parliamentary system policy-making is straightforward. Though this is in general a good thing, it is clear that there must be some times when we would wish that the government had been slowed down and had been prevented from taking hasty action or action that did not have fairly broad support. A parliamentary system, because of its efficiency, does not do this.

2. A second disadvantage to the parliamentary system is that it *may* produce unstable government. I have spoken above of the "party or parties" that control a parliament. If no one party holds a majority of the seats, then two or more parties must form a *coalition* to control the parliament. In forming a coalition, they will divide up the positions of the cabinet among themselves (party A gets to name the premier, the minister of economics, the foreign minister, and the minister for agriculture; party B gets to name the minister for defense and the minister for industry, etc.). In the parliament, they agree that their combined parties' votes will always be cast on behalf of legislation proposed by the cabinet.

This is fine if the partners of the coalition are in general agreement on most issues. But if the coalition is strictly a marriage of convenience and the parties in it disagree on enough things, it may be hard to keep them together and cooperating for very long. A socialist party may pull out because the coalition has not been able to agree on a program to stimulate employment, a Hindu party may pull out over a question of religious policy, or whatever. At that point the government "falls," and a new coalition must be negotiated.

If this happens only occasionally, it is no problem. Political change obviously must come from time to time. But in a parliamentary system it sometimes happens that the numerical strength of the parties and their relationships with each other are such that it is always difficult to keep a coalition together. This may lead to a paralyzing succession of governmental breakups, in which governmental control is so unstable that people lose confidence in the whole process. Germany suffered from this problem from 1918 to 1933, when Hitler overthrew the weakened democracy. France suffered from it until 1958, when the military intervened and imposed a presidential system. Italy has suffered from it chronically since 1945; in fifty-one years (as of 1996) Italians have had fifty-five different governments. On the other hand most parliamentary systems have not had this problem. The Scandinavian countries, the Low Countries, Germany, and others have had long histories of generally stable government by coalitions.

## CABINET CONTROL

If parliamentary government is to function smoothly, the cabinet must be able to control what goes on in the parliament. If a cabinet could be voted out casually just because the mood of the parliament had changed, no one would find that a satisfactory situation; government would be far too unstable. Particularly if the cabinet is based on a coalition of parties, the basis for bargaining on the makeup of the cabinet is the number of votes each party can deliver. If the cabinet was, in fact, not able to count regularly on the votes of one or another of the parties, the rest of the coalition would feel cheated and the coalition would not last long. As it happens, this is a large part of the problem in Italy; the Christian Democratic party has been an important part of every coalition since 1945, but it is a fragmented party and has never been able to guarantee its parliamentary support very well.

On the basis of this reasoning, we might expect to see, in the many smoothly functioning parliamentary systems, that the cabinets dominate their parliaments. This is indeed the case. The usual situation is that legislation is proposed by the cabinet and is *debated* in the parliament; after all, it is only there that the opposition parties have their innings. But aside from the addition of minor amendments, there is rarely any question but that the legislation will be passed by the parliament. In effect, the parliament is a rubber stamp for the cabinet.

It is ironic that a body that is elected by the parliament and can be brought down at any time by it—a body that is, in effect, created by the parliament—can turn around and control what the parliament does. It is readily understandable that this should be the case, however, if we recall that the members of the cabinet are top leaders of their parties. They are skillful politicians, and they have every reason to find ways to control what happens in the parliament so as to protect the power they enjoy as cabinet members.

In Chapter 11 we saw that a side effect of political parties was that, as organizations, they bind a number of people together and provide a channel by which some of those people can control others. It is by this channel that cabinets control their parliaments. The members of a cabinet participate in parliamentary debates; they vote in parliament; but most important, they are leaders or powerful members of their party organizations in the parliament. For the other members, the party provides the avenue for advancement in the parliament. Debate time, committee assignments, the chance of a cabinet post someday—all these are controlled for members of parliament by their party. Those who do not cooperate with their party's leaders generally do not advance. It is by this source of discipline, in their capacity as the leaders of their party, that the cabinet are able to impose their will on the parliament.

## WHAT DOES A PARLIAMENT DO?

Because it is so controlled by the cabinet, the governmental role of a parliament is difficult for students from the United States to appreciate. With regard to the passage of legislation, most parliaments are indeed "rubber stamps." From 1945 to 1978, for instance, of bills that the British cabinet submitted to the House of Commons for consideration, 97 percent were approved by the House. And amendments to bills are also tightly controlled by the cabinet in Britain. From 1967 to 1971, the cabinet proposed 1,772 amendments to various bills; of these, 1,770 were approved. By contrast, other members of the House proposed 4,198 amendments during the same period, but only 210 of these passed.[1]

---

[1]Rose, Richard, "Still the Era of Party Government," *Parliamentary Affairs* 36 (Summer 1983); 284–285.

## "DELEGATE" AND "TRUSTEE" MODELS OF REPRESENTATION

An enduring debate in political science centers on what role representatives should assume vis-à-vis their constituents. In the "delegate" model, they should regard themselves as simply speaking for the constituents and should cast each vote as they think the constituents would wish it to be cast. In the "trustee" model, it is assumed that representatives learn more about an issue than any of their constituents could possibly know and have also been chosen on the basis of their superior judgment; we would then expect that on at least a few occasions they would vote differently than their constituents would wish them to vote.

Edmund Burke put the case for the trustee model beautifully in a speech to the electors of Bristol on November 3, 1774, after they had chosen him to represent them:

Certainly, gentlemen, it ought to be the happiness and glory of a representative to live in the strictest union, the closest correspondence, and the most unreserved communication with his constituents. Their wishes ought to have great weight with him; their opinion, high respect; their business, unremitted attention. It is his duty to sacrifice his repose, his pleasures, his satisfactions, to theirs; and above all, ever, and in all cases, to prefer their interest to his own. But his unbiased opinion, his mature judgment, his enlightened conscience, he ought not to sacrifice to you, to any man, or to any set of men living. These he does not derive from your pleasure; no, nor from the law and the constitution. They are a trust from Providence, for the abuse of which he is deeply answerable. Your representative owes you, not his industry only, but his judgment; and he betrays, instead of serving you, if he sacrifices it to your opinion.

My worthy colleague says, his will ought to be subservient to yours. If that be all, the thing is innocent. If government were a matter of will upon any side, yours, without question, ought to be superior. But government and legislation are matters of reason and judgment, and not of inclination; and what sort of reason is that, in which the determination precedes the discussion; in which one set of men deliberate, and another decide; and where those who form the conclusion are perhaps three hundred miles distant from those who hear the arguments?

To deliver an opinion, is the right of all men; that of constituents is a weighty and respectable opinion, which a representative ought always to rejoice to hear; and which he ought always most seriously to consider. But *authoritative* instructions; *mandates* issued, which the member is bound blindly and implicitly to obey, to vote, and to argue for, though contrary to the clearest conviction of his judgment and conscience,—these are things utterly unknown to the laws of this land, and which arise from a fundamental mistake of the whole order and tenor of our constitution.

---

It is apparent that whatever things parliaments do, deciding what legislation is to become law is not chief among them. In the unified governmental arrangement of a parliamentary system, it is expected that the executive and legislative parts of government will work together to make legislation; and because over the years cabinets have learned to protect themselves by controlling their parliaments, it is by now generally accepted that cabinets call the tune in designing laws.

Is parliament then a useless appendage? No, because it still serves a number of purposes that are similar to those of the U.S. Congress, and one further purpose that is peculiar to parliamentary systems.

First, a parliament furnishes a forum for the public debate of bills. The opposition parties have a chance, before a bill is passed into law, to present their position on it and to stimulate public discussion.

Second, a parliament is a place where a bill that the cabinet wants to enact into law is submitted to detailed scrutiny by the friends of the cabinet as well as by its enemies. It may well be that a number of small problems may be uncovered in a complicated bill, problems that the cabinet is happy to have brought to its attention. In the British example above, almost all of the 1,772 amendments introduced by the cabinet were amendments to its *own bills*, since virtually no legislation is considered by the House of Commons except legislation submitted by the cabinet. Most of those amendments were cabinet responses to problems that were brought to their attention in the course of parliamentary consideration of their bills.

Third, a parliament is one of the few parts of the governmental apparatus that has an interest in keeping a critical eye on how the cabinet is administering public policy. The opposition parties are especially eager participants in this, for obvious reasons, but there is also a general tradition that the cabinet must report regularly to the parliament how it is managing the affairs of the state. This sort of accounting takes many forms. In most parliamentary systems, there is some sort of annual speech made to the parliament describing in broad outlines the state of things and the cabinet's plans for the coming year. In addition, many parliaments use a device called "question time," in which various cabinet members appear regularly to answer questions from other members of the parliament about the way their ministry is being run. The answers they give may spark lively debates.

This third function of parliaments—watching what the executive part of the government does—is not generally met as well in parliamentary as in presidential systems. The reason is that committees are not generally very strong in parliaments, as will be seen below. Committees in a legislature may provide a powerful site for overseeing the executive. They are groups of legislators who specialize in a particular area of policy and who may become quite expert in it over the years. Furthermore, if they have a good professional staff, they may be able to match the offices of the executive in expertise and in the ability to handle evidence. If the committee can hold hearings and subpoena witnesses, it can provide a strong investigative force. But committees in parliamentary systems are generally weak, and so the oversight function devolves primarily on individual members of the parliament, who are usually not much of a match for the experts of the executive office.

From the discussion up to this point, it might seem that a parliament is a poor fish indeed. It has little control over legislation except inasmuch as the cabinet can be persuaded to amend its own bills, and it is not as powerful in oversight of the executive as legislatures elsewhere. The one thing we have so far noted that it does well is to conduct public debate of bills. All in all, this looks meager as compared, say, with the Congress of the United States. But there is another function of parliaments that is peculiar to parliamentary systems.

The fourth function of a parliament in a parliamentary system is to provide a pool of trained people for service in the executive and a setting in which they operate while serving in the executive; a legislature like the U.S. Congress does not do this. In most parliamentary systems, nearly all members of the cabinet and other political appointments in the executive are members of parliament. In Britain at any given time, about two hundred members of the House of Commons are serving in such positions as prime minister, minister for defense, first lord of the admiralty, other cabinet positions, or lesser executive positions such as parliamentary secretary to the minister for defense. All of these are members from the party that has a majority in the House, and so at the same time something like another two hundred members of the opposition parties are hoping for electoral success that will give *their* parties control of parliament and put them into executive positions. Thus, at any given time, about two-thirds of the members of the House of Commons either hold executive positions or are waiting for them.

The members of the political executive in a parliamentary system are men and women who have been selected by the other members of their party for executive tasks, and that selection is based largely on how well they have performed in debate and other tasks in the House. They are selected after some years of service in the House, which, like any organization, imposes norms of behavior on its members and in many subtle ways changes their behavior and the manner in which they react to things. Once they are in executive positions, these people are still sitting members of the House and take part in its daily business of debate, voting on bills, and so on. Even while they hold executive office, they rub shoulders daily with their colleagues in the House.

Thus an important task of parliament in a parliamentary system is to produce those who will hold executive office, train them in the ways of politics, select them, and then serve as the site from which they conduct the executive functions. In a presidential system, the legislative part of government exercises its strength in *opposing* the executive; but in a parliamentary system, it exercises its strength *through* the executive.

## THE LIFE OF A MEMBER OF PARLIAMENT

What is it like to serve in such a body? Consider the situation of a young member of the British House of Commons:

> In the 1974 general election, Mr. Dorrell offered himself as the Conservatives' sacrificial lamb in the solidly Labor dockside district of East Hull. "They want you to make your first mistakes in an area where it doesn't matter," he remarks. "But you make them all over again where it does."
>
> Then in 1976, he was chosen out of 105 applicants for what he saw as the "reasonably winnable" seat in Loughborough, a pleasantly diversified manufacturing and farming district in the East Midlands, about 120 miles north of London. The local party organization didn't particularly care for his youth and bachelorhood—he will be married in September—but his energy and articulateness carried the day. Once nominated, he bought a house in the district.
>
> In a typical parliamentary week, Mr. Dorrell first reads the morning papers in his small apartment a few minutes' walk from Westminster. Most MPs have some quarters, from a shared apartment to an elegant town house, "within the sound of the bells"; when the bells ring for a Commons vote, as they may a dozen times a night, MPs have eight minutes to get to the voting "lobbies."

### Routine Work

After breakfast he is off to the tiny, sparsely furnished office he shares with another Tory freshman, Timothy Eggar, a block from Parliament. His secretary is two floors away in a crowded office shared with other secretaries. Mornings usually go to correspondence and constituent work or research for a magazine or a speech to a private group (junior MPs don't get many chances to speak on the Commons floor). Or there may be a routine committee meeting, where Mr. Dorrell's main role is to vote periodically for government motions to speed a bill along.

Afternoons bring more tiresome committee work, and for the rest of the day he may sit around the House chamber, the tearoom or a dinner table discussing problems with other backbenchers. With the late-night sessions and frequent votes, MPs don't have much of a London social life.

Few members attend the unconsequential Friday sessions, so on most Fridays Mr. Dorrell drives 2 1/2 hours to Worcester, where the family business is, and later another hour and a half to Loughborough "to talk to any group that wants to hear me." After the Saturday "surgery," he stops by a local fair or other social gathering. Sunday he tries to keep free for family or friends.

Why would anyone put up with such drudgery? The obvious reason must be that it is through good soldiering in the supporting role that one may advance to interesting and powerful positions in the executive.

## PARLIAMENTARY COMMITTEES

Committees of the U.S. House of Representatives and Senate are well known as independent, bristly bodies that presidents, bureaucrats, and even other members of the Congress defy only at their own risk. The State Department quivered in the 1950s when the House UnAmerican Affairs Committee investigated some of its younger personnel. Most bills that are introduced in the U.S. Congress are killed by a committee that refuses to vote them out with a recommendation, or else they die through delay in committees. This is true of many bills originating in the presidential office as well as those that are projects of individual members of Congress.[2]

Such independent bodies within a parliament would greatly weaken the central unity of parliament with the executive, because as independent sources of power the committees would make it more difficult for the executive leaders to control what happened in the parliament. For a parliamentary system to work well, power must as much as possible be lodged with the leaders of the parties and no one else.

For this reason, committees of a parliament are generally a good deal weaker and less assertive than those in the U.S. Congress. All parliaments must have committees, of course. If hundreds of bills are to be submitted to a parliament in a year, the work of scrutinizing those bills carefully must be divided up among the membership in some way or other; there is simply not time for each member of the parliament to do a careful job on all bills that come down in a year. But care is generally taken that the committees do not operate too independently in doing their work.

As an extreme example of this, consider committees in the British House of Commons. Where the U.S. Congress uses "standing committees"—such as the Committee

---

[2]For example, see Bruce I. Oppenheimer's analysis of the role of congressional committees in blocking President Carter's attempt to form a new energy policy. Lawrence C. Dodd and Bruce I. Oppenheimer, *Congress Reconsidered*, 2nd ed. (Washington, D.C.: Congressional Quarterly, Inc. 1981), pp. 275–295.

Debate in the Canadian House of Commons. (Canapress Photo Service)

on Foreign Affairs, with a set group of members who serve for years and may become quite expert in the areas of policy that they cover—the British set up an ad hoc committee for each bill as it comes in. The members of this committee are not people who regularly work together; they have been put together just to consider this bill. They have not had years of specialized experience in a particular area of policy. They cannot subpoena witnesses and, in fact, do not hold open hearings on their bill. They have no permanent staff. As one might imagine, their ability to transform legislation and put their own stamp on it is quite limited. The cabinet need not fear that its bill will be stopped or mangled by a committee in the House of Commons.

Other parliamentary systems are not so extreme. It is generally more convenient to use standing committees, so that a new group does not have to be constituted for each bill. Even the British, in recent years, have set up limited standing committees for the House of Commons (to oversee the executive and bureaucracy, not to review proposed bills). But in smoothly working systems, standing committees still do not operate with the independence of the committees in the U.S. Congress.

## EXCEPTIONS TO PARLIAMENTARY SUPREMACY

We have described here a "pure case" of parliamentarism, which is probably not met with exactly in any country of the world, although Great Britain comes close. Most parliamentary systems have incorporated one institution or another that divides the political power of the state and thus compromises the principle of parliamentary supremacy. For instance, Germany, Canada, India, and some other parliamentary systems are federal states; this means that important areas of policy are taken out of the hands of the cabinet and parliament. Germany and some other parliamentary systems tolerate fairly strong and independent committees in parliament. A few parliamentary systems—Austria and Germany are two examples—have courts that can overrule an act of parliament; we will look at this in more detail in Chapter 14.

In these and other ways, most parliamentary systems incorporate a few exceptions to the basic principles listed at the opening of this chapter. They are still "parliamentary systems," however.

## PARLIAMENTS IN NONDEMOCRATIC SYSTEMS

Many states that are not parliamentary systems as described above still have a parliamentary body. We saw in Chapter 10 that many nondemocratic systems have found it

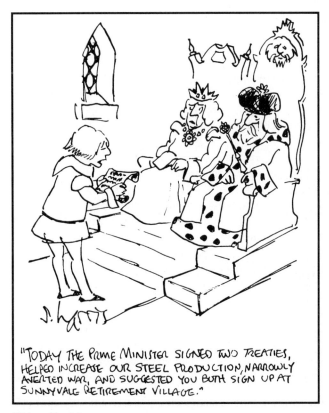

"TODAY THE PRIME MINISTER SIGNED TWO TREATIES, HELPED INCREASE OUR STEEL PRODUCTION, NARROWLY AVERTED WAR, AND SUGGESTED YOU BOTH SIGN UP AT SUNNYVALE RETIREMENT VILLAGE."

(Sidney Harris)

useful to hold elections for a variety of reasons; similarly, many of them find it useful to have a parliament. All a parliament is, after all, is a set of people who are designated to represent other groups of people, usually with some sort of geographic focus to the represented groups. It is not necessary that the parliament be able to operate independently or that it have discretion over laws. It can still sit and do a number of things.

The former Soviet Union's parliament, for instance, was the Supreme Soviet. In the Soviet system, almost all governmental decisions were taken elsewhere, within the Communist party, and the parliament was set up so that it could not be a rival to the party. The parliament met only twice a year for just a few days. It spent most of its time hearing long reports from the Central Committee of the party, reports that it ratified unanimously by a show of hands. A sizable number of the members were not members of the Communist party, but few of them were repeaters from the preceding parliament. This made it unlikely that they would have the experience or confidence to act independently. Selection to the parliament was generally a token of honor for good citizenship in one's community, factory, or collective farm.

This parliament looks to us to have been a triviality, yet the Soviet Union made a great fuss about it. It was one of the chief bodies to result from the elections they conducted so enthusiastically, and they set great store by it. It must have been doing something, but what?

One thing it did was to serve as a symbol of a unified nation. As you recall, the Soviet Union sprawled over a vast area in which a number of different languages were spoken. The people of the Soviet Union ranged from nomadic deer herders in the north to Moslems in the south and very European peoples on the Baltic coast. A parliament that drew individuals from all the regions of the country and was further drawn so as to give extensive play to such groups in the population as women, peasants, and blue-collar workers could serve as a potent symbol of a unified population. This helps to explain the amount of fuss that was made over it as the Soviet authorities advertised this symbol of unity.

The Supreme Soviet also served other purposes. One need of the Soviet regime was to provide means for complaints and suggestions from the population at large to work their way into the decision-making process. We saw in an earlier chapter that the Communist party itself served this need quite actively, but the members of the Supreme Soviet were also expected to be alert to problems of their constituents, and they could bring these to the attention of appropriate ministries in speeches, if they were able to get the floor, or through less formal means. The Supreme Soviet, like the Communist party itself, served as a useful conduit for popular feeling in a governmental system that did not permit either a free press or the formation of organizations that might serve as rival foci of power.[3]

## CONCLUSION

We have presented here a form of government, parliamentary government, that is closely approximated in a majority of democracies. Its two central principles are that

---

[3]A good review is Stephen White, "The U.S.S.R. Supreme Soviet: A Developmental Perspective," *Legislative Studies Quarterly* 5 (May 1980): 247–274.

power is unified rather than divided and that it is lodged with a democratically elected parliament and a cabinet that is formed from and works within that parliament.

An irony of parliamentary government is that for members of the parliament who are not serving in its cabinet or in executive posts associated with the cabinet, this unity makes their job rather dull. Unlike a divided system like that of the United States, their main job is not to *decide* whether the cabinet should be doing what it is doing and writing the laws it is writing. That decision has been pretty well taken care of by the basic decision of the parties in the parliament to install this particular cabinet and not to bring it down. It follows that the cabinet's bills must almost always be passed in the end, or else the cabinet would fall. The task of ordinary members of the parliament, then, is to operate on the edges of bills as they come in, to discuss their merits, to suggest amendments that the cabinet may choose to accept, to question members of the cabinet on what they are doing, and—all the while—to groom themselves for eventual participation in cabinets of the future.

### Example: Parlimentary Government in India

 The general constitutional arrangement chosen for the new state of India in 1947 was largely drawn from the British parliamentary models, but a few devices were also borrowed from the United States. As is the case with any new state, including the United States itself in the early nineteenth century, India provides an interesting example of the evolution of governmental structure through custom and practice. It has taken the first four decades of politics in India to straighten out the relative power of the various parts of the government.

In the general outline of its constitution, India has a parliament consisting of two houses: The lower house is the Lok Sabha, or Council of the People, and the upper house is the Council of the States. A powerful prime minister and cabinet are responsible to the Lok Sabha, and a rather weak president oversees the whole structure. Thus far, India is a fairly standard parliamentary system, but it departs from common practice in two ways: (1) It is a federal system, with state governments which have a good deal of programmatic discretion, and (2) it has a powerful Supreme Court that can overturn actions of the rest of the government.

India is a state that faced grave problems on independence. Its people are among the poorest in the world, with an average annual income per person of $330. This places the country among the twenty most impoverished states of the world. At the same time, India's population of 846 million makes it the second largest state in the world and an important power on the international stage. India is deeply divided internally along lines of religion and language, with three major religions (Hindu, Sikh, and Moslem) and over fifteen major languages.

Until 1947, India was a colony of Great Britain. The pacifist leader Mohandas K. Gandhi and his Congress party led a prolonged movement for independence, which succeeded in 1947. The Congress party dominated early elections in the young democracy, and it was only in 1977 that an opposition coalition was able to break

Congress's hold on power. Until 1989 a somewhat changed Congress party ruled under Prime Minister Rajiv Gandhi, but a non-Congress coalition replaced him then and ruled until the 1991 elections. In those elections, marked by the tragic assassination of Gandhi, Congress regained control. At this point the situation is clearly one of competition, rather than a dominant-party system.

Against this background, let us look at the development of India's governmental institutions and particularly the Lok Sabha. One important issue that had to be worked out in practice over the early decades of independence was the power of the president, who is elected by an electoral college consisting of the members of both houses of Parliament plus the members of the state legislatures. Thus it is conceivable that a president could be of a different party than the party that controlled the Lok Sabha and cabinet. The written constitution initially gave the president broad powers—among others, the power to rule by decree when Parliament was not in session, to declare a state of emergency and rule directly, and to dissolve Parliament or any state government and declare new elections. It might have happened that a strong, independent presidency would have evolved in India.

However, the dominance of the Congress party ensured that this did not happen. Since Congress controlled both houses of Parliament and most state governments, a series of Congress party presidents were selected by electoral colleges. And the prime ministers, who were leaders of the Congress party, made certain that weak and unaggressive people, who would be willing to do what the prime minister told them to do, were put into the presidency. Thus the presidency developed into an office much like that of the queen in Great Britain. In a formal sense, all of the powers enumerated above are the president's, but the president will exercise them only on the advice of the prime minister. This was formalized in an amendment to the constitution in 1976, stating that the president "shall" act in accordance with the advice of the cabinet and prime minister. The practice was fixed even more firmly during a constitutional crisis the next year. In 1977, the Janata coalition won a majority of seats in the Lok Sabha and put its own cabinet into place. This cabinet asked the president—B. D. Jatti, of the Congress party—to dissolve the legislatures of the nine states which had Congress majorities and force new elections in those states. He hesitated for a day in doing what the cabinet requested, amid demonstrations and uproar, but finally gave in. Thus the cabinet's supremacy over the president was established by something more dependable than words in a constitution; it was established by practice and precedent.

A second important question that had to be settled during this period was the relative power of Parliament and its cabinet vis-à-vis the Supreme Court. This question came to a point of crisis in 1967, when the Supreme Court ruled that an earlier amendment under which government land reforms were being administered was itself unconstitutional because it violated the Fundamental Rights guaranteed elsewhere in the constitution.[4] (Among other things, the Fundamental Rights guarantee a right against the expropriation of property.) Thus, the government could not consti-

---

[4]Under the Indian constitution, Parliament is responsible for initiating amendments to the constitution. Many sorts of amendment can be passed by a simple majority in both houses, while certain sensitive areas require a two-thirds majority in both houses. Ratification by half the states is then necessary for the amendment to become law.

tutionally carry out land reform programs of the sort it wanted, and there was no way in which the constitution could be amended that would allow it to do so. In effect, the Court ruled that the Fundamental Rights constituted a special part of the constitution that was above all parliamentary action.

As one might expect, this ruling caused considerable uproar. Over the next few years, the Court held to its position that the Fundamental Rights occupied a special place in the constitution and struck down various acts of Parliament in their name. A crisis was finally reached in 1971, when Prime Minister Indira Gandhi, frustrated at her inability to pass her reform programs, asked the president to dissolve the Lok Sabha and call for new elections. The single theme of this election was the question of parliamentary supremacy over the Court. When her Congress party swept to victory with 352 of the 518 seats in the Lok Sabha, the prime minister had a popular mandate to establish Parliament as supreme. Parliament amended the constitution with this simple addition:

> Notwithstanding anything in this constitution, Parliament may, in exercise of its constituent power, amend by way of addition, variation or repeal, any provision of this Constitution in accordance with the procedure laid down in this Article.

The next year this amendment was challenged in the Supreme Court. After the longest series of arguments ever heard there, the Court gave in and sustained Parliament's right to amend any part of the constitution.

Between these two developments—the establishment of the supremacy of Parliament and its cabinet first over the president and then over the Supreme Court—a basically parliamentary framework similar to that of Britain's was ensured. A third crisis was required, however, to establish firmly the principle of democratic government itself. In 1975, Prime Minister Indira Gandhi was found guilty in a state court of minor campaign irregularities. While her case was pending appeal in the Supreme Court, the opposition parties in Parliament, and some members of her own party, pressed her to resign as prime minister. To forestall such efforts, Mrs. Gandhi struck first. She persuaded the president to declare a state of emergency so that she could rule dictatorially through him. She then had most of the leaders of the opposition arrested, banned a number of opposition organizations, and introduced a considerable degree of censorship for the press. In all, perhaps 50,000 people were arrested for political reasons.[5]

This crisis for democracy was resolved in 1977, when Mrs. Gandhi called for a new election to the Lok Sabha. Presumably, she thought that her party would win this election, but in a massive rejection of her seizure of power, the voters reduced the Congress party to 153 out of the 543 seats in the Lok Sabha. Congress was out of power for the first time since 1945. Though Congress and Indira Gandhi returned to power in 1980 after the opposition parties had proved incapable of governing effectively, the point had been made.[6] The 1977 election was a strong reaffirmation by the Indian people of their desire for democratic government.

---

[5]D. C. Gupta, *Indian Government and Politics*, 4th ed. (New Delhi: Vikas, 1978), p. 657.

[6]Indira Gandhi was assassinated in 1984 by her Sikh bodyguards, as a result of tensions with militant Sikhs. Her son Rajiv took her place as prime minister and leader of the Congress party, but he was in turn assassinated in 1991, by Tamil separatists.

To focus more specifically on the Parliament of India and how it operates, let us first note that the upper house, the Council of States, has less power than the lower house. This is typical of parliamentary systems; another good example is the British House of Lords, whose mainly hereditary members have the power only to delay, not block, bills passed by the House of Commons. The members of the Council of States are not directly elected by voters, which would give them more prestige and legitimacy, but rather are chosen by the state legislatures and are sent to the Council of States to represent their states. Most bills require the Council of States' assent to become law, but there is an important limitation on this power. No money bills, including the annual budget and all tax laws, require the assent of the Council of States. The Council discusses each money bill and may make suggestions to the Lok Sabha, but the Lok Sabha has sole authority to pass the bill. Finally, the most important of all limitations on the power of the Council of States is that the prime minister and cabinet are responsible only to the lower house. This is almost universally true of parliamentary systems. It means that the prime minister and cabinet require the support of a majority of the Lok Sabha to exercise their power (they can be ousted at any time by a majority vote on a motion of "no confidence"), but they cannot be ousted by the Council of States.

The Lok Sabha plays a role much like that of the House of Commons in Britain. It has full powers to pass or deny legislation, and the cabinet depends on it for its power. However, because of party discipline, the Lok Sabha is controlled by the cabinet and its members do not feel individually all that powerful. From 1989 to 1991, for instance, of 81 bills introduced by the cabinet, 63 were passed; of 156 bills introduced by individual members, not one was passed.[7]

Aside from the usual informal cabinet domination of Parliament via party discipline, the Indian constitution also gives the cabinet some formal powers that allow it further to dominate the parliament. The most important of these is the power to rule by decree when Parliament is not sitting. This was originally intended to allow for small matters that might need immediate attention when Parliament was not in session, but cabinets have come to use it as a device for taking measures they are not sure they could get through Parliament. Such actions as wage freezes, excise taxes, and rules to regulate smuggling have become law in this way, sometimes just days before or after Parliament was in session.

Still, the Lok Sabha functions importantly as a place for debate and one where the opposition can regularly scrutinize what the cabinet is doing. "Question time" has been borrowed from the British and has taken on a vigorous life in India. During the first hour of each parliamentary day, members of the cabinet are questioned by members of the house and their answers debated. From 1989 to 1991, over 1,847 questions were debated in this way. All in all, though the Lok Sabha has had the usual rocky road of an institution with a new constitution that is being "broken in," the parliamentary system of which it is a part seems to have established itself reasonably well in India.

---

[7]Lok Sabha Secretariat, *The Ninth Lok Sabha, 1989–1991: A Study* (New Delhi: Lok Sabha Secretariat, 1992), pp. 112–113.

### Example: Parliamentary Government in Germany

 Germany has a parliamentary system that is similar to the general model of parliamentary government presented in this chapter except that, in a number of important ways, the power of the parliament is limited so that the line of power and responsibility is not as clean as in a pure parliamentary system. The system was first set up in West Germany and has been extended, since German reunification in 1990, to the new eastern portion of the state as well. When the system was first set up in 1949, the disaster of Hitler's rule was still vivid in everyone's mind. The occupying forces from France, Britain, and the United States were anxious to prevent the rise of another dictator, as were the Germans who wrote the new constitution with them. Accordingly, power was deliberately fragmented, so that it would be hard for any one person to seize it all. The resulting system of "checks and balances" may seem natural to American readers, but it blends awkwardly with parliamentary government and gives Germany a rather unusual form of parliamentarism.

Parliament is not wholly supreme in Germany, as it should be in a "pure" parliamentary system and as it nearly is in India. First of all, Germany, like India, is a federal system, and so there are many areas of governmental activity that are not controlled by the national government. And compared with India, the national government has not devised as many ways of controlling what the state governments do. Furthermore, there is a very active system of judicial review in Germany, with perhaps the most accessible Supreme Court in the world.[8] Among other things, the Court has, for example, barred national administrations from outlawing the Communist party and from establishing a national television network. Both federalism and the system of judicial review were new constitutional devices for Germany in 1949, inserted into the constitution in order to diffuse and limit the exercise of power.

Another limitation on the power of the lower house and its cabinet is that Germany's parliament has a powerful upper house that may bar the lower house from many actions. We have seen that the House of Lords in Britain and the Council of States in India actually have little power to block a bill. But the upper house of the German parliament, the Bundesrat, does have the power to block bills of many kinds.

The Bundesrat was strengthened in the new constitution to protect the powers of the newly established states. Its members are not directly elected but are appointed by the governments of the states. Under the constitution, its consent is required for all constitutional amendments and for any law that affects the administrative, tax, or territorial interests of the states. In practice, a series of Supreme Court decisions have established that about 60 percent of all bills fall into these categories and require the support of a majority in the Bundesrat to become law. On all other bills, the lower house may override a Bundesrat veto, but it requires more than a simple 50 percent majority in the lower house to do this.

---

[8]Any German citizen may bring a case directly to the Supreme Court by simple petition; it does not even require a lawyer.

As a result of these provisions, the lower house and its cabinet often do not have the free play to make policy that should theoretically be theirs in a parliamentary system. Whole areas of policy, such as education, may be under the control of the states. Or the cabinet and lower house may find that what they wish to do is ruled unconstitutional by the Supreme Court. Finally, if the Bundesrat is controlled by a different party than the lower house, the cabinet may find that it continually has to compromise with the opposition in order to get its bills through. This was the case in the late 1970s, when a cabinet led by the Social Democratic party was faced with a Bundesrat controlled by the Christian Democratic party; and again after 1991 when the Social Democrats gained control of the Bundesrat, often blocking the cabinet—now led by the Christian Democrats.

The lower house, or Bundestag, is set up along the familiar lines of parliamentary government. The cabinet is responsible only to the lower house, as is standard parliamentary practice, and so the lower house controls who sits in the executive. In its turn, the cabinet uses its control of party organization to ensure strict party voting in support of its bills. From 1961 to 1980, there were only fifteen instances in which a member of the party broke ranks and voted against the party position in the Bundestag.[9]

Even within the lower house, however, there are more checks and balances than we generally find in a pure parliamentary system. While party leaders expect total support for their parties' positions, ordinary members have more influence over what those positions will be than is the case in Britain.

First, the parties meet regularly as caucuses to determine their positions on bills. Members actually spend more of their time in meetings of the party caucus than in full meetings of the house. Policies are debated extensively within the party caucus, and the parties have full committee structures within the caucus to give careful and skilled scrutiny to each proposed bill. Thus, the party position on bills is not simply dictated to ordinary members by the party leaders.

Second, unlike the British House of Commons, there are about two dozen specialized standing committees with full staffs, which scrutinize bills before they go to the full house. Parties are given strength on the committees proportional to their strength in the house, and each committee selects its own chair. Each bill must be considered twice by one of these committees before it comes before the full house for a vote, and it may be heavily amended by the committee.

The general tone of the Bundestag is businesslike and rather dull, with a strong overtone of interest-group neocorporatism. The members are highly skilled (about one-third hold doctorates) but tend not to be politically combative. In a survey in the late 1970s, 47 percent of the members were civil servants who had gone on leave to serve in the parliament, while a further 13 percent were officials of interest groups.[10]

---

[9]Tony Burkett, "Developments in the West German Bundestag in the 1970s," *Parliamentary Affairs* 34 (Summer 1981): 302.

[10]Ibid., p. 305. Interest-group officials generally take a special interest in their group's concerns, seeking positions on useful committees and in general binding the parliament and the interest-group system tightly together. This helps to produce a "neocorporatist" blending of interest groups and government.

Full sessions of the house do not provide ringing rhetoric. For example: The Bundestag, like many parliaments, has a "question hour," but answers are generally provided in writing by the minister rather than in person and are read to the Bundestag by an assistant.

The end result of this is that German parliamentarism does not provide the clean line of responsibility we generally expect from parliamentary government. Even a defeat of the cabinet on a major bill in the lower house does not necessarily lead to the fall of the cabinet, since the constitution provides for the ouster of a cabinet only under carefully specified conditions.[11]

The ruling parties cannot necessarily be held responsible by the electorate for the state of public policy, because the policy may actually not have been their choice. It may have been forced on them by the Bundesrat or the Supreme Court, or it might be policy of the "states" rather than of the central government. German parliamentarism, while it retains the general form and most of the flexibility of parliamentarism in general, lacks the usual advantage of a clean line of responsibility.

## FURTHER READING

Abraham, Henry J. *The Judicial Process: An Introductory Analysis of the Courts of the United States, England and France*. 5th ed. New York: Oxford University Press, 1986.

Birch, Anthony H. *Representation*. New York: Praeger, 1971.

Brand, Jack. *British Parliamentary Parties: Policy and Power*. New York: Oxford University Press, 1992.

Cox, Gary W., and McCubbins, Mathew D. *Legislative Leviathan: Party Government in the House*. Los Angeles: University of California Press, 1993.

Crossman, R. H. S. *The Myths of Cabinet Government*. Cambridge, Mass.: Harvard University Press, 1972.

Fenno, Richard F., Jr. *Learning to Legislate: The Senate Education of Arlen Specter*. Washington, D.C.: Congressional Quarterly Press, 1991.

Jennings, Ivor. *Cabinet Government*. 3rd ed. New York: Cambridge University Press, 1969.

Kommers, Donald P. *Judicial Politics in West Germany*. Beverly Hills, Calif.: Sage, 1976.

Laver, Michael, and Schofield, Norman. *Multiparty Government: The Politics of Coalition in Europe*. Oxford: Oxford University Press, 1990.

Loewenberg, Gerhard. *Parliament in the German Political System*. Ithaca, N.Y.: Cornell University Press, 1967.

———, and Patterson, Samuel C. *Comparing Legislatures*. Boston: Little, Brown, 1979.

Olson, David M., and Mezey, Michael L., eds. *Legislatures in the Policy Process: The Dilemmas of Economic Policy*. New York: Cambridge University Press, 1991.

Pitkin, Hanna Fenichel. *The Concept of Representation*. Berkeley: University of California Press, 1967.

Rose, Richard. *The Problem of Party Government*. New York: Free Press, 1974.

Searing, Donald D. *Westminster's World: Understanding Political Roles*. Cambridge, Mass.: Harvard University Press, 1994.

---

[11]The only way a cabinet can be brought down is for the opposition to propose a motion of no confidence, including a statement of who the new chancellor would be; the motion requires a majority to pass. The cabinet are not required to resign if one of their major bills fails to pass.

Strom, Kaare. *Minority Government and Majority Rule.* New York: Cambridge University Press, 1990.

———. "The Presthus Debacle: Intraparty Politics and Bargaining Failure in Norway," *American Political Science Review* 88 (March 1994): 112–127.

*Parliamentary Affairs* and *Legislative Studies Quarterly* are useful specialized journals relevant to this chapter.

# 14

# NATIONAL DECISION-MAKING INSTITUTIONS: PRESIDENTIAL GOVERNMENT

Presidential government is a democratic system in which the legislature and the executive exist independently and are elected independently of each other. Since both parts of the governmental apparatus are responsible for the making and carrying out of law and yet are independent, it often happens that they compete and find themselves in conflict. The executive and the legislature are not forced into the kind of cooperation that tends to be ensured in a parliamentary system, where the two depend closely on one another.

Just as the political party provides a glue that allows the parliament and its cabinet to function in intimate cooperation, so, in a presidential system, the political party may operate to soften the natural competition between independent executives and legislatures. In the United States, for example, the president, as head of one of the two great parties, is always guaranteed a large number of friends in the Congress. The system does not force the sort of unity on the president and his party's members of Congress that we would see in a parliamentary system, but still the bond of party allows for a good deal of coordination and cooperation.

However, note two things about presidential-legislative cooperation via party ties:

**1** Parties may often be more loosely unified in presidential systems than in parliamentary systems. In parliamentary systems, the premier and cabinet hold over the heads of ordinary members of parliament the threat that they may not advance into executive office if they do not cooperate with the leadership. In a presidential system, the president has little control over the careers and advancement of members of the legislature and thus cannot force unity on them. Even when the president's party has a majority of the seats in the legislature, the president will usually not be able to control what happens in the legislature as closely as most cabinets can control their parliaments in parliamentary systems.

**2** Also, there is no guarantee that the party that holds the presidency will also control the legislature. Since the two parts of the governmental apparatus are elected independently, it may well happen that one party will have prevailed in the presidential election and another in elections for the legislature. For instance, throughout the 1980s, the Republican party held the U.S. presidency and at times controlled the Senate, but the Democratic party controlled the House of Representatives. When this happens, cooperation between the two branches of government is even more fragile.

The most famous presidential system in the world, of course, is that of the United States. A number of Latin American states also use versions of the presidential system, as do several other states around the world, including France and Turkey. In some of these, unified parties provide for more coordination than is found in the United States. In Mexico, for instance, the huge Party of the Institutionalized Revolution has held the presidency and controlled the Chamber of Deputies continually since 1929. Mexico's Constitution also provides the president with a great deal of independent power; under these circumstances, it has not been difficult to provide coordinated policymaking. But as a rule, presidential systems exhibit a good deal less coordination between the executive and the legislature than we see in parliamentary systems.

Since the legislature is a coequal body to the executive in a presidential system, how is the legislature organized and how does it function? In a parliamentary system, the cabinet organizes the business of the legislature, but in a presidential system, the legislature must organize itself. How is this done? The U.S. Congress provides a good example.

The U.S. Congress consists of two equal houses, the House of Representatives and the Senate. Each house is governed by leaders who are elected by the party that has a majority in the house and by strong, independent committees whose chairs are appointed from among members of the majority party. Seniority—the length of time one has served in the house—is the dominant factor in deciding who will chair committees. For instance, as of 1995, the Republican party had majorities in both the U.S. Senate and the House of Representatives. The majority leader of the Senate was Robert Dole of Kansas, and the Speaker of the House was Newt Gingrich of the state of Georgia. These two men exercised considerable influence over the business of their two houses, partly through their ability to persuade and partly through formal powers, such as the power to influence appointments to committees, to assign bills to committees, and to preside over debate. Gingrich, in particular, exercised strong control of his party members, and through them, the House, by his strong ideological vision and leadership.

However, the leaders cannot dominate their houses. Any bill must first be considered by a committee, and these committees operate independently and put their own considerable mark on bills that they bring to the full house. Power in each of the houses is so diffused—among leaders, committees, the minority party, and so on—that no one can be said really to control what happens in either one.

The absence of control is heightened by the fact that voting in Congress is much less a party affair than it would be in a parliament. As we have seen, in a parliamentary system, regular failure by members to support their party's position would lead to collapse of the cabinet; for this reason, among others, members generally vote tightly along party

(Reprinted with permission of United Feature Syndicate)

lines. In the Congress, this incentive for discipline is lacking, and so members of Congress choose their votes more individually. Through the 1970s and 1980s, fewer than half of all bills passed by the House of Representatives were "party votes" even in the very modest sense that over half the Democrats voted on one side and over half the Republicans on the other.

## PRESIDENTIAL AND PARLIAMENTARY SYSTEMS COMPARED

What difference does it make whether a state is a parliamentary or a presidential system? Some differences include the following (we will expand on each of these in the next several sections):

• Policy leadership is often more clearly lodged with a president than with a parliamentary cabinet.
• Responsibility for policy is more difficult to identify in a presidential system.
• Comprehensive policy is more difficult to accomplish in a presidential system than in a parliamentary system.
• Recruitment of executive leaders differs in the two systems.
• There are special problems for review and control of the executive in a presidential system.
• The symbolic and political aspects of the executive are unified in a presidential system, but split in a parliamentary system.
• Constitutional review of some sort seems to be more necessary in a presidential system, as is true in general of divided systems of power.

Let us first consider the question of policy leadership. Because presidents have a personal mandate from the voters, they are able to take more direct personal charge of policy than the cabinet can do in a parliamentary system. A parliamentary cabinet owes its position to its parties' members in the parliament, and it must operate with them as a team. The president, on the other hand, is personally elected by all the voters of the nation, and this is true of no other public official. This personal mandate focuses attention on the president, who is accordingly thrust into a position of policy leadership.

Unlike the cabinet in a parliamentary system, the presidential cabinet does not consist of party notables whose appointments are generally obligatory. Rather, presidents appoint a group of cabinet officials who will be beholden to them personally. Often, these officials come from positions in which they have had little political exposure: In recent years, presidential cabinets in the United States have included college professors, lawyers, auto company executives, a president's brother, and other relatively nonpolitical figures as well as politicians. In general, prominent political figures are *not* included, and this helps to focus attention directly on the president and the president's staff.

In most presidential systems, the president is constitutionally designated as the commander in chief of the state's armed forces and is personally charged with the responsibility to direct the affairs of the state, dictatorially if necessary, in the event of war or emergency. The president is also generally given personal responsibility for the direction of foreign policy.

Finally, in the making of laws, the legislative branch in a presidential system habitually puts itself in a passive stance, simply waiting to respond to proposals that the president is expected to put forward.

A presidential system, then, provides for a coherent and unified policy leadership that may be lacking in a parliamentary cabinet, especially if that cabinet is formed of a coalition of parties and most especially if the state suffers from cabinet instability.

## GOVERNMENTAL RESPONSIBILITY

A presidential system provides a clear focus for *leadership*, but—ironically—it blurs the final *responsibility* for policies. In a presidential system, no one part of the governmental apparatus can be held responsible for any particular policy or any particular lack of policy. If the president proposes a new energy tax and the tax is defeated in Congress, who is responsible for the lack of tax reform? Is the Congress obstinate? Should the president have proposed a tax that would have been more liable to pass? Should the president have lobbied harder for the bill? It might also happen that the bill would pass, but with amendments that changed it substantially. Is it now the president's bill? Congress's? No one's?

Since they do not present a clear picture of the responsibility for policies, presidential systems exhibit two important weaknesses. First, when voters cannot pin the responsibility for policies on any particular official, their electoral choices become less significant. Should a voter in the United States in 1948 who was upset at inflation have voted Republican? That would have been a vote against the party of President Truman, who should perhaps have been held responsible for the inflation. But what if the "do-nothing" Republican-controlled Congress were at fault, as Truman claimed? Faced with a choice like this, the poor bewildered voter must vote on less policy-related criteria, such as a candidate's personality or personal favors that an incumbent candidate has been able to do while in office. Eventually, elections come to function less and less as vehicles by which voters can affect the making of policy.[1]

A second weakness of presidential government caused by its blurring of responsibility is that when public officials do not have clear responsibility for a policy, they may literally begin to behave irresponsibly. If Congress is not directly held responsible for producing a balanced budget, it is easy for members of Congress to vote simultaneously to cut taxes (which will look good to their constituents) and to build highways (which will also look good). "Through the fault of no one in particular," the government usually spends more than it takes in.

Campaign platforms of U.S. parties provide another example of the chronic irresponsibility of presidential systems. Because a party's president cannot be blamed for failing to enact into law the party's promises—after all, Congress might not cooperate—it becomes easy for the parties to promise in their campaign platforms whatever they think the voters would like to hear. With power as fragmented as it is in a presidential system, the party will never lack for an alibi if the voters should take them to task for not delivering on their promises.

## PRESIDENTIAL SYSTEMS AND COMPREHENSIVE POLICY

It is generally more difficult to make comprehensive policies in a presidential system than in a parliamentary one. Policies are more likely to be patched together of varied compromises or perhaps not to be put together at all. The United States is one of the few democracies that lacks a national energy power, though this has not been for want of trying. Presidents have proposed energy policies to Congress but have never been able to get agreement on anything recognizable as a policy.

Because of the many points in a fragmented system at which a bill can be blocked, it is generally not enough that a mere majority of the people want something done; considerably more than a majority is required if all the defensive positions provided by a fragmented system are to be overrun. Handgun control, prayer in the schools, and the equal rights amendment are all examples of policies that a majority of the U.S. population want but which have been impossible to enact into law.

If you are suspicious of majorities, as many of the authors of the U.S. Constitution were, this may be seen as a good effect of the fragmentation of power. But there is no denying that it makes the government slow to respond to change.

## RECRUITMENT OF EXECUTIVE LEADERS

There is a significant difference between the sorts of leaders who emerge in parliamentary and presidential systems. In a parliamentary system, all or almost all the leaders in

---

[1]A large body of literature has long urged that the United States should try to accomplish "responsible party government" similar to that of Britain. Generally, the argument has been that U.S. parties should become more tightly disciplined, not that the constitutional division of power should be changed. A good example is E. E. Schattschneider, *Party Government* (New York: Holt, Rinehart and Winston, 1942).

the executive have emerged from careers in parliament; indeed, they continue to serve in the parliament while they hold executive office. This means that they will all have had fairly similar lives before they entered the executive. For a decade or two or three, their jobs will have consisted of the wording of bills and of service to the voters in their constituency. They will have had a long period of exposure to the wide range of issues facing the state in diplomacy, tax policy, education, defense, and so on.

The similarity of these executive officers is made greater by the fact that they are mostly selected from among the members of the parliament on the basis of a common set of criteria. Members who move up to executive office are those who do a good job of being a member of parliament: They debate well, they keep their noses to the grindstone, they do not make waves.

Recruitment in a parliamentary system has the virtue that officials are chosen *by those who know them and their work* (their fellow members of parliament) *during a career that has made them familiar with most of the issues they will have to face.* It has the disadvantage that *there is not much variety among the types of people chosen, that they have by and large had little experience in managing things* (legislators spend most of their time responding to initiatives of others), *and that there are few "mavericks" or adventurers included.*

In a presidential system, recruitment into executive office is fairly independent of the legislative parts of government. While a president may have started off with a legislative career, this is by no means necessary. Consider the last nine presidents of the United States:

| PRESIDENT | BACKGROUND |
|---|---|
| Dwight D. Eisenhower | Army general |
| John F. Kennedy | Senator |
| Lyndon B. Johnson | Senator |
| Richard M. Nixon | Senator; vice-president |
| Gerald Ford | Member of Congress |
| Jimmy Carter | Farmer; governor of Georgia |
| Ronald Reagan | Film actor; governor of California |
| George Bush | Appointee to various foreign policy positions; vice-president |
| William Clinton | Governor of Arkansas |

Half of these men had established themselves with the public by something other than service in one of the houses of Congress.

Furthermore, the recruitment of other officials to staff the executive does not draw heavily on Congress in the United States or in most other presidential systems. Only a minority of the membership of recent U.S. presidents' cabinets have been drawn from careers in the Senate or House. Many of the most distinctive and interesting cabinet members have been drawn from careers that were far from Congress, careers that gave them interesting points of view of their own. Three examples are Robert McNamara, secretary of defense under Kennedy and Johnson, who had been a Ford Motor Corporation executive; Henry Kissinger, secretary of state under Nixon and Ford, who had been a university professor; and Donna Shalala, secretary of health and human services under Clinton, who had been chancellor of the University of Wisconsin.

This sort of selection has the advantage that it brings varied talents and backgrounds to the task of executive and that, through the introduction of new blood, problems may come to be seen in a new light. New points of view and the zeal of amateurs may thus be brought into policymaking at a high level, as in Jimmy Carter's campaigns on behalf of human rights.

On the other hand, selection is often haphazard, since it is not generally done by those who have worked directly with the candidates; candidates may have little previous experience in important areas (Carter, Reagan, and Clinton, for instance, had had no experience with foreign policy before they became president); and inappropriate choices are more likely than in a parliamentary system.[2]

In short, in a parliamentary system you know much more what you are getting than in a presidential system. Executive officials are not going to surprise you in a parliamentary system, but they will not disappoint you, either.

## REVIEW AND CONTROL OF THE EXECUTIVE

Most organizations have some sort of plural board to which the executive leader is responsible and reports regularly. The president of a business corporation must report reg-

---

[2]An argument for the desirability of recruitment in the parliamentary mode is made in Harold W. Chase, Robert Holt, and John Turner, *American Government in Comparative Perspective* (New York: Franklin Watts, 1980), Chapter 2.

(Dana Summers/The Orlando Sentinel)

ularly to a board of directors, the president of a university reports to the board of trustees of the university, a superintendent of schools reports to a school board, and so on.

In a parliamentary system, the parliament serves this purpose. The prime minister and cabinet regularly report to the parliament on the conduct of their business, questions are asked, and so on. There is regular and frequent contact between the cabinet and the parliament regarding the conduct of government.[3]

In a presidential system, however, the members of the executive operate in relative isolation. The press looks over their shoulder constantly, of course, and there is occasionally contact between them and the legislature regarding a particular bill or investigation. But there is no broader body to which the president or other members of the executive regularly report.

This isolation of the presidency often leads to an inward-looking presidential office, with "inside" staff persons accused by those on the outside of arrogance and insensitivity. More seriously, the lack of some regular device for review and control of the president made the Watergate crisis a good deal more traumatic for the United States than it might otherwise have been. When President Nixon was implicated in petty crimes at the Watergate office complex and it became apparent that some airing of the question was needed, there was no regular stage available for this, and extraordinary procedures for impeachment were required. Had he been a prime minister, he would have been called to task in the parliament as a matter of ordinary business.

## THE SPLIT EXECUTIVE OF PARLIAMENTARY SYSTEMS

Oddly enough, given that in general parliamentary systems are based on the principle of unifying power, the executive itself is generally split in parliamentary systems into the prime minister and cabinet, on the one hand, who are responsible for political and administrative leadership, and some other office that is responsible for the symbolic leadership of the state. In a presidential system all these functions are united in the president.

In Britain the prime minister and cabinet are responsible for political and administrative leadership, but it is the queen who carries on all the ceremonies and personifies the state. It is she who opens new hospitals and bridges, it is her health and that of her family that the press subjects to ghoulish scrutiny, it is she at whose death the nation will go into deep mourning. Like the president of the United States, she is greeted by a special song when she enters a room, and crowds press in on her wherever she goes. The prime minister remains much more a mundane figure, one who goes about the daily business of governing but does not personally represent the state.

It is clear why the two kinds of executive function are united in one person in a presidential system. The executive is weakened in a presidential system by virtue of the fact that its legislature is not under its control; in order for strong leadership to be available to the state, almost everything that *can* be done to strengthen the president's hand *must* be done. One such thing, an important one, is to give presidents an aura of majesty that

---

[3]For further comparison along these lines, see William S. Livingston, "Britain and America: The Institutionalization of Accountability," *Journal of Politics* 38 (November 1976): 870–894.

they can use to bolster their political power. More than one member of Congress has gone into the White House and walked out shaken, muttering, "When the president of the United States asks you to vote in the country's interest, what can you do?"

In a parliamentary system there is no need to add to the power of the cabinet in this way, since the cabinet is capable of providing effective leadership without it. If it is not necessary to combine the two faces of the executive in a single office, as is done in presidential systems, there are some obvious advantages to separating them.

First, the symbolic representation of the state in a person appears to fill a deep need of a modern people. The devotion people feel for those who personify their state is real. Consider the following examples. At John F. Kennedy's assassination in 1963, many Americans felt what they later reported as an almost religious experience. In Britain the most disturbing political event of the twentieth century, with the sole exception of the two world wars themselves, occurred when Prince Edward VIII left the throne in order to marry a divorced American. Norwegians credit King Haakon VII with having almost singlehandedly kept the government from surrendering to Germany in 1941, taking his family into exile and making it possible for Norwegians to fight on in the Resistance. Finally, consider the heart-wrenching difficulty with which Americans faced what would have been a fairly simple task if they had not revered the presidency so much—the ouster of Richard M. Nixon in 1974 when he had been implicated in petty crimes.

If modern peoples need a person on whom to focus their reverence for the state, it seems obvious that this had best be someone who has little involvement in day-to-day politics. The queen of Britain, the king of Sweden, the emperor of Japan, the "president" of Germany (not a president as the term is used in this chapter, but an almost purely ceremonial figure)—these people have virtually no political power and are not involved in routine decision making. This allows them to serve as unblemished objects of national affection. Presidents of the United States, in contrast, must excite mixed feelings among the many people who find themselves in political disagreement with them. On the one hand, these people want to revere the president, but on the other hand, they find themselves faced with a political leader whose policies they may despise. Corporation executives and Republicans in general were in many ways deprived of an object for national reverence during the presidency of Franklin Delano Roosevelt, as were welfare recipients and Democrats in general during the presidency of Ronald Reagan.

Thus, one problem of blending the political executive and the symbolic executive in a single office is that the symbolic function cannot be performed as well when it is located in an office that is inevitably involved in controversy.

The flip side of this problem is that political leadership does not operate as cleanly when reverence for the state gets mixed up with it. A president of the United States gains unfair political advantage from serving as the symbol of the state. Franklin Roosevelt, Lyndon Johnson, Richard Nixon, and Ronald Reagan were quite adept at taking positions that had questionable public support, appearing on radio or television with all the sober attention that a president can command, and selling that endangered program to the public. After all, this man is the president of the United States! Whom can we trust more than him?

We may welcome this as a way to cut through the confusion of the divided powers of a presidential system, but it is still unfortunate that, on any public issue at a given time, only one side is able to take advantage of this reverential response. In a parliamentary system, the cabinet and the opposition operate on more even terms in seeking public support for their political positions.[4]

## WHY AREN'T ALL DEMOCRACIES PARLIAMENTARY SYSTEMS?

Let us review for a moment what we have looked at so far in this chapter. We first described fairly simply how presidential government operates, and we noted the main difference between a parliamentary system and a presidential system: that the one unifies power and the other divides it. We then examined several aspects of presidential government that result from this difference:

- Concentration of policy leadership with the president
- Difficulty of locating responsibility for policies
- Difficulty of making comprehensive policy
- A different pattern of recruitment for executive leaders
- Special problems for review and control
- A merger of the symbolic and political aspects of the executive in a single office

While not every one of these differences showed the presidential system to disadvantage, most did. Overall, you have probably been left with the impression that parliamentary systems are better than presidential ones. The parliamentary system is a simpler, more direct, and generally more efficient way of making public choices. Why aren't all democracies parliamentary systems?

The main reason lies in the very faithfulness with which a parliamentary system transposes political divisions into the policymaking machinery. Policy is set and administered in a parliamentary system by a party, or a cooperative coalition of parties, that controls a majority of the votes in the parliament. This makes for straightforward policymaking if a stable majority is possible in the parliament. But if the country is divided into numerous parties that are intensely hostile to each other, it may be impossible to find a large enough number of members of parliament who can work together cooperatively as a governing coalition. It may be that no working majority is available.

Under these circumstances, a parliamentary system may limp along with an unstable government, as Italy has done since 1945, or the country may prefer to use some system that divides power but is more stable than what parliamentarism could provide.

France after World War II was plagued by parliamentary instability similar to that of Italy. The Communists could not cooperate with any of the other parties, Catholic parties had trouble cooperating with Socialists, and so on. In 1958, the regime collapsed through a revolt by French settlers in Algeria. The military terminated the 4th Republic, and asked Charles de Gaulle to design a new system; his new constitution replaced parliamentary government with a version of presidential government.

---

[4]Related arguments may be found in Edward Shils and Michael Young, "The Meaning of the Coronation," *Sociological Review* 1 (December 1953): 63–81; and in Lewis Lipsitz, "If, as Verba Says, the State Functions as a Religion, What Are We to Do Then to Save Our Souls?" *American Political Science Review* 52 (June 1968): 527–535.

In much of the South, too, democracies, whether or not they started out as parliamentary systems, have often found that they must provide a more stable base for executive leadership than is possible under parliamentarism, even at the cost of fragmenting and complicating public decision-making processes. Many Latin American democracies, under the influence of the United States, used presidential systems from the start; Mexico and Cost Rica are good examples. But many African and Asian democracies—faced with the political stresses of poverty, modernization, and ethnic diversity—have had to modify what started out as parliamentary systems. Nigeria, for example, abandoned parliamentarism when democratic government was reestablished in 1975 and set up a system with an independent presidency rather like that of the United States.[5] Turkey has established a presidential system similar to that of France.

Perhaps the message of this chapter, in the end, is that a parliamentary system is the best form of democracy *if* a country is sufficiently unified to cooperate in parliamentary politics.

## CONSTITUTIONAL REVIEW AND THE FRAGMENTATION OF POWER

Wherever power is fragmented, whether in a presidential system (which divides power between different parts of a national government) or a federal one (which divides power between a central government and regional governments), there seems to be a need for some institution that can operate as a referee to adjudicate disputes among the various holders of power. If a president has part of the power and a legislature has another part, how do we resolve the kind of dispute that must inevitably occur when the legislature says to the president, "You've just done something that's supposed to be left up to us"—or vice versa? How do we resolve disputes over whether the central government or the regional governments have jurisdiction in a particular question? The obvious solution is to have some third institution that is empowered to serve as a referee. In the United States, this is the Supreme Court.

Over the last two centuries the U.S. Supreme Court has established that it has the right to annual acts of presidents and laws passed by Congress whenever it deems either body to have exceeded its proper powers. Although there is occasional grumbling about the Court and its power, it is striking how readily this essentially undemocratic arrangement is tolerated. Think of it! Nine people who are appointed by the president and the Senate and thereafter serve for the rest of their lives without ever being subject to popular election—these nine people wield huge power in our otherwise democratic system. The only explanation for Americans' ready toleration of this is their recognition that the fragmentation of power requires something like this to make their system work.

Constitutional review is found in almost all systems that fragment power and is rare in those that do not. There are two main ways by which a constitution may fragment power: by establishing a presidential system, as has been discussed here; or by establishing a federal system to divide power between a central government and regional governments. (See Chapter 9.) In Table 14–1 the states of western Europe and North

---

[5]This, in turn, succumbed to a military coup in 1983.

PRESIDENTIAL CHARACTER

Presidents have not been studied as much as members of cabinets or parliaments simply because there have been so few of them. In over two hundred years of presidential government, the United States has had only forty-one presidents; in almost thirty years of presidential government, France has had only four. Across so few cases it is difficult to trace any patterns of behavior. The picture is dominated by the personal idiosyncrasies of the relatively few people who have so far filled the role of president. As a result, scholars have analyzed the office of president a good deal in the abstract, thinking about what presidents should be or might be; but few have looked at what presidents *are*.

One exception is James David Barber, who, in his book *The Presidential Character*, 2nd ed. (Englewood Cliffs, N.J.: Prentice-Hall, 1977), draws on the tradition of psychoanalysis, in which people are in any case usually analyzed one at a time.

Barber presents a twofold typology that, he asserts, is useful in understanding the performance of American presidents. He examines the degree to which each president has been active or passive in his role and the extent to which each is positive or negative (likes it or dislikes it) about his work. This typology produces four types of presidents: *active-negatives*, whose basic motive is to obtain and maintain power and who engage in compulsive activity because of a lack of personal self-esteem; *passive-negatives*, who are motivated by a sense of civic duty and citizen virtue and who do not work very hard at being president but agree to do it because they feel a duty to serve the people; *passive-positives*, who are motivated by a need for love and affection and feel that they can meet this need by obtaining the approval of others through their political activities; and finally, *active-positives*, who are problem solvers, are flexible and productive, and have high self-esteem.

Barber characterizes the presidents encompassed by his study as follows: Eisenhower, passive-negative; Kennedy, active-positive; Johnson, active-negative; Nixon, active-negative; Ford, active-positive; Carter, active-positive. His analysis has been widely criticized simply because it is so subjective. One person's "active-positive" might well be another's "active-negative." At the very least, though, setting out these categories organizes the way we look at presidents and offers insights into their careers we might not otherwise have gained.

America are divided according to whether the governmental system is parliamentary or presidential, and according to whether power is unified geographically or fragmented federally; we then note for each state whether or not it has a system of constitutional review. Switzerland is the only system with fragmented power of either sort that does not provide for judicial review. While most unitary parliamentary systems do not provide for constitutional review, Ireland and Italy do.

The main exception to this rule of thumb (that fragmented power is the reason for constitutional review) is that constitutional review has also had some popularity since World War II as a means of protecting individuals from the arbitrary use of state power. That is, constitutional review has been seen as a tool of "constitutionalism," in which a relatively nonpolitical court can help to place limits on the authority of the government.[6] This helps to explain the popularity of constitutional review in Germany after the Nazi dictatorship, although the federal system there probably would have required it in any case. More to the point, it also helps to explain the institution of constitutional review in Ireland and Italy, which have neither federal systems nor presidential governments.

---

[6]See the discussion of constitutionalism in Chapter 9.

**TABLE 14–1**
CONSTITUTIONAL REVIEW, FEDERALISM, AND PRESIDENTIAL GOVERNMENT: WESTERN
EUROPE AND NORTH AMERICA

|  | Constitutional review |
|---|---|
| States with a federal system and/or presidential government | |
| Austria | Yes |
| Canada | Yes |
| France | Yes |
| Mexico | Yes |
| Portugal | Yes |
| Spain | Yes |
| Switzerland | No |
| U.S.A. | Yes |
| Germany | Yes |
| | |
| States with neither a federal system nor presidential government | |
| Belgium | No |
| Denmark | No |
| Great Britain | No |
| Iceland | No |
| Ireland | Yes |
| Italy | Yes |
| Luxembourg | No |
| Netherlands | No |
| Norway | No |
| Sweden | No |

## A NOTE ON CONSTITUTIONS AND POWER

Having looked at formal governmental arrangements in this chapter and the preceding one, we should note an important principle of constitutions that is well illustrated by the development of some of the governmental institutions we have examined.

We saw in Chapter 9 that written constitutions are not static but change and develop as they are put to use. One predictable way in which constitutions change is this: *If power is given constitutionally to a body that lacks the resources to exercise it, informal mechanisms usually develop, leading to the de facto loss of that power* even though the formality of power remains.

One excellent example of this principle at work is the domination of parliaments by their cabinets. Parliaments are vested with supreme authority in the constitutions of parliamentary systems, but a parliament is too large and diverse a group to actually take charge of governmental policy by itself. Over the years, cabinets have developed ways to bully parliaments through the informal mechanism of the disciplined political party. This has shifted actual power from the parliament to its cabinet, which allows policy to be made coherently; but the parliaments remain *formally* supreme. Political parties are rarely even mentioned in the constitutions of democracies, but they have obviously become an important part of living constitutions.

Presidential power? The President does many things for public effect; here Bill Clinton displays his technique on a weight machine.

A second example of this general principle is the problem of "localism" in the French parliament before 1958. France had long had a tradition of central governmental dominance over towns and regions. If a town wished to build a new school or pave a new set of streets, it generally needed to get the permission of the government in Paris to do so. These arrangements gave the central government great formal power, but its exercise involved such a huge number of minuscule decisions that it was simply impossible for any central operation to do a good job of making them. In self-defense, over the late nineteenth and early twentieth centuries, town governments devised ways in which they could get special treatment from the Paris government. Because the members of the parliament were elected from local districts, parliament was a special target of these efforts. Town governments tried, with a great deal of success, to convince the local members of parliament to take as one of their chief tasks in Paris the furthering of local causes. Members of parliament eventually spent much of their time and effort in making deals—trading votes with other members so that their towns could get the necessary permission and funds to build town halls or install streetlights. Party discipline declined, and many members' votes were heavily influenced by the deals they had cut with other members, so that the directions of party leaders were often ignored. This trend was a major cause of the increasing instability of the national government. (France had twenty-five different cabinets in the thirteen years from 1945 to 1958.) Thus the formal power over localities' decisions, which was supposed to *strengthen* the central government, in fact helped to weaken it.

A third example is provided by the Bundesrat, the upper house of the German parliament, which was described in the previous chapter. The Bundesrat, you will recall, was established in the constitution in order to protect the independence of the new "states" from the central government. If Germany was to be a federal system, it was reasoned, the states needed a lever in the central government itself to allow them a veto over actions that would take away their rights. Therefore the Bundesrat was established. It consists of representatives from the state governments and must give its consent to any action affecting their tax, administrative, or territorial interests.

Ironically, setting up the Bundesrat and giving it these powers has made it, and the states that appoint its members, sufficiently important to national political leaders that they now try to control what goes on in state politics and have undermined the independence of state leaders in important ways. Elections for state governments often turn on a national issue rather than on those of the state. Figures from the central government campaign hard in the state, not for local figures or for the local party but in terms of national political questions. And once a state election is over, national leaders often put pressure on local leaders to form a particular sort of coalition in the state parliament solely because of the effect the nature of the local coalition will have on the state's votes in the Bundesrat.[7] The existence of the Bundesrat has arguably had an effect just the opposite of what was intended by the framers of Germany's constitution. The states' prerogatives would have probably been protected adequately by the Supreme Court if the Bundesrat had never been set up, and local political leaders would operate more independently of national leaders than is now the case.

In all three of these examples, actual power relationships—the living constitution—have fit themselves to the power of groups in ways quite different from what was intended by those who designed the formal document. Such mismatches between reality and formal rules generally result from a failure to appreciate fully the "power" in "power and choice." If one thinks of politics primarily as a question of working out choices for the state, it will seem that an appropriate set of procedures should do that, and the choice making will follow from the procedures. This ignores the necessities of power and can lead to surprises for those who write rules.

### Example: Presidential Government in France

After World War II, France set up a fairly standard parliamentary system. It was immobilized, however, by the hostility of various parties to each other and by weak discipline within many of them, which made it difficult for coalitions to form and hold together. The average life of a cabinet was about six months, and because ministers did not stay in place long enough to get full control of their offices, France was, in effect, governed by its bureaucracy rather than by its elected leadership.[8] There was a sense of drift, and when in 1958 tensions associated

---

[7]For an early example, see Arnold J. Heidenheimer, "Federalism and the Party System: The Case of West Germany," *American Political Science Review* 52 (September 1958): 809–828.

[8]Ironically, France was actually governed rather well. During this period, France pioneered in establishing the European Economic Community, and its per capita income grew at a rate of 3.5 percent annually in real terms throughout the 1950s.

with Algeria's war for independence were added to the mix, things fell apart. The military took over, and Charles de Gaulle, the hero of World War II, was brought in to set up a new system.

De Gaulle and his advisers designed a new kind of democracy with elements of both presidential and parliamentary government in which, however, the presidential elements have gradually come to dominate things. As first designed, the system consisted of a cabinet responsible to the National Assembly (the lower house of parliament) and of a rather powerful but nonpolitical president. The president, indirectly elected by an assembly of parliament and of mayors, was, in turn, to designate the premier and to preside over the affairs of government, especially foreign affairs and defense policy. The president could bring issues before the French electorate in the form of a referendum and could, if necessary, declare a state of emergency and take over all power for up to six months at a time.

Although this obviously was a powerful position, it did not actually provide much more than what is implicit in the powers of the queen of England or what was implicit in the powers of the French president from 1945 to 1958. The key question was whether the French president would act as a primarily symbolic figure, performing these functions only on the advice of the cabinet, or would realize the full potential of the office's powers. De Gaulle himself served as the first president under the new system from 1958 to 1969. He exercised his potential power strongly and added to that power in three important ways:

• In 1962 he had the constitution changed so that the president was directly elected. The president has since then carried great prestige as the only official elected by all the people of France.

• He set up an executive office with a structure that paralleled the ministries of the cabinet. Any bill that a ministry wished to submit to parliament had to be cleared by its counterpart bureau in the executive office. Eventually many important policies began to be set in the executive office even without the knowledge of the minister involved.

• He established the principle that a president could dismiss a premier at will. The constitution states that the president "designates" the premier but says nothing about dismissal. In 1962, de Gaulle asked his first premier, Michel Debre, to resign, and Debre did so. From that point on, another important element of presidential power had been established.

Today, as long as the same party simultaneously holds the presidency and controls the parliament, the premier and cabinet function as agents of the president, conducting much of the day-to-day business of the state and representing the president in relations with the parliament.

The new constitution included a large number of constraints on the independence of the parliament, which were intended to prevent the immobility that had characterized French government before 1958. An absolute majority of members is required to overthrow a cabinet, so that abstentions or absent members in effect count as votes in favor of the cabinet on a motion of confidence. When the cabinet submits a bill to the parliament, the cabinet has the right to list the priority within which the bill will be debated as well as the rules of debate; thus the cabinet is given considerable power in scheduling the work of the parliament. (Among other rules, the cabinet can require that a bill be voted on as a whole, rather than having a separate vote on any amendment; this frequently used device makes it difficult to amend a bill.) Members of the parliament are constitutionally barred from offering amendments to a bill that would have the effect of either adding to state expenditures or decreasing state revenues; an amendment requiring new expenditure, for instance, must include within itself either a compensating cut in some other expenditure or an increase in taxes. Finally, the independence and power of parliamentary committees was decreased by the simple device of limiting their number to six. This assured that they would be large bodies (the average size of committees is over a hundred members) with broad areas of policy and that they would never again be able to develop into tight-knit groups of specialists.

In effect, by laying down these rules, the new French constitution brought about executive supremacy of the sort that in most parliamentary systems is achieved informally through the political party. Since parties had failed to establish the necessary discipline, constitutional design was used to ensure executive supremacy. One could argue that the informal device is better because it is more flexible, but the constitutional devices appear to have worked well in France.

These rules established executive domination over the parliament, and—as things have developed in France—"executive" generally means the president. However, an oddity of the French hybrid of parliamentary and presidential systems is that, since the president governs through a cabinet which can be turned out of office at will by the National Assembly, it is crucial whether or not the same party controls the presidency and the National Assembly. If the president's party has a majority (or close to it) in the National Assembly, things work smoothly in the way I have describe above; the president names a cabinet, and the party's majority in the National Assembly supports it. This has been the situation for all but five of the more than thirty-six years since the establishment of the Fifth Republic.

However, if the president's party does not control the National Assembly, there is an obvious possibility of deadlock. It is at least theoretically possible that the president could name cabinet upon cabinet, which would be voted down by the National Assembly as quickly as they were named. The president could not rule under these circumstances.

Split control of the presidency and National Assembly has occurred twice so far. In 1985 conservatives won a majority in the National Assembly, and President Mitterrand, a socialist, had to appoint Jacques Chirac, a Gaullist, to the premiership. No one really knew how this would work; but it turned out that when the premier and the president are of different parties, more of the executive power rests with the premier than with the president, although both are then powerful. Mitterrand chose the ministers for defense and foreign affairs, while Chirac chose all the rest; legislative initiatives lay wholly with Chirac and his cabinet, although Mitterrand limited Chirac's ability to promulgate decrees; and at international conferences both Mitterrand and Chirac represented France, dividing allotted speaking time between them(!).

This period of split control, dubbed "cohabitation" by the French, lasted only three years. In 1988, a newly reelected President Mitterrand took advantage of the enthusiasm over his victory and dissolved the National Assembly, calling for a new election of its members. The Socialists regained control, and the old constitutional system of presidential dominance was reestablished. Cohabitation emerged for a second time, however, when in 1993 the Socialists once again lost control of the National Assembly. This time it proceeded with less friction as the prickly Chirac decided not to involve himself, and the new premier, Edouard Balladur, got along well with Mitterand while still establishing clear dominance in the executive. In 1995 the system returned to "normal" when Chirac himself was elected president with a conservative majority in the National Assembly.

In all sorts of ways, the constitution of France (constitution with a small "c") changes abruptly when different parties come to control the National Assembly and the presidency. It is almost as if France has two constitutions, which switch on and off like light bulbs.

### Example: Presidential Government in Mexico

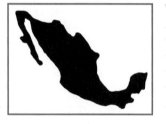

The present Mexican system arose out of a decade and a half of chaos, from 1910 to 1925. In a swirling tumult of banditry, revolutionary battles, and civil war, approximately a million Mexicans starved or were killed. The period of violence ended in the establishment of the dominant Party of the Institutionalized Revolution, which we examined in Chapter 11. By the 1930s the rule of the party had come to be centered on a very strong presidency, and that regime has continued to the present time.

The President of Mexico dominates all politics. Although the constitution provides for an independent Congress and Supreme Court much like those of the United States, neither of these bodies has operated very independently of the president. Until 1988 all but a handful of members of the Congress were from the PRI (the dominant party; see Chapter 11), and since 1988 the PRI has still always had clear majorities in both houses. The opposition is divided in the Congress, so that in the rare instances in which the president needs help (passing a constitutional amendment, for example, which requires a two-thirds majority), he may easily be able to get support form one of the other parties. Presidential dominance since 1988 may partly be due to the fact that a Congress with more than a handful of opposition members is such a new thing that the opposition has not yet learned to use its potential power.[9]

The Supreme Court is somewhat more insulated from the power of the president and has not infrequently ruled in favor of citizens who were suing the presidential office on minor technical matters. But the Court has always avoided confrontation with the president on important questions of policy. Like the U.S. Supreme Court, the Mexican court refuses to hear cases that it considers "political"; but unlike the U.S.

[9]Martin C. Needler, *Mexican Politics*, 2nd ed. (New York: Praeger, 1990), p. 88.

Court, it has interpreted this stricture broadly to include almost any important area of presidential activity.

A president in office has great power. What has saved the system from an unbearable concentration of power is the firm tradition that presidents must step down after a single six-year term. For six years, a single person rules, but then the party (influenced strongly by the incumbent president) chooses another person to serve the next six years.[10] It is at this point that the system has shown some flexibility over the years. The outgoing president has based his decision on a combination of negotiations among party leaders, consultations with the PRI's three "sectors," interest-group pressures, and consideration of the popular mood, or "temper of the times."[11] Thus, when the mood is to the left, a president generally emerges from the left; corrupt presidents are often succeeded by reformers; and so on. Not only the holder of the presidential office changes, but most other executive officers change as well, as the new president finds jobs for the members of his faction. The holder of a job under one president has in the past had only a 30 percent chance of holding a job under the next president.[12]

Such concentration of power, even if it is temporary, does encourage corruption and personal gain, which is a chronic problem of Mexican politics. Mexico appears to go through alternate waves of corruption and reform. The administration of President Alemán from 1946 to 1952 was marked by large-scale corruption, as was that of López Portillo from 1976 to 1982. Various officials of the López Portillo administration are widely thought to have taken $3 billion or more from public funds; his successor, President Miguel de la Madrid Hurtado, came to office pledged to a clean government and prosecuted some of the offenders of the previous regime. Although the corruption is obviously costly and broad, some have speculated cynically that it has the hidden virtue of making possible the regular six-year transition in power. If it were not for the illicit wealth on which they could retire, so this reasoning goes, some officials would by now have devised a way of subverting the six-year rule so that they could stay in office.

Just as the weakening of the PRI is opening up Mexico to greater political competition, however, the old system of corruption is now also under attack. The present president, Ernesto Zedillo, is a clear "reform" president and is the third such president in a row.

## FURTHER READING

Abraham, Henry J. *The Judicial Process*. 5th ed. New York: Oxford University Press, 1986. Chapters on judicial review.

Andrews, William G. *Presidential Government in Gaullist France*. Albany, N.Y.: State University of New York Press, 1982.

---

[10]Again, with increasing competition from opposition parties, the party's nomination may never again confer the office as automatically as it did through and including the 1988 election. In the election of 1994 the outcome was truly open, although the PRI's candidate still won.

[11]Rubio F. Luis, "The Presidential Nomination Process," in George W. Grayson, ed., *Prospects for Democracy in Mexico* (New Brunswick, N.J.: Transaction Publishers, 1990), p. 76.

[12]Peter H. Smith, "Does Mexico Have a Power Elite?" in Jose L. Reyna and Richard S. Weinert, eds., *Authoritarianism in Mexico* (Philadelphia: Institute for the Study of Human Issues, 1977), p. 139.

Bond, Jon R., and Fleisher, Richard. *The President in the Legislative Arena.* Chicago: University of Chicago Press, 1990.

Brichta, Avraham, and Zalmanovitch, Yair. "Proposals for Presidential Government in Israel." *Comparative Political Studies* 19 (October 1986): 57–68.

Dibacco, Thomas V., ed. *Presidential Power in Latin American Politics.* New York: Praeger, 1977.

Edwards, George C. III; Kessel, John H.; and Rockman, Bert A., eds. *Researching the Presidency: Vital Questions, New Approaches.* Pittsburgh: University of Pittsburgh Press, 1993.

Fiorina, Morris P. *Congress: Keystone of the Washington Establishment.* 2nd ed. New Haven: Yale University Press, 1989.

Linz, Juan J., and Valenzuela, Arturo, eds. *The Failure of Presidential Democracy.* Baltimore: Johns Hopkins University Press, 1994.

Neustadt, Richard E. *Presidential Power and the Modern Presidents.* New York: Free Press, 1991.

Nwabueze, Benjamin O. *Presidentialism in Commonwealth Africa.* London: Hurst, 1974.

Pious, Richard M. *The American Presidency.* New York: Basic Books, 1979.

"Presidential and Parliamentary Democracies: Which Works Best?" Special Conference Issue, *Political Science Quarterly* 109 (no. 3, special issue, 1994).

Rose, Richard. *The Postmodern President.* Chatham, N.J.: Chatham House, 1989.

———, and Suleiman, Ezra N., eds. *Presidents and Prime Ministers.* Washington, D.C.: American Enterprise Institute, 1980.

Rossiter, Clinton. *The American Presidency.* 2nd ed. New York: New American Library, 1964.

Schlesinger, Arthur M., Jr. *The Imperial Presidency.* Boston: Houghton Mifflin, 1973.

Shugart, Matthew Soberg, and Carey, John M. *Presidents and Assemblies: Constitutional Design and Electoral Dynamics.* New York: Cambridge University Press, 1992.

Skowronek, Stephen. *The Politics Presidents Make: Leadership from John Adams to George Bush.* Cambridge, Mass.: Harvard University Press, 1993.

Wills, Gary. *Cincinnatus: George Washington and the Enlightenment.* Garden City, N.Y.: Doubleday, 1984.

# 15

# BUREAUCRACY AND THE PUBLIC SECTOR

In the last few chapters we have reviewed the structure of governments. But a great deal goes into policymaking beyond what government leaders do. The government may establish by law that the speed limit on highways is 55 miles per hour, but what this means in detail is determined by hundreds of thousands of traffic patrol officers across the country. It is they who decide whether this means that you are ticketed if you drive 56 miles per hour or whether there is a "zone of grace" so that you are ticketed only for speeds of 60 miles per hour or above. It is they who decide whether a woman with a bleeding wound in her arm is in bad enough shape that she is justified in speeding to the hospital at 75 miles per hour. It is they who decide whether to treat a well-dressed man in a dark-blue sedan differently from a youth in blue jeans who is driving a red sports car, warning the one and ticketing the other.

The local police officer, the public health inspector, the president of the state university, the teacher in a public school—these are just as much a part of the policymaking machinery as the legislator, judge, or U.S. president. In fact, for most citizens, it is *these* people—and not the legislator, judge, or president—who embody the state and its policies. People receive the policies of the state from police officers, immigration officials, I.R.S. agents, schoolteachers, agricultural extension agents, and members of fire departments, not from the nation's president or members of Congress.

Any state, if its operations are at all complex, must have a large number of people like this—people who are not directly involved in politics in the sense that they share in making major decisions but who are involved in the construction and implementation of the policies that carry out those decisions. These are collectively called the *public administration* of the state. A modern state has a large number of people in its public ad-

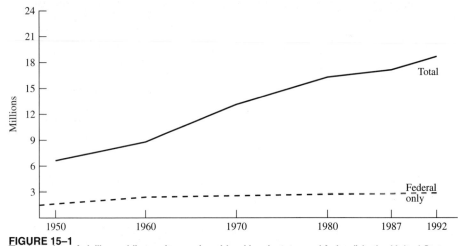

**FIGURE 15–1**
Total number of civilian public employees (combined local, state, and federal) in the United States, 1950–1992.

*Source:* U.S. Department of Commerce, Bureau of the Census, *Statistical Abstract of the United States.*

ministration. Figure 15–1 charts the growth of the public administration of the United States since 1950.

The number of public employees in the United States climbed from 6,400,000 in 1950 to 18,653,000 in 1992, almost wholly from increases at the state and local levels. (Federal civilian employment increased over this period by about 1,200,000.) Public employment climbed not only in absolute numbers but also as a proportion of the total civilian labor force. In 1950, 11 percent of all employed civilians were public employees; by 1992, this had risen to 15 percent. In other words, by 1992 better than 1 out of 7 employed persons was a member of the U.S. public administration.

Actually, all this understates the growth of government *operations* by a good deal. Federal operations obviously grew by much more than the growth in federal employment shown in the chart. What happened is that the federal government has tended over the years to expand its operations by contracting jobs out to private research firms and other organizations not directly in the government. The rapid growth of Washington, D.C., over the last few decades has been driven more by the growth of "beltway bandit" firms associated with the government than by growth of the government itself.

## PUBLIC ADMINISTRATION AS A POLITICAL PROBLEM

The fact that some part of policymaking is done by such a large number of people poses something of a problem for the state. Public administrators as a group obviously have significant governmental power, yet they are too numerous and individually too unimportant to be controlled very effectively. Thus, *a significant part of the governmental power of any state is necessarily not under close political control.*

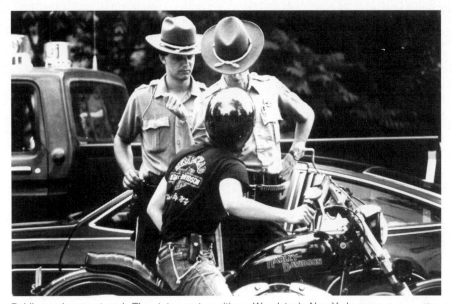

Public employees at work. The state meets a citizen, Woodstock, New York. (Mark Antman/Stock, Boston)

Examples of the governmental discretion of administrators are numerous. American police officers have a good deal of discretion, for instance, in whom they stop to search for weapons or illegal substances, and numerous studies of American police in the 1960s and 1970s showed that the rate at which black youths were stopped was far higher than that for white youths under similar circumstances.[1] As another example, consider the agents of the I.R.S. in the United States who audit taxpayers' returns. Inevitably, given the complexity of our tax laws, interpretation of the laws will vary from one agent to the next. As a result, the outcome of a tax audit depends at least to some extent on which agent handles it. Finally, consider the fact that the teachers of America determine, by their individual actions, the grading system that has such important ultimate effects on students' careers.

These and other examples show that even rather minor administrators make a good deal of governmental policy. The politically responsive part of government (elected officials, party leaders, military juntas, courts, or whatever), must be concerned to make certain that, at least in broad outline, they control the policies implemented by administrators. This control is not easy to design, however. An early study in this area illustrates the problem. In 1948 the U.S. Supreme Court ruled that it was unconstitutional for school districts to schedule certain hours during the day in which religious groups would come to school and provide classes in religion for those students who desired it. (Students who did not wish to have religious instruction were sent to study hall.) The

---

[1] For example, Irving Piliavin and Scott Briar, "Police Encounters with Juveniles," *American Journal of Sociology* 70 (September 1964): 206–214.

(Sidney Harris)

Court ruled that this practice violated the constitutional separation of church and state. Nearly ten years later, in a survey of Pennsylvania school superintendents, one-tenth of those responding stated that their school districts continued this practice, even though it was unconstitutional. The survey also ascertained that the superintendents understood the Court decision fully; they were acting not out of ignorance, but deliberately.[2]

## CHARACTERISTICS OF GOOD PUBLIC ADMINISTRATION

The way in which we organize our public administration should be intended to help us maximize some desirable traits. Among these are the following:

**1** *Honest, accurate translation of political leaders' decisions into more specifically designed policies:* This addresses the problem referred to above, of making sure that political leaders control at least the broad outlines of policy.

**2** *Flexibility in dealing with special cases at the point of delivery:* While adminis-

[2]Frank J. Sorauf, "Zorach v. Clausen: The Impact of a Supreme Court Decision," *American Political Review* 53 (September 1959): 777–791.

trators should be obedient to directions from above, they should not be slavishly obedient. If a police officer pulls a driver over for speeding and discovers that the driver is trying to get a child with a gaping wound to the hospital, we do not want the officer to write a ticket.

**3** *But this flexibility should not be used arbitrarily:* "Arbitrary" action is action taken capriciously, without regard to the truly important circumstances of a case. Stopping and searching blacks because of their race is an arbitrary act, for example. Another example would be to allow some students to take a makeup examination but to deny the makeup to others who had had the same excuse.

**4** *Feedback of expert advice; active imagination, and assertive inquiry on the part of administrators:* We hope that administrators will know more about their areas of work than anyone else and that they will not hang back from sharing their expertise with the public and with their political leaders.

**5** *Efficiency:* We hope that all this can be done without costing too much.

Now, we have said that all of these are desirable traits. So they are, but it is important to note that some of them are to a certain extent mutually contradictory, so that all of them cannot be fully met simultaneously. For instance, there is some tension between item 1 (honest, accurate translation) and item 2 (in which we expect administrators to follow their own judgment). Item 3 is difficult in and of itself, since one person's capriciousness is another person's courageous judgment. And item 4 (feedback of expert advice) assumes an independent-minded set of administrators who fit oddly with the task of honest, accurate translation.

It follows that there is no one best way to organize public administration; various modes of organization will emphasize one or another of these good things. Therefore, under varying circumstances, varying modes may be preferred.

## "BUREAUCRACY": A REFORM OF THE LAST CENTURY

Bureaucracy is one way to organize the public administration. The word "bureaucracy" is often used in common language simply to mean the public administration, usually with a connotation of distaste. But social scientists have a precise meaning for it—a particular mode of administrative organization that was developed as a reform in the nineteenth century and has spread widely to be the most generally used mode today.

Let us first set the stage of the eighteenth and early nineteenth centuries to show how bureaucracy developed as a reform of the systems then in place. Generally at that time, in both Europe and North America, positions in the public administration were treated as pieces of property, to be exchanged among people. In the United States, this took the form of the infamous "spoils system," by which administrative jobs were treated as commodities with which victorious candidates rewarded their party's workers. When the presidency changed hands, for instance, all post-office managers in the country were fired and new people from the victorious party were put in their place. The same thing happened with state highway and surveyor jobs when one party replaced another in a state capital; so also with fire and police jobs when city hall changed hands.

In Europe, positions in the public administration were individually bought and sold more or less as investments. A wealthy family wishing to establish a son in a comfortable life would buy him a position in the customs service, an officer's commission in the army, or some similar position.

Needless to say, such loose arrangements produced inefficient service, and there was little control over the quality of officials. In the United States, for example, some post-office managers could not read. And since, for most officials, getting the job in the first place was the only trick (what they did once they were there did not bear consequences for them), controlling officials' acts was difficult.

In the nineteenth century there arose a new method of organizing public administration, one that social scientists have come to call "bureaucracy."[3] Under a system of bureaucracy:

**1** Members of the public administration are appointed and promoted on the basis of their qualifications for the job they are to do.

**2** Special requirements of training or experience are set for the position.

**3** Administrative procedures are standardized, so that relatively little is left to individual officials' biases or passions.

**4** Clear lines of command are established, in which an order from a high official goes to a lower official, who then passes the order on to the next level, and so on until it reaches the point of operation. This arrangement is called a *hierarchical command structure*.

**5** Finally, public administrators are shielded from day-to-day political pressure, usually with a system of tenure.

This new, cleaner, and more efficient way of organizing the public administration was first used in appointments for procurement officers with the French and Prussian armies in the eighteenth and early nineteenth centuries. It demonstrated its usefulness in this area and spread rapidly. In the United States, the coming of the bureaucratic mode was embodied in the move for civil service reform at the turn of the century, which eventually took most administrative positions out of party control and based them on competitive civil service exams. By World War II, some form or another of bureaucracy was the usual method of organizing public administration throughout Europe and North America. And as new states attained their independence, they also generally adopted some form of bureaucracy. It is today the usual mode of administrative organization throughout the world, although there are many variations on its general themes.

## BUREAUCRACY VS. FLEXIBILITY

As noted above, there is no ideal way to organize administration. Of the various things that may be desirable in public administration, bureaucracy is particularly strong on the accurate translation of leaders' decisions and on preventing arbitrary behavior. Believe it or not, it is also rather efficient. (Bureaucracy has to some extent been identified in the public mind as wasteful because the public has high expectations for how cheaply one

---

[3]For the definitive statement, see Max Weber, "Bureaucracy," in H. H. Gerth and C. Wright Mills, *From Max Weber* (New York: Oxford University Press, 1958), pp. 196–244.

might expect administration to be done. Compared with private businesses, the administrative costs of public agencies are usually not all that far out of line.)

However, the very standardization and clarity of command that accomplish these good things mean that bureaucracy does not very well provide for local flexibility. Also, although the requirements for training and for decisions based on merit generally produce well-qualified officials, the system of standardization does not encourage independent-mindedness on their parts, and so bureaucracy does not especially tend to produce helpful expert advise to political leaders. Administrators under most versions of bureaucracy tend to hold their advice until it is asked for.

This means that the bureaucratic form of organization will fit some sorts of administrative needs better than others. Where standardization and obedience are especially important, bureaucratic organization fits well. Where independent and flexible judgment are especially important, it does not. Military service is one area in which standardization and obedience are important, because if a general is conducting a wheeling motion on a battlefield, everything could be lost if one battalion wheeled in the wrong direction. The bureaucratic model fits military operations well, and indeed the military—with its clean lines of command and its tendency to "do things by the book"—exemplifies the bureaucratic model. On the other hand, public enterprises in which obedience is less important than individuality are not as well served by bureaucratic organization. The university or college is such a place: The object here is to put a gifted individual in the lab or in front of a class and let that person do creative things.

It follows that bureaucracy is a better form of organization for some areas of the public administration than for others, depending on the relative needs for smooth obedience and for individualistic judgment. To a considerable extent, these differences are reflected in the organization of various agencies; almost universally the armed forces are the most bureaucratically organized agencies in any state's public administration, and universities tend to be rather decentralized.

However, there is in general a tilt *toward* bureaucracy, with most operations being organized more bureaucratically than would really be necessary. Most public administrators appear to incline toward standardization and away from individual initiative, a natural result of the human desire for safety and security. An official working within standardized procedures, unlike one who is supposed to make independent choices, cannot be blamed for the results. Procedures shelter bureaucracies, and so bureaucracies foster procedures. Impressionistic evidence for this, at least, is offered by the fact that there are apparently no armed forces in the world set up in anything but a pretty straightforward bureaucratic mode; whereas universities, which would not require bureaucratic organization and would almost surely benefit by its absence, are nonetheless often hemmed in by tight rules.[4]

## THE PROBLEM OF PROTECTED INCOMPETENCE

Another common problem of bureaucratic organization stems from a combination of two factors: (1) the difficulty in *public* administration, as compared with private busi-

---

[4]For example, in some European universities there are official limits on the number of pages that students may be required to read. In Norway in 1983, the limit for a fifteen-week political science course was 600 pages.

ness, of evaluating how well a person has performed a job, and (2) the requirement in a bureaucracy that administrators be shielded from direct political pressure, usually by a system of tenure.

In private business, a standard yardstick is available to evaluate how well a person has done in a job. If profits have gone up in that person's sector, if sales have been high, or whatever—if the person has made money for the company—then the job has been done well. But how do we evaluate the performance of public administrators? There is no notion of "profit" in the operations of a public school, of the army, or of a state's department of highways. A professor is supposed to teach well, but there is no dollar figure that can tell us *how* well the professor has taught. A highway superintendent is supposed to maintain the roads well, but there is no dollar figure that can tell us how well they have been maintained.

Combine this with the fact that political intervention against members of the bureaucracy is difficult and unlikely, and you have a situation in which incompetent administrators will rarely be removed from their positions. Few unambiguous standards of their performance are available, and—in the absence of clear-cut evidence—superiors will be reluctant to take action for fear that they will be accused of favoritism or political interference.

As a result, although bureaucracies do not particularly attract incompetent people—and although, by their entrance requirements, they have some success at selecting unusually competent people—those incompetents who do get in are less likely to be removed than they would be in private businesses.

## ADJUSTMENTS TO BUREAUCRACY

Although bureaucracy is only one way to organize the public administration, it is the dominant mode of organization across the world, as we have seen. Indeed, it is so dominant that the word "bureaucracy" has become almost a synonym for public administration, in much the way that "Kleenex" has come to be synonymous with facial tissues or "Xerox" with photocopies.

As a term loosely signifying public administration, "bureaucracy" has a number of unpleasant connotations. "Bureaucrats" are thought to be lazy, arrogant, inflexible, shortsighted—and too numerous. Partly this derives from the fact that it is impossible to construct an ultimate, best form of organization for the public administration; as we have seen, the various characteristics we would wish to see in a good public administration are to some extent mutually contradictory. Partly it derives from real weaknesses of bureaucracy.

In various parts of the world, adjustments have evolved or have been invented that can soften bureaucracy when it is excessively "bureaucratic." Among these are the office of *ombudsman*, provisions for opening government files for inspection, informal interference in the bureaucracy by political leaders, and—in general—pressure from public opinion.

1. *The office of ombudsman* is a Swedish invention. An ombudsman is a government official whose primary duty is to seek out citizens' complaints of abuse by public administrators and to negotiate changes in the offending practices. The ombudsman idea

has been picked up and copied in many other countries. In the United States, it has not been used at the national level; but Hawaii, Florida, and other states have established ombudsman offices. Many nongovernmental institutions have also found it an attractive idea. Universities have established ombudsman offices for their students or faculty, newspapers have set up a readers' ombudsman, and so on.

2. *Freedom of information* laws have been passed in many countries, and the United States has been a pioneer in this direction. Under such laws, individuals are guaranteed the right to examine most kinds of "internal" governmental documents, including dossiers that may have been gathered on them personally. The intent of the laws is to allow citizens to find out generally what procedures administrators are following in processes that are of interest to them; more specifically, it allows citizens to check and correct any information the government has gathered about them.

3. *"Interference" in administration by political leaders* may act as a safety valve to help correct abuses. You will recall that in the bureaucratic mode of organization, administrators are shielded from much direct intervention by political leaders. This was intended to avoid the excesses of a spoils system.

However, it does not compromise the bureaucratic model greatly if political leaders take advantage of their potential power over administrative budgets to seize bureaucrats' attention and get them to deal with a constituent's problem. In the United States, in particular, this has become a major part of the job of a member of Congress and has developed into an important correction of bureaucratic inflexibility. It is well understood that if you are having trouble getting a passport or your social security check has been held up, you should call your member of Congress for help. In 1976, for instance, members of the U.S. Congress each handled an average of 11,954 personal problems for constituents, and the caseload has grown immensely since then.[5]

4. *Pressure from public opinion* can help to correct bureaucratic sluggishness and abuse. Administrators are ultimately dependent on political processes for their offices' budgets, and so they must be attentive to public opinion. Also, since they are human, they want to be liked and admired for what they do. Public criticism hurts them and will usually lead to improvements where there have been problems. Agricultural agencies, welfare services, research agencies, the postal service—all are worried by stories in the press about shortcomings in their operations and all keep in reasonably close touch with their "clients," the groups most affected by their policies.

Perhaps the best evidence that public opinion serves as an important corrective to bureaucracy may be found by looking at an agency that is *not* under much direct pressure from public opinion. In democracies all over the world, immigration services are relatively free from pressures of public opinion because their "client group"—those who wish to enter the country as immigrants—cannot vote in elections and usually lack powerful friends. It is almost universally true that these offices are less responsive to their clients and more inclined to make arbitrary judgments than other government agencies.

• *Item:* The United States Immigration Service several years ago tried to save about $20 million by setting a rule that no visas could ever be renewed under any circum-

---

[5]U.S. Congress, House, Commission on Administrative Review, *Final Report,* House Document 95–272, 95th Cong., 1st sess., 1977, vol. 2. See also John Johannes, *To Serve the People: Congress and Constituency Service* (Lincoln: University of Nebraska Press, 1984).

stances. They would have saved the money by eliminating the positions of clerks who at that time handled applications for renewal. This decision ignored several important things: the hundreds of millions of dollars that would now not have been spent in the United States by visitors who were unable to prolong their stay, the human hardship and ill will that would have resulted, and the fact that there would still have had to be some provision for emergency cases, such as heart attacks and appendectomies on the day of departure. The Immigration Service was eventually talked out of it, as it was a silly idea.

• *Item:* Within the last several years, a German visiting the United States on a valid visa was turned back at the Minneapolis airport and forced to return home because he had a pornographic homosexual magazine in his suitcase.

• *Item:* When the Norwegian government in 1980 decided to reduce the number of work permits they would grant to foreigners by 50 percent, the Norwegian Immigration Service also reduced the staff to deal with those requests by 50 percent. They forgot that although they were going to say yes only half as often, just as many people would be *asking* as before. It was not long before the office had such a backlog that applicants were required to wait nine months to a year for an answer.

• *Item:* In the late 1970s, until they were dissuaded by embarrassing publicity, the British Immigration Service required a virginity test of women who were applying for permission to immigrate to Britain.

## SOCIAL REPRESENTATIVENESS OF PUBLIC ADMINISTRATION

Because members of the public administration are not under very direct political control and adjustments such as those described above can go only so far, there has been recurrent concern over how socially representative top bureaucratic decision makers are; that is, there has been a concern that they should not be too different from the population as a whole in such things as class background, race, or gender. There has been some controversy over this. On the one hand, advocates of "representative bureaucracy" urge that if administrators are not politically responsible, we should at least do all we can to ensure that they will look at things in the same ways that the common people would. On the other hand, skeptics have responded that we should not want "common people" in positions of uncommon importance and that we should not expect top public administrators to be any more socially representative than the leaders of corporations, universities, or other large institutions.[6]

Whatever our feelings on this, certainly many governments have made efforts to ensure that top public administrators will be reasonably representative. Since the 1970s, the United States has tried by affirmative action programs to increase numbers of minority and women officials. Decades earlier, after World War II, many European countries (France, for example) attempted to increase the proportion of their officials who

---

[6]See discussions in Samuel Krislov, *Representative Bureaucracy* (Englewood Cliffs, N.J.: Prentice-Hall, 1974); and Kenneth John Meier, "Representative Bureaucracy: An Empirical Analysis," *American Political Science Review* 69 (June 1975): 526–542.

**TABLE 15–1**

BACKGROUNDS OF EUROPEAN AND AMERICAN SENIOR CIVIL SERVANTS

|                              | Britain | Germany | Italy | Sweden | U.S.A. |
|------------------------------|---------|---------|-------|--------|--------|
| Social class origin (percent) |         |         |       |        |        |
| Upper                        | 35      | 42      | 42    | 42     | 47     |
| Middle                       | 47      | 50      | 49    | 43     | 35     |
| Working                      | 18      | 8       | 9     | 15     | 18     |
| Sex (percent)                |         |         |       |        |        |
| Female                       | 2       | 1       | 0     | 3      | 2      |
| Male                         | 98      | 99      | 100   | 97     | 98     |

*Source:* Robert D. Putnam, "The Political Attitudes of Senior Civil Servants in Britain Germany, and Italy," in Mattei Dogan, ed., *The Mandarins of Western Europe* (New York: Wiley, 1975).

were from the working class. They did this by changing their entrance procedures and providing for internal promotions from less important administrative posts.

Generally speaking, the effectiveness of such attempts is limited. As Table 15–1 shows, the sex and class backgrounds of senior administrative officials are remarkably similar across a fairly varied set of countries. These figures are based on a study conducted in 1970, and so the effects of recent efforts to increase the number of women at this level are not reflected. However, a 1987 study showed only 6 percent of department heads and 9 percent of deputy department heads were women, across all Western industrialized countries.[7]

## CORRUPTION

In the most general sense, "corruption" means that something has been changed so that it no longer meets its proper purpose. (Thus when meat spoils, we say that corruption has set in.) Specifically regarding politics, our concern is with officials performing their public tasks improperly in order to receive personal benefits: elected officials selling their votes, police overlooking crimes in return for a bribe, a housing inspector ignoring an unsafe building in return for a favor, and so on.

Obviously, this is not limited to the bureaucracy, though it does concern bureaucrats. Elected officials may also be involved, and even corruption in the private sector (business officials taking kickbacks to steer an order to a particular company, for instance) may concern public policy matters. But since the question of corruption often involves bureaucrats, this seemed as good a place as any to discuss it.

One might ask, first of all, why bother about corruption? It has always been present in human exchange, and there does not seem to be much we can do about it. It may even be the case that corruption occasionally serves good purposes by greasing the skids for commerce. The answer to this is twofold. First, the effects of corruption are horrid, and

[7]United Nations Office of Vienna, Centre for Social Development and Humanitarian Affairs, *Women in Politics and Decision-Making in the Late Twentieth Century* (Dordecht, Netherlands: Martinus Nijhof, 1992), p. 63.

it is not something society should tolerate. Second, while it does surely exist everywhere, it is worse in some places than in others, so there are things we can do about it.

What does corruption do to the community? The worst cost may be cynicism, lack of faith, and disregard for the rule of law that widespread corruption breeds. This can also contribute to broader political instability; from the earlier description of Nigerian state building (p. 40), recall that the Nigerian military overthrew the democratic government over charges of corruption—and it was largely because of the corruption of the civilian government that the military takeover was widely accepted.

But corruption also has direct economic costs. Some of these are obvious and dramatic, such as the billions of dollars the dictator Ferdinand Marcos apparently extracted from the impoverished Philippine economy for himself and his family. But more generally, the cost of government services not properly provided and the inflated cost of government programs due to corruption reduce both economic growth and the benefits we get from governmental services. According to Hong Kong's Independent Commission Against Corruption, bribes to Chinese government officials add 3 to 5 percent to operating costs for businesses investing in China.[8] And it is estimated that corruption has added as much as 15 percent, or $200 billion, to Italy's national debt.[9] Corruption does not always have to involve bribes. "Personal gain" may result from cozy relationships between vendors and government purchasing agents in the form of job prospects for the purchasing agents when they leave the government; or from the connection between moneyed interests and candidates to whom they made large contributions. These may be part of the background on the recurrent miniscandals in government purchasing in the United States ($100+ toilet seats) and some of the spectacularly failed savings and loan associations in the late 1980s.

What can be done about corruption? First, it is worth noting that corruption is not equally pervasive everywhere, and that should give us some hope. If it varies, there must be reasons that cause it to be greater in one place than another. Unfortunately, a number of these reasons do not offer much leverage. Societies undergoing rapid change often appear susceptible to corruption, partly because norms of behavior are in flux so people do not have stable moral guides for behavior and partly because there are so many opportunities for corruption in a situation of rapid economic change. Two good examples of this today are China and Russia, where corruption has exploded in the shift away from planned economies. This doesn't help us much, though—should we tell societies not to undergo rapid change?

The presence of foreign businesses has also been noted as a catalyst for corruption, since they may seem like easy marks and are often better situated financially than local officials, so that what may be a huge bribe to the official may look like a normal expense to the foreign business.

It is also generally the rule that industrialized states have less corruption than nonindustrialized Southern states—though Italy is a glaring exception, and there is certainly enough corruption to go around even in industrialized states.

Robert Klitgaard offers a number of practical suggestions.[10] Based on several case

---

[8]"The Destructive Cost of Greasing Palms," cited in *Business Week*, 6 December 1993, p. 136.
[9]Ibid., p. 138.
[10]Robert Klitgaard, *Controlling Corruption* (Berkeley: University of California Press, 1988).

CORRUPTION, ON A SCALE OF 0 TO 10

Transparency International, an international organization dedicated to documenting and tracing levels of governmental corruption, has ranked countries for 1995 by their level of corruption. The ranking was done by combining seven polls of bankers and businesspeople as to how much corruption there is in governments they've worked with. A score of 10 means politics is totally clean, 0 means that it is totally corrupt. Here are the scores of the forty countries for which they were able to develop a measure:

| | | | |
|---|---|---|---|
| New Zealand | 9.55 | Portugal | 5.56 |
| Denmark | 9.32 | Malaysia | 5.28 |
| Singapore | 9.26 | Argentina | 5.24 |
| Finland | 9.12 | Taiwan | 5.08 |
| Canada | 8.87 | Spain | 4.35 |
| Australia | 8.80 | Korea | 4.29 |
| Switzerland | 8.76 | Hungary | 4.12 |
| Netherlands | 8.69 | Turkey | 4.10 |
| Norway | 8.61 | Greece | 4.04 |
| Ireland | 8.57 | Colombia | 3.44 |
| Great Britain | 8.57 | Mexico | 3.18 |
| Germany | 8.14 | Italy | 2.99 |
| Chile | 7.94 | Thailand | 2.79 |
| United States | 7.79 | India | 2.78 |
| Austria | 7.13 | Philippines | 2.77 |
| Hong Kong | 7.12 | Brazil | 2.70 |
| France | 7.00 | Venezuela | 2.66 |
| Belgium | 6.85 | Pakistan | 2.25 |
| Japan | 6.72 | China | 2.16 |
| South Africa | 5.62 | Indonesia | 1.94 |

Note that industrialized states tend to have the cleanest politics, though the industrializing state of Singapore (score of 9.26) shows that states of the South are not necessarily corrupt; and Italy (2.99) shows that the industrialized states are not necessarily clean. The United States, ranked fourteenth of the forty states, does not show up especially well with its score of 7.79.

studies, including the anticorruption programs of Justice Effren Plana of the Philippines and Hong Kong's Independent Commission Against Corruption, his recommendations include public education programs (if stable behavioral norms are part of the problem, perhaps these can be reinforced); acting as watchdogs; making examples of some high officials; changing incentive programs and professionalizing the bureaucracy (these appear to be part of the explanation for the better performance of industrialized states). International pressure can also help. The 1977 Foreign Corrupt Practices Act, which bans U.S. multinationals from including bribes as part of their operating budgets, has probably helped to reduce corruption in other countries. Recently, a new international organization, Transparency International, was founded to help states around the world reduce corruption in their governments.

Relative to its importance in people's lives, corruption is one of the least-studied problems in the world, and one which governments have bestirred themselves the least to improve. There is no excuse for continuing to avoid the situation.

## CONCLUSION

The members of the public administration pose a dilemma to a state's political leaders. They are too numerous and individually too minor to control very effectively, yet collectively they have a major impact on policies. We have reviewed in this chapter various ways by which the state may address its dilemma—establishment of the bureaucratic model, adjustments to the bureaucratic model, attempts to achieve "representative bureaucracy"—but none of these can be fully successful. This is a problem of politics in which "half a loaf" may truly be the best one can hope for.

### Example: The French Bureaucracy

The "ordinary" bureaucracies of industrialized states do not vary greatly from one country to another. Mail carriers, teachers, agricultural extension agents, and so on, are organized and do their jobs in fairly similar ways around the industrialized world. Where there is considerable variation is in how the higher civil service—the managers, diplomats, specialists, and so on—are organized and work. In this realm the French are quite distinctive; theirs is arguably the best civil service in the world.

In this section we shall address almost solely the higher civil service. First, however, it should be noted that one thing *is* unusual about the "ordinary" French civil service: It is relatively small. In 1980 there were only approximately 2.5 million full-time local and national civil servants in France outside of the military. This compared, for example, with 3.2 million in Great Britain.[11]

The higher civil service of France consists of about four to six thousand highly trained persons. Most of these work within one of the ministries (defense, health, etc.), but at any given time over a thousand of them are working in more independent ways, either as staff advisers to the premier or ministers or in relatively autonomous administrative bodies, which I shall describe below. Furthermore, a certain number of them are at any time on loan to businesses, universities, or local government.

One of the things that distinguishes the French higher civil service is the training and ability of its members, which leads also to a high degree of self-confidence and pride. There are two main routes of entry into the higher civil service. If one wishes

[11]Douglas E. Ashford, *Policy and Politics in France* (Philadelphia: Temple University Press, 1982), p. 69.

to be a specialist, such as a scientist or statistician, one normally receives a university education from one of the "great" technical schools, such as the Polytechnic or the School of Agronomy, followed by more specialized training at an institution such as the School of Mines or School of Statistics and Economic Administration. If one wishes to be a generalist, after university one enters the famous National School of Administration (the ENA). One of the most difficult schools in the world to enter, the ENA gives its graduates a general training in administration and in the social sciences. Whether from one of the "great schools" or the ENA, higher civil servants in France are noted for their verbal skill and for a tendency to abstraction and mathematical reasoning. They are pragmatic rather than ideological and usually emphasize economics over politics.

The second thing that sets French higher civil servants apart is the tradition of "detached service," whereby they may leave the national civil service for periods of time either on personal leave or on loan by the national government to work in business, local government, or the universities or to hold elective office. In the 1970s, for example, about one-fourth of the members of the parliament were civil servants on leave from their administrative posts, and as of 1984 there were twenty-five national civil servants on loan to the city of Paris.

Under these circumstances, the French have developed a more politicized civil service than that of most countries, one that lives on the frontier between "politics" and administration.[12] When François Mitterrand became president in 1981, for instance, about four hundred high administrators were replaced with others who would be more compatible with the new regime, although Mitterrand took pains to demonstrate that this was not done solely on the basis of party connections. This politicization appears to have added vigor to the higher civil service and has allowed French civil servants to lead aggressively in the development of such new political thrusts as the campaign for a tunnel under the English Channel, the adoption of the value-added tax, and the formation of the Common Market.

It was stated above that the French higher civil service is "arguably" the best in the world. The other side of the "argument" is raised by those who see the civil service as too insulated from the rest of the population, too haughty, and overly given to technical fixes:

> Instead of a homogenous administration equally open to everyone, one sees established an aristocracy of a few thousand young men produced through privileged channels; the isolation of their education easily persuades them that they are destined to retain among themselves (and for themselves) the administration of the state, and above all its best jobs. Less and less are they touched by doubts; the assurance of their elders and their own success convinces them that it is enough to advance confidently under cover of their technique to make obstacles disappear. The sharing of a certain exoticism of language or of modern administrative techniques or of economics; the sense of making up a kind of network between the bosses and dauphins of the great public and private businesses; the exhilaration, still

---

[12]This also fits the more general culture of the French and other continental Europeans. English is the only European language that distinguishes between "politics" and "policy"; in French, both are called *politique*.

hardly acknowledged, of feeling in their hands such means of action, and such docile un-derlings; all these make up the psychology of a senior civil servant, young and ardent, certainly devoted to what he considers the public good, but more inclined to define it him-self, or to let it be defined by the boss, than to listen on this subject to the aspiration of the country.[13]

## Example: The Saudi Arabian Bureaucracy

A severe problem facing most states of the South is that their bureaucracies are newly established and often had to be assembled hurriedly as the state was formed. Technical expertise is scarce, and the bureaucracies have also not had time to build up an esprit de corps, with high expecta-tions for performance, such as that seen in France. As a re-sult, states of the South seem to be especially burdened with sluggish, cautious, inefficient administration.

The bureaucracy of Saudi Arabia illustrates these problems. Saudi Arabia is not a poor country, and so it is spared the problems of poverty that many other states of the South endure. Like most of the States of the South, however, the Saudi government and

---

[13]"Le Regime des 'Jeunes Messieurs,'" *Courrier de la Republique*, November 1965, quoted in An-thony Sampson, *The New Europeans* (London: Hodder and Stoughton, 1968), p. 345.

**TABLE 15–2**
ATTITUDES OF SAUDI BUREAUCRATS

|  | Strongly agree (percent) | Agree (percent) | Disagree (percent) | Strongly disagree (percent) | Number answering question |
|---|---|---|---|---|---|
| It is best to change or cancel programs that cause social conflict. | 25 | 59 | 14 | 2 | (282) |
| Social change should not be instituted at the expense of traditional values. | 37 | 53 | 8 | 2 | (287) |
| It is best to consult with one's superior before making a decision. | 26 | 57 | 15 | 1 | (288) |
| In making decisions, no one should violate rules and regulations. | 21 | 55 | 21 | 2 | (286) |

*Source:* Saud al Nimir and Monte Palmer, "Bureaucracy and Development in Saudi Arabia: A Behavioral Analysis," *Public Administration and Development* 2 (April-June 1982): 93–104.

public administration were established in their present form only in the last few decades; before that, the Saudis had had little experience in modern public administration.

A study of the values and attitudes of middle-range Saudi bureaucrats reveals a group of people who are cautious, wedded to routine, and not very ambitious.[14] Table 15–2 presents the bureaucrats' answers to several questions.

Answers to other questions were consistent with the four given in the table. For instance, 78 percent of the bureaucrats would prefer a low-paying job with few risks to a high-paying job with high risks. There is, of course, no "typical" state of the South. Saudi society is a conservative one, in which traditional values are strongly enforced. This may help to explain the bureaucrats' caution about social change, but it should not have much to do with their caution in dealings with their superiors, and in this the Saudi bureaucrats seem to be similar to those in most of the South. This caution, of course, may not be wholly a bad thing. It fits the standard bureaucratic model and should ensure the faithful transmission of orders. However, we saw earlier in this chapter that an emphasis on any one virtue in administration is purchased at the cost of other virtues. In this case, flexibility and innovation are lost—virtues that are important to states of the South which, like Saudi Arabia, are undergoing great social and economic change.

### Example: Battling the Bureaucracy in Brazil[15]

 Wherever modern government structures are built on an already highly developed legal and administrative system, bureaucracies are bound to multiply. Brazil is no exception. What is exceptional is the degree to which Brazilians have managed to circumvent the more rigid and obstructive bureaucratic rules. In addition, the government has recently had some success in attacking the rules themselves.

Brazilians have described their federal administrative system as excessively centralized, formal, and distrustful of the public. This view dates back at least to the temporary transfer to Brazil of the Portuguese kingdom and its centralized administration in 1808, and perhaps even further, to 1549, when the first governor-general arrived with a framework of laws and regulations even before there were people to conform to them. The formalism embodied the prejudice that documents are more important than facts. The distrust showed in the controls that required endless lists of certificates, attestations, licenses, and other documents. Not many years ago the case was reported of an export license that required 1,470 separate legal actions and involved thirteen government ministries and fifty agencies.

The *jeito* was employed to overcome such difficulties. This Portuguese term, corresponding roughly to "knack," "way," or "fix" in English, refers to the varied ways

---

[14]Saud al Nimir and Monte Palmer, "Bureaucracy and Development in Saudi Arabia: A Behavioral Analysis," *Public Administration and Development* 2 (April–June 1982): 93–104.
[15]World Bank, *World Development Report 1987* (Oxford, England: Oxford University Press, 1987), p. 73, reprinted by permission.

that Brazilians, like people in other countries, get around the maze of regulations and legal requirements. The jeito principle has been remarkably effective. It relies significantly on the *despachante* (roughly, an expeditor), who has counterparts in many countries but has been especially active in Brazil, where the lubrication of sticky administrative processes has been essential for social mobility and rapid economic development.

The despachante is an intermediary who, in return for a commission or fee, purchases and fills out the multiplicity of legal forms, delivers them to the proper persons, and extracts the needed permission or document. The system developed when the simplest transactions, such as obtaining a marriage license or identity card, could take ages or days or hours, depending on whether one used despachantes and how much they were paid. The despachantes are thriving, specialized professionals and have their own union and competitive examinations. Some specialize in police work, naturalizations, auto licenses, marriages, or "legalization of real estate." The despachantes who arrange imports and exports have long enjoyed a legal monopoly. Each typically has several employees, and almost all sizable businesses maintain their own despachantes.

Brazil's rapid economic growth and social evolution demonstrate that a complex bureaucracy need not be a barrier to development. The costs are nevertheless substantial. Moreover, such resourceful adaptations of the jeito may have been too effective and undermined attempts to reform public administration.

The most recent efforts to reform the system, rather than live with it, began in 1979. A National Debureaucratization Program was designed to simplify administrative procedures and, more broadly, to reverse what was seen as the relentless trend toward growth in government, excessive centralization, and abundant regulation.

The results in 1979–84 were impressive. On the basis of citizens' project (which surveyed all the points of contact of individuals, throughout their lives, with bureaucratic requirements) it was possible to eliminate, or simplify, a long list of documents and procedures ranging from notarization requirements and driver's licenses to passport extensions, university enrollment processes, and income tax returns. Evidence of residence, economic dependence, and so on, could be established with simply a written statement by the interested party rather than legal certificates and third-party attestation. Thus a "presumption of truth" displaced the "rule of distrust." Other legal procedures were simplified. In all, more than 600 million documents a year were removed from circulation. The savings have been estimated at close to $3 billion a year, equivalent to about 1.5 percent of Brazil's GDP.[16]

In the economic field the main achievements were to simplify rural credit procedures, to change commercial registration procedures so that forming a company could take three days rather than three to six months, and to bring relief from bureaucracy to 1.5 million small enterprises. For the time being, however, the program has left many areas of regulation untouched, including some that are important to industrialization and trade.

---

[16]The GDP (Gross Domestic Product) is the sum of all goods and services produced in the state. See also its entry in the glossary.

It is significant that, although a minister of debureaucratization was appointed, no new government department was formed. The program was implemented by an executive secretary and just twelve assistants. At the very least—and on a limited front—some progress has been made in simplifying the rules and changing the relationship between citizens and civil servants.

## FURTHER READING

Aberbach, Joel D.; Putnam, Robert D.; and Rockman, Bert A. *Bureaucrats and Politicians in Western Democracies*. Cambridge, Mass.: Harvard University Press, 1981.

Allison, Graham T. *Essence of Decision: Explaining the Cuban Missile Crisis*. Boston: Little, Brown, 1971.

"Bureaucracy." In the *International Encyclopedia of the Social Sciences*.

Crozier, Michel. *The Bureaucratic Phenomenon*. Chicago: University of Chicago Press, 1963.

Dogan, Mattei, ed. *The Mandarins of Western Europe: The Political Role of Top Civil Servants*. New York: Wiley, 1975.

Gruber, Judith E. *Controlling Bureaucracies*. Berkeley: University of California Press, 1987.

Heidenheimer, Arnold J., et al., eds. *Political Corruption: A Handbook*. 2nd ed. New Brunswick, N.J.: Transaction, 1988.

Kaufman, Herbert. *Red Tape: Its Origins, Uses, and Abuses*. Washington, D.C.: Brookings, 1977.

Knott, Jack H., and Miller, Gary J. *Reforming Bureaucracy: The Politics of Institutional Choice*. Englewood Cliffs, N.J.: Prentice-Hall, 1987.

Ostrom, Vincent. *The Intellectual Crisis in American Public Administration*. University, Ala.: University of Alabama Press, 1973.

Smith, Bruce L. R., ed. *The Higher Civil Service in Europe and Canada: Lessons for the United States*. Washington, D.C.: Brookings, 1984.

Suleiman, Ezra N. *Politics, Power, and Bureaucracy in France*. Princeton, N.J.: Princeton University Press, 1974.

Wilson, James Q. *Bureaucracy: What Government Agencies Do and Why They Do It*. New York: Basic Books, 1989.

# 16

## LAW AND THE COURTS

The *law* is a collection of rules laid down by the government, binding all members of the state, including members of the government itself. The law does two things: (1) It sets society's norms and rules for behavior; for instance, it may state that one may not steal others' property, that one may not expose oneself indecently, or that religious practice other than the state religion is illegal. And (2) it sets the rules by which individuals in the state must relate to each other—rules governing divorce procedures, rules for the honoring of contracts, and so on.

The rules making up the "law" may reside in the state's constitution; or may be statutes passed by the state's legislature; or decrees announced by the state's executive officers such as the president, a military junta, dictator, or whatever. They may also, in some states, develop out of decisions of courts.

Courts are an odd part of the government in that they have the responsibility for interpreting all parts of the law and adjudicating—when various parts of the law are in conflict—which part takes precedence. Their oddity lies in the fact that they are themselves part of the government but must judge fairly among all citizens of the state, including those in the government. Thus, while they are part of the government, they must be to some extent independent of it. This independence has even developed so far in some states, as noted above, that the courts themselves are able to share in creating the law.

The tension implicit in being part of the government but at the same time independent of the government, and how this tension is resolved, is an important aspect of the world's major legal systems, which we shall examine below. *Legal systems* are general, organized sets of legal principles that form the basis of law and adjudication in states. They organize legal practice for states in a way somewhat parallel to the role ideologies play in organizing the thought processes of individuals.

## ANGLO-SAXON CASE LAW

The legal system that is most familiar to Americans and Canadians is Anglo-Saxon case law. This is the system that developed in England during the late Middle Ages and early modern period and spread further to such former British colonies as the United States, Canada, India, and Nigeria.

In the system of case law, courts are seen as largely independent of the state's government, so independent that in the cases they decide they share to some extent in the making of the law, since those cases serve as precedents for future decisions. This is why the system is called "case law."

The heart of the system is the belief that the law is something that exists partially independent of the government itself. From this there follow several important aspects of case law:

- The task of judges is to find proper law, and the law evolves over time with a certain degree of flexibility. Thus, the United States Supreme Court in its landmark *Brown v. Board of Education* decision took note of changing sociological evidence to decide that segregated schools (which had once been considered legal) were now against the law.[1]
- Training of judges and lawyers proceeds in special schools, separate from the rest of the university; their training—largely by other lawyers—emphasizes clarity of thought and expression, and skills at searching out and applying precedents.
- The role of the judge is to be a neutral arbiter, ruling on behalf of the law after listening fairly passively to opposed arguments by the lawyers.
- Especially where the government brings charges against an individual (a criminal case), the law protects the individual against the disproportionate power of the government. The burden of proof lies with the government (the defendant is "considered innocent until proven guilty"), and a whole series of protections hold: An individual may not be held more than twenty-four hours without being charged (right of habeas corpus), spouses may not be forced to testify against each other, and so on.

I do not mean to suggest here that in case law systems the law is simply manufactured by judges. The courts base their decision not only on precedents but on statutes passed by the government, including (in the case of the United States) the Constitution. If the government changes the law by statute, the courts follow its directions, and so the government is the *final* authority on the law. If the United States government were to amend the Constitution so as to make segregated schools constitutional, for instance, *Brown* v. *Board of Education* would be annulled. However, in the absence of government action, and by filling in the details of government statutes, the courts work with the government to make the law. For instance, when a tax code revision is passed in the United States, commentators generally say that we will need to wait for two or three years of court cases to know exactly what the new law means. In a case law system, then, courts operate largely independently of the rest of the government, even though statutes and the constitution have the final word.

---

[1]Brown v. Board of Education, 347 U.S. 484 (1954).

## CONTINENTAL EUROPEAN CODE LAW

Case law developed in England out of local customs and was popular especially with the same emerging commercial elites who would help to develop the ideology of liberalism.[2] With its emphasis on the law as something existing at some remove from the government, and on the law's capacity to restrain illegal governmental action, case law has a clear affinity with liberalism's desire for limited government.

On the continent of Europe, forces for limitations on governmental power were never as strong as in England, probably because the establishment and maintenance of the continental states was usually more difficult than the establishment of a secure state in England, protected as it was by the English Channel. The legal tradition on the continent has generally been to rely on variants of the Roman system of law, which involves a detailed code of law produced and interpreted by the government. The law, in this tradition, is an expression of governmental policy. Napoleon, when he was building his French Empire in the early nineteenth century, gave this tradition added life by encoding existing French law in the Code Napoleon; he later imposed similar codes in many of the European states he conquered. In one way or another, code law eventually dominated across the continent.

From the basic principle that the law is an instrument of the government, there follow several notable characteristics of code law:

• It is not based nearly as much as case law on the accumulation of precedents. While code law judges obviously try to keep in step with each other, lest the law itself degenerate into chaos, they rely more on the statute or code itself as an authority—not on previous judges' decisions. They do not "make the law" as case law judges do.

• The training of code law lawyers and judges, accordingly, is more general and not as specialized as what one finds in case law systems. Since legal officials are seen primarily as just another kind of civil servant, they are trained in the general university by professors rather than being trained in a separate school by lawyers.

• The distinction between law as a tool of the state and law as something above the state is most marked in criminal cases, where the state itself (in the person of the prosecutor) is a party to the case. Under most code law systems, in a criminal case the judge is not a neutral arbiter of the arguments between the prosecution and defense; rather, as a servant of the state, the judge enters directly into argument, questioning witnesses and even, in some systems, directing the police investigation of the crime. The judge's role is not to pass judgment on the state's case but rather, as a servant of the state, to try actively on behalf of the state to learn the truth in the case. There is no presumption of innocence, as in case law; actually, there is no presumption at all. The state, through the court, simply tries to find out what happened. And finally, in most code law systems there do not exist the elaborate structures of protection for the accused that we see under case law—right of habeas corpus, right against self-incrimination, right against spouse's testimony, and so on. The task of the court is not to "prove guilt beyond any reasonable doubt"; rather, it is simply to decide what is most probably true in the case.

[2]See Chapter 3.

To an American raised on "innocent until proven guilty" this may seem strange.

The original code law systems were European. As new states were established in other parts of the world, unless they were former British colonies, they generally adopted some form of code law. When a revolutionary government or a new state based on an independence movement has needed to make an abrupt break with the past, it has seemed more straightforward to design a code of law directly, rather than build one gradually through an accretion of judicial decisions.

In communist states, the spirit of law as servant of the state—or, in this case, the revolution—was carried to an extreme form of code law. In criminal law, for instance, where in case law many barriers are raised to protect the accused from the state, and in code law there are generally no presumptions either way, in the communist variants of code law barriers were often raised against the accused, to make it certain that the state could convict a person if that was thought necessary. For instance, in the Soviet Union a defendant was not told what the state's evidence was until the day before the trial; this obviously made it difficult to prepare a defense. A person charged with a crime did not personally choose a defense lawyer. Rather, a lawyer was assigned from the collective, and that lawyer was not supposed to put the client's interests ahead of the state. If the lawyer found evidence of guilt, it was the lawyer's duty to bring that evidence forward.

## RELIGIOUS LAW: THE SHARIA

Generally, states of the world have some version of case law or code law, often referred to as "Western law," introduced by the European powers or borrowed from them. A number of other legal systems survive partially, however. The most enduring are various forms of religious law; and of these, the most important is the Sharia—Islamic law—which makes up part of the legal system of such Islamic states as Morocco, Tunisia, Egypt, Syria, Iraq, Mauritania, Yemen, Afghanistan, and Pakistan.

No state is governed exclusively by the Sharia, and this is true of other traditional legal systems in use today; rather, where it is used, it supplements and blends with Western law. For instance, the code systems of Egypt, Syria, and Iraq instruct judges to fill any gaps in the code according to principles of Islamic law.

Islamic law centers on obligations—to God and to other people—rather than on any sort of rights or entitlements. It is based on central Islamic principles of justice, good deeds, equality, and human brotherhood, as these were applied in the first few centuries after Muhammad to specific questions of behavior. The law was pretty well set by the tenth century A.D.; many elements which seem odd in modern society made sense for the medieval society in which they developed, but they have not changed since. For instance, polygamy apparently originated after the battle of Uhud in which many men were lost and their widows had to be provided for.[3] And what seem to us unbearably harsh punishments, such as cutting off a hand for thievery, were common and perhaps enlightened in the tenth century; certainly, they did not differ from European practice of that time.

---

[3]Noor Mohammed, "An Introduction to Islamic Law," in Kenneth Robert Redden, *Modern Legal Systems Cyclopedia* (Buffalo, N.Y.: Hein, 1990), p. 5a. 100.9.

## EMILE DURKHEIM'S THEORY OF LAW

Law is the set of rules that bind a society together, and so theorists of society have often looked to law as the critical point for analyzing society itself. Emile Durkheim, a great French sociologist of the nineteenth century, analyzed law in his work *The Division of Labor in Society* to address the question, "How do societies hold themselves together?" He saw law as functioning in varying ways at different stages of societal development, to provide the mechanism for maintaining the society intact. In analyzing the role of law, he had a lot to say about why law develops as it does.

He first asked the question, "Why would people be moved to stay together as a society?" As an answer, he pointed to two bases for staying together: "Mechanical solidarity," or the similarity among people of the same society which makes them feel akin to each other and comfortable with each other, and different from people not in that society; and "organic solidarity," the benefits of economic cooperation by which, for instance, a group of people with varying specialized skills are able by cooperating to build an automobile—something no one of them could possibly have done alone.

These two reasons for staying together as a society, however, operate under a natural tension. To build the kind of division of labor that yields large returns of organic solidarity it is necessary for people to be *different* from each other. One person must be a designer, another a capable machinist, and so on. This must diminish the similarity that builds mechanical solidarity. Thus, as society comes to rely more on organic solidarity, it must rely less on mechanical solidarity.

What does this imply for law? Durkheim points out that the two kinds of solidarity require different things of the law. Mechanical solidarity, which is based on people feeling similar to each other, requires law that makes people behave like each other and—when this similarity is broken—law that gives dramatic, public punishment. This reemphasizes the rules and reassures the public that the break has been compensated for. Laws will prescribe sexual practice, dietary practice, religion, dress, and so on; and punishment will be revengeful and memorable.

Organic solidarity, based on cooperation, needs law that ensures and regulates that cooperation—law enforcing the fulfillment of contracts, law regulating ownership of property, and so on. Where a law has been broken, what is needed is monetary compensation or enforcement of a contract, rather than societal retribution.

The development of law in modern societies—as improved technology makes the payoffs of cooperation ever greater, and we appear to rely more and more on "organic" rather than "mechanical" solidarity—does seem to bear Durkheim out. Punishments for crimes have generally become less dramatic and emphasize rehabilitation more than revenge. Public hangings were common in criminal cases in the United States in the nineteenth century, for instance, but are not used today. And the vast body of contract law is a relatively "recent" addition of the last few centuries.

Note, incidentally, that Durkheim is squarely on the "choice" side of "power and choice." He sees legal structures arising to suit the needs of individuals making up society, not because someone imposes them. And the very question Durkheim poses at the beginning is based on the idea that people choose to be in a society, that the very existence of society is based not on the use of power but on an accumulation of individual choices.

Trial in Kuwait of those who allegedly collaborated with Iraqi invaders.(Gelin/Sipa Press)

Unfortunately, since Islamic law is based on divine inspiration, it is not easily adapted by judges. It is not totally inflexible, however. New circumstances can be adjudicated by analogy to older cases, and complex evasions can be worked out that honor the letter if not the spirit of the old laws. For instance, the Sharia bars charging interest on loans, since loans should be given out of a generous heart; but various evasions are used to get around this today, such as giving a valuable gift in return for the "gift" of a loan. At its heart, however, a God-given law cannot be a flexible as human law.

It is perhaps the flexibility of Western systems that has led them to be so widely used. Modern commercial transactions, especially, require rules of a kind that most traditional legal systems never envisioned: enforcement of contracts, for instance. Where traditional law is used today, it is always combined with many elements of Western law.

## THE BLENDING OF CASE LAW AND CODE LAW

I have probably exaggerated so far how sharp the distinction is between case law and code law. It is important to realize that the differences between them are mostly differences of *degree*. For instance, case law is not *simply* "made by judges"; statute is also an important part of the law, and the state can always change "judge-made" law by passing a new law or amending the constitution. In code law, similarly, judges do not totally ignore precedent. They cannot decide a case simply by looking at the code and ignoring what all other judges are doing, or else things would become quite chaotic; nobody would know what the law was, since different judges might decide similar cases quite differently.

Thus the distinction between these two types of cases is a matter of degree. Still, matters of degree can matter a great deal, as we have seen in comparing how criminal cases are handled in the two systems.

In the late twentieth century, we find that even the somewhat fuzzy distinction between the systems is becoming still less clear, as code law systems adopt some aspects of case law, and vice versa. For instance, in the general spirit of "constitutionalism," protections of individuals against abuse by the state have become popular even in many code law systems.[4] In 1959 France, for instance, established for the first time the right of habeas corpus.

Furthermore, most industrialized states with complex governmental structures have found it necessary to set up some sort of avenue for individuals to sue the state; if the state was supposed to pay you a pension through the social security system but did not, for example, you need some way to force them to honor their obligation. In standard code law systems this was difficult, since the law was a tool of the state and could not stand judge over it. Furthermore, faced with the complex governmental regulations of the twentieth century, government agencies often find themselves operating in quasijudicial roles. An antitrust office, for instance, must rule on whether a proposed merger of companies will restrict trade unduly. Such decisions require "judicial" procedures within an administrative agency.

To handle questions like these a wholly separate system of *administrative courts* has developed in many states, and these generally make law by precedent. In France, the administrative court system has a case load larger than that of the regular courts, and its law is developed on a case basis.

Thus many code law systems are evolving to look more like case law systems. The opposite process is not as marked, but some case law systems are becoming more like code law in certain ways. Legislatures and parliaments in some case law systems have begun to write codes in various areas to which judges are bound. For instance, many states in the United States have set up codes of uniform sentencing guidelines which set narrow ranges within which a judge may set the sentence of a person convicted of any particular crime. Also, in Great Britain—where case law started—there has been some discussion of late about setting a code of basic legal and human rights which all judges would be bound to enforce.

The historic differences in how legal systems originated in Europe may be receding far enough now that the differences they produced are being overridden by the great *similarity* of conditions across modern industrialized states. These states need the strong coherence that code law can provide, but at the same time their governmental operations are so large and complex that individuals feel a need for some protection against abuse by government. It may be that under these circumstances, a blend of code and case law is most appropriate.

---

[4]For "constitutionalism," see Chapter 9.

## COURTS

Courts are organized in sometimes rather complicated ways to take care of the variety of questions that come before them. The one common element to all courts is that, to the extent that a state has a tradition of constitutionalism, the courts are organized so as to be at some remove from other sources of political power. This is necessary if the courts are to be *independent* and thus able to give fair decisions no matter who is involved in a case.

Thus, judges and other court officials in most of Europe are professional civil servants and are protected by the traditions of the bureaucratic model from political pressure.[5] In the United States federal judges are appointed by the president with approval of the Senate, but the appointments are lifetime appointments so that no judge can be threatened with expulsion for having made an unpopular decision. Judges for state and local courts are elected in many states, but those elections are usually set for long terms in office and are formally nonpartisan, to emphasize the removal of the judges from the ordinary give-and-take of politics.

Where constitutionalism is less well established, however, the judiciary may have little independence. In Paraguay under Stroessner's military government, for example, the courts were subordinate to the military, and the president's office directed judicial decisions in all cases involving political prisoners.[6]

Courts are often organized separately to handle different kinds of law, especially:

• *Criminal law*, which involves a charge that a person has disobeyed a law prescribing proper conduct. In such cases, the state (through a prosecutor, district attorney, etc.) is the party that brings the case, and the person charged is the "defendant." The outcome of a criminal case is either acquittal of the defendant, or punishment such as imprisonment or a fine.

• *Civil law*, which regulates relations between people. Civil cases may include disputes about the meaning of a contract, suits for damages in cases of injury, questions of mutual responsibility in marriage or divorce, and so on. The outcome of a civil case is some decision by the court as to mutual responsibilities—how much money is to be paid in child support, how a contract is to be met, or whatever. Because civil cases usually involve private disputes rather than the breaking of a law that affects the broad public, civil cases are normally conducted between individuals, without the state being involved as a party to the case.

It is possible in civil law not only to get compensation for something that has happened in the past but to prevent a person from doing something in the future that will harm you, or force them to do something that you wish. To do this, the court declares an "injunction" that the person should (or should not) do the thing required. An example would be an injunction against a neighbor draining a marsh that you share; the injunction might be necessary if the marsh, once drained, could never be the same again biologically, so that undoing the damage after the fact would not be possible.

---

[5]For the "bureaucratic model," see Chapter 15.
[6]George Thomas Kurian, *Encyclopedia of the Third World* (New York: Facts on File, 1987), p. 1572.

(Sidney Harris)

• *Constitutional law*, which involves disputes about the nature of the political process itself and about whether laws themselves are consistent with the constitution.

Aside from being organized by *substance*, as above, courts may also be organized by *jurisdiction:*

• *Lower courts,* which handle disputes directly.

• *Appeals courts,* which handle disputes about whether lower courts have decided cases properly.

• *Juvenile courts,* which handle criminal cases involving defendants who are not yet adults. Using separate courts here allows for more flexible, private proceedings for defendants who are considered not yet fully responsible for their actions.

• *"State" courts* (federal systems only), which handle cases under the separate "state" laws in a federal system.

• *Religious courts*, used in a state such as Iran, where religious law coexists with Western law.

• And many others.

The "law" has a paradoxical character to it in that it is made by the government but, since it controls all parts of the state, it must control the government as well. Arrangements have been worked out to give varying degrees of independence to the law, but ultimately the paradox remains.

### Example: The Law in China

Chinese law today is shaped by China's Confucian tradition and by the needs of the state's leaders. For thousands of years, until the end of the nineteenth century, China was dominated by Confucian thought. In the Confucian view of the world, society was meant to be in harmony. This harmony was thought to be maintained by leaders' continual demonstration of virtue, which instilled a sense of virtue into the rest of the people; and it was maintained also by complex networks of rites and mutual obligations based on the family and clan.

Problems were supposed to be worked out among disputants, perhaps with the help of a local person of superior rank, in a way that was conciliatory and that left everyone in agreement. No one was to lose; no one was to lose face. There were lawyers and law in China then, but they were to be appealed to as a last resort. The truth is, Confucian China *did not like law* and disapproved of it. Legal proceedings were made so unpleasant that most Chinese would go to any lengths to avoid them; and avoiding them was all the easier for the fact that the alternative of mediation and conciliation was pressed on the disputants by their families and communities with a good deal of social pressure. Proceedings were deliberately made difficult and dangerous by Confucian rulers, to discourage use of the law. The seventh-century Emperor K'ang Hsi is quoted as saying:

> Lawsuits would tend to increase to a frightful amount, if people were not afraid of the tribunals, and if they felt confident of always finding in them ready and perfect justice. As man is apt to delude himself concerning his own interests, contests would then be interminable, and the half of the Empire would not suffice to settle the lawsuits of the other half. I desire, therefore, that those who have recourse to the tribunals should be treated without any pity, and in such a manner that they shall be disgusted with law, and tremble to appear before a magistrate.[7]

When the Communists gained power in China after World War II, they continued the tradition of minimizing use of the law and legal procedures. From 1949 until 1976 the government passed little legislation, preferring to govern less formally through enunciation of doctrines by party leaders. Courts and the legal process were rarely used. In 1981, on the eve of Deng Xiaoping's opening of the system, there were only 5,000 lawyers for a Chinese population of approximately 1 billion, compared with half a million lawyers for a U.S. population a quarter the size of China's.[8]

---

[7]Cited in René David and John E. C. Brierly, *Major Legal Systems in the World Today*, 3rd ed. (London: Steven, 1985), p. 520n.

[8]Xinhua General Overseas News Service, Item 1009065, 9 October 1990.

Of course, the Communist government changed the Confucian system markedly. The old aristocratic leadership and old networks of obligation and ancestral rites were replaced by factory committees, neighborhood committees, and party officials. But the basic principle remained, that disputes were resolved by conciliation and mediation processes with a great deal of social pressure on the disputants to reach a mutually acceptable consensus.

With the death of Mao Tse-tung in 1976 a power struggle developed between Mao's supporters, who had pushed society in a radical left direction during the Cultural Revolution of 1966–1976, and more centrist leaders such as Deng Xiaoping, who had been victims of the Cultural Revolution. Deng and his supporters prevailed, and among the changes they introduced was a much greater reliance on law and legal proceedings than what had gone before. The body of statutes was expanded dramatically, with codes of law for many areas previously not ruled by law, including industrial safety, environmental protection, and patents; criminal law, marriage law, and many areas of civil law were expanded. The legal profession expanded dramatically as well, with a tenfold increase by 1990. Especially in criminal law, changes were dramatic, with procedures set up rather along the lines of European code law.

These changes were probably made for two reasons:

1 *To establish a "rule of law":* The informal procedures of Confucian China, once the Confucian structure of society had been destroyed, left the way open for purely arbitrary power. Deng and his friends had suffered grievously from informal, arbitrary proceedings during the Cultural Revolution—Deng, for instance, was sentenced to hard labor, and his son was permanently crippled when his back was broken during interrogation—and they wanted to set up somewhat greater protections for the individual.

2 *To handle the problem of economic disputes:* Deng wished to liberalize the Chinese economy, introducing large elements to market choice. Before 1976 there was little civil law in China; since there was practically no individual property under communism, there were few private disputes except for matters like marriage that could be handled reasonably in conciliation by local bodies. With the development of a partial market economy, however, there would be long-distance disputes between suppliers and customers, partners, and so on, and these could not be handled locally. Also, economic exchanges required precise, dependable rules—not informal social processes for resolution. With the use of market mechanisms, civil law was necessary, and this could not easily be provided without building a more formal legal structure.

Economic development proved Deng right in this; by 1995, just in the first eight months of the year, Chinese courts saw 697,000 cases involving disputes between businesses.[9]

Such changes cannot occur overnight, of course. Even with a tenfold increase in the number of lawyers over the 1980s, there were only 50,000 lawyers in China in 1990, and a number of them were part time and not fully trained. These are clearly

[9]"China's Litigation Boom." *Business Week,* October 9, 1995, p. 64.

insufficient to operate a full-scale legal system in a country of a billion people. Furthermore, old Confucian attitudes of disdain for the legal process die hard. In 1986, for instance, a woman who had been beaten by members of another clan petitioned the supreme court for compensation. When nothing came of the petition, she gave a copy of it to an editor of *People's Daily*. The editor sent it to the police, and she was sent to a concentration camp, beaten, and sent home. "The police said they would beat me to death for being a petitioner. Petitioners are all bad people, they said."[10]

### Example: The European Court of Justice

 As you saw in the example at the end of Chapter 2, the European Union is an organization of fifteen western European states which are attempting to merge their markets and economies. The Union has an elaborate governing structure, although the members remain independent, sovereign states.

One of the governing structures is a court, the European Court of Justice; observing this court provides us with a fascinating case of how a court may develop a body of law in "new ground"—fifteen independent states that are bound together to form a common market. The Court consists of thirteen justices, who are appointed by the unanimous consent of the fifteen member states. A justice serves a term of six years and is sworn to act on behalf of the Union as a whole.

The original basis of the European Union is the 1957 Treaty of Rome, which comes as close as anything to serving as the Union's constitution. The treaty was rather vague about the status and duties of the Court. It stated that the Court must ensure that "the law is observed" in applying the treaty (Article 164), and at various other points it suggested that the Court should apply general principles of law; but it did not spell out clearly the Court's jurisdiction or powers.

Much like John Marshall's Supreme Court in the early days of the United States, the Court of Justice has made its place in the order of things through a series of decisions, in effect defining its powers by what it has been able to get away with. It has moved cautiously, but steadily, to make its law supreme within the European Union.

In an important early decision, the Court ruled that the Rome Treaty set up a new order for the members which was not governed by international law. The key question was whether a member state could retaliate in kind if another member violated the Rome Treaty and injured it. Under international law, this would be permitted; and so if the Rome Treaty were simply a treaty among sovereign states, a member could do this. The Court ruled, however, that one member could not retaliate against another but must instead seek relief through the Union's institutions. It thereby transformed the Treaty of Rome from just a treaty into a constitution.

In a later decision the Court of Justice expanded the right to bring cases from

[10]*The Economist*, vol. 316, no. 7669, 25 August 1990, p. 28.

member states to include also individuals and corporations in those states. Thus citizens of states in the Union could bring cases against their own governments. Most cases in the Court have involved trade regulations because the Union is, after all, primarily an organization to enforce free trade within its borders. But perhaps the most dramatic development of law by the Court of Justice has been in the area of individual rights.

The Treaty of Rome did not specify many rights for individuals. It was a document intended to set up a free market, and most of the few rights that are mentioned in it are economic: the right to free movement of capital, the right to bargain collectively, the right of women to earn pay equal to that of men, and so on. The Court, however, has gradually developed across several dozen cases a set of rights based on "the constitutional traditions common to the Member States" and on other treaties that member states may have signed, such as the European Convention on Human Rights—even though the Court is nowhere directly empowered to enforce those treaties. Some of these cases have gone deeply into what would be considered the independent responsibilities of member states: British schools have been directed to stop using corporal punishment, the Dutch army has had to change its disciplinary procedures, German courts have had to provide access to lawyers before a suspect is charged with a crime. Among general rights that the Court has written into Union law are freedom to practice religion; a right against *any* kind of discrimination based on gender, not simply discrimination in pay; the right to education; and freedom from arbitrary governmental decision.

Since so little was written into the Treaty of Rome along these lines, the Court of Justice has proceeded by building a body of case law. As is usually true where case law develops, the Court has been tolerated in this because it has generally been seen as a constructive force in the development of the Union and because the alternative—states retaliating against each other for trade violations, for instance—could bring chaos.

Like courts everywhere, a basic problem for the European Court is enforcing its decisions. Its authority could never have developed as it has if member states did not heed it when it ruled on a case. It has no power to force compliance and must rely on member states' governments to enforce its rulings, which could have posed grave problems except that there has been a remarkable record of compliance. There have been exceptions, though. An order to France to desist from restricting imports of mutton was defied for a couple of years. But in general, states have followed the Court's directions, and the more often this happens, the more solidly the Court's power becomes rooted in habit and expectations.

## FURTHER READING

Abraham, Henry J. *The Judicial Process*. 5th ed. New York: Oxford University Press, 1986.
Bartlett, Katherine T., and Kennedy, Rosanne, eds. *Feminist Legal Theory*. Boulder, Colo.: Westview, 1991.

Barton, John H.; Gibbs, James Lowell, Jr.; Hao Li, Victor; and Merryman, John Henry. *Law in Radically Different Cultures*. St. Paul, Minn.: West, 1983.

David, René, and Brierly, John E. C. *Major Legal Systems in the World Today*. 3rd ed. London: Steven, 1985.

Glendon, Mary Ann; Gordon, Michael W.; and Osakwe, Christopher. *Comparative Legal Traditions*. St. Paul, Minn.: West, 1982.

Redden, Kenneth Robert. *Modern Legal Systems Cyclopedia*. Buffalo, N.Y.: Hein, 1990.

# PART FIVE

# INTERNATIONAL POLITICS

# 17

---

# POLITICS AMONG STATES

---

In the preceding chapters, we have looked at the manner in which politics—the use of power to make collective choices for a group of people—is carried on within states. But states also carry on politics *among* themselves. For instance, they sign trade agreements setting up special arrangements for the exchange of goods between firms in two or more countries. Or a number of states may agree to coordinate their military activities, as in the NATO alliance. Regular exchanges of scientific information are set up among states. Agreements are drawn up committing all those who sign to such things as a promise not to test nuclear weapons in the open air. Treaties are drawn up to protect wildlife that migrates across state borders. Wars are fought, and are settled. All these are examples of politics—the use of power to make collective choices—*among* states rather than within any one state. This is commonly called "international politics."

## THE EVOLUTION OF THE INTERNATIONAL SYSTEM SINCE WORLD WAR II

Before analyzing international politics abstractly, it will be useful to review the development of the international system since World War II.

From the seventeenth century until the twentieth, most of the world's wealth and military power were concentrated in Europe and various European states used that power to subjugate large populations around the world and form them into colonial empires. By the early twentieth century, European dominance was already weakening, especially because of the increasing power of the United States. The Europeans then hastened their slide from power by squandering their wealth and slaughtering their youth in World Wars I and II. Although other powers such as the United States and Japan were eventually involved in these wars and they have been called "world wars," almost all of the fighting and destruction centered in Europe. The European states emerged from World War II in 1945 exhausted, with only enough strength left to reconstruct themselves internally.

Two major changes in international politics resulted from this exhaustion of Europe: (1) Two new superpowers—the Soviet Union and the United States—arose to fill the power vacuum, and (2) the European states' empires threw off European rule, since the Europeans no longer had the power to hold them in subjugation.

The rise of the Soviet Union and the United States to dominate world politics created quite a different kind of system than what had gone before. When Europe dominated world politics, a number of substantial powers were involved in the system because Europe itself was so fragmented. Britain, France, Germany, Italy, and to some extent the Soviet Union, Japan, and the United States could figure in alliances. Many varying combinations of states in alliance were possible, and patterns of alliance shifted as states jockeyed for position. In the world after 1945, however, and especially from 1945 to about 1960, the system of politics consisted simply of a bipolar rivalry between the United States and the Soviet Union.

The two superpowers had been allies in the war against Hitler and initially set out into their domination of the world with pledges to cooperate in building a new, peaceful political order. However, they differed deeply in political philosophy, and they had conflicting political and economic goals. The Soviet Union used its dominating military force in the region to bring most of eastern Europe under its control, both for economic advantage and in order to insulate itself militarily and politically from western European states such as Germany and France (which had frequently attacked it earlier in the century). By 1946, Winston Churchill had coined the phrase "Iron Curtain" in his famous speech at Westminster College, Missouri:

> From Stettin in the Baltic to Trieste in the Adriatic, an iron curtain has descended across the continent. Behind that line lie all the capitals of the ancient states of Central and Eastern Europe. Warsaw, Berlin, Prague, Vienna, Budapest, Belgrade, Bucharest and Sofia, all these famous cities and populations around them lie in what I must call the Soviet sphere, and all are subject in one form or another not only to Soviet influence but to a very high and, in many cases, increasing measure of control from Moscow.[1]

In 1947 President Harry S Truman announced that the United States was sending economic aid to the embattled anticommunist government of Greece, and the Cold War was joined.

The period of rivalry between the Soviet Union and the United States from 1945 on into the 1960s (and periodically still until 1989) is called the "Cold War" because while at times it involved intense animosity, it never developed into full-scale "hot" warfare. Various skirmishes were fought—the Soviet blockade of West Berlin in 1948, war between the United States and the Soviet client state of North Korea in 1950—but there was never direct fighting between the two superpowers. There is a clear reason for this. Not only was the international system turned into a bipolar system after 1945 but the

---

[1]Randolph S. Churchill, ed., *The Sinews of Peace: Post-War Speeches by Winston S. Churchill* (London: Cassell, 1948), p. 100.

two superpowers of that system were armed with a new kind of weapon that made a war between them essentially unwinnable. Nuclear weapons are so destructive that, in an all-out nuclear war, either combatant would be able to ruin the other.[2] As a result, the bipolar system that followed World War II was marked by a frustrated rivalry in which the two superpowers chewed on their animosity toward each other but were not able to do much about it.

The other main result of Europe's exhaustion after World War II was the breakup of the old colonial empires. Fully 100 of today's 190 states were colonies of European states at the outbreak of World War II. In other words, there are more than twice as many states in the world now as there were in 1941. These new states receive sympathy and support from some of the older states—such as China, Egypt, and the states of Latin America—which, although they were independent before World War II, find that they share a common set of problems with the newer states. Together, these new and older states make up the South.

The growth in numbers and importance of the Southern states has changed the international system markedly. The South commands many of the world's natural resources and comprises about three-fourths of its population. However, it does not command anything close to a proportional share of wealth or military power. Most of the states of the South are individually weak, although some, like India, China, and Brazil, have developed into moderately important powers. However, as a group they account for so much of the world that they cannot be ignored. Many Southern states, as they grow in wealth and military strength, appear to have a great potential as future powers. The United States, Japan, and the states of western Europe all court states of the South as important markets for the goods they buy and produce, and as important powers for the future.

## THE NEW WORLD ORDER

As of the early 1970s, then, the world could have been described as a fairly stable system of states dominated by two main conflicts—a military standoff in the Cold War animosity between the Soviet bloc and the bloc led by the United States, and an economic and political "north-south" tension between the South and the industrialized states of both blocs. Over the next two decades, however, three major developments changed this system into the more fluid, more complicated, but less tense one we face today:

1. *Steadily over the last couple of decades the set of actors involved in international politics expanded and became more varied.* At the beginning of this period international

---

[2]A revisionist literature has questioned whether nuclear weapons really prevent war. This literature points out that in the 1920s many people thought that the existence of poison gas, in combination with the development of modern air forces, had made all-out war unwinnable. Any power, even if it were going down in defeat, could launch such deathly attacks with gas canisters that the winner of the war would be destroyed. Therefore, it was agreed, no one would dare to wage war against a power that had poison gas weapons. As it turned out, full-scale war was waged in World War II, but without gas. All the participating powers had chemical weapons, but none ever used them for fear of retaliation in kind. The revisionist literature argues that all-out conventional warfare could similarly occur today without the use of nuclear weapons. See, for example, John Ellis van Courtland Moon, "Chemical Weapons and Deterrence: The World War II Experience," *International Security* 8 (Spring 1984): 3–35.

War and famine in Ethiopia caused this Eritrean mother and child to flee to an intensive feeding clinic in the Sudan. (Sarah Putnam/The Picture Cube)

politics was conducted pretty much just by the states of the world, plus the United Nations and its agencies. Starting in the early 1970s, however, the number of nongovernmental international organizations began to grow explosively—growth that continues today, as we see in Figure 17–1.

Not all of these organizations are actively engaged in international politics. The International Political Science Association, for instance, exists mainly to promote communication among scholars, although it will occasionally act to promote or defend academic freedom in various parts of the world. But many others—Amnesty International, the International League for the Repatriation of Soviet Jews, the Pugwash Conferences on Science and World Affairs, the Union of National Radio and Television Organizations of Africa, the International Federation of Journalists, to name only a few—are active in all sorts of ways.

In addition to formal organizations, other kinds of new actors have joined the scene. We noted in Chapter 2 that many corporations today are so large, and their operations spread across so many states' boundaries, that they bargain directly with the states almost as equals. Terrorist groups, too, have become significant actors in international politics. Throughout the 1980s, terrorist groups in Lebanon, not directly associated with any government, were an important factor because of the leverage they gained by taking and holding hostages from Western states.

2. *The interdependence of the world's states grew enormously.* One way this has shown up is in the dependence of states' economies on their trade with each other. For the United States, for instance, trade as a proportion of economic activity was fairly sta-

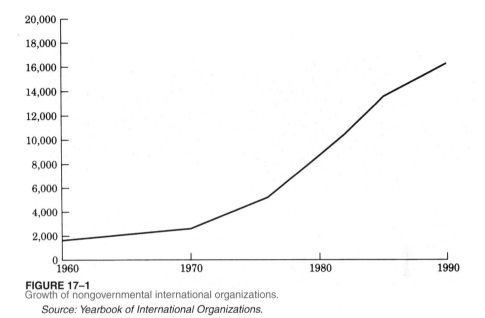

**FIGURE 17–1**
Growth of nongovernmental international organizations.
*Source: Yearbook of International Organizations.*

ble through the 1950s and 1960s, but it became an increasingly significant part of our economy in the 1970s. As seen in Figure 17–2, it doubled as a proportion of our gross national product between 1970 and 1980. Not only did international trade play a larger role in states' economies, but since many of a state's largest corporations were spread across numerous countries, states' economies now depended more on what was going on in other states than was the case, say, in the first half of the twentieth century.

Environmental policy is another area in which interdependence has increased explosively. As the world becomes more industrialized, the environmental impact of what we do is less a matter of concern only for the polluting state and perhaps its nearest neighbors. The depletion of the ozone layer, as well as the increase in carbon dioxide in the atmosphere that causes global warming, affects all states' populations. These and other problems are the ultimate "externality"; as we saw earlier (pp. 99–100), any externality forces a search for collective decisions.

Finally, partly through the expansion of worldwide communications such as Cable News Network and partly because the people of the world are more literate and better educated than they were twenty years ago, we all seem more aware of what happens in other states than we used to be. What would once have been claimed as "internal affairs" of sovereign states—apartheid in South Africa, human rights abuses in many other states—are now part of international politics.

It is a cliché, but still a good one, that the world is indeed becoming a smaller place.

3. *Finally, the bipolar system of rivalry between the Soviet Union and the United States disappeared.* This had already been happening, fairly slowly, for about twenty years as the U.S.S.R. and the U.S.A. gradually weakened economically and lost their

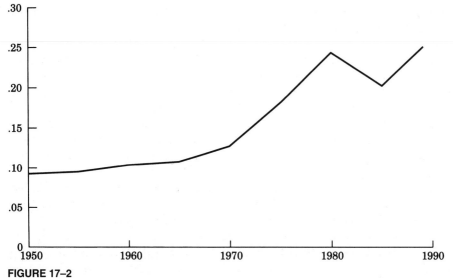

**FIGURE 17–2**
Trade (exports plus imports) as a proportion of United States gross national product.
*Source: World Almanac 1994* (Mahwah, N.J., 1993: Funk & Wagnalls, pp. 104, 184).

monopolies of economic and military power to such upstarts (both communist and non-communist) as Japan, China, Germany, and France. But the system of rivalry finally ended rather suddenly about 1989 with the economic exhaustion of the Soviet Union and its internal collapse after the failed coup of 1991.

The results of this shift are momentous. The very way we defined the system of states—West, East, "Third World"—had been based on the old rivalry. Defense establishments suddenly found themselves searching for a new raison d'etre. Client states, like Cuba and Pakistan, found themselves abandoned by their superpower partners.

We are still only beginning to work out the implications of all these changes in the international system. There are, of course, many dangers inherent in some of the changes. There are likely to be more "small wars," for instance, as the superpowers no longer feel a need to keep a lid on boundary disputes around the world; and while these may be "small" wars, we have seen in Bosnia, Somalia, and other instances that they can be dirty and cruel. But the new, fluid system also offers opportunities. It may be that with increased interdependence and the disappearance of bipolarity, the world will be able to search more cooperatively for collective decisions to address its collective problems.

In this regard we have seen both hopeful and unhopeful signs. The 1991 Gulf War was an indication of the possibilities of cooperation. In August 1990, Iraq blatantly invaded and seized its neighbor Kuwait. It is true that the separate existence of the two states was as usual the result of a colonial past (Iraq had long argued a claim on Kuwait), and so the boundary issues were not altogether clear. But the invasion *was* sudden. And as the same sort of claims Iraq made could have justified hundreds of other invasions by other states in other parts of the world, most of the world's states united in condemnation of Iraq's action.

Things might have stopped there, as they so often had in the past, with international condemnation. But partly because of worldwide concern for supplies of oil ("interdependence" again) and partly because the U.S.S.R. and the U.S.A. did not veto each other's proposals in the United Nations (the end of bipolarity), the UN was able to function as its original designers had intended—to provide collective protection to small states threatened by larger ones. The protection was concrete: initially, a program of economic sanctions against Iraq, followed by military action.

On the other hand, one should not conclude that international relations in the post-Cold War era will necessarily be based on cooperation most—or even much—of the time. A cautionary example is provided by the tragic brutality that followed the breakup of Yugoslavia.

Yugoslavia was a state composed of quite disparate ethnic groups: Roman Catholic Slovenians and Croatians; Greek Orthodox Serbs, Montenegrens, and Macedonians; and Moslems who were mostly Bosnians but included Croatians and Serbs as well. Tensions were exacerbated by the fact that the Croatians had sided with the occupying German troops during World War II against guerrilla troops that were primarily Serbian. This multinational state had held together as a loose federation throughout the post-War period at least partly because of bipolarity, with both the United States and the Soviet Union fearful of what would happen if the country were allowed to disintegrate.

In 1991, Slovenia and Croatia signalled their intention to declare independence. Serbia, which was the largest part of Yugoslavia and controlled most of the army, tried to block their secession. Slovenia established its independence after a few sharp battles; but in Croatia, a Serbian minority, supported by the Yugoslav army, tried to prevent Croatia from seceding, or at least tried to isolate large areas of Croatia and add them to Serbia.

A prolonged civil war broke out in Croatia. In 1992, the situation turned from awful to horrible when Bosnia also declared its independence of Serbia and a complex four-party war ensued, with Croatians, Bosnian Moslems, Croatian and Bosnian Serb minorities, and Serbia all fighting in varying combinations. At times, Croatia and the Serbs ganged up on the Moslems; at other times, Croatia shifted sides and attacked the Serbs. There were nauseating atrocities on all sides, and the prolonged siege and bombardment of the Moslem city of Sarajevo focused international attention on the events.

The rest of the world repeatedly declared their wish to help stop the fighting and return seized lands to the Bosnian Moslems, but they were quite ineffective in pursuing either goal. The United Nations declared an embargo on arms exports to any part of Yugoslavia, but this mostly hurt the Bosnian Moslems since Croatia and Serbia had ways to obtain arms despite the embargo. The European Union offered to mediate the conflict and discouraged American offers (admittedly halfhearted) to become involved. The Europeans appeared to believe Yugoslavia was in their sphere of interest and that they should take responsibility for it. While the EU formed a common policy toward the region and sent troops to dispense humanitarian aid under United Nations auspices, they were never able to take a tough stance toward any of the combatants that might have actually stopped the fighting.

Finally in 1995, after years of terrible bloodletting, the EU and the United States, under the auspices of their common NATO organization, decided to use massive air power

PEACE COMES TO BOSNIA

(Auth © 1995 The Philadelphia Inquirer. Reprinted with permission of Universal Press Syndicate.
All rights reserved.)

to punish those who resisted peace accords. With this threat as a tool, and with the offer
of Russian, American, and west European troops to thelp police any peace agreements,
all participants were finally brought to serious negotiations. A peace treaty was signed
in November 1995 in Dayton, Ohio, though the Bosnian Serbs' reservations about it still
left some uncertainty whether it would work.

Even taking into account that this part of the world has been famously difficult to
work with throughout history, the international system cannot be said to have worked
well to prevent destruction and human suffering in this long, sad, and possibly pre-
ventable war.

## INTERNATIONAL POLITICS

Certainly, the world has a full agenda of problems to address: the problem of environmental degradation; the peaceful transformation of the socialist societies in eastern Europe and the former Soviet Union; help for the poorest states of the world (mostly in
Africa), which are getting poorer rather than better off; the population explosion, which
again is occurring most rapidly in the poorest countries; the maintenance of international trade in the face of protectionist competition; the control of nuclear arms; and
many more.

How are these to be addressed? I have argued in the above section that the changes of the last two decades may—*may*—provide new opportunities to find solutions to common problems. However, international politics has some special characteristics that make it unusually difficult to find common solutions, as compared with other kind of politics. These enduring weaknesses may, or may not, stymie any hopes of a "new world order."

Let us look a bit more abstractly at international politics. We will first consider a few ways in which politics *among* states differs from politics *within* a state, the sort of politics with which we have been concerned so far in this book. It will be necessary, in doing this, to add one new concept, the "fiduciary political role." After we have looked at this question, we will conclude by examining the nature of power in international politics and, again, the question of power and choice.

How is international politics like that which we have been looking at so far in this book, and how is it different? In its main outlines, politics among states is a good deal like politics within states. The same general sorts of policy questions are addressed in both—regulation of potentially harmful behavior, aid programs for the weak, guarantees of standard weights and measures, and so on. And like politics within states, politics among states is marked both by the use of force and by appeals to mutual self-interest, that is, by power and choice. Political decisions—decisions on behalf of groups of people—are reached in both kinds of politics. But in important ways international politics differs from politics within a state. *The most important difference is that there is no single central authority to provide ultimate settlement of a dispute among states. Also, political figures are more likely to follow overtly selfish* (selfish on behalf of their states' interests) *strategies in politics among states. And finally, political interchange does not proceed as easily in politics among states as it does in politics within a state.* Let us look at each of these points.

## THE ABSENCE OF CENTRAL AUTHORITY

In politics as it is carried on within a state, the various antagonists are all subject to a central authority that has enough power to settle a question firmly. If environmentalists square off in conflict with a mining company, both sides know that ultimately their dispute will be resolved by some higher authority that has the power to make them accept that decision, even if they do not agree with it. In the United States, that authority would be Congress, the President, or perhaps the Supreme Court; in Britain, it would be the Parliament; in Saudi Arabia, it would be the King. The point is, within any state there is a central authority, more powerful than any single political force, that can enforce decisions on any question that comes up. The only exception to this would be a state involved in a civil war, which is precisely a situation in which there is no clearly established central authority.

In politics conducted *among* states, however, there is generally no central position of authority. Therefore states that become involved in disputes must ultimately settle them themselves, whether by negotiations or through war. Other states may give helpful advice and exert pressure on the disputants, but there is no body of any sort that can impose a settlement.

The United Nations would be a potential body of authority. It is an organization of 179 states, most of the states of the world, that accepts responsibility for many of the things a government would do within a state. That is, it is concerned to preserve law and order by preventing violent solutions to disputes (i.e., wars); it promotes health programs, education, and research; it tries to see that poorer states are helped.

But while the United Nations tries to do the *things* a government does, it cannot do them *the way a government would do them.* It has no army or police force of its own to enforce its decisions. Rather, it must depend on voluntary help from its member states. And, since few states are going to send their soldiers voluntarily into a place where they are not wanted—and thus risk war with the people on whom they are enforcing the United Nations' decision—this has effectively meant that the UN can almost never send in a police force unless the disputants all agree voluntarily to accept it. (The Gulf War was the first exception to this rule in decades.) The UN's attempt to pacify Somalia is a bit different question, since that involved bringing order to a region where the government had broken down, rather than a case of interceding between warring parties. Even there, though, the organization found it difficult to marshal the will to impose solutions.

Despite these limitations the UN has frequently been able to play a helpful role when the nations involved in a dispute want to bring in a neutral group to police their negotiated settlement. For instance, small United Nations forces supervised the initial disengagement of Egyptian and Israeli forces after their 1967 war. This is a far cry from the real policing power that would give the United Nations the authority to force a decision on the parties in dispute, but it has helped on occasion to reduce international violence.[3]

Another potentially ultimate authority in the system of states is the International Court of Justice, headquartered in the Netherlands. The Court is a branch of the United Nations, but the body of "international law" over which it decides goes back far beyond the United Nations, which was founded only in 1945. Since that time, about fifty cases have been tried in the Court, but again, any solution laid down by the Court sticks only if the parties of the dispute voluntarily abide by the Court's ruling. In 1984, for instance, Nicaragua brought suit against the United States for mining its harbors. When the United States refused to admit that the Court had jurisdiction, the Court could do little. Most cases that come to the Court are not of this sort but are cases in which all who are involved have agreed in advance to accept the Court's decision, whatever it may be. In these circumstances, the Court can serve as a useful tool for resolving disputes. Overall, however, it cannot play the role a government would play.

Since there is no ultimate governmental authority in the world, politics among states is in many ways what we might expect politics within a state to be if that state had no government. States that are large and strong are able to bully smaller states, and they usually get what they want. Small states must attach themselves to stronger states, through alliances, for protection. In effect, gangs of states join together for mutual protection just as, in a governmentless state, people would form gangs.

---

[3]For a good discussion of the UN's role, see Indar J. Rikhye, Michael Harbottle, and Bjørn Egge, *The Thin Blue Line: International Peacekeeping and Its Future* (New Haven, Conn.: Yale University Press, 1974).

(By Toles for The Buffalo News)

## FIDUCIARY POLITICAL ROLES AND INTERNATIONAL MORALITY

Before we consider the second special aspect of international politics, we must define a new concept—*the fiduciary role in politics*.[4] We say that someone acts in a fiduciary role if that person operates as an agent on behalf of another person's interest. A real estate agent acts in a fiduciary role on behalf of a person who wishes to sell a house, or a lawyer acts in a fiduciary role for a client.

The important thing about fiduciary roles for our purposes is that a person acting in a fiduciary role stands in a peculiar moral position. Let us assume that the fiduciary agent is personally upright and moral and that among the agent's "upright" traits is a strong sense of duty toward the person whose interests are being represented. Now let us suppose that the agent is caught in circumstances in which doing the thing that is personally moral will hurt the interests of the person who is represented. Consider the lawyer, for instance, who may need to browbeat a timid witness in order to defend a client. What is

---

[4]William H. Riker presents the concept of fiduciary role in much the way it is used here in *A Theory of Political Coalitions* (New Haven, Conn.: Yale University Press, 1962), pp. 24–27.

the right thing to do? We hope such a lawyer would never browbeat a timid person on her own behalf, but is it right for her to impose her personal scruples on the client's case, and thereby injure the client's interests?

This sort of situation arises frequently in modern life, because today we have given more and more of our activities over to agents. A corporation president might be generous personally and wish to pay the company's workers more than the going rate, but it is the stockholders who will pay if the company does this, not the president. Is it right for the president to be generous with their money? A real estate agent might not remain silent about that tiny leak in the north gable in trying to sell his own house, but is he right to impose his openness on his client? In general, we recognize that a different moral situation exists when people do something on behalf of others than when they do it to help themselves. We feel differently about a prostitute who is in the trade as a normal occupation than we do about a mother who, in dire straits, prostitutes herself in order to get food for her children.

How does all this relate to international politics? It is important to international politics because here, more than in the politics within a state, almost all decisions are made by those who see themselves as acting in fiduciary roles, on behalf of the people in the state they represent. In politics as it occurs *within* a state, political figures act to some extent as fiduciary agents (members of Congress, for instance, represent their constituents); but they are largely personal decision makers who represent no clear single interest. Leaders of states, however (and the diplomats and others who help them to construct the state's position in international politics), work on behalf of a single clear "client," the people of that state. It is well understood that a state's leader owes first duty in international politics to the state and its interests, and that anything or anyone else in the world for whom the leader feels affection must run a distant second. We expect Bill Clinton to serve the interests of the United States, Jacques Chirac to serve the interests of France, Hosni Mubarak to serve the interests of Egypt.

This gives a different and colder moral tone to international politics than we find in politics within states. We expect leaders of states to be more cold-blooded in international politics than they would be domestically. And what is regarded as personal virtue in domestic affairs may be seen as perverse and harmful in international politics.

Leaders of states have often been forgiven for official acts that, if done for personal gain, would have blackened their names forever. Harry Truman, for instance, killed many thousands of Japanese civilians when he ordered atomic bombs dropped on Hiroshima and Nagasaki, and Churchill launched devastating firebomb attacks on German cities. But they were judged at least partly in light of their official positions. The fact that leaders of states see themselves as filling fiduciary roles is reinforced by *nationalism*, which generally sees other peoples as being less human, less deserving of justice and mercy, than our own. This makes both the leaders and general populations of states more comfortable than they might otherwise be with their states' amoral behavior.

This case should not be overstated, however, since the political actions of states are not *solely* based on calculations of cold rationality. Emotions play a role, and some of these may be generous. For instance, U.S. support for Great Britain in World War II was based on more than just rational considerations, although there were certainly elements of rationality involved as well. And clearly, U.S. support of Israel over the last few decades has involved something beyond rationality. But in its broad outlines, international politics is distinguished from politics within states by its relatively greater tone of calculation.

## IMPEDIMENTS TO INTERNATIONAL COMMUNICATION

A third major difference between international politics and politics within states is that communication between leaders is more cumbersome and more vulnerable to misunderstanding than communication within any one state. Within a state, the various political leaders generally speak the same language. More important, they "speak the same language" in that they know each other fairly well, generally have a common fund of experiences and stories, and share the same culture.

In international politics, the people involved must often use interpreters to converse, which makes the proceedings more formal and slow and also leaves a good deal of room for misunderstanding. The problem of interpretation can lead to amusing moments, as when President Jimmy Carter's statement that he was happy to be in Poland was translated as "I lust for Poland." But the formalization of interchanges can produce more important glitches than that.

More serious yet is the frequent lack of shared assumptions and motivations, which may lead to a failure of communication between states. After World War I, U.S. diplomacy was deeply flawed by Woodrow Wilson's inability to understand the motives of its allies, Britain, France, and Italy. The leaders of Britain and France in the 1930s responded to Hitler in what was probably an inappropriately gentle way because they did not understand what he wanted to do. In the postwar period, U.S. and Soviet leaders had continual trouble dealing with one another appropriately because they approached their mutual interchanges with such different historical and political assumptions.

## POWER AND INTERNATIONAL POLITICS

Under these circumstances—with most decisions made by reciprocal bargaining or through conflict, with a relatively naked rationality operating, and with severe difficulties of communication—international politics is a rough game. More simply and directly than in politics within a state, the raw power of the participants determines the outcomes.

On what is this power based? First and foremost, a state's *military power* determines its overall power in international politics. Military power is hard to assess. Different states emphasize different kinds of arms. Israel does not have much of a navy, but it has an excellent small army and air force. How do we compare it with Great Britain, which has an excellent small navy? And how does nuclear capacity figure in our calculations? Beyond this problem of comparing apples and oranges, there are imponderable questions such as toughness, morale, and battle readiness that must be considered. Israel's armed forces are much stronger than their small size would suggest, simply because of their spirit and their level of training and because they have had frequent combat experience; they are "tried and true." Finally, any armed force will fight better when defending its home soil. A smaller and weaker army may well be able to defend itself successfully against a stronger army under some circumstances.

A good example of this is the tough resistance that Argentina was able to maintain in 1982 against the more imposing and experienced British armed forces in the Falkland Islands war, even though Argentina eventually lost. An even better example is the defeat dealt to the large and powerful U.S. forces by North Vietnam in the 1960s.

Table 17–1 displays a few aspects of the military strength of the ten states that are probably the strongest military powers in the world.

### Population

A state with a large number of people—like India, Indonesia, or Nigeria—gains power just from the mass of its population. Nigeria is the leading state of sub-Saharan Africa primarily because it has the largest population of the region. This large population gives it sufficient "critical mass" that it is the natural center for cultural and economic activity in the region; it thus becomes a hub of communication.

Another reason why population per se serves as a basis of power is that in wartime, even if a state does not have a particularly good army, it may be difficult to defeat if it has a large population. Hitler discovered this when he invaded the Soviet Union in 1941. The Soviet army was initially no match for the Germans and retreated rapidly. But the Germans kept going, and going, and going and were still only part of the way into Russia. Their lines of communication stretched over a thousand miles, they were sitting in the midst of a hostile population, winter came on, and still there was a large population left in regions they had not yet occupied. From the remnant of Russia, Stalin was able to build a powerful army that eventually defeated the Germans.

Of course, population alone will not make a state strong. In the nineteenth century,

**TABLE 17–1**
TEN MAJOR MILITARY POWERS

|  | Persons in uniform | Of these, Air Force | Defense budget (billions of dollars, 1993) | Nuclear weapons? |
|---|---|---|---|---|
| China | 2,930,000 | 470,000 | 27.4 | Yes |
| France | 409,600 | 89,800 | 37.2 | Yes |
| Germany | 367,300 | 82,900 | 35.3 | No |
| Great Britain | 254,300 | 75,700 | 35.1 | Yes |
| India | 1,265,000 | 110,000 | 7.3 | Yes |
| Israel | 172,000 | 32,000 | 7.2 | Rumored |
| Italy | 322,300 | 73,300 | 24.4 | No |
| Japan | 237,700 | 44,500 | 42.1 | No |
| Russia | 1,714,000 | 170,000 | 79.0 | Yes |
| U.S.A. | 1,650,500 | 433,800 | 280.6 | Yes |

*Source:* International Institute for Strategic Studies, *The Military Balance, 1994–1995* (London: International Institute for Strategic Studies, 1994).

China, the largest state in the world, was dominated easily by the smaller European powers. Today the two largest states in the world, India and China, are still only intermediate powers.

### Economic Power

Even if it is not militarily powerful, a state may figure importantly in international politics if it controls something of economic importance. Saudi Arabia has only a small military force, for instance, but it has often been able to get other states to do what it wishes because they depend on it for their oil imports. Germany's army is large and effective, but it is constitutionally limited to defense and so cannot realistically be used as a threat to make other states do what it wishes. Greater leverage for Germany comes from the fact that, for most of the last twenty years (until its economic problems caused by reunification in 1990), it has had the strongest, most stable economy in Europe. Its central bank has so dominated the European economies that Germany has, in effect, set economic policy for many of them.

Economic position may also *fail* to provide a political tool, however, as is illustrated by the various attempts of the United States in the 1970s to use threats of economic punishment to get the Soviet Union to do what it wanted. Because the United States could not credibly threaten the Soviet Union militarily (a war between the two superpowers would be so destructive that no one would dare to start it), the United States at various times tried to use its economic muscle to influence the Soviets. When the Soviet Union invaded Afghanistan, the United States canceled its exports of grain to the Soviets, promising to start them up again if the Soviets changed their policy. Similarly, in the 1970s the United States tried through economic sanctions to get Soviet and Polish leaders to liberalize the regime in Poland. These efforts did not work because the United States was simply not important enough economically to the Soviet bloc countries, whose economies were rather self-contained, to force them to back down on policies that were important to them. On the other hand, during the 1980s economic sanctions by the world's states were successful at breaking down the South African system of apartheid; the key was that almost all states simultaneously closed their economies to South Africa.

### Geography

Many states are protected by natural formations that render them more secure militarily than their armed power alone would suggest they should be.[5] Great Britain has always benefited from the fact that it is an island, separated from the rest of Europe by the English Channel. It was this that prevented Hitler from invading England during World War II. Similarly, Switzerland has always been rather secure in its rough mountains. Until the coming of air transportation, the United States was sufficiently isolated from Europe

---

[5]An interpretation of international politics that emphasizes economic and especially geographic sources of power is Harold and Margaret Sprout, *The Ecological Perspective on Human Affairs, with Special Reference to International Politics* (Princeton, N.J.: Princeton University Press, 1965).

that it could get by with a very small army. Germany has suffered over the centuries from the fact that it sits in the middle of a wide plain stretching from northern France into Russia, a plain along which armies can move easily.

### Leadership

Finally, skilled leadership may make a difference in the actual weight a state carries in international politics. Charles de Gaulle, by skillful diplomacy and a flair for public relations, was able to make France the leading state of western Europe in the late 1960s and 1970s. Woodrow Wilson's leadership probably diminished the influence of the United States at the end of World War I. Hitler and Mussolini led their states into disastrous, overreaching wars of conquest.

## POWER AND CHOICE IN INTERNATIONAL POLITICS

It is easy to see the "power" side of international politics, but with no central authority to define common goals for the international system, it is not so easy to see that international politics may also involve "choice." Some theorists think that the international system may work toward certain common goals, however, even in the absence of a coordinating authority. Two examples are balance-of-power theory and regime theory.

Hans Morgenthau developed in the 1950s an elegant analysis of international politics based on the concept of the "balance of power," which assumes that the international system has a natural tendency to prevent any one state from dominating the system.[6]

This tendency, which is a characteristic of the system as a whole, is supposed to result if all the states within it individually try to maintain their own power. If any one state begins to grow too large, other states become alarmed and combine against it, thus keeping power balanced. In this way the system operates with a "hidden hand" to maintain itself as a multiple set of competitive states. Historic examples of the balance of power at work include the fairly evenly matched alliance structure in Europe on the eve of World War I; the combination of numerous European states to balk an ambitious Napoleon; and the role of Britain over four centuries, throwing its support first to one, then to another European power, always on the weaker side, in order to prevent any one power from dominating the continent of Europe. The Cold War between the Soviet Union and the United States, with their rather evenly matched alliances, may be interpreted as a natural working out of the balance of power. Morgenthau credits the balance of power with a number of good things: the maintenance of a varied system of states; in particular, the protection of small states; and, under some circumstances, a decrease in warfare.

Regime theory is quite a different kettle of fish, but it, too, sees international politics as transcending the simple power relationships of states. A "regime" is:

(a set of) principles, norms, rules, and decision-making procedures around which actors' expectations converge in a given issue-area.[7]

---

[6]Hans Morgenthau, *Politics Among Nations,* 5th rev. ed. (New York: Knopf, 1978), Chapters 11–14.
[7]Stephen D. Krasner, ed., *International Regimes* (Ithaca, N.Y.: Cornell University Press, 1983), p. 1.

In other words, above and beyond the power relationships of states and other international actors, there may emerge a set of values and principles in the international community that modifies the behavior of the members of the community. States may be moved by a shared vision of the common good, not just by narrow interpretations of their individual interests. Since the Second World War, for instance, a basic assumption of the international order, embodied in institutions such as the International Monetary Fund, has been that trade should expand so that all economies may operate more efficiently. This "regime" has not been uncontested; leaders of the South have argued that the regime should instead emphasize redistribution of wealth, rather than taking the disparities between North and South as a given, and simply striving for maximal exchange and overall efficiency of the world economy. The point is, though, that there may be a set of values that has had a power of its own, and has affected how states act above and beyond the power relationships of those involved.

Proponents of regime theory see it as a way to address common problems in a more hopeful way than my bleak description of the "fiduciary role" might lead us to expect. Critics argue that regimes are froth on the international system, that they simply are expressions of the power relationships of those involved—that the international regime on trade, for instance, has been what it was because that suited Western and especially United States interests.

At this point, balance-of-power analysis and regime theory are important for us because they suggest that even in the anarchy of international politics, politics may be interpreted as more than simply the exercise of power. As we have tried to show throughout this book, a proper understanding of politics always requires that we remain simultaneously aware of its two sides. With some of the recent changes described in this chapter, the bleak picture of traditional international politics may have acquired some cooperative highlights. The growth of interdependence, and the entry of more nonstate actors (which softens somewhat the starkness of the fiduciary role), may make international politics in the future a more balanced mix of "power" and "choice."

## CONCLUSION

The unpredictability and danger of international politics can be awesome, especially now, in the nuclear age. Politics on this level can be analyzed in the same ways that we analyze other kinds of politics, but the high stakes involved put a greater edge on that analysis than we feel in the study of politics within states. In a general text such as this, we can touch only briefly on international politics, but I hope that you will have developed a taste for more. We urgently need to build a better understanding of international politics.

## A PERSONAL NOTE

Let me close this book with a personal note. We tend, when analyzing politics, to think of it in the abstract and rather dispassionately. We analyze people's actions according to the resources available to them and according to a rational application of those resources to their goals. By and large this analysis works well. We can generally tell which of two countries will be able to impose its will upon another, what sort of people will turn out to vote in greater numbers at election time, how a change in party finance will affect candidates' strategies, and so on. But sometimes passionate belief can cut through all this. Ideas and ideology can take on a power of their own, which transcends all analysis. No political scientists in the early 1960s predicted the tumultuous events of the civil rights movement. And who would have thought that little Vietnam would be able to best the United States in a war? Or that primitive Afghanistan would be able to defy the Soviet Union for years on end? Or that the democratic opposition would eventually triumph over the Communist party in eastern Europe and the Soviet Union?

Just as a small dog, if it is on its home ground, may be able to send a larger one running away with its tail down, so may the weaker side—even a very weak side—prevail in politics if its supporters believe strongly enough that they are right.

This book has emphasized the analysis of politics, and surely this is important. But I hope you will also remember the importance of passion and belief. As Marshall McLuhan so aptly put it, "Nothing is inevitable as long as one person is aware that it is happening."

### Example: A Failure of the New World Order: Ethnic Conflict in Rwanda

Rwanda is a small, land-locked state in central Africa, about the size of Massachusetts. It is an agricultural country with significant exports of coffee and tea, and with milk production and grain for local consumption. The country is one of the most densely populated in Africa, with over seven hundred people per square mile—a population density slightly greater than that of Massachusetts.

Before Rwanda came into contact with Europeans at the end of the nineteenth century, it was already a fairly well-developed state ruled by a king. The population was ethnically divided between two tribes. The Tutsis were a tribe of cattle herders and warriors. They controlled politics (the king and most warriors were Tutsi), even though they were numerically a distinct minority. The much larger Hutu tribe were land-based farmers, raising crops rather than grazing cattle on the open range. As of the 1956 census, 16 percent of Rwandans were Tutsi, 83 percent Hutu.

The "tribal" distinction was to some extent physical, with Tutsis generally taller and longer-faced, but there had been a good deal of intermarriage over the years, and this had blended such physical differences a good deal. The operating distinction was in part also an economic one, between haves and have-nots. A Hutu could become a Tutsi if he acquired large numbers of cattle, and a Tutsi could become so impoverished that he sank to being a Hutu.

When Rwanda was colonized, first by the Germans and then by the Belgians, the colonizers found a state in which a Tutsi king ruled, but with a good deal of autonomy for localities, many of which were led by Hutus. In setting up a rationalized bureaucracy for tax collection and road-building, the Belgians relied exclusively on the Tutsis to control the population and rewarded them with weapons and power. In so doing, they greatly sharpened the distinction between Tutsi and Hutu and the hierarchical organization of the state. At the same time, by introducing Western ideas of justice and equality, they helped to develop a sense of grievance among the Hutus. When they granted the country independence in 1962, the Belgians left behind a powder keg of ethnic power relationships and resentments.

Even before independence, a brief, bloody civil war in 1959 had led to the overthrow of the monarchy and had given effective political power to the Hutus. Thousands of Tutsis had fled Rwanda at that time. After independence, there were periodic outbursts of ethnic violence. In 1964 approximately 20,000 Tutsis were killed in massacres by the Hutu. In 1972 the military (dominated by Tutsis) led a massacre of over 100,000 Hutus; they concentrated on the better educated, who were seen as the greatest threat.

Throughout the 1980s about 250,000 mainly Tutsi refugees lived outside Rwanda in neighboring countries. In the early 1990s a Tutsi-led rebel force known as the Front Patriotique Rwandais (FPR), based on these refugee groups, began to have significant success against the Hutu-led government, and by 1993 they occupied much of the northern part of the country. The government and the rebels reached a peace accord that called for democratic, multiparty elections, but it was a fragile peace. Especially ominous was the fact that the (now predominantly Hutu) army refused to honor some of the peace directives from the government, even though the government was nominally in charge of the army.

On April 6, 1994, newly elected President Juvénal Habyarimana, who had been actively promoting reconciliation, was assassinated when the plane in which he and the president of neighboring Burundi were passengers was shot down over Rwanda's capital. Immediately a well-organized campaign of assassinations and massacres began in which Habyarimana's allies (including the prime minister and the president of the Constitutional Court) were murdered, along with other Hutus who favored reconciliation, educated Tutsis, and a number of United Nations personnel. Over the following several weeks an organized campaign to kill all Tutsis was carried out, in which an estimated 500,000 Tutsis—half the total population, and including many children—died. The killings were brutal. Some of the tall Tutsis had their feet chopped off "to bring them down to our size."

Meanwhile, the rebel Tutsi force continued to gain ground on the government, although it was too late to save many Tutsis from murder. By July they effectively controlled the country. Millions of Hutus fled the country to live as refugees in neighboring Zaire. They were kept there by rumors their leaders spread of Tutsi vengeance, even though there was remarkably little evidence of any revenge by the new Tutsi-led government.

A chilling history! Yet the United States and other Western countries did not generally pay much attenton to it, except for brief expressions of horror at moments when the violence periodically erupted at its worst. Rwanda is not of great economic importance and lacks natural resources such as oil, and is not strategically located with regard to shipping lanes or to international conflicts. In the words of Neville Chamberlain at the time that France and Britain acquiesced in Hitler's dismemberment of Czechoslovakia, Rwanda's suffering was "a quarrel in a far-away country between people of whom we know nothing."

The general lack of Western attention to the continuing problems of Rwanda is exemplified by the fact that until the horrendous genocide of 1994, the press in the United States consistently showed more concern for the mountain gorillas of Rwanda (who had been filmed in the popular movie *Gorillas in the Mist*) than for the people of that unfortunate country. A key-word search in June 1994 found 1,123 articles combining the key-words "gorilla" and "Rwanda," but only 138 combining "guerrilla" and "Rwanda."[8] Yet, 1993 was a year in which hundreds of Rwandan civilians were killed by both sides, and hundreds of thousands were made homeless. The major coverage of Rwanda that year consisted of stories in *The New York Times, Newsweek, The Houston Chronicle,* and Reuters News Service, warning that Dian Fossey's camp (featured in the movie) was threatened by the war:

> [*The Houston Chronicle* article] mentioned the war's human toll only in writing that "the hunger and desperation of a million war refugees" had made Rwanda a less "enticing place for visiting scientists to work." Just as tragically, the war had "ruined the eco-tourism trade that made gorilla sightseeing . . . one of Rwanda's leading sources of overseas income."[9]

The Western response even to the 1994 genocide was half-hearted. The French, who had had a continuing relationship with the Hutu government, consistently had the largest Western military presence in the area. Though at times they intervened to protect the Tutsis, it was usually late and sporadic. As late as May, after hundreds of thousands had been killed, the French continued to ship arms to the Hutu militias who were carrying out the organized murders. The strongest French effort eventually came in protecting the Hutu government as it fled the victorious rebels in July.

Britain offered fifty unarmored trucks to aid in helping prevent the slaughter.

The United States was not bathed in glory, either. American diplomats as a matter of stated policy denied the term "genocide" in reference to Rwanda until late in the killings, by which time over a third of all Tutsis had been killed. America offered only slow-arriving logistical support to help move troops from other African countries to restore order. In the end, little was done, and order settled on the deathly country without much help from anyone.

After the victory of the Tutsi rebels, a massive exodus of Hutus began. Today, one-fourth of the population of Rwanda lives in squalid refugee camps on its border, mainly in neighboring Zaire. They are Hutus, afraid to return home because they believe they will be attacked by Tutsi hard-liners in the army. In the meantime they are often terrorized by the Zairean army—which wants to force them back to Rwanda to ease the burden of caring for them—and by their own defeated Hutu army, which is now preparing a new invasion of Rwanda. The United Nations has tried to be helpful by offering humanitarian aid, building camp shelters, and sending observers to check on conditions in Rwanda's prisons. But in the end, there is little the United Nations can do there.

I titled this "A Failure of the New World Order," but this may have been unfair. Perhaps there was little the rest of the world could do about the ethnic poison in Rwanda.

---

[8]Ken Silverstein, "Guerrillas in the Mist," *The Washington Monthly* (September 1994), p. 21.
[9]*Ibid.,* p. 23.

And yet, much of the poison was created by the rest of the world during the colonial period. It just does not feel right to throw up our hands at a problem like this.

## FURTHER READING

Claude, Inis. *States and the Global System.* New York: St. Martin's Press, 1988.

Goldstein, Judith, and Keohane, Robert O., eds. *Ideas and Foreign Policy: Beliefs, Institutions, and Political Change.* Ithaca, N.Y.: Cornell University Press, 1993.

Jacobson, Harold K. *Networks of Interdependence: International Organizations and the Global Political System.* 2nd ed. New York: Knopf, 1984.

Kennedy, Paul. *The Rise and Fall of the Great Powers.* New York: Random House, 1987.

Keohane, Robert. *After Hegemony: Cooperation and Discord in the World Political Economy.* Princeton, N.J.: Princeton University Press, 1984.

———, ed. *Neorealism and Its Critics.* New York: Columbia University Press, 1986.

———, and Nye, Joseph S. *Power and Interdependence.* 2nd ed. Glenview, Ill.: Scott, Foresman, 1989.

Krasner, Stephen D., ed. *International Regimes.* Ithaca, N.Y.: Cornell University Press, 1983.

Nye, Joseph S. *Bound to Lead: The Changing Nature of American Power.* New York: Basic Books, 1990.

Pirages, Dennis. *Global Technopolitics: The International Politics of Technology and Resources.* Pacific Grove, Calif.: Brooks/Cole, 1989.

Porter, Gareth, and Brown, Janet Welsh. *Global Environmental Politics.* Boulder, Colo.: Westview, 1991.

Rosecrance, Richard. *Rise of the Trading State.* New York: Basic Books, 1986.

Rosenau, James N. *Turbulence in World Politics.* Beverly Hills, Calif.: Sage, 1990.

Snyder, Jack. *Myths of Empire: Domestic Politics and International Ambition.* Ithaca, N.Y.: Cornell University Press, 1991.

Sullivan, Michael P. *Power in Contemporary International Politics.* Columbia, South Carolina: University of South Carolina Press, 1990.

Ullman, Richard H. *Securing Europe.* Princeton, N.J.: Princeton University Press, 1991.

Urquhart, Brian. *Decolonization and World Peace.* Austin: University of Texas Press, 1989.

Waltz, Kenneth. *Theory of International Politics.* Reading, Mass.: Addison-Wesley, 1979.

Young, Oran R. *International Cooperation: Building Regimes for Natural Resources and the Environment.* Ithaca, N.Y.: Cornell University Press, 1989.

# Appendix

## PRINCIPLES OF POLITICAL ANALYSIS

There are a number of basic principles of argument and logic that students should learn in an introductory political science course. In part, these should have shown up implicitly in much of the material you have already read and discussed in this course, but it is also helpful to look at them more directly. They are included here not as a tag end or afterthought but because this seems to be the best way to handle them. Some instructors may prefer to use this section at the beginning of a course, some at the end, others at some other point. Locating this discussion in an appendix leaves to the instructor the decision of how to handle it.

### FALSIFIABILITY

The most basic principle of political argument is that in order to be useful, any statement about politics must be *falsifiable*. That is, it must be at least potentially possible that the statement is not true and could therefore be falsified. For example, the statement "two-party systems tend to produce less redistribution of income than multiparty systems" would be falsified if we compared the two-party and multiparty systems of the world and found that there was little difference between the two in the degree of income redistribution they produced. Or the statement "Ted Kennedy has shown little sympathy for blacks" would be falsified if one produced a long list of statements and actions in which Ted Kennedy demonstrated sympathy for blacks.

On the other hand, some statements about politics are true by definition. "Michael Dukakis lost the 1988 presidential election because most of the voters chose George Bush" is one example. "The poor countries of the world are more backward economically than rich countries" is another. Think about it: How would you go about falsifying either of these statements? They are true by definition.

Since these statements could not possibly be demonstrated to be false, they are automatically true. Such a statement does not tell anything about the world that we did not already know before we read the statement. Literally, a statement that is not falsifiable says nothing about the world. Such statements are called *tautologies*.

343

The two examples given above are fairly obvious, and so you might wonder why the importance of falsifiability is emphasized here. Surely, mustn't it be obvious when a statement says nothing new? If so, it wouldn't seem to be much of a problem. As it happens, though, it is not always immediately clear that a statement is a tautology. Consider the following: "A country with a large agricultural sector and a large industrial sector to its economy will tend to have a small service sector." Such a country will not "tend" to have a small service sector, it will *always* have a small one, because this statement is true by definition. To have a large agricultural sector means that a large percentage of the labor force is employed in agriculture; if the country also has a large industrial sector, then another large percentage of the labor force is employed in industry. What's left is the service sector. Since the percentages employed in different sectors must always sum to 100 percent, this means that if the first two percentages are large, there cannot be much left for the service sector. Its percentage must by definition be small, and so the statement is a tautology—although to most people it would not be obvious, at first glance, that such was the case.

As you become involved in the analysis of politics, you will be surprised by how often statements about politics turn out, on closer examination, to be true by definition.

We have now cleared the underbrush a bit and know that we are to deal only with statements that are at least potentially falsifiable. Clearly, however, some of these statements will be more interesting than others, and we don't want to waste our time with the uninteresting ones. This leads us to the following question:

## WHAT MAKES A STATEMENT INTERESTING?

There are three kinds of statements about politics:

• *Statements of fact:* These state what *is*, they *describe* reality. Examples: "The American president is elected for a four-year term." "There are two major political parties in West Germany." "Chile and Argentina have been engaged in a dispute over boundaries for decades."

• *Statements of value:* These state *how good* something is; they *evaluate* reality. Examples: "The U.S. Constitution provides the best governmental system in the world." "Sales taxes are not as good as income taxes because they are regressive." "A planned economy provides a better life for people than a free-market economy."

• *Explanatory statements:* These state *why* something is as it is; they *analyze* reality. Examples: "Bill Clinton defeated George Bush in the 1992 presidential election because most voters were dissatisfied with the economy." "People whose parents were very interested in politics tend to be especially interested in politics themselves." "The sending of unclear diplomatic signals increases the likelihood that war will break out."

All three types of statement are appropriate areas for political investigation and argument. Whatever sort of statement you make, however, you want it to be an interesting one. A statement will be relatively interesting to the extent that it offers your readers something that (1) is of concern to them and (2) would have been difficult for them to accomplish for themselves. The fact that the statement must be of concern to your readers is obvious and requires no further comment. (Most American readers, for instance, would not be much concerned about the precise arrangements for choosing a king in Sweden, and statements about it would not be especially interesting to them.) However, note the further condition for interest—that the statement should offer your readers something that would have been difficult for them to accomplish for themselves. This is not so obvious.

Consider two descriptive statements about Congress: "Congress has 535 members," and "Three-fourths of the members of Congress have cast a vote at one time or another on direct instructions from a lobbyist." (The second of these is imaginary and, one hopes, false!) These two statements would be of equal *concern* to students of Congress, but the second statement would be more interesting to them because it is something that would have been difficult for them to learn for themselves. They could have learned how many members there are in Congress by a quick glance in any encyclopedia, but it would take a clever investigator, working for a long time, to ascertain the truth of the second statement.

Similarly, "justice is good" is not a very interesting statement of value. Presumably, everyone would be able to agree with it without much thought, and so it does not provide us with much that is new. However, the statement "discrimination is good" is a challenging statement, one that goes against the grain. It would not automatically occur to most of your readers and would require a good deal of argument to be rendered plausible for them. Arguing for this statement requires a lot of thought, which you must provide for your readers, and will thus be proportionately more interesting to them.

As a final example, the explanatory statement, "Rich countries will tend to have bigger armies than poor countries" is not a very interesting explanation of the size of armies, because it is so obvious that coming up with it did not require much thought. "Countries with high unemployment, and therefore cheap labor, will tend to have large armies" is a more interesting explanation of the same thing. A thoroughly obvious, hence uninteresting, explanation is called a *trivial explanation*.

As a general rule, statements of value and explanatory statements require more thought on the part of the writer than descriptive statements and they are thus more likely to be interesting statements. Students writing papers are often tempted to write descriptive papers, laying out a set of descriptive statements, simply because this is easier that justifying statements of value or explanation. You should remember that unless you choose a *challenging* descriptive problem, your work will not be a particularly interesting one. Often you will be given a particular descriptive investigation as an exercise; you might, for instance, be asked to trace the progress of a bill through the legislative process. If so, describe away! But if you are simply asked to "write a term paper about some aspect of the legislative process," you will generally be able to write a more interesting paper if you choose a question of value or of explanation.

## CAUSATION AND EXPLANATION

Let us look a bit more closely at explanation. An explanatory statement necessarily involves the notion of causation. We *explain* a certain thing by saying that another thing *causes* it. For example, we might explain the fact that the U.S. government has difficulty making broad, systematic policy in areas such as energy by blaming it on the separation of powers in the American system. That is, we *explain* the existence of the difficulty by saying that the difficulty is *caused* by the separation of powers. (Presumably this would be because there are many points at which the political power of opponents can be decisive—the presidency, either house of Congress, or the courts. As a result, "difficult" programs are hard to pass.)

In the example above, we cannot conceive of any way to explain the American difficulty except to assert one or another possible cause of the difficulty. So to explain is to analyze causes.

But what is causation? What does it mean to say that one thing causes another? In general, we think that to cause something is to *bring it about*, to bring it forth, to produce it. Turning a key causes my car to start. The Soviet Union's opposition to a proposal causes the defeat of the proposal in the United Nations. The increasing electoral advantages of incumbents in U.S. congressional elections have caused an increase in the average seniority of members of Congress. And so on.

We think of causation as working only forward in time. In order for one thing to produce another thing, the "producer" has to precede the "product" temporally. So it doesn't make sense to think of Ronald Reagan's electoral victory in 1984 as having caused Walter Mondale to argue for tax increases during the 1984 campaign; but it does make sense to think of Mondale's position as one of the causes of Reagan's electoral victory.

However, temporal precedence is not enough to establish one thing as a cause of another. We do not think of winter as causing spring, for instance, even though we know that "when winter comes spring can't be far behind." Although the seasons unfold together, we do not think of one season as bringing the other about. Similarly, it is probably true that brunettes tend to be Democrats, since for historical reasons a number of ethnic groups with dark hair—blacks, Native Americans, Chicanos, southern Europeans—have gravitated to the Democratic party. Yet even though people acquire their hair color long before they give a thought to which party they will support, we do not think of hair color as causing people's party preferences. It is only a coincidence that the two tend to vary together.

Political scientists put a great deal of effort into trying to sort out what things cause the things in which we are interested. Why does the United States have only two major parties? Why are so few Third World states democracies? Why do communist economies not grow more quickly than they do? If we could experiment with politics in a laboratory, as chemists or physicists do in their specialties, we could hold all other possible factors constant; we could allow only the one we wished to examine to vary and then see whether, when it varied, the thing we were trying to explain also varied. For instance, a physicist may place two identical weights on identical wheelchairs on slopes of different angles and measure the effect of the angle of slope on the speed of descent; since nothing else varies, it is clear in this case that only differing angles of slope can be causing differing speeds of descent. If we could manipulate things in this way, we would feel confident in stating that the one thing was causing the other to vary. However, with rare exceptions, we cannot experiment with the things we are examining in political science. We cannot change the electoral system of the United States in order to see what effect this would have on the number of parties, or change Third World states to industrial states in order to see whether their political regimes would change, or change command economies to market economies in order to see whether they would become more productive.

What we *can* do is observe variations and changes as they occur around us and try to figure out which variations or changes actually cause other things to happen. For instance, many Third World states, especially in East Asia, are now becoming industrialized. The challenge in basing analysis on such changes is that no one thing ever changes in isolation from everything else, in the way a physicist can arrange it in the laboratory. Everything is always changing at once, and we must use our creative sense to try to sort out *which* changes have caused *which* others.

For example, in 1961, France changed its electoral system to one based on a presidency, which should, in principle, tend to bring about a two-party system. Over the years since then, France has indeed seen a coalescence of its party system into five parties, organized in two well-defined blocs. But did the new electoral system bring about the coalescence? At the same time that France was adjusting to its new electoral arrangements, it was also experiencing unprecedented prosperity, which might perhaps have made people less likely to support small radical parties. Also, it was at this time that the very popular Charles de Gaulle served as president. He drew a large political party about himself—something he could probably have done no matter what the electoral system was, and which knocked out several smaller parties. What, then, was the effect of the change in electoral arrangements on the number of parties?

Under such circumstances, we cannot be certain of the effects of one thing on another. We can and do use our common sense, asking, for example, what the effects of electoral systems *should* be. And we can look at overall patterns across many cases, asking what has happened after changes of electoral system in other countries. The end result is not a firm, indisputable finding but rather something to be argued about. There is nothing wrong with this.

## HISTORICAL EXPLANATION

A natural affinity between the field of history and what we have been discussing here should be apparent to you. Historians follow a series of events as they move forward in time, linking them to one another. This is much like the analysis of causation that political scientists frequently engage in.

There is a difference in emphasis between the two fields, however. Historians are more often concerned to present a single train of events—a biography of Lincoln, a history of negotiations at the Council of Europe, a military history of World War II, and so on—with causal analysis left somewhat implicit. Political scientists, on the other hand, are more likely to be looking for overall patterns (embodied in theories) and less concerned with tracing carefully through any single case or train of events.

The important thing to note is that this is only a difference of degree. Both political historians and political scientists are engaged in the same task—to make sense out of the myriad political events occurring around us—and historians as well as political scientists do this by *explaining* certain things, showing that they are caused by other things.

Remember from our earlier discussion that it is not enough just to show that one thing happened before another. If we are to treat the earlier event as causing the later one, we must also establish some basis for treating it as having brought the other about, or having produced it. *This necessity holds just as much for the historian as for the political scientist.*

This is an important point for students in political science courses, because as you are assigned research papers to write, a deceptively simple route may appear to be a paper that traces the history of something: a history of the arms race between the Soviet Union and the United States, a biography of Senator Dole, a history of the diplomacy leading up to the Camp David peace accords, a description of how the National Security Council developed, a tracing of changes in French fiscal policy after the Socialists came to power, and so on. Any of these could make an excellent topic for a paper, but if you do it right, it will be neither easier nor more difficult than any other topic would be. To do the job right is to try to establish causal relationships among the events as they transpire. If, in attempting to write a paper of this sort, you simply lay out the events—first X happened, then Y, then Z—you will have merely described things. And as noted above, you will not have a very interesting paper. However, if you operate here as all good historians do—that is, if you try to explain why the train of events occurred as it did—you will have an interesting and not necessarily easily written paper.

## A FEW COMMON PITFALLS IN ANALYSIS

As you analyze politics, you must think straight. For the most part, common sense will carry you well; and practice, and criticism from your readers, will help to sharpen your abilities. As an introductory help, you may find it useful to consider three common flaws in analysis that you should watch out for in both your own writing and the work of others.

1. *Begging the Question.* Frequently writers answer a question with an answer that simply restates the question. It looks as though it has answered the question, but it has not. It has simply turned the question into another form and does not produce much forward progress. This is called "begging the question."

For example, a person analyzing the victory of North Vietnam in the Vietnam War might state that North Vietnam won because it was more powerful than South Vietnam. But this does not really answer the question we want to see addressed; it simply changes it slightly into the question: Why was North Vietnam more powerful than South Vietnam? Similarly, an analysis of American voting behavior concluding that people vote for candidates they prefer would not seem to have brought us forward. It would simply leave us with the further question: Why do people prefer certain candidates over others? Questions of value can also be begged. For instance, a paper arguing that socialism is a better system than capitalism because it is more just—unless it expanded on this to show what was meant by "justice"—would simply leave us with the question: What makes socialism more just than capitalism?

These examples may have all seemed rather simple, and you may have wondered why you would need to be cautioned to watch out for a flaw that is so easily avoided. But begging a question is actually easy to do. Not all instances of it are as obvious as the examples used here. For instance, people often argue about policy on the basis of "natural rights," rights so basic to the nature of humanity that they take priority over all else. The Declaration of Independence appeals to "certain inalienable rights, [among which are] life, liberty, and the pursuit of happiness," and argues that because the king of England had violated these rights, his rule was outlaw; hence it was proper to rise in revolution against him. At a later period, administrators in Hitler's Germany were charged with the crime of having obeyed and enforced Hitler's laws. This was a crime because the laws themselves were in violation of natural rights. Basic privacy, the right of a woman to control her own body, and the fetus's right to life are other things that have been defended at one time or another as natural rights.

This sort of argument comes readily to us, and we slip easily into it. It is, in fact, a useful rhetorical device. But we should realize, when we assert the existence of natural rights, that unless we accompany this assertion with an analysis of human nature, we are begging the question in the following way: "X should be defended because it is a natural right." But what makes it a natural right? The fact that it is basic to the very nature of a human being. But how do we know what is basic to the nature of a human being?

2. *Circular Argument.* A circular argument is one in which a person proves A from B, but we know that B is true only because of A. In other words, B implies A, but we believe B only if we first believe A. The argument goes in a circle and does not offer any new reason to believe either A or B.

Suppose, for example, we argued that political influence of the military is a major cause of the size of defense budgets, but that we measured "military influence" by the size of the armed forces. In this case, we would be asserting that military influence is what causes defense budgets to be large, but since our measure of "military influence" is something that itself is a direct result of the size of defense budgets, finding that the two things tend to rise and fall together would give us no new reason to believe the original statement.

3. *Post hoc Explanation.* A post hoc explanation is the "Monday-morning quarterback" of explanation. It consists of taking a set of things that have already happened, showing that one of them plausibly could have resulted from the others, and, on the basis of this, asserting that those others are in general a cause of the thing in question.

For example, many commentators have looked at the sequence of events leading up to World War II and have asserted that it was the appeasement of Britain and France that led Hitler on and resulted in his frantic war of conquest. This is certainly plausible, but it is post hoc.

The danger in post hoc explanations is that for *any* event there will be some set of things that happened at more or less the same time and that may look like a plausible explanation for it. If those same things happen again in the future, they may or may not produce that same result. It is not that a post hoc explanation is *wrong*, but that it leaves us with a greater feeling of certainty than we should have. We confuse the set of events that first suggested an idea to us with verification of the idea. What has suggested that appeasement encourages aggressors? The events leading up to World War II. How do we know that it's true? Just look at Hitler!

The three problems of argument noted here are by no means the only ones you will learn to watch for, but they are three common problems. In the end, these three, and all of the rest, boil down to a matter of simple common sense. If you are endowed with some of that, you won't go wrong.

# GLOSSARY

Following most terms, the first page on which the term is introduced substantively appears in parentheses.

**American conservatism** *(p. 48)*   The rather loose ideology known in the United States as "conservatism." Since it is really a variant of the more general ideology of liberalism and has relatively little to do with the more general ideology of conservatism, it has been distinguished in this book by the name *American conservatism.* American conservatism is particularly suspicious of governmental intervention to make people more equal but is often willing to entrust government with power in order to maintain codes of moral behavior.

**American liberalism** *(p. 48)*   The rather loose ideology known in the United States as "liberalism." Since it is only a variant of the more general ideology of liberalism, it has been distinguished in this book by the name *American liberalism.* American liberalism is particularly concerned to make people equal, and it is relatively willing to entrust government with power in order to bring this about; it is also particularly concerned to maintain freedom of expression.

**anomic interest group** *(p. 228)*   Politically relevant groups with no formal organizational structure and no obvious leaders that come together only temporarily and with the loosest of coordination to their efforts.

**arbitrary action** *(pp. 90 and 289)*   Action that is taken capriciously. The people affected do not know what to expect before the action and do not learn afterward the grounds on which the action was chosen.

**associational interest group** *(p. 230)*   The "typical" interest group—an organized group of citizens, one of whose primary purposes is to affect the policies of the state.

**authority** *(p. 109)*   Power based on a general agreement that the holder of the power has the right to issue certain sorts of commands and that those commands should be obeyed.

**balance of power** *(p. 336)*   The idea that the international system works in a natural way to keep the power of states balanced so that no one state can ever achieve domination of the entire system.

**begging a question** *(p. 347)*   "Answering" a question (actually, failing to answer it) by offering a rephrasing of it as an answer. Example: "Why did Britain win the Falkland Islands war?" "Because Britain was more successful militarily than Argentina." (This leaves us with the question "Why was Britain more successful militarily than Argentina?" which just restates the original.)

**"behavioralist" political science** *(p. 15)*   Political science that emphasizes statistical analysis and abstract theories seeking out basic, essential regularities across a whole set of events.

**bureaucracy** *(p. 289)*   A way of organizing the public administration that emphasizes professionalism, recruitment and promotion on the basis of merit, standardization of procedures, and the smooth flow of commands.

**cabinet (in parliamentary system)** *(p. 246)*   The executive portion of a parliamentary government. It consists of ministers, most of whom are usually members of the parliament. Each minister is responsible for the administration of some part of the government's services, such as health or defense. The cabinet leads the parliament, proposing legislation, conducting the country's foreign policy, and so on. It serves at the pleasure of the parliament and can be ousted by a majority vote of no confidence.

**case law** *(p. 305)*   A legal system emphasizing the independence of the judiciary from the rest of the government. Under case law the ongoing stream of prior decisions (precedents) becomes itself an important part of current law. Predominant in Britain and her former colonies.

**causation** *(p. 345)*   An interpretation of relations between events in which one event "brings about" or produces another event. Example: "Poverty is a major cause of communist support in the Third World."

**circular argument** *(p. 348)*   An argument in which one proves A from B, but in which A itself provides our only evidence that B is true.

**coalition** *(p. 248)*   A tactical combination of varied groups, constructed so that the groups will in combination be large enough to command power that they can then share among themselves. Frequently applied to parliamentary government, in which 50 percent of the votes in parliament are required in order to form a cabinet, but in which it may be necessary to combine two or more parties in order to amass 50 percent of the votes.

**code law** *(p. 306)*   A legal system emphasizing a relative subordination of the judiciary to the rest of the government. Legal interpretation consists primarily of reading and applying codes of legal statute passed by the parliament, rather than looking to the precedent of prior court decisions. Used in various forms in most parts of the world except Britain and her former colonies.

**collective good** *(p. 100)*   A thing that benefits all members of the collectivity and which no one can be prevented from using. Because it is difficult to get individuals voluntarily to pay part of the cost of the good, it is usually chosen by governmental authority.

**committees (legislative)** *(p. 251)*   Small group of legislators whose task (usually) is to review carefully a proposed piece of legislation and recommend to the full legislature what action should be taken on it. In many legislatures, bills may be amended by the committee or killed in entirety. Committees may also perform other tasks, such as investigating an area of possible legislation.

**communism** *(p. 58)*   The more militant branch of socialism. Communists generally argue that the only way to build a socialist state is by revolution. Therefore, they are sometimes less interested in electoral activity than the democratic socialists. After the 1920s, communists generally acknowledged the leadership of the Soviet Union in the formulation of their goals and strategies. See also *socialism; democratic socialism.*

**conservatism** *(p. 51)*   An ideology positing that the most important goal of politics is to create stable communities based on a hierarchy of power, in which leaders and followers have reciprocal responsibilities and obligations. Unlike liberalism, conservatism is not suspicious of power and does not seek to limit the power of the state. Rather, the point of conservatism is that that power should be in the hands of a traditional class of rulers. See also *American conservatism.* *(p. 161)*

**constitution** *(p. 161)*   A set of rules by which power is distributed in a political group, such as the state. This generally consists in part of a formal set of rules, but it always contains as well various informal mechanisms, traditions, and understandings by which power is assigned to people.

**constitutional review** *(p. 275)*   A system under which a judicial or quasijudicial part of the government can annul acts of other parts of the government if, in its judgment, those acts violate the constitution of the state.

**constitutionalism** *(p. 172)*   The doctrine that states' constitutions should be designed fairly, not so as to give undue advantage to any particular group, and that the government should then be faithful to that constitution. In this way, individuals are protected against arbitrary governmental action.

**corruption** *(p. 295)*   Performing one's public tasks improperly in order to receive personal benefits (bribes, etc.).

**coup** *(p. 145)*   The forceful deposition of a government by all or a portion of the armed forces and installation of a new military government.

**court politics** *(p. 150)*   The political process in a state where great power is vested in a single person, as in traditional monarchy or in a personal dictatorship.

**courts** *(p. 304)*   Governmental institutions charged with interpreting the law.

**democracy** *(pp. 114 and 129)*   A state in which all fully qualified citizens vote at regular intervals to choose, among alternative candidates, the people who will be in charge of setting the state's policies.

**democratic socialism** *(p. 58)*   The branch of socialism that supports electoral democracy and holds that the proper way for workers to control society is to win elections. Democratic socialists are also generally more moderate than communists in the goals they set, being more willing to settle for piecemeal progress rather than holding out for a complete remaking of society. See also *socialism; communism.*

**dictatorship**   A governmental arrangement in which those who hold power did not gain power by any regular constitutional process and are not responsible in their exercise of power to any formal set of rules.

**dominant-party system** *(p. 212; contrast "one-party system")*   A political party system in which various parties are allowed to function openly and with reasonable effectiveness but in which a single party nonetheless holds power all the time.

**due process** *(p. 90)*   An expectation that certain set procedures must always be followed in making a policy and that if they were not, the policy should be void.

**efficient policies** *(p. 93)*   Policies that produce the greatest good at the least cost.

**electoral system** *(p. 184)*   A set of rules by which the outcomes of an election (a set of officers elected, or whatever) is determined from the distribution of votes cast by the electorate.

**empirical theory** *(p. 15)*   A theory describing how things work in the world we observe.

**established church**   A church or other organized religion that is established by law as the official church or religion of a state and which has political and legal ties to the government of the state. Examples are the Anglican church, which is established in Great Britain; the Roman Catholic church, which is established in Italy and many other countries; and Judaism, which is established in Israel.

**European Union** *(p. 41)*   An organization of fifteen western European states that have set up a rather weak common government and have coordinated many of their economic policies.

**externality** *(p. 100)*    A situation in which there are social costs or benefits beyond the individual costs and benefits involved in a transaction.

**fairness** *(p. 87)*    A situation in which all people are treated as they deserve.

**fascism** *(p. 59)*    A political movement that appeared in many countries in the 1920s and 1930s. Fascism stressed militaristic pageantry and a strident nationalism as ways of binding the people to a single dramatic dictator. Franco, Mussolini, and Hitler were fascist dictators.

**federal state** *(p. 168)*    A state in which the constitution grants to regional governments a legal monopoly over certain political decisions, such as educational policy. Thus, two different governments will control the same group of people, but with regard to different political questions.

**fiduciary role** *(p. 331)*    A role in which one acts as an agent on behalf of someone else's interests. This role often places the agent in problematic positions.

**glasnost** *(p. 218)*    Mikhail Gorbachev's campaign in the late 1980s to make politics in the Soviet Union more open and competitive, ending tight control of politics by the Communist party.

**government** *(p. 28)*    The group of people within the state who have the ultimate authority to act on behalf of the state.

**gross domestic product, or GDP** *(p. 302)*    The total value of all goods and services exchanged in a society. That is, the sum of such things as the value of all food sold, the value of all mechanics' work on automobiles, the value of all educational activity, and so on. The higher the GDP, the greater the total amount of economic activity in the society. Per capita GDP divides GDP by the population, to measure how economically well-off the average person is.

**habeas corpus** *(p. 305)*    The right not to be held indefinitely by the police without being formally charged with a crime.

**higher civil service** *(p. 298)*    Specialized and executive members of the public administration, corresponding to professionals and managers in the private sector.

**ideology** *(p. 46)*    A set of ideas that are related and that modify one another, that is, an organized set of ideas about something.

**implicit power** *(p. 7)*    Power in which A does what B desires not because of anything B says or does, but because (1) A senses that B wants something done and (2) for any of a variety of reasons, A wishes to do what B wants done.

**incentive compatibility** *(p. 165)*    A situation in which those who make decisions on behalf of society benefit personally when their decisions benefit society. When incentive compatibility is present, society does not need to depend on nobility of character in its officials; it can depend on a more reliable force—their concern for their own self-interest.

**incrementalism** *(p. 95)*    A policy of making decisions cautiously and implementing them through small staged changes rather than in bold sweeps.

**institutional interest group** *(p. 230)*    A group that is primarily set up for some purpose other than political activity but which becomes politically active in order to defend its own interests in the policy decisions of the state.

**interest group** *(p. 222)*    An organized group of citizens one of whose goals is to ensure that the state follows certain policies.

**International Court of Justice** *(p. 330)*    The court that hears cases at law between states. It has no power to enforce its ruling.

**international politics** *(p. 321)*    Politics conducted among states rather than within a single state.

**interpretive political science** *(p. 15)*    Political science that emphasizes historical, anthropological, and (sometimes) legal methods, and the complex whole that is being studied.

**justice** *(p. 87)*    Rewarding people on the basis of the contributions they make to common efforts, of their need for the reward, or at least approximate equality of treatment. How these three criteria are weighted is important in determining the justice of a policy and will vary from one person to another.

**legal systems** *(p. 304)* General, organized sets of legal principles.

**legitimacy** *(p. 111)* A belief on the part of large numbers of people in a state that the existing governmental structure and/or the particular persons in office should appropriately wield authority.

**liberalism** *(p. 49)* An ideology positing that the most important goal of politics is to help individuals develop their capacities to the fullest. To this end, people should be regulated and aided by governments as little as possible, so that they will learn from the experience of being responsible for their own decisions. Liberalism may be summarized by the slogan, "That government is best which governs least." See also *American liberalism.*

**manifest power** *(p. 7)* Power based on an observable action by A that causes B to do what A wants.

**market mechanism** *(p. 96)* A mechanism whereby social choice results from choices of all members of the collectivity rather than a decision made by the central governing unit.

**mobilization** *(p. 202)* The systematic stimulation of concerted effort by large numbers of people, as in elections or demonstrations. This term is used especially in reference to such stimulation conducted on its own behalf by the government.

**multinational corporations** Corporations like Exxon or ITT, which have become so large and conduct their operations in so many different states that we can no longer realistically think of them as belonging to any particular state.

**multiparty system** *(p. 214)* A democratic system in which there are more than two major parties.

**nation** *(p. 30)* A large group of people who are bound together and recognize a similarity among themselves because of a common culture; in particular, a common language seems important in creating nationhood. Nations often but not always coincide with the political boundaries of states. The Kurdish language and culture is spread across parts of Turkey, Iraq, and Iran; Irish nationalists and British nationalists are mixed together in Northern Ireland, where they are at each other's throats. There are many similar examples of mismatches between national "boundaries" and the boundaries of states. Such mismatches are a potent source of political turmoil.

**nationalism** *(p. 27)* Passionate identification with a state on the part of its citizens.

**nationalization of industry** *(p. 71)* The acquisition of an industrial operation by the government, which then operates it directly as part of the governmental administration.

**neocorporatism** *(p. 238)* A system of government and interest groups in which all interests are organized but—instead of simply responding to groups' pressures—the government actively involves the groups themselves in the job of governing. This active governmental role distinguishes neocorporatism from pluralism.

**nonassociational interest group** *(p. 229)* One or another category of people who are not formally organized in any way but are treated by others as if they represented an interest.

**normative theory** *(p. 15)* A theory that involves making a judgement about the world, not describing how it works.

**ombudsman** *(p. 292)* A government official whose primary duty is to seek out citizens' complaints of abuse by public administrators and to negotiate changes in the offending practices.

**one-party system** *(p. 212; contrast "dominant-party system")* A political system in which only a single political party is allowed to be active.

**one-party state** *(p. 149)* A state in which the government is based on, and in turn supports, a single political party. No other party is allowed to function in other than a token way.

**pacts** *(p. 134)* In general, agreements; specifically, with regard to democratization, agreements between the leaders of the new democracy and supporters of the older authoritarian system that soften the change for the latter and help them to accept the democracy.

**paradox of participation** *(p. 190)* The paradox that no one should really vote if their only reason for voting is that they wish to help their favored candidate win. The odds that all the rest of the voters will produce a tie are incredibly small, and that is the only circumstance in which the person's vote will make any difference at all to the candidate.

**parliamentary government** *(p. 246)*    A democracy in which the executive and legislative functions are merged in one institution, the parliament. The parliament is the state's supreme legislature, but it also appoints a committee (the cabinet) to serve as the political executive for the state.

**party identification** *(p. 204)*    A personal identification with a political party, not just agreement with its policies or candidates of the moment but an enduring identification with the party itself.

**pluralism** *(p. 237)*    A system of government and interest groups in which all interests organize and compete freely, with no one group dominating, and in which the government is open to pressure from the groups so that policy is largely the outcome of groups' competing pressures.

**political culture** *(p. 120)*    The set of all attitudes and beliefs held communally by a people, forming the basis for their political behavior.

**political party** *(p. 199)*    A group of officials or would-be officials who are linked with a sizable group of citizens into an organization; a chief object of this organization is to ensure that its officials attain power or are maintained in power.

**political science** *(p. 14)*    The academic field that takes as its sole and general task the analysis of politics, especially the politics of the state.

**political socialization** *(p. 121)*    The process of learning the facts, assumptions, and attitudes we use in responding to politics. Political socialization occurs most rapidly in childhood and youth, but continues throughout life.

**politics** *(p. 4)*    The making of common decisions for a group of people through the exercise of power by some members of the group over other members.

**post hoc explanation** *(p. 348)*    An explanation tailored to the particular set of events to be explained. ("Post hoc" means "after this.") A danger in this is that mere coincidences may be treated as general relationships in the explanation.

**power** *(p. 6)*    The ability of one person to cause another to do what the first wishes, by whatever means. (See also *implicit power* and *manifest power.*)

**presidential government** *(p. 265)*    A democratic system in which the legislature and executive exist independently and are elected independently of each other. Generally the president takes a leading role in forming policy but must have the consent of the legislature if that policy is to be enacted. A presidential system divides power, whereas a parliamentary system unifies it.

**privatization**    Selling to the public or by some other means transforming to private ownership economic enterprises that were previously owned and managed by the state.

**progressive taxation** *(p. 79)*    A system of taxes that takes a greater proportion of a person's income if the income is high than if the income is low.

**proportional representation electoral system, or PR** *(p. 184)*    An electoral system in which parties receive a number of seats in the legislature roughly proportional to the number of votes that were cast for them among the electorate.

**public administration** *(p. 285)*    The set of people who are not involved directly in the making of major political decisions but who construct and implement the policies that carry out those decisions. Examples are police officers, public health nurses, IRS agents, public university presidents.

**question time** *(p. 260)*    A device, originating in the British House of Commons and since imitated in many parliaments, by which cabinet members appear regularly in the parliament to answer questions from members about the administration of their offices. These questions and answers often spark hot debate.

**radicalism** *(p. 95)*    Making decisions in bold sweeps and changing policies rapidly, so as not to miss opportunities that might disappear if one moved slowly.

**referendum** *(pp. 183 and 188)*    An election in which voters choose directly whether a particular proposal will become law; this contrasts with other kinds of elections, in which voters choose among various candidates for a political office.

**regime theory** *(p. 336)*    A theory of international relations emphasizing the importance of "regimes," or sets of principles and values that transcend state boundaries and regulate in an informal way areas of policy such as trade, development of the polar regions, and so on.

**regional integration** *(p. 36)*    A partial merging of the political and economic structures of several states in the same region of the world. The most successful attempt at regional integration to date has been the formation of the European Community.

**regressive taxation** *(p. 79)*    A system of taxes that takes a greater proportion of a person's income if the income is low than if the income is high.

**regulation** *(p. 70)*    Direct laying down of rules by the government as to how people may conduct their affairs. This is distinguished from *indirect* governmental direction of choices, as when a government taxes liquor heavily to discourage its use but does not actually make its use illegal. The latter would constitute regulation.

**representative bureaucracy** *(p. 294)*    The idea that members of the public administration should be similar to the groups they serve in such characteristics as class, race, and gender, so that they will be able to serve them better.

**selective incentive** *(p. 227)*    Benefits that an organization offers its members in addition to the central purposes of the organization. A trade union, for example, may offer its members such added benefits as low-cost package vacations.

**Sharia** *(p. 307)*    Islamic law, based on a set of rules for moral conduct developed over the first few centuries after the death of Muhammad.

**single-member-district plurality electoral system, or SMDP** *(p. 184)*    An electoral system in which the state is divided into geographic subdivisions, each subdivision is represented by a single member in the legislature, and the candidate who attains a plurality of votes in that subdivision is the one who fills the seat.

**socialism** *(p. 54)*    An ideology positing that society consists of classes (groups of people who are similarly placed economically) which are constantly in conflict. In order to create a just society in which people are equal, the working class should take over the state and direct all industries.

**sovereignty** *(p. 31)*    The legal capacity of a geographic unit to maintain ultimate responsibility for the conduct of its own affairs.

**state** *(pp. 13 and 28)*    The basic unit by which people are organized politically; often casually called "country" or "nation." States are militarily independent of each other and are guided by governments that typically regulate the economy, set the laws of the state, and so on. States in the twentieth century tend to be relatively large territories with stable boundaries whose populations are bound together by intimate political ties. In marginal cases such as the European Community, it can be a bit tricky to say exactly whether a unit is or is not a "state." In the United States, "state" also has a second meaning, referring to one of the fifty regional divisions (California, Alaska, Florida, Minnesota, etc.) into which the United States is divided.

**tautology** *(p. 343)*    A statement that is logically true and thus cannot be shown false by an examination of evidence. Example: "All brunettes have dark hair."

**theory** *(p. 15)*    A statement linking specific instances to broader principles.

**trivial explanation** *(p. 344)*    An explanation that is obvious to the audience and therefore not very interesting to them. Example: "Why does John eat so much?" "Because he's hungry."

**two-party system** *(p. 214)*    A democratic system in which two parties regularly receive 90 percent or more of votes cast, but in which it is rare for either of them very often to receive more than 55 or 60 percent of the votes. These two parties will replace each other in office fairly frequently.

**unitary state** *(p. 168)*    A state in which no other governmental body but the central government has any areas of policy that are exclusively under its control. In a unitary state, local and regional governments may potentially be overruled by the central government in any political decision they make.

**United Nations** *(p. 330)*    An organization of almost all the world's states. The UN provides a forum at which complaints can be aired; it has occasionally helped to cool off conflicts between states; and its specialized committees seek to improve world standards of health, education, and so on.

**welfare state**    A state in which the government seeks, by a complex set of policies, to ensure that its citizens will not suffer great economic insecurity or grievous want. Such policies may include guaranteed pensions, public provision of health care, public attempts to prevent unemployment, public help in the care of children, and so on. Most industrialized states have established welfare states in the period since World War II.

# BIBLIOGRAPHY

Aberbach, Joel D.; Putnam, Robert D.; and Rockman, Bert A. *Bureaucrats and Politicians in Western Democracies.* Cambridge, Mass.: Harvard University Press, 1981.

Abraham, Henry J. *The Judicial Process: An Introductory Analysis of the Courts of the United States, England, and France.* 5th ed. New York: Oxford University Press, 1980.

Adams, John Clarke, and Barile, Paolo. *The Government of Republican Italy.* 3rd ed. Boston: Houghton Mifflin, 1972.

Alba, Victor. *Politics and the Labor Movement in Latin America.* Stanford, Calif.: Stanford University Press, 1968.

Alexander, Herbert and Shiratori, Rei. *Comparative Political Finance Among the Democracies.* Boulder, Colo.: Westview Press, 1994.

Alford, Robert R. *Health Care Politics.* Chicago: University of Chicago Press, 1975.

Allison, Graham T. *Essence of Decision: Explaining the Cuban Missile Crisis.* Boston: Little, Brown, 1971.

Almond Gabriel A. *A Discipline Divided: Schools and Sects in Political Science.* Newbury Park, Calif.: Sage, 1990.

———, and Coleman, James S., eds. *The Politics of the Developing Areas.* Princeton, N.J.: Princeton University Press, 1960.

———, and Verba, Sidney. *The Civic Culture.* Boston: Little, Brown, 1965.

———, eds. *The Civic Culture Revisited.* Boston: Little, Brown, 1980.

Anderson, Charles. *Statecraft.* New York: Wiley, 1977.

Andrews, William G. *Presidential Government in Gaullist France.* Albany: State University of New York Press, 1982.

Anglin, Douglas. "Southern African Responses to Eastern European Developments." *Journal of Modern African Studies* 28 (no. 3, 1990): 431–456.

Arendt, Hannah. *The Origins of Totalitarianism.* New York: Harcourt Brace, 1951.

Arian, Alan, and Barnes, Samuel. "The Dominant Party System: A Neglected Model of Democratic Stability." *Journal of Politics* 36 (August 1974): 592–614.

357

Ashford, Douglas E. *Policy and Politics in France.* Philadelphia: Temple University Press, 1982.

Bachrach, Peter, and Baratz, Morton S. "The Two Faces of Power." *American Political Science Review* 56 (December 1962): 947–953.

Badie, Bertrand, and Birnbaum, Pierre. *The Sociology of the State.* Chicago: University of Chicago Press, 1983.

Baker, Kendall; Dalton, Russell; and Hildebrandt, Kai. *Germany Transformed.* Cambridge, Mass.: Harvard University Press, 1981.

Baker, Pauline H. "Nigeria: Lurching Toward Unity." *Wilson Quarterly* 4, no. 1 (Winter 1980): 70–80.

Bakvis, Herman, and Chandler, William M. *Federalism and the Role of the State.* Toronto: University of Toronto Press, 1987.

Ball, A., and Millard, F. *Pressure Politics in Industrial Societies.* Atlantic Highlands, N. J.: Humanities Press International, 1987.

Barber, Benjamin. *Strong Democracy.* Berkeley: University of California Press, 1984.

Barber, James David. *The Presidential Character.* 2nd ed. Englewood Cliffs, N.J.: Prentice-Hall, 1977.

Barnes, Samuel H.; Kaase, Max; and Allerbeck, Klause. *Political Action: Mass Participation in Five Western Democracies.* Beverly Hills, Calif.: Sage, 1979.

Bartlett, Katherine T., and Kennedy, Rosanne, eds. *Feminist Legal Theory.* Boulder, Colo.: Westview, 1991.

Barton, John H.; Gibbs, James Lowell, Jr.; Li, Victor Hao; and Merryman, John Henry. *Law in Radically Different Cultures.* St. Paul, Minn.: West, 1983.

Bates, Robert H. *Markets and States in Tropical Africa.* Berkeley: University of California Press, 1981.

———; Przeworski, Adam; and Tarrow, Sidney. "Understanding Political Change in Eastern Europe." *PS* 24 (no. 1, March 1991): 12–27.

Bauer, Raymond A.; Pool, de Sola Ithiel; and Dexter, Lewis Anthony. *American Business and Public Policy.* New York: Atherton, 1963.

Beer, Samuel. *British Politics in the Collectivist Age.* New York: Knopf, 1965.

Berger, Suzanne, ed. *Organizing Interests in Western Europe: Pluralism, Corporatism, and the Transformation of Politics.* Cambridge, England: Cambridge University Press, 1981.

Bienen, Henry. "Military Rule and the Political Process: Nigerian Examples." *Comparative Politics* 10 (January 1978): 205–225.

———; with Fitton, Martin. "Soldiers, Politicians and Civil Servants." In *Soldiers and Oil,* edited by K. Panter-Brick. London: Frank Cass, 1978.

Birch, Anthony H. *Nationalism and National Integration.* London: Unwin Hyman, 1989.

———. *Representation.* New York: Praeger, 1971.

Bond, Jon R., and Fleisher, Richard. *The President in the Legislative Arena.* Chicago: University of Chicago Press, 1990.

Brand, Jack. *British Parliamentary Parties: Policy and Power.* New York: Oxford University Press, 1992.

Brichta, Avraham, and Zalmanovitch, Yair. "Proposals for Presidential Government in Israel." *Comparative Political Studies* 19 (October 1986): 57–68.

Burkett, Tony. "Developments in the West German Bundestag in the 1970s." *Parliamentary Affairs* 34 (Summer 1981): 291–307.

Burnham, Walter Dean. *Critical Elections and the Mainsprings of American Politics.* New York: Norton, 1970.

Cameron, David. "The Expansion of the Public Economy: A Comparative Analysis." *American Political Science Review* 72 (December 1978): 1243–1261.

Campbell, Angus; Converse, Philip; Miller, Warren E.; and Stokes, Donald. *The American Voter.* New York, Wiley, 1960.

Cassels, Alan. *Fascism.* Arlington Heights, Ill.: Harlan Davidson, 1985.

Chase, Harold W.; Holt, Robert; and Turner, John. *American Government in Comparative Perspective.* New York: Franklin Watts, 1980.

Chrines, S. B. *English Constitutional History.* London: Oxford University Press, 1947.

Chubb, John E., and Moe, Terry M. *Politics, Markets, and America's Schools.* Washington, D.C.: Brookings Institution, 1990.

Churchill, Randolph S., ed. *The Sinews of Peace: Post-War Speeches by Winston S. Churchill.* London: Cassell, 1948.

Claude, Inis. *States and the Global System.* New York: St. Martin's, 1988.

Collier, David, ed. *The New Authoritarianism in Latin America.* Princeton, N.J.: Princeton University Press, 1979.

Conover, Pamela Johnston, and Feldman, Stanley. "Belief System Organization in the American Electorate: An Alternate Approach." In *The Electorate Reconsidered,* edited by John Pierce and John L. Sullivan. Beverly Hills, Calif.: Sage, 1980.

Conradt, David. *The German Polity,* 5th ed. New York: Longmann, 1993.

Coulter, Philip B. *Measuring Inequality.* Boulder, Colo.: Westview Press, 1989.

Cox, Gary W., and McCubbins, Mathew D. *Legislative Leviathan: Party Government in the House.* Los Angeles: University of California Press, 1993.

Cronin, Thomas E. *Direct Democracy: The Politics of Initiative, Referendum and Recall.* Cambridge, Mass.: Harvard University Press, 1989.

Crossman, R. H. S. *The Myths of Cabinet Government.* Cambridge, Mass.: Harvard University Press, 1972.

Crozier, Michel. *The Bureaucratic Phenomenon.* Chicago: University of Chicago Press, 1963.

Dahl, Robert. *Who Governs?* New Haven, Conn.: Yale University Press, 1961.

———. *Modern Political Analysis.* 4th ed. New York: Prentice-Hall, 1984.

———. *Democracy and Its Critics.* New Haven: Yale University Press, 1989.

Dalton, Russell J., et al., eds. *Electoral Change in Advanced Industrial Democracies: Realignment or Dealignment?* Princeton, N.J.: Princeton University Press, 1984.

David, René, and Brierly, John E. C. *Major Legal Systems in the World Today.* 3rd ed. London: Steven, 1985.

Davis, Otto; Dempster, M. A. H.; and Wildavsky, Aaron. "A Theory of the Budgetary Process." *American Political Science Review* 60 (September 1966): 529–547.

Delli Carpini, Michael X., and Keeter, Scott. *What Americans Know About Politics and Why It Matters.* New Haven: Yale University Press, 1995.

Deutsch, Karl. *Nationalism and Social Communication.* Cambridge, Mass.: MIT Press, 1953.

Dibacco, Thomas V., ed. *Presidential Power in Latin American Politics.* New York: Praeger, 1977.

Digeser, Peter. "The Fourth Face of Power." *Journal of Politics* 54 (November 1992): 977–1007.

Dodd, Lawrence C., and Oppenheimer, Bruce I. *Congress Reconsidered.* 2nd ed. Washington, D.C.: Congressional Quarterly, 1981.

Dogan, Mattei, ed. *The Mandarins of Western Europe: The Political Role of Top Civil Servants.* New York: Wiley, 1975.

Doron, Gideon, and Goldberg, Giora. "No Big Deal: Democratization of the Nominating Process," in Asher Arian and Michal Shamir, eds., *The Elections in Israel—1988.* Boulder, Colo.: Westview Press, 1990.

Downs, Anthony. *An Economic Theory of Democracy.* New York: Harper & Row, 1957.

Duchacek, Ivo D. *The Territorial Dimensions of Politics Within, Among and Across Nations.* Boulder, Colo.: Westview Press, 1986.

Duverger, Maurice. *Political Parties.* New York: Wiley, 1954.

Easton, David; Gunnell, John G.; and Graziano, Luigi, eds. *The Development of Political Science: A Comparative Survey.* New York: Routledge, 1991.

Eckstein, Harry, and Gurr, Ted Robert. *Patterns of Authority.* New York: Wiley, 1975.

Edwards, George C. III; Kessel, John H.; and Rockman, Bert A., eds. *Researching the Presidency: Vital Questions, New Approaches.* Pittsburgh: University of Pittsburgh Press, 1993.

Ehrmann, Henry. *Politics in France.* 4th ed. Boston: Little, Brown, 1983.

Epstein, Leon D. *Political Parties in the American Mold.* Madison: University of Wisconsin Press, 1986.

Evans, P. B.; Rueschmayer, D.; and Skocpol, Theda, eds. *Bringing the State Back In.* Cambridge, England: Cambridge University Press, 1985.

Fenno, Richard F. *Home Style: House Members in Their Districts.* Boston: Little, Brown, 1978.

———. *Learning to Legislate: The Senate Education of Arlen Specter.* Washington, D.C.: Congressional Quarterly Press, 1991.

Finer, S. E. *The Man on Horseback: The Role of the Military in Politics.* New York: Praeger, 1962.

———, ed. *Five Constitutions.* Harmondsworth, Middlesex: Penguin, 1979.

Fiorina, Morris P. *Congress: Keystone of the Washington Establishment.* 2nd ed. New Haven: Yale University Press, 1989.

Flanigan, William H., and Zingale, Nancy. *Political Behavior of the American Electorate.* 7th ed. Washington, D.C.: Congressional Quarterly Press, 1991.

Freeman, John R. *Politics and Markets: The Politics of Mixed Economies.* Ithaca, N.Y.: Cornell University Press, 1989.

Frieden, Jeffrey A. *Debt, Development and Democracy.* Princeton, N.J.: Princeton University Press, 1991.

Friedrich, Carl. *Limited Government: A Comparison.* Englewood Cliffs, N.J.: Prentice-Hall, 1974.

Fukuyama, Francis. "The End of History?" *The National Interest* 16 (Summer 1989): 3–19.

Gellner, Ernest. *Culture, Identity and Politics.* Cambridge, England: Cambridge University Press, 1987.

Gerth, H. H., and Mills, C. Wright. *From Max Weber.* New York: Oxford University Press, 1958.

Ginsberg, Benjamin. *The Consequences of Consent: Elections, Citizen Control, and Popular Acquiescence.* Reading, Mass.: Addison-Wesley, 1982.

Glendon, Mary Ann; Gordon, Michael W.; and Osakwe, Christopher. *Comparative Legal Traditions.* St. Paul, Minn.: West, 1982.

Goldstein, Judith, and Keohane, Robert O., eds. *Ideas and Foreign Policy: Beliefs, Institutions, and Political Change.* Ithaca, N.Y.: Cornell University Press, 1993.

Goldwin, Robert A.; Kaufman, Art; and Schambra, William A., eds. *Forging Unity out of Diversity: The Approaches of Eight Nations.* Washington, D.C.: American Enterprise Institute, 1989.

Goodman, David S. G., ed. *Groups and Politics in the People's Republic of China.* Armonk, N.Y.: M. E. Sharpe, 1984.

Graber, Doris. *Mass Media and American Politics.* Washington, D.C.: Congressional Quarterly Press, 1980.

Gramsci, Antonio. *Letters from Prison.* New York: Columbia University Press, 1994.

Grayson, George W., ed. *Prospects for Democracy in Mexico.* New Brunswick, N.J.: Transaction, 1990.

Gruber, Judith E. *Controlling Bureaucracies.* Berkeley: University of California Press, 1987.

Gupta, D. C. *Indian Government and Politics.* 4th ed. New Delhi: Vikas, 1978.

Hah, Chong-do, and Martin, Jeffrey. "Toward a Synthesis of Conflict and Integration Theories of Nationalism." *World Politics* 27, no. 3 (April 1975): 361–386.

Hardin, Garret. "The Tragedy of the Commons." *Science* 162 (13 December 1968): 1243–1248.

Hartz, Louis. *The Liberal Tradition in America.* New York: Harcourt Brace, 1955.

Harvey, Jack, and Bather, L. *The British Constitution.* 3rd ed. London: Macmillan, 1972.

Heclo, Hugh. *Modern Social Politics in Britain and Sweden.* New Haven, Conn.: Yale University Press, 1974.

Heidenheimer, Arnold J. "Federalism and the Party System: The Case of West Germany." *American Political Science Review* 52 (September 1958): 809–828.

——— et al., eds. *Political Corruption: A Handbook.* 2nd ed. New Brunswick, N.J.: Transaction Books, 1988.

———; Heclo, Hugh; and Adams, Carolyn. *Comparative Public Policy.* 2nd ed. New York: St. Martin's, 1983.

Heisler, Martin O., ed. *Politics in Europe.* New York: David McKay, 1974.

Hendel, Samuel. *The Soviet Crucible.* Boston: Duxbury, 1980.

Herz, John H. *The Nation-State and the Crisis of World Politics.* New York: David McKay, 1976.

Hirschman, Albert O. "On Democracy in Latin America." *New York Review of Books* 10 (April 1990).

Hobsbawm, E. J. *Nations and Nationalism Since 1780: Programme, Myth, Reality.* Cambridge: Cambridge University Press, 1990.

Hochschild, Jennifer. *What's Fair?: American Beliefs About Distributive Justice.* Cambridge, Mass.: Harvard University Press, 1981.

*Human Rights Watch World Report 1990.* New Haven, Conn.: Yale University Press, 1991.

Hunter, Floyd. *Community Power Structure.* Chapel Hill: University of North Carolina Press, 1953.

Huntington, Samuel P. *The Soldier and the State.* Cambridge, Mass.: Harvard University Press, 1957.

———, and Moore, Clement. *Authoritarian Politics in Modern Society.* New York: Basic Books, 1970.

———, and Nelson, Joan M. *No Easy Choice: Political Participation in Developing Countries.* Cambridge, Mass.: Harvard University Press, 1976.

Ichilov, Orit. *Political Socialization, Citizenship Education, and Democracy.* New York: Teachers College Press, 1990.

Inglehart, Ronald. *Culture Shift in Advanced Industrial Society.* Princeton, N.J.: Princeton University Press, 1990.

Iyengar, Shanto, and Kinder, Donald R. *News That Matters: Television and American Opinion.* Chicago: University of Chicago Press, 1987.

Jackman, Robert. "Politicians in Uniform." *American Political Science Review* 70 (December 1976): 1098–1109.

———. *Power Without Force: The Political Capacity of Nation-States.* Ann Arbor, Mich.: University of Michigan Press, 1993.

Jackson, Robert H., and Rosberg, Carl G. *Personal Rule in Black Africa.* Berkeley: University of California Press, 1982.

Jacobs, Lawrence R. *The Health of Nations: Public Opinion and the Making of American and British Health Policy.* Ithaca, N.Y.; Cornell University Press, 1993.

Jacobson, Harold K. *Networks of Interdependence: International Organizations and the Global Political System.* 2nd ed. New York: Knopf, 1984.

Janda, Kenneth. *A Conceptual Framework for the Comparative Analysis of Political Parties.* Beverly Hills, Calif.: Sage, 1970.

———. *Political Parties: A Cross-National Survey.* New York: Free Press, 1980.

Jaros, Dean. *Socialization to Politics.* New York: Praeger, 1973.

Jennings, Ivor. *Cabinet Government.* 3rd ed. New York: Cambridge University Press, 1969.

Jennings, W. Ivor. *The British Constitution.* 3rd ed. Cambridge, Eng.: Cambridge University Press, 1950.

Johannes, John. *To Serve the People: Congress and Constituency Service.* Lincoln: University of Nebraska, 1984.

Johnson, John J., ed. *The Role of the Military in Underdeveloped Countries.* Princeton, N.J.: Princeton University Press, 1962.

Kaufman, Herbert. *Red Tape: Its Origins, Uses, and Abuses.* Washington, D.C.: Brookings, 1977.

Kennedy, Paul. *The Rise and Fall of the Great Powers.* New York: Random House, 1987.

Keohane, Robert. *After Hegemony: Cooperation and Discord in the World Political Economy.* Princeton, N.J.: Princeton University Press, 1984.

———, ed. *Neorealism and Its Critics.* New York: Columbia University Press, 1986.

———, and Nye, Joseph S. *Power and Interdependence.* 2nd ed. Glenview, Ill. Scott, Foresman, 1989.

Klitgaard, Robert. *Controlling Corruption.* Berkeley: University of California Press, 1988.

Knott, Jack H., and Miller, Gary J. *Reforming Bureaucracy: The Politics of Institutional Choice.* Englewood Cliffs, N.J.: Prentice-Hall, 1987.

Kommers, Donald P. *Judicial Politics in West Germany.* Beverly Hills, Calif.: Sage, 1976.

Krasner, Stephen D., ed. *International Regimes.* Ithaca, N.Y.: Cornell University Press, 1983.

Krislov, Samuel. *Representative Bureaucracy.* Englewood Cliffs, N.J.: Prentice-Hall, 1974.

Kurian, George Thomas. *Encyclopedia of the Third World.* New York: Facts on File, 1987.

Kvavik, Robert. *Interest Groups in Norwegian Politics.* Oslo: Universitetsforlaget, 1976.

Lane, Robert E. *Political Ideology: Why the American Common Man Believes What He Does.* New York: Free Press, 1962.

Lange, P., and Garrett, G. "The Politics of Growth: Strategic Interaction and Economic Performance in the Advanced Industrial Democracies, 1974–1980." *Journal of Politics* 47 (August 1985): 792–827.

LaPalombara, Joseph. *Interest Groups in Italian Politics.* Princeton, N.J.: Princeton University Press, 1964.

———, and Weiner, Myron. *Political Parties and Political Development.* Princeton, N.J.: Princeton University Press, 1966.

Laqueur, Walter, ed. *Fascism: A Reader's Guide.* Berkeley: University of California Press, 1976.

Lasswell, Harold R., and Kaplan, Abraham. *Power and Society.* Yale Law School Studies, vol. 2. New Haven, Conn.: Yale University Press, 1950.

Lave, Charles A., and March, James G. *An Introduction to Models in the Social Sciences.* New York: Harper & Row, 1975.

Laver, Michael, and Schofield, Norman. *Multiparty Government: The Politics of Coalition in Europe.* Oxford: Oxford University Press, 1990.

Lehmbruch, Gerhard, and Schmitter, Philippe C., eds. *Patterns of Corporatist Policy-Making.* Beverly Hills, Calif.: Sage, 1982.

Lenin, V. I. "State and Revolution." In *Sources in Twentieth-Century Political Thought,* edited by Harry Kariel. New York: Free Press, 1964.

Levi, Margaret. *Of Rule and Revenue.* Berkeley: University of California Press, 1988.

Levite, Ariel, and Tarrow, Sidney. "Legitimation of Excluded Parties in Dominant Party Systems: A Comparison of Israel and Italy." *Comparative Politics* 15 (April 1983): 295–327.

Lewis-Beck, Michael S. *Economics and Elections.* Ann Arbor: University of Michigan Press, 1988.

Li, Richard P. Y., and Thompson, William R. "The 'Coup Contagion' Hypothesis." *Journal of Conflict Resolution* 19 (March 1975): 63–88.

Lindblom, Charles. *The Intelligence of Democracy.* New York: Free Press, 1965.

———. *Politics and Markets.* New York: Basic Books, 1977.

Linz, Juan J. "Transitions to Democracy." *Washington Quarterly* (Summer 1990): 143–164.

———, and Stepan, Alfred. *The Breakdown of Democratic Regimes.* Baltimore: Johns Hopkins University Press, 1978.

———, and Valenzuela, Arturo, eds. *The Failure of Presidential Democracy.* Baltimore: Johns Hopkins University Press, 1994.

Lipset, Seymour Martin, and Rokkan, Stein. *Party Systems and Voter Alignments.* New York: Free Press, 1967.

———; Trow, Martin A.; and Coleman, James S. *Union Democracy.* Garden City, N.Y.: Doubleday, 1962.

Lipsitz, Lewis. "If, as Verba Says, the State Functions as a Religion, What Are We to Do Then to Save Our Souls?" *American Political Science Review* 52 (June 1968): 527–535.

Lipsky, Michael. "Protest as a Political Resource." *American Political Science Review* 62 (December 1968): 1144–1158.

Little, Richard D. "Mass Political Participation in the U.S. and the U.S.S.R." *Comparative Political Studies* 8 (January 1976): 437–460.

Livingston, William S. "Britain and America: The Institutionalization of Accountability." *Journal of Politics* 38 (November 1976): 870–894.

Loewenberg, Gerhard. *Parliament in the German Political System.* Ithaca, N.Y.: Cornell University Press, 1967.

———. "The Remaking of the German Party System." *Polity* 1 (Fall 1968): 86–113.

———, and Patterson, Samuel C. *Comparing Legislatures.* Boston: Little, Brown, 1979.

Lok Sabha Secretariat, *The Ninth Lok Sabha, 1989–1991: A Study.* New Delhi: Lok Sabha Secretariat, 1992, pp. 112–113.

Loomis, Burdett A., and Cigler, Allan J., eds. *Interest Group Politics.* Washington, D.C.: Congressional Quarterly, 1983.

Luis, Rubio F. "The Presidential Nomination Process." In George W. Grayson, ed., *Prospects for Democracy in Mexico.* New Brunswick, N.J.: Transaction, 1990.

Lukes, Steven. *Power: A Radical View.* London: Macmillan, 1974.

MacIver, R. M. *The Web of Government.* New York: Macmillan, 1947.

Maier, Charles S., ed. *Changing Boundaries of the Political.* Cambridge: Cambridge University Press, 1987.

Maisel, L. Sandy, ed. *The Parties Respond: Changes in the American Party System.* 2nd ed. Boulder, Colo.: Westview, 1994.

Mandel, Ernest. *Late Capitalism.* London: NLB, 1975.

Mansbridge, Jane J. *Why We Lost the ERA.* Chicago: University of Chicago Press, 1986.

McCloskey, Herbert. "Consensus and Ideology in American Politics." *American Political Science Review* 58 (June 1964): 361–382.

McCormick, Richard L., ed. *Political Parties and the Modern State.* New Brunswick, N.J.: Rutgers University Press, 1984.

Medish, Vadim. *The Soviet Union.* 2nd ed. Englewood Cliffs, N.J.: Prentice-Hall, 1984.

Meier, Kenneth John. "Representative Bureaucracy: An Empirical Analysis." *American Political Science Review* 69 (June 1975): 526–542.

Michels, Robert. *Political Parties.* New York: Free Press, 1962.

Migdal, Joel. *Strong Societies and Weak States.* Princeton: Princeton University Press, 1988.

Miller, Arthur H., and Borrelli, Stephen A. "Confidence in the Government During the 1980s." *American Politics Quarterly* 19 (April 1991): 147–173.

Millet, Kate. *Sexual Politics.* Garden City, N.Y.: Doubleday, 1970.

Moe, Terry. *The Organization of Interests.* Chicago: University of Chicago Press, 1980.

Moon, John Ellis van Courtland. "Chemical Weapons and Deterrence: The World War II Experience," *International Security* 8 (Spring 1984): 3–25.

Moore, Stanley W., et al. *The Child's Political World: A Longitudinal Perspective.* New York: Praeger, 1985.

Morgenthau, Hans. *Politics Among Nations.* 5th rev. ed. New York: Knopf, 1978.

Nagel, Jack H. *The Descriptive Analysis of Power.* New Haven, Conn.: Yale University Press, 1975.

Needler, Martin C. "Political Development and Military Intervention in Latin America." *American Political Science Review* 60 (September 1966): 616–626.

———. "The Logic of Conspiracy: The Latin American Military Coup as a Problem in the Social Sciences." *Studies in Comparative International Development* 13 (Fall 1978): 28–40.

———. *Mexican Politics.* 2nd ed. New York: Praeger, 1990.

Nettl, J. P. "The State as a Conceptual Variable." *World Politics* 20 (July 1968): 559–592.

Neumann, Franz. *Behemoth: The Structure and Practice of National Socialism, 1933–1944.* New York: Oxford University Press, 1944.

Neustadt, Richard E. *Presidential Power and the Modern Presidents.* New York: Free Press, 1991.

al Nimir, Saud, and Palmer, Monte. "Bureaucracy and Development in Saudi Arabia: A Behavioral Analysis." *Public Administration and Development* 2 (April–June 1982): 93–104.

Nordlinger, Eric A. *Soldiers in Politics.* Englewood Cliffs, N.J.: Prentice-Hall, 1976.

Nwabueze, Benjamin O. *Presidentialism in Commonwealth Africa.* London: C. Hurst, 1974.

Nye, Joseph S. *Bound to Lead: The Changing Nature of American Power.* New York: Basic Books, 1990.

O'Donnell, Guillermo. *Modernization and Bureaucratic Authoritarianism: Studies in South American Politics.* Berkeley: Institute of International Studies, University of California Press, 1973.

———; Schmitter, Philippe; and Whitehead, Laurence. *Transitions from Authoritarian Rule: Prospects for Democracy.* Baltimore: Johns Hopkins University Press, 1986.

Oliver, James. "Citizen Demands in the Soviet System." *American Political Science Review* 63 (June 1969): 465–475.

Olsen, David M., and Mezey, Michael L., eds. *Legislatures in the Policy Process: The Dilemmas of Economic Policy.* New York: Cambridge University Press, 1991.

Olson, Mancur. *The Logic of Collective Action.* Cambridge, Mass.: Harvard University Press, 1965.

———. *The Rise and Decline of Nations: Economic Growth, Stagflation and Social Rigidities.* New Haven: Yale University Press, 1982.

Olson, Susan M. *Clients and Lawyers, Securing the Rights of Disabled Persons.* Westport, Conn.: Greenwood, 1984.

Ornstein, Norman J., and Elder, Shirley. *Interest Groups, Lobbying and Policymaking.* Washington, D.C.: Congressional Quarterly Press, 1978.

Ostrogorski, M. *Democracy and the Organization of Political Parties.* Garden City, N.Y.: Doubleday, 1964.

Ostrom, Elinor. *Governing the Commons: The Evolution of Institutions for Collective Action.* Cambridge: Cambridge University Press, 1991.

Ostrom, Vincent. *The Intellectual Crisis in American Public Administration.* University, Ala.: University of Alabama Press, 1973.

Padgett, L. Vincent. *The Mexican Political System.* 2nd ed. Boston: Houghton Mifflin, 1976.

Page, Benjamin I. *Who Gets What from Government.* Berkeley: University of California Press, 1983.

Paltiel, Khayam. "Campaign Finance: Contrasting Patterns and Reforms." In David Butler, ed., *Democracy at the Polls.* Washington, D.C.: American Enterprise Institute, 1981.

Pastor, Robert A. "Post-Revolutionary Mexico: The Salinas Opening," *Journal of Interamerican Studies and World Affairs* 32 (Fall 1990): 10.

Pateman, Carole. *Participation and Democracy Theory.* Cambridge, England: Cambridge University Press, 1970.

Patterson, Thomas E. *The Mass Media Election.* New York: Praeger, 1980.

———. *Out of Order: How the Decline of Political Parties and the Growing Power of the News Media Undermine the American Way of Electing Presidents.* New York: Knopf, 1994.

Perlmutter, Amos. *The Military and Politics in Modern Times.* New Haven, Conn.: Yale University Press, 1977.

Peterson, Paul. *City Limits.* Chicago: University of Chicago Press, 1981.

Phillips, Kevin R. *The Politics of Rich and Poor: Wealth and the American Electorate in the Reagan Aftermath.* New York: Random House, 1990.

Pierce, John C., and Sullivan, John L., eds. *The Electorate Reconsidered.* Beverly Hills, Calif.: Sage, 1980.

Piliavin, Irving, and Briar, Scott. "Police Encounters with Juveniles." *American Journal of Sociology* 70 (September 1964): 206–214.

Pious, Richard M. *The American Presidency.* New York: Basic Books, 1979.

Pirages, Dennis. *Global Technopolitics: The International Politics of Technology and Resources.* Pacific Grove, Calif.: Brooks/Cole, 1989.

Pitkin, Hanna Fenichel. *The Concept of Representation.* Berkeley: University of California Press, 1967.

Piven, Frances Fox, and Cloward, Richard A. *Regulating the Poor.* New York: Pantheon, 1971.

Porter, Gareth, and Brown, Janet Welsh. *Global Environmental Politics.* Boulder, Colo.: Westview, 1991.

Powell, G. Bingham, Jr. "American Voter Turnout in Comparative Perspective." *American Political Science Review* 80 (March 1986): 17–44.

Pridham, Geoffrey, and Vanhanen, Tatu, eds. *Democratization in Eastern Europe.* London: Routledge, 1994.

Przeworski, Adam. "Some Problems in the Study of the Transition to Democracy." In Guillermo O'Donnell, Philippe C. Schmitter, and Laurence Whitehead, eds. *Transitions from Authoritarian Rule: Comparative Perspectives.* Baltimore: Johns Hopkins University Press, 1986, pp. 47–63.

———. *Democracy and the Market.* Cambridge: Cambridge University Press, 1991.

———, and Sprague, John. *Paper Stones: A History of Electoral Socialism.* Chicago: University of Chicago Press, 1986.

Quinton, Anthony, ed. *Political Philosophy.* Oxford, England: Oxford University Press, 1967.

Rawls, John. *Political Liberalism.* New York: Columbia University Press, 1993.

———. *A Theory of Justice.* Cambridge, Mass.: Belknap, 1971.

Redden, Kenneth Robert. *Modern Legal Systems Cyclopedia.* Buffalo, N.Y.: Hein, 1990.

Reshetar, John S., Jr. *The Soviet Polity.* 3rd ed. New York: Harper & Row, 1989.

Reyna, Jose L., and Weinert, Richard S., eds. *Authoritarianism in Mexico.* Philadelphia: Institute for the Study of Human Issues, 1977.

Rigby, Thomas H. *Communist Party Membership in the U.S.S.R., 1917–1967.* Princeton, N.J.: Princeton University Press, 1968.

Riker, William. *A Theory of Political Coalitions.* New Haven, Conn.: Yale University Press, 1962.

———. *Federalism: Origin, Operation, Significance.* Boston: Little, Brown, 1964.

———, and Ordeshook, Peter C. *An Introduction to Positive Political Theory.* Englewood Cliffs, N.J.: Prentice-Hall, 1973.

Rikhye, Indar, J.; Harbottle, Michael; and Egge, Bjørn. *The Thin Blue Line: International Peace-keeping and its Future.* New Haven, Conn.: Yale University Press, 1974.

Rogowski, Ronald. "Political Cleavages and Changing Exposure to Trade." *American Political Science Review* 81 (December 1987): 1121–1137.

Rokeach, Milton. *The Open and Closed Mind: Investigations Into the Nature of Belief Systems and Personality Systems.* New York: Basic Books, 1960.

Rose, Richard. *Do Parties Make a Difference?* Chatham, N.J.: Chatham House, 1980.

———. "Still the Era of Party Government." *Parliamentary Affairs* 36 (Summer 1983): 282–299.

———. *The Postmodern President.* Chatham, N.J.: Chatham House, 1989.

———, and Suleiman, Ezra N., eds. *Presidents and Prime Ministers.* Washington D.C.: American Enterprise Institute, 1980.

———. *The Problem of Party Government.* New York: Free Press, 1974.

Rosecrance, Richard. *Rise of the Trading State.* New York: Basic Books, 1986.

Rosenau, James N. *Turbulence in World Politics.* Beverly Hills, Calif.: Sage, 1990.

Rosenstone, Steven J., and Hansen, John Mark. *Mobilization, Participation and Democracy in America.* New York: Macmillan, 1993.

Rossiter, Clinton. *The American Presidency.* 2nd ed. New York: New American Library, 1964.

Rouiquie, Alain. *The Military and the State in Latin America.* Berkeley: University of California Press, 1987.

Rudolph, James D. *Peru: The Evolution of a Crisis.* Westport, Conn.: Praeger, 1992.

Sabatier, Paul, and Mazmanian, Dan. "The Implementation of Public Policy: A Framework of Analysis." *Policy Studies Journal* 8 (Special Issue, no. 2, 1980): 538–559.

Salisbury, Robert. "An Exchange Theory of Interest Groups." *Midwest Journal of Political Science* 13 (February 1969): 1–32.

Sampson, Anthony. *The New Europeans.* London: Hodder and Stoughton, 1968.

Sartori, Giovanni. *Parties and Party Systems.* Cambridge, England: Cambridge Universtiy Press, 1976.

Schapiro, Leonard. *The Communist Party of the Soviet Union.* New York: Random House, 1960.

Schattschneider, E. E. *Party Government.* New York: Holt, Rinehart and Winston, 1942.

———. *The Semisovereign People.* New York: Holt, Rinehart and Winston, 1960.

Schlesinger, Arthur M., Jr. *The Imperial Presidency.* Boston: Houghton Mifflin, 1973.

Schlesinger, Joseph. *Ambition and Politics: Political Careers in the United States.* Chicago: Rand McNally, 1966.

———. *Political Parties and the Winning of Office.* Ann Arbor: University of Michigan Press, 1991.

Schlozman, Kay Lehman, and Tierney, John T. *Organized Interests and American Democracy.* New York: Harper & Row, 1986.

Schmidt, Vivien A. *Democratizing France: The Political and Administrative History of Decentralization.* Cambridge: Cambridge University Press, 1991.

Schmitter, Philippe, and Lehmbruch, Gerhard, eds. *Trends Toward Corporatist Intermediation.* Beverly Hills, Calif.: Sage, 1979.

Schulman, Paul R. "Nonincremental Policy Making: Notes toward an Alternative Paradigm." *American Political Science Review* 69 (December 1975): 1354–1370.

Schwartz, Barry. *George Washington: The Making of an American Myth.* New York: Free Press, 1987.

Scott, James C. *Weapons of the Weak: Everyday Forms of Peasant Resistance.* New Haven: Yale University Press, 1985.

Searing, Donald D. *Westminster's World: Understanding Political Roles.* Cambridge, Mass.: Harvard University Press, 1994.

Shamir, Michal, and Sullivan, John. "The Political Context of Tolerance: The United States and Israel." *American Political Science Review* 77 (December 1983): 911–928.

Shils, Edward, and Young, Michael. "The Meaning of the Coronation." *Sociological Review* 1 (December 1953): 63–81.

Shively, W. Phillips. "From Differential Abstention to Conversion." *American Journal of Political Science* 36 (May 1992): 309–330.

———. "The Nature of Party Identification." In *The Electorate Reconsidered,* edited by John C. Pierce and John L. Sullivan. Beverly Hills, Calif.: Sage, 1980.

Shonfield, Andrew. *Modern Capitalism.* Oxford, England: Oxford University Press, 1965.

Shugart, Matthew Soberg, and Carey, John M. *Presidents and Assemblies: Constitutional Design and Electoral Dynamics.* New York: Cambridge University Press, 1992.

Sigel, Roberta S. *Political Learning in Adulthood.* Chicago: University of Chicago Press, 1989.

Silverstein, Ken. "Guerillas in the Mist," *The Washington Monthly* (September 1994): 21.

Sisk, Timothy. *Democratization in South Africa: The Elusive Social Contract.* Princeton, N.J.: Princeton University Press, 1995.

Skidmore, Thomas E. *The Politics of Military Rule in Brazil, 1964–1985.* Oxford: Oxford University Press, 1988.

Skilling, H. Gordon, and Griffiths, Franklyn, eds. *Interest Groups in Soviet Politics.* Princeton, N.J.: Princeton University Press, 1971.

Skinner, B. F. *Walden Two.* New York: Macmillan, 1948.

Skocpol, Theda. *States and Social Revolutions.* Cambridge, England: Cambridge University Press, 1979.

Skowronek, Stephen. *Building a New American State: The Expansion of National Administrative Capacities, 1877–1920.* Cambridge: Cambridge University Press, 1982.

———. *The Politics Presidents Make: Leadership from John Adams to George Bush.* Cambridge, Mass.: Harvard University Press, 1993.

Smith, Bruce L. R., ed. *The Higher Civil Service in Europe and Canada: Lessons for the United States.* Washington, D.C.: Brookings, 1984.

Smith, Hedrick. *The New Russians.* New York: Random House, 1990.

Sniderman, Paul. *Personality and Democratic Politics.* Berkeley: University of California Press, 1975.

Snyder, Jack. *Myths of Empire: Domestic Politics and International Ambition.* Ithaca, N.Y.: Cornell University Press, 1991.

Solomon, Robert C., and Murphy, Mark C., eds. *What is Justice? Classic and Contemporary Readings.* Oxford: Oxford University Press, 1990.

Solzhenitsyn, Alexander. *The Gulag Archipelago, 1918–1956.* New York: Harper & Row, 1974.

Sorauf, Frank J. *Inside Campaign Finance.* New Haven: Yale University Press, 1992.

———. "Zorach vs. Clausen: The Impact of a Supreme Court Decision." *American Political Science Review* 53 (September 1959): 777–791.

———, and Beck, Paul A. *Party Politics in America.* 7th ed. New York: HarperCollins, 1992.

Speer, Albert. *Inside the Third Reich.* New York: Macmillan, 1970.

Sprout, Harold and Margaret. *The Ecological Perspective on Human Affairs, with Special Reference to International Politics.* Princeton, N.J.: Princeton University Press, 1965.

Stokes, Susan C. *Cultures in Conflict: Social Movements and the State in Peru.* Berkeley, Calif.: University of California Press, 1995.

Strom, Kaare. *Minority Government and Majority Rule.* New York: Cambridge University Press, 1990.

———. "The Presthus Debacle: Intraparty Politics and Bargaining Failure in Norway." *American Political Science Review* 88 (March 1994): 112–127.

Suleiman, Ezra N. *Politics, Power, and Bureaucracy in France.* Princeton, N.J.: Princeton University Press, 1974.

Sullivan, John L.; Piereson, James; and Marcus, George E. "An Alternative Conceptualization of Political Tolerance." *American Political Science Review* 73 (September 1979): 781–794.

———; Walsh, Pat; Shamir, Michal; Barnum, David G.; and Gibson, James L. "Why Politicians are More Tolerant: Selective Recruitment and Socialization Among Political Elites in Britain, Israel, New Zealand, and the United States." *British Journal of Political Science* 23 (January 1993): p. 60.

———, Shamir, Michal; Walsh, Patrick; and Roberts, Nigel S. *Political Tolerance in Context: Support for Civil Liberties in the United States, Israel, and New Zealand.* Boulder, Colo.: Westview Press, 1985.

Sullivan, Michael P. *Power in Contemporary International Politics.* Columbia, S.C.: University of South Carolina Press, 1990.

Taagepera, Rein, and Shugart, Matthew S. *Seats and Votes: The Effects and Determinants of Electoral Systems.* New Haven, Conn.: Yale University Press, 1989.

Teixeira, Roy A. *The Disappearing American Voter.* Washington: Brookings Institution, 1992.

Thomas, Clive S. *First World Interest Groups: A Comparative Perspective.* Westport, Conn.: Greenwood Press, 1993.

Tilly, Charles, ed. *The Formation of National States in Western Europe.* Princeton, N.J.: Princeton University Press, 1975.

Tinker, Irene, ed. *Persistent Inequalities: Women and World Development.* Oxford: Oxford University Press, 1990.

Titmuss, Richard M. *The Gift Relationship: From Human Blood to Social Policy.* New York: Pantheon Books, 1971.

Tribe, Lawrence H., and Dorf, Michael C. *On Reading the Constitution.* Cambridge, Mass.: Harvard University Press, 1991.

Truman, David B. *The Governmental Process.* 2nd ed. New York: Knopf, 1951.

Tuchman, Barbara W. *A Distant Mirror: The Calamitous Fourteenth Century.* New York: Knopf, 1978.

Tufte, Edward R. *Political Control of the Economy.* Princeton, N.J.: Princeton University Press, 1978.

Ullman, Richard H. *Securing Europe.* Princeton, N.J.: Princeton University Press, 1991.

Urquhart, Brian. *Decolonization and World Peace.* Austin: University of Texas Press, 1989.

United Nations Office of Vienna, Centre for Social Development and Humanitarian Affairs. *Women in Politics and Decision-Making in the Late Twentieth Century.* Dordrecht, Netherlands: Martinus Nijhof, 1992.

U.S. Senate, Committee on Governmental Operations. *Confidence and Concern: Citizens View American Government.* Washington, D.C.: Government Printing Office, 1973.

Valenzuela, J. Samuel, and Valenzuela, Arturo. "Modernization and Dependency." *Comparative Politics* 10 (July 1978): 535–557.

Verba, Sidney; Kim, Jae-on; and Nie, Norman H. *Participation and Political Equality.* London: Cambridge University Press, 1978.

———, and Nie, Norman H. *Participation in America.* New York: Harper & Row, 1972.

———; Schlozman, Kay Lehman; Brady, Henry. *Voice and Equality: Civic Voluntarism in American Politics.* Cambridge, Mass.: Harvard University Press, 1995.

Voegelin, Eric. *Order and History.* Baton Rouge: Louisiana State University Press, 1956.

Wahlke, John C. "Liberal Learning and the Political Science Major." *PS* 24 (March 1991): 48–60.

Walker, Jack L., Jr. *Mobilizing Interest Groups in America.* Ann Arbor: University of Michigan Press, 1991.

Wallerstein, Immanuel. *The Capitalist World Economy.* Cambridge, England: Cambridge University Press, 1979.

Waltz, Kenneth. *Theory of International Politics.* Reading, Mass.: Addison-Wesley, 1979.

Weissberg, Robert. *Public Opinion and Popular Government.* Englewood Cliffs, N.J.: Prentice-Hall, 1976.

Wesson, Robert, ed. *Democracy: A Worldwide Survey.* New York: Praeger, 1987.

Wheare, K. D. *Federal Government.* 4th ed. London: Oxford University Press, 1963.

White, Stephen. "The U.S.S.R. Supreme Soviet: A Developmental Perspective," *Legislative Studies Quarterly* 5 (May 1980): 247–274.

Wiarda, Howard, ed. *New Directions in Comparative Politics,* rev. ed. Boulder, Colo.: Westview Press, 1991

———. "Mexico: The Unravelling of a Corporatist Regime?" *Journal of Interamerican Studies and World Affairs* 30 (Winter 1988–89): 7.

Wildavsky, Aaron B. *Speaking Truth to Power.* New Brunswick, N.J.: Transaction Books, 1987.

Williamson, John, ed. *Latin American Adjustment: How Much Has Happened?* Washington, D.C.: Institute for International Economics, 1990.

Wills, Gary. *Cincinnatus: George Washington and the Enlightenment.* Garden City, N.Y.: Doubleday, 1984.

Wilson, Frank L. "French Interest Groups: Pluralist or Neocorporatist?" *American Political Science Review* 77 (December 1983): 895–910.

Wilson, James Q. *Bureaucracy: What Government Agencies Do and Why They Do It.* New York: Basic Books, 1989.

———. *Political Organizations.* New York: Basic Books, 1973.

Wrong, Dennis. *Power.* New York: Harper & Row, 1979.

Young, Oran R. *International Cooperation: Building Regimes for National Resources and the Environment.* Ithaca, N.Y.: Cornell University Press, 1989.

# INDEX